Down to Earth Sociology

Down to Earth Sociology

Introductory Readings

FOURTH EDITION

JAMES M. HENSLIN, Editor

THE FREE PRESS
A Division of Macmillan, Inc.
NEW YORK

In Memory of Erving Goffman

1922–1982

From Whom I Learned So Much

The Free Press
A Division of Macmillan, Inc.
866 Third Avenue, New York, N. Y. 10022

Collier Macmillan Canada, Inc.

Printed in the United States of America

printing number

6   7   8   9   10

Library of Congress Cataloging in Publication Data

Main entry under title:

Down to earth sociology.

   Includes indexes.
   1. Sociology—Addresses, essays, lectures.   2. United
States—Social conditions—Addresses, essays, lectures.
I. Henslin, James M.
HM51.D68   1985   301   84-25841
ISBN 0-02-914290-3 (pbk.)

Credits
and Acknowledgments

Grateful acknowledgment is made to the authors and publishers who have granted permission to reprint the following selections:

ARTICLE
NUMBER

1   Excerpt from *Invitation to Sociology* by Peter L. Berger. Copyright © 1963 by Peter Berger. Reprinted by permission of Doubleday & Company, Inc.

2   "Sociology and the Social Sciences" by James M. Henslin. Copyright © 1985 by James M. Henslin. Written for this volume.

3   "The Promise" by C. Wright Mills. From *The Sociological Imagination* by C. Wright Mills, pp. 3–13. Copyright © 1959 by Oxford University Press, Inc. Reprinted by permission.

4   "One Hundred Percent American" by Ralph Linton. From *The American Mercury*, 40 (1937), pp. 427–29.

5   "Body Ritual Among the Nacirema" by Horace Miner. Reprinted by permission of the author and the American Anthropological Association from *American Anthropologist*, 58 (1956), pp. 503–7.

6   "The Sounds of Silence" by Edward T. Hall and Mildred R. Hall. Reprinted by permission of the authors from *Playboy*, June 1971, pp. 139–40, 204, 206. Copyright © 1971 by Edward T. Hall and Mildred Reed Hall.

7   "The Presentation of Self in Everyday Life" by Erving Goffman. Reprinted by permission of Doubleday & Co., Inc., and Penguin Books

20   "Drag Queens" and "Fag Hags" by Diane E. Taub and Robert G. Leger. Reprinted by permission of the authors and Hemisphere Publishing Corporation.

21   "Pronoia" by Fred H. Goldner. Reprinted by permission of the author and publisher from *Social Problems*, Vol. 30, No. 1 (October 1982), pp. 82–91. Copyright © 1982 by The Society for the Study of Social Problems.

22   "Techniques of Neutralization" by Gresham M. Sykes and David Matza. Reprinted by permission of the authors and publisher from *American Sociological Review*, Vol. 22 (December 1957) pp. 664–70. Copyright © 1957 by the American Sociological Association.

23   Robert Lejeune, "The Management of a Mugging," *Urban Life*, Vol. 6, No. 2 (July 1977), pp. 123–48. Copyright © 1977 by Sage Publications, Inc. Reprinted by permission of Sage Publications, Inc.

24   "The Pathology of Imprisonment" by Philip G. Zimbardo. Published by permission of Transaction, Inc. from *Society*, Vol. 9, No. 6. Copyright © 1972 by Transaction, Inc.

25   Specified abridgement from pages 1–96 of *The Bohemian Grove and Other Retreats: A Study in Ruling-Class Cohesiveness* by G. William Domhoff. Copyright © 1974 by G. William Domhoff. Reprinted by permission of Harper & Row, Publishers, Inc.

26   "The Uses of Poverty: The Poor Pay All" by Herbert J. Gams. From *Social Policy*, July/August 1971, pp. 20–24. Published by Social Policy Corporation, New York. Copyright © 1971 by Social Policy Corporation. Reprinted by permission.

27   "Some Hidden Injuries of Class" by Richard Sennett and Jonathan Cobb. Reprinted by permission of Alfred A. Knopf, Inc., from *The Hidden Injuries of Class*, pp. 119–35. Copyright © 1972 by Richard Sennett and Jonathan Cobb.

28   "The Doctor–Nurse Game" by Leonard J. Stein. Reprinted by permission of the author and publisher from *Archives of General Psychiatry*, Vol. 16 (1967), pp. 699–703. Copyright © 1967 American Medical Association.

29   "Tally's Corner" by Elliott Liebow. Reprinted by permission of the publisher from *Tally's Corner*, pp. 50–71. Copyright © 1967 by Little, Brown and Co., Inc.

30   "Good People and Dirty Work" by Everett C. Hughes. Reprinted by permission of the publisher from *Social Problems*, Vol. 10, No. 1 (Summer 1962), pp. 3–11. Copyright © 1962 by The Society for the Study of Social Problems.

31   "The Family as a Company of Players" by Annabelle B. Motz. Published

by permission of Transaction, Inc. from *Transaction*, Vol. 2, No. 3. Copyright © 1965 Transaction, Inc.

32   "The Military Academy as an Assimilating Institution" by Sanford M. Dornbusch. Reprinted by permission of the publisher from *Social Forces*, Vol. 33 (May 1955), pp. 316–21. Copyright © 1955 by The University of North Carolina Press.

33   Lawrence K. Hong and Marion V. Dearman, "The Streetcorner Preacher," *Urban Life*, Vol. 6, No. 1 (April 1977), pp. 53–68. Copyright © 1977 by Sage Publications, Inc. Reprinted by permission of Sage Publications, Inc.

34   "The Wrestling Referee" by Charles W. Smith. From "Performances and Negotiations: A Case Study of a Wrestling Referee," *Qualitative Sociology*, Vol. 6, No. 1 (Spring 1982), pp. 33–45. Copyright © 1982 by Human Sciences Press, Inc. 72 Fifth Avenue, NY, NY 10011. Reprinted by permission.

35   "After Death in the Hospital" by Barney G. Glaser and Anselm L. Strauss. Reprinted by permission of the authors and Aldine Publishing Co. from *Time for Dying*, pp. 207–18. Copyright © 1968 by Barney G. Glaser and Anselm L. Strauss.

36   "Violence and the Police" by William A. Westley. Reprinted by permission of the author and publisher from *American Journal of Sociology*, Vol. 59 (July 1953), pp. 34–41. © 1953 by The University of Chicago Press. All rights reserved.

37   "The Structure of Power in American Society" by C. Wright Mills. From *Power, Politics and People: The Collected Essays of C. Wright Mills*. Edited by Irving Horowitz. Copyright © 1963 by the Estate of C. Wright Mills. Reprinted by permission of Oxford University Press, Inc.

38   "Future Shock" by Alvin Toffler. Reprinted by permission from Random House, Inc. from *Future Shock*, p. 9–12. Copyright © 1970 by Alvin Toffler.

39   "Searching for Roots in a Changing World" by Richard Rodriguez. Reprinted by permission of the publisher from *Saturday Review*, February 8, 1975, pp. 147–49. Copyright © 1975 by *Saturday Review*. All rights reserved.

40   "The American Family in the Year 2000" by Andrew Cherlin and Frank F. Furstenberg, Jr. Reprinted by permission of the publisher from *The Futurist*, June 1983, pp. 143–47.

41   "Life in the 21st Century" by Charles J. Leslie. Reprinted from *USA Today*, November 1982. Copyright by Society for the Advancement of Education.

Contents

Preface to the Fourth Edition

IT IS WITH PLEASURE that I introduce the fourth edition of *Down to Earth Sociology*, a pleasure akin to seeing a dear friend reach another cheerful milestone in his or her life. Adopters of earlier editions will find themselves at home, I believe, in this latest edition. They will see many selections they have already successfully used in the classroom, and I trust they will welcome the many newcomers.

Following the suggestions of those who have used the earlier editions of *Down to Earth Sociology*, I have strived to continue to present down to earth articles in order to make the student's introduction to sociology enjoyable and meaningful. These selections reflect the experiences of people who have "been there" and who, with a minimum of jargon and quantification, insightfully share those experiences with the reader.

Focusing on social interaction in ordinary or everyday activities and situations, these selections share some of the fascination of sociology. They reflect both the individualistic and the structural emphases of our discipline. Social structure is not simply an abstract fact of life; it vitally affects our lives. The decisions of the rich, the politically powerful, and the bureaucrats provide social constraints that augment those dictated by birth, social class, and other circumstances. By social structure our vision of life is lifted or limited, our chances of success closed or opened. Social structure concretely brings tears and laughter, hopes and despair.

Yet so much of sociology goes about its business as though data were unconnected to people, as though the world consisted of analysis of abstract social facts. From my own experiences I know this is far from the truth—divorced from life—and I have sought authors who share the realities that people directly experience. At least as I see it, sociology is the most fascinating of the social sciences, and it is this fascination that these selections are designed to convey.

It is my hope that I have succeeded in accomplishing this goal, because I believe that sociology is able to open new windows of perception that can touch every aspect of the individual's world. If these readings achieve at least part of this goal, I owe a great debt to the many who adopted the earlier editions, especially to those whose reactions and suggestions have helped give shape to the contents of *Down to Earth Sociology.*

In response to those reactions, the selections are organized to make them compatible with most introductory textbooks. Through subjects inherently interesting, we cover the major substantive areas of sociology. Part I is an introduction to the sociological perspective; it invites students to view the world in a new way by participating in the exciting enterprise we call sociology. Part II examines the cultural underpinnings of social life, the taken-for-granted assumptions and contexts that provide the contours of our everyday life in society. In Part III that essential component of our beings—sexuality—is the focus, including an analysis of both the processes by which we assume the social identity of male or female and how those identities provide the basis for interaction among adults.

Part IV examines social groups and social structure, looking behind the scenes to see how people's assumptions, the features of social settings, individuals' previous relationships with one another, their location in the social hierarchy, and the structuring of work relationships establish both constraints and freedoms. The process of becoming deviant, the broader social context that shapes deviance and social reactions to violations of social control are the subjects of Part V. We examine social stratification in Part VI, looking at the power, wealth, educational, sexual, occupational, and racial dimensions of social inequality. In Part VII the social institutions of the family, education, religion, sports, medicine, law, and our intertwining political, military, and economic interests are analyzed. Social change is the focus of Part VIII; after an introduction to the concept of future shock, the search for personal roots in a rapidly changing social world and life in the future are discussed.

These selections bring the student face to face with the dual emphases of contemporary sociological research: the focus on the individual's experience and the analysis of social structure. Uncovering the basic expectations that underlie routine social interactions, these articles emphasize the ways in which social institutions are interrelated. It is to these authors' credit that we lose sight of neither the people who are interacting nor the structural base that so directly influences the form and content of their interactions.

About the Contributors

George E. Arquitt (article 16) was awarded his Ph.D. at the University of Tennessee. He is an Associate Professor of Sociology at Oklahoma State University.

Peter L. Berger (article 1) received his Ph.D. from the New School for Social Research. He is a Professor of Sociology at Boston University and the author of numerous books, including *The Noise of Solemn Assemblies, The Sacred Canopy, A Rumor of Angels*, and *Invitation to Sociology*, from which the selection in this book is taken.

Mae A. Biggs (article 14) earned her M.A. at Southern Illinois University Edwardsville and is an associate of the Masters-Johnson Institute (Biological Research Institute) in St. Louis, Missouri.

William J. Chambliss (article 19) earned his Ph.D. at Indiana University. He is a Professor of Sociology at the University of Delaware and has written many books, including *Crime and the Legal Process, Criminal Law in Action, On the Take*, and *Whose Law? What Order?*

Andrew Cherlin (article 40), who received his Ph.D. from the University of California at Los Angeles, is an Associate Professor of Sociology at Johns Hopkins University. He has written *Marriage, Divorce, Remarriage.*

Jonathan Cobb (article 27) earned his Ph.D. at Columbia University. He does research on the working class at the Center for the Study of Public Policy in Cambridge, Massachusetts. He has edited (with Stephan Thernstrom) *Nineteenth Century Cities* and has written (with Richard Sennett) *The Hidden Injuries of Class*, from which the selection in Part VI is taken.

Nannette J. Davis (article 18) earned her Ph.D. at Michigan State University and is a Professor of Sociology at Central Michigan University. She is the author of *Sociological Constructions of Deviance, Women and Deviance*, and (with Bo Anderson) *Social Control*.

Marion V. Dearman (article 33) received his Ph.D. from the University of Oregon. He is an Assistant Professor of Sociology at California State University at Los Angeles.

G. William Domhoff (article 25) earned his Ph.D. at Miami University in Oxford, Ohio. He is a Professor of Sociology at the University of California, Santa Cruz. Among his books on the power structure of American society are *Who Rules America?*, *The Higher Circles: The Governing Class in America*, and *The Bohemian Grove and Other Retreats: A Study in Ruling-Class Cohesiveness*, from which the selection here is taken.

Sanford M. Dornbusch (article 32) was awarded his Ph.D. at the University of Chicago and is a Professor of Sociology at Stanford University. He has written (with W. Richard Scott) *Evaluation and the Exercise of Authority*, (with Louis Schneider) *Popular Religion*, and (with Calvin F. Schmid) *A Primer of Social Statistics*.

Elaine Fox (article 16) earned her M.A. at San Diego State University and is the author of *The Marriage-Go-Round: An Exploratory Study of Multiple Marriages*.

Frank F. Furstenberg, Jr. (article 40), earned his Ph.D. at Columbia University and is a Professor of Sociology at the University of Pennsylvania. His books include *Recycling the Family: Remarriage After Divorce, Unplanned Parenthood: The Social Consequences of Teenage Childbearing, Teenage Sexuality, Pregnancy, and Childbearing*, and *Burdens and Benefits: The Impact of Early Childhood on the Family*.

Herbert J. Gans (article 26) received his Ph.D. from the University of Pennsylvania. He is a Professor of Sociology at Columbia University and has written such books as *The Levittowners*, *Deciding What's News*, and *The Urban Villagers*.

Barney G. Glaser (article 35) earned his Ph.D. at Columbia University and is a Professor of Sociology at the University of California at San Francisco. His many books include *Anguish: Chronic Illness and the Quality of Life*, *Status Passage*, (with Anselm L. Strauss) *The Discovery of Grounded Theory*, and (with Anselm L. Strauss) *Time for Dying*, from which the selection in this book is taken.

Erving Goffman (article 7) earned his Ph.D. at the University of Chicago and at the time of his death in 1982 was the Director of the Center for Urban Ethnography at the University of Pennsylvania. His many books include *Stigma*, *Behavior in Public Places*, *Frame Analysis*, and the book from which a selection in Part II is taken, *The Presentation of Self in Everyday Life*.

Fred H. Goldner (article 21) received his Ph.D. from the University of California at Berkeley and is a Professor of Sociology at Queens College of the City University of New York.

Edward T. Hall (article 6) was awarded his Ph.D. at Columbia University. He is a Professor of Anthropology at Northwestern University and has written several books, including *The Silent Language*, *The Hidden Dimension*, *Beyond Culture*, and *The Dance of Life: The Other Dimension of Time*.

Mildred R. Hall (article 6) received her B.A. from Barnard College and (with Edward T. Hall) has written *The Fourth Dimension in Architecture* and (with Edward T. Hall) *Hidden Differences*.

James M. Henslin (articles 2, 8, 12, and 14) earned his Ph.D. at Washington University in St. Louis. He is a Professor of Sociology at Southern Illinois University, Edwardsville. He is the editor of several books including *Marriage and Family in a Changing Society* and (with Edward Sagarin) *The Sociology of Sex* and has written *Sociology: Toward Understanding Life in Society* and (with Donald W. Light, Jr.) *Social Problems*.

Lawrence K. Hong (article 33) earned his Ph.D. at the University of Notre Dame. He is an Associate Professor of Sociology at California State University in Los Angeles.

Everett C. Hughes (article 30) received his Ph.D. at the University of Chicago. At the time of his death in 1983 he was Professor Emeritus of Sociology at Boston College. He wrote such books as *French Canada in Transition*, *Collective Behavior*, and *The Sociological Eye*, and edited (with others) *The Collected Papers of Robert Park*.

Robert G. Leger (article 20) was awarded his Ph.D. at the University of Iowa. He is an Associate Professor of Sociology at East Tennessee State University and has edited *The Sociology of Corrections*.

Robert Lejeune (article 23) received his Ph.D. from Columbia University and is an Associate Professor of Sociology at Herbert H. Lehman College. He is the author of *Class and Conflict in American Society*.

Charles J. Leslie (article 41) received his M.S. from Purdue University, where he is the Associate Director of the Office of Public Information.

Janet Lever (article 10) earned her Ph.D. at Yale University and is an Assistant Professor of Sociology at Northwestern University. She is the author of *Soccer Madness* and (with Pepper Schwartz) *Women at Yale*.

Elliot Liebow (article 29) earned his Ph.D. at the Catholic University of America. He is a social anthropologist with the National Institute of Mental Health and the author of *Tally's Corner*, the book from which his selection is taken.

Ralph Linton (article 4) earned his Ph.D. at Harvard University, and at the time of his death in 1953 was a Professor of Anthropology at Yale University. His many books include *Culture and Mental Disorders, The Material Culture of the Marquesas Islands, The Cultural Background of Personality*, and *The Study of Man*.

David Matza (article 22) was awarded his Ph.D. at Princeton University and is a Professor of Sociology at the University of California at Berkeley. He is the author of *Delinquency and Drift* and *Becoming Deviant*.

C. Wright Mills (articles 3 and 37) received his Ph.D. from the University of Wisconsin. His scathing criticisms of American society in such books as *White Collar, The Power Elite, The Causes of World War III*, as well as the book from which article 3 is taken, *The Sociological Imagination*, made him one of the most controversial sociologists in the United States. At the time of his death in 1962, he was a Professor of Sociology at Columbia University.

Horace Miner (article 5) earned his Ph.D. at the University of Chicago. He is a Professor Emeritus of Anthropology at the University of Michigan and the author of several books, including *The Primitive City of Timbuctoo, Oasis and Casbah, The City in Modern Africa*, and *Cave Hollow*.

Annabelle B. Motz (article 31) earned her Ph.D. at the University of Chicago and is a Professor of Sociology at American University. She has written (with Kurt Finsterbusch) *Social Research for Policy Decisions*.

Ann Oakley (article 9) earned her Ph.D. at the University of London and is the author of a number of books on feminism, including *Housewife, Becoming a Mother*, and *The Sociology of Housework*, as well as *Subject: Women*, the book from which her selection is taken.

Mimi Rodin (article 11) received her Ph.D. at the University of Illinois and is an Associate Professor at the University of Illinois School of Public Health.

Richard Rodriguez (article 39) wrote this piece while he was a Ph.D. candidate in the Department of English at the University of California at Berkeley. Since then he has written a book, *Hunger of Memory: The Education of Richard Rodriguez*.

Barry Schwartz (article 13) was awarded his Ph.D. at the University of Pennsylvania. He is an Associate Professor of Sociology at the University of Georgia.

Pepper Schwartz (article 10) earned her Ph.D. at Yale University and is an Associate Professor of Sociology at the University of Washington. She is the author of *Sexual Scripts: The Social Construction of Female Sexuality,* (with Janet Lever) *Women at Yale,* and (with Philip Blumstein) *American Couples: Money, Work, and Sex.*

Richard Sennett (article 27) earned his Ph.D. at Harvard University. He is a Professor of Sociology at New York University and the author of such books as *The Fall of a Public Man, Families Against the City,* and *The Use of Disorder.*

Charles W. Smith (article 34) received his Ph.D. at Brandeis University. He is an Associate Professor of Sociology at Queen's College of the City University of New York and has written *A Critique of Sociological Reasoning.*

Leonard I. Stein (article 28) earned his M.D. at the Medical School of the University of Wisconsin, where he is a Professor of Medicine. He has written *Community Support Systems for the Long-Term Patient.*

Anselm L. Strauss (article 35) received his Ph.D. from the University of Chicago and is a Professor of Sociology at the University of California at San Francisco. He is the author of such books as *Where Medicine Fails, Mirrors and Masks: The Search for Identity,* (with Barney G. Glaser) *The Discovery of Grounded Theory,* and (with Barney G. Glaser) *Time for Dying,* from which the selection in this book is taken.

Gresham M. Sykes (article 22) was awarded his Ph.D. at Northwestern University. He is a Professor of Sociology at the University of Virginia. His books include *Crime and Society, Criminology, Society of Captives: A Study of a Maximum Security Prison,* and *The Future of Crime.*

Diane E. Taub (article 20) is a Ph.D. candidate in Sociology at the University of Kentucky, where she is also an Instructor of Sociology.

William E. Thompson (article 17) earned his Ph.D. at Oklahoma State University and is an Assistant Professor of Sociology at Emporia State University.

Alvin Toffler (article 38) received his A.B. degree at New York University. He has received a number of faculty appointments as Visiting Professor and is the author of such books as *The Culture Consumers, The Eco-Spasm Report, The Third Wave,* and *Future Shock,* the book from which his article is taken.

William A. Westley (article 36) earned his Ph.D. from the University of Chicago. He is a Professor of Sociology at McGill University and has written (with Nathan B. Epstein) *The Silent Majority: Families of Emotionally Healthy College Students, Violence and the Police,* and (with Margaret W. Westley) *The Emerging Worker.*

William Foote Whyte (article 15) received his Ph.D. from the University of Chicago. He is a Professor Emeritus of Sociology at Cornell University and has written several books, including *Men at Work, Industry and Society, Organizing for Agricultural Development*, and *Street Corner Society*, the book from which his article is taken.

Philip G. Zimbardo (article 24) earned his Ph.D. at Syracuse University and is a Professor of Clinical Psychology at Stanford University. His books include *Psychology and Life, The Shyness Workbook*, and *Influencing Attitudes and Changing Behavior*.

PART I The Sociological Perspective

I WOULD LIKE TO BEGIN THIS FIRST INTRODUCTION ON A PERSONAL NOTE. Since my early school days, I enjoyed reading immensely. I read almost anything I could lay my hands on and was especially fascinated by books that helped me understand people better—that described their life situations, their thoughts, their relationships, their hopes and dreams and the obstacles to their realization. Without knowing it, I was gaining an appreciation for understanding the context of people's lives—for seeing how important that context is in determining what they are like.

When I went to college and took my first course in sociology, I was "hooked." I found that there was a name for my interests: *sociology*.

This was an exciting discovery for me. In college I found an entire academic discipline centered on understanding the general context in which people live and analyzing how their lives are influenced by that context. I could not help wanting to read sociology, to take more courses, to immerse myself in it.

The intention of this book is to share some of the excitement and fascination of sociology, to make more visible the context of social life that affects us all, and to whet the appetite for more sociology.

This then, is an invitation to sociology, to look behind the scenes to a different way of viewing life.

As Peter L. Berger says in the opening selection, the discovery of sociology can change one's life. It can help one to understand better the social forces one confronts, the forces that constrain and free. This understanding has a liberating potential; by examining these forces one can stand somewhat apart from at least some aspects of society and exert more creative control over one's own life.

1

But just what is sociology? I have found in my teaching that initially, introductory students sometimes find this a vexing question. To provide a better grasp of what sociology is, in the second selection James M. Henslin compares and contrasts sociology with the other social sciences. The comparison shows how, for some, sociology casts an intellectual net that provides an unparalleled approach to understanding social life.

In the third article, C. Wright Mills focuses on the liberating potential offered by sociology. As he points out, this centers on understanding three main issues: (1) the structure of society—that is, how the essential components of society are related; (2) where one's society stands in human history and what changes are occurring in it; and (3) what type of people prevail in one's society, how they are selected for prevalence, and what types are coming to prevail.

Thinking of life in these terms, says Mills, is a quality of mind worth striving for. It is this "sociological imagination," to use his term, that allows us to see beyond our immediate confines, to seek out and understand the broader social and historical forces at work in our lives. As a consequence, he says, we are able to see ourselves more accurately through that perspective.

It is the goal of this first Part, then, to let students dip their feet in the sociological waters, so to speak—to challenge them to venture into sociology and to stimulate their sociological imagination.

1 Invitation to Sociology

PETER L. BERGER

Motivated by an intense desire to know what is "really happening," what goes on "behind the scenes," sociologists study almost every aspect of life in society. As Berger indicates, nothing is either too sacred or too profane to be spared the sociologist's scrutiny. But when one penetrates the surface and peers behind the masks that individuals and organizations wear, one finds a reality quite unlike the one that is so carefully devised and, just as carefully, put forward for public consumption.

It is this changed angle of vision that Berger says is so dangerous, for once one has peered behind the scenes and viewed life in a new light, it is nearly impossible to revert to complacent assumptions. The old, familiar, and so very comfortable ways of looking at life are upset when one's angle of vision changes. This potential of sociology is, of course, part of its excitement.

THE SOCIOLOGIST (that is, the one we would really like to invite to our game) is a person intensively, endlessly, shamelessly interested in the doings of men. His natural habitat is all the human gathering places of the world, wherever men come together. The sociologist may be interested in many other things. But his consuming interest remains in the world of men, their institutions, their history, their passions. And since he is interested in men, nothing that men do can be altogether tedious for him. He will naturally be interested in the events that engage men's ultimate beliefs, their moments of tragedy and grandeur and ecstasy. But he will also be fascinated by the commonplace, the everyday. He will know reverence, but this reverence will not prevent him from wanting to see and to understand. He may sometimes feel revulsion or contempt. But this also will not deter him from wanting to have his questions answered. The sociologist, in his quest for understanding, moves through the world of men without respect for the usual lines of demarcation. Nobility and degradation, power and obscurity, intelligence and folly—these are equally *interesting* to him, however unequal they may be in his personal values or tastes. Thus his questions may lead him to all possible levels of society, the best and the least known places, the most respected and the most despised. And, if he is a good sociologist, he will find himself in all these places because his own questions have so taken possession of him that he has little choice but to seek for answers.

It would be possible to say the same things in a lower key. We could say that the sociologist, but for the grace of his academic title, is the man who must listen to gossip despite himself, who is tempted to look through keyholes, to read other people's mail, to open cabinets. Before some otherwise unoccupied psychologist sets out now to construct an aptitude test for sociologists on the basis of sublimated voyeurism, let us quickly say that we are speaking merely by way of analogy. Perhaps some little boys consumed with curiosity to watch their maiden aunts in the bathroom later become inveterate sociologists. This is quite uninteresting. What interests us is the curiosity that grips any sociologist in front of a closed door behind which there are human voices. If he is a good sociologist he will want to open that door, to understand these voices. Behind each closed door he will anticipate some new facet of human life not yet perceived and understood.

The sociologist will occupy himself with matters that others regard as too sacred or as too distasteful for dispassionate investigation. He will find rewarding the company of priests or of prostitutes, depending not on his personal preferences but on the questions he happens to be asking at the moment. He will also concern himself with matters that others may find much too boring. He will be interested in the human interaction that goes with warfare or with great intellectual discoveries, but also in the relations between people employed in a restaurant or between a group of little girls playing with their dolls. His main focus of attention is not the ultimate significance of what men do, but the action in itself, as another example of the infinite richness of human conduct. So much for the image of our playmate.

In these journeys through the world of men the sociologist will inevitably encounter other professional Peeping Toms. Sometimes these will resent his presence, feeling that he is poaching on their preserves. In some places the sociologist will meet up with the economist, in others with the political scientist, in yet others with the psychologist or the ethnologist. Yet chances are that the questions that have brought him to these places are different from the ones that propelled his fellow-trespassers. The sociologist's questions always remain essentially the same: "What are people doing with each other here?" "What are their relationships to each other?" "How are these relationships organized in institutions?" "What are the collective ideas that move men and institutions?" In trying to answer these questions in specific instances, the sociologist will, of course, have to deal with economic or political matters, but he will do so in a way rather different from that of the economist or the political scientist. The scene that he contemplates is the same human scene that these other scientists concern themselves with. But the sociologist's angle of vision is different. When this is understood, it becomes clear that it makes little sense to try to stake out a special enclave within which the sociologist will carry on business in his own right. Like Wesley the sociologist will have to confess that his parish is the world. But unlike some latter-day Wesleyans he will gladly share this parish with others. There is, however, one traveler whose path the sociologist will cross more often than anyone else's on his journeys. This is the historian. Indeed, as soon as the sociologist turns from the present to the past, his preoccupations are very hard indeed to distinguish from those of the historian. However, we shall leave this relationship to a later part of our considerations. Suffice it to say here that the sociological journey will be much impoverished unless it is punctuated frequently by conversation with that other particular traveler.

Any intellectual activity derives excitement from the moment it becomes a trail of discovery. In some fields of learning this is the discovery of worlds previously unthought and unthinkable. This is the excitement of the astronomer or of the nuclear physicist on the antipodal boundaries of the realities that man is capable of conceiving. But it can be the excitement of bacteriology or geology. In a different way it can be the excitement of the linguist discovering new realms of human expression or of the anthropologist exploring human customs in faraway countries. In such discovery, when undertaken with passion, a widening of awareness, sometimes a veritable transformation of consciousness, occurs. The universe turns out to be much more wonderful than one had ever dreamed. The excitement of sociology is usually of a different sort. Sometimes, it is true, the sociologist penetrates into worlds that had previously been quite unknown to him—for instance, the world of crime, or the world of some bizarre religious sect, or the world fashioned by the exclusive concerns of some group such as medical specialists or military leaders or advertising executives. However, much of the time the sociologist moves in sectors of experience that are familiar to him and to most people in his society. He investigates communities, institutions and activities that one can read about every day in the newspapers. Yet there is another excitement of discovery beckoning in his investigations. It is not the excitement of finding the familiar becoming transformed in its meaning. The fascination of sociology lies in the fact that its perspective makes us see in a new light the very world in which we have lived all of our lives. This also constitutes a transformation of consciousness. Moreover, this transformation is more relevant existentially than that of many other intellectual disciplines, because it is more difficult to segregate in some special compartment of the mind. The astronomer does not live in the remote galaxies, and the nuclear physicist can, outside his laboratory, eat, and laugh and marry and vote without thinking about the insides of the atom. The geologist looks at rocks only at appropriate times, and the linguist speaks English with his wife. The sociologist lives in society, on the job and off it. His own life, inevitably, is part of his subject matter. Men being what they are, sociologists too manage to segregate their professional insights from their everyday affairs. But it is a rather difficult feat to perform in good faith.

The sociologist moves in the common world of men, close to what most of them would call real. The categories he employs in his analyses are only refinements of the categories by which other men live—power, class, status, race, ethnicity. As a result, there is a deceptive simplicity and obviousness about some sociological investigations. One reads them, nods at the familiar scene, remarks that one has heard all this before and don't people have better things to do than to waste their time on truisms—until one is suddenly brought up against an insight that radically questions everything one had previously assumed about this familiar scene. This is the point at which one begins to sense the excitement of sociology.

Let us take a specific example. Imagine a sociology class in a Southern college where almost all the students are white Southerners. Imagine a lecture on the subject of the racial system of the South. The lecturer is talking here of matters that have been familiar to his students from the time of their infancy. Indeed, it may be that they are much more familiar with the minutiae of this system than he is. They are quite bored as a result. It seems to them that he is only using more pretentious words to describe what they already know. Thus he may use the term "caste," one commonly used now by American sociologists to describe the Southern racial system. But in explaining the term he shifts to traditional Hindu society, to make it clearer. He then goes on to analyze the magical beliefs inherent in caste tabus, the social dynamics of commensalism and connubium, the economic interests concealed within the system, the way in which religious beliefs relate to the tabus, the effects of the caste system upon the industrial development of the society and vice versa—all in India. But suddenly India is not very far away at all. The lecture then goes back to its Southern theme. The familiar now seems not quite so familiar any more. Questions are raised that are new, perhaps raised angrily, but raised all the same. And at least some of the students have begun to understand that there are functions involved in this business of race that they have not read about in the newspapers (at least not those in their hometowns) and that their parents have not told them—partly, at least, because neither the newspapers nor the parents knew about them.

It can be said that the first wisdom of sociology is this—things are not what they seem. This too is a deceptively simple statement. It ceases to be simple after a while. Social reality turns out to have many layers of meaning. The discovery of each new layer changes the perception of the whole.

Anthropologists use the term "culture shock" to describe the impact of a totally new culture upon a newcomer. In an extreme instance such shock will be experienced by the Western explorer who is told, halfway through dinner, that he is eating the nice old lady he had been chatting with the previous day—a shock with predictable physiological if not moral consequences. Most explorers no longer encounter cannibalism in their travels today. However, the first encounters with polygamy or with puberty rites or even with the way some nations drive their automobiles can be quite a shock to an American visitor. With the shock may go not only disapproval or disgust but a sense of excitement that things can *really* be that different from what they are at home. To some extent, at least, this is the excitement of any first travel abroad. The experience of sociological discovery could be described as "culture shock" minus geographical displacement. In other words, the sociologist travels at home—with shocking results. He is unlikely to find that he is eating a nice old lady for dinner. But the discovery, for instance, that his own church has considerable money invested in the missile industry or that a few blocks from his home there are people who engage in cultic orgies may not be drastically different in emotional impact. Yet we would not want to imply that sociological discoveries are always or even usually outrageous to moral sentiment. Not at all. What they have in common with exploration in distant lands, however, is the sudden illumination of new and unsuspected facets of human existence in society. This is the excitement and, as we shall try to show later, the humanistic justification of sociology.

People who like to avoid shocking discoveries, who prefer to believe that society is just what they were taught in Sunday School, who like the safety of the rules and the maxims of what Alfred Schutz has called the "world-taken-for-granted," should stay away from sociology. People who feel no temptation before closed doors, who have no curiosity about human beings, who are content to admire scenery without wondering about the people who live in those houses on the other side of that river, should probably stay away from sociology. They will find it unpleasant or, at any rate, unrewarding. People who are interested in human beings only if they can change, convert or reform them should also be warned, for they will find sociology much less useful than they hoped. And people whose interest is mainly in their own conceptual constructions will do just as well to turn to the study of little white mice. Sociology will be satisfying, in the long run, only to those who can think of nothing more entrancing than to watch men and to understand things human.

It may now be clear that we have, albeit deliberately, understated the case in the title of this chapter. [The chapter title from which this selection is taken is "Sociology as an Individual Pastime,"] To be sure, sociology is an individual pastime in the sense that it interests some men and bores others. Some like to observe human beings, others to experiment with mice. The world is big enough to hold all kinds and there is no logical priority for one interest as against another. But the word "pastime" is weak in describing what we mean. Sociology is more like a passion. The sociological perspective is more like a demon that possesses one, that drives one compellingly, again and again, to the questions that are its own. An introduction to sociology is, therefore, an invitation to a very special kind of passion.

2 Sociology and the Social Sciences

JAMES M. HENSLIN

Introductory students often wrestle with the question of what sociology is. If you continue your sociological studies, however, that vagueness of definition—"Sociology is the study of society" or "Sociology is the study of social groups"—that frequently so bothers introductory students will come to be appreciated as one of sociology's strengths and values. That sociology encompasses almost all human behavior is, indeed, precisely the appeal that attracts many to sociology.

To help make clearer at the outset what sociology is, however, Henslin compares and contrasts sociology with the other social sciences. After examining the salient similarities and differences in their approaches to understanding human behavior, he looks at how social scientists from these related academic disciplines would approach the study of juvenile delinquency.

HUMAN BEINGS ARE FASCINATED with the world in which they live. They appear always to have felt this fascination—along with an intense desire to unravel its mysteries—for people in ancient times also attempted to understand their world. Despite the severe limitations which confronted them, the ancients explored the natural or physical world, developing explanations that satisfied them. They also developed an understanding of the social world, the ways in which people organize themselves and deal with one another. Their explanations, however, were based largely on a mixture of magic and superstition which they imposed upon their naturalistic observations.

Contemporary people are no less fascinated with the world within which they live out their lives. They continuously investigate both the mundane and the esoteric. They cast a quizzical eye at the common rocks they find embedded in the earth, as well as at some rare variety of insect found only in some almost inaccessible region of remote Tibet. People subject their world to the constant probings of the instruments and machines they have developed to extend their senses. In their attempt to decipher their observations, they are no longer satisfied with traditional explanations of origins or of relationships. No longer do people unquestioningly accept explanations that earlier generations took for granted. Utilizing observations derived through such technical aids as electronic microscopes and the latest generation of computers, people derive testable conclusions concerning the nature of their world.

As the ancients could only wish to do, our contemporaries have been able to expand their objective study of the world beyond the confines of this planet. In their relentless pursuit of knowledge, people are no longer limited to guesses concerning the nature of other planets. In the last couple of centuries the telescope has enabled people to make detailed and repetitive observations of the planets and other heavenly bodies. From these observations, they have been able to draw startlingly different conclusions from those which people traditionally held concerning the relative place of the earth in our galaxy and the universe. In just the past few years, by means of space technology, we have been able to extend our senses, as it were, beyond anything we had before dreamed possible. We are now able to reach out by means of our space ships, observational satellites, and space platforms to record data from distant planets. We have also been able to dig up and return to the earth samplings of soil from the surface of the moon as well as send space ships to the radiation and magnetic belts of Jupiter, over a distance so great (or, conversely, with technology still so limited) that they must travel eighteen months before they can send back reports.

Such feats a generation ago existed only in the brains of "mad" scientists, who at that time seemed irrelevant to the public but who are today producing fascinating and frequently fearful consequences for our life on earth. Some of these scientists are now giving serious thought to plans for colonizing space, providing still another area of exciting exploration whose consequences will probably be only inadequately anticipated. Others are drawing plans for real space wars, with the potential for results so terrifying we can barely imagine them. In any event, science directly impinges on life in society, leaving none of us unaffected.

In satisfying these basic curiosities concerning the world around us, we have developed what are called the *natural sciences*, the intellectual-academic endeavors designed to comprehend, explain, and predict the events in our *natural environment*. The endeavors of the natural sciences are divided into major specialized fields of research according to their subject matter, such as biology, geology, chemistry, and physics. These are further subdivided into even more highly specialized areas, with a further narrowing of content—biology is divided into botany and zoology, geology into mineralogy and geomorphology, chemistry into its inorganic and organic branches, and physics into biophysics and quantum mechanics. Each of these divisions, in turn, has its own further specialized areas. Each area of investigation examines a particular "slice" of natural reality or the reality of nature.

In their pursuit of an adequate understanding of the world, people have not limited themselves to investigating nature. They have also explored, by means of what are called the social sciences, the social world, the ways in which people relate to each other. The term *social sciences* refers to the subject upon which they focus—the social aspects of people, that is, human relationships. The social sciences are an attempt to objectively understand the social world. Just as the world of nature contains ordered (or lawful) relationships that are not obvious but must be abstracted from nature through controlled observations, so the human or social world is made up of ordered relationships that are also not obvious and must be abstracted by means of controlled and repeated observations.

The social sciences, like the natural sciences, are also divided into specialized fields based on their subject matter. The usual or typical divisions of the social sciences are anthropology, economics, psychology, political science, and sociology, with history sometimes included in this enumeration, depending primarily on the preference of the person drawing the list. To be inclusive, I shall count history as a social science.

Since our focus is sociology, we shall take a brief look at each of these social sciences and contrast each with sociology. I should point out that the differences I shall elaborate are not always this clear in actual practice and that there is much that social scientists do as they practice their crafts which greatly blurs the distinctions I am making.

History, the social science focusing on past events, is perhaps the easiest to deal with. Historians attempt to unearth the facts surrounding an event that they feel is in some way of social significance. They attempt to establish the context, or social milieu, relevant to the event—the important persons, ideas, social movements, and preceding events that appear to have in some way influenced the outcome they are attempting to explain. From this context that they re-establish from the records of the past, they abstract what they consider to be the most important elements, or *variables*, that caused the event. By means of these "causal" factors or variables, historians "explain" the past.

Political science focuses on the study of politics or government. The political scientist studies the ways people govern themselves: the various forms of government, their structures, and their relationships to other institutions of society. The political scientist is especially interested in how people attain the ruling position in their society, how they maintain this position once they secure it, and the social consequences of the activities of rulers for those who are governed. In studying a government which has a constitutional electorate, such as ours, the political scientist is especially concerned with voting behavior.

Economics is another discipline in the social sciences which is primarily concerned with the study of a single social institution. Economists concentrate on the production, distribution, and allocation of the material goods and services of a society. They want to know what goods are being produced at what rate at what cost, the factors that influence their distribution to the consumer, and the variables that determine who gets what. They are also interested in the factors that underlie decisions to produce the particular items in the first place—for example, why with limited resources a certain type of item is being produced instead of another. Some economists, but not nearly enough in my judgment, are also interested in the consequences for human life of facts of production, distribution, and allocation of goods and services.

Anthropology primarily focuses on the study of preliterate peoples. The primary concern of anthropologists is understanding *culture*, the total way of life of a group of people. Culture includes (1) the artifacts people produce, such as their tools, art, and weapons; (2) the way the group is structured, that is, the hierarchy and other patterned organizations of the group that determine people's relationships to their fellow members of the group; (3) ideas and values, especially the belief system of a people, that is, the major things that members of a group believe and the effects of these beliefs on their lives; and (4) their patterns or forms of communication, especially the language used by human groupings. Although some anthropologists now deal with modern societies, this has not traditionally been one of their major efforts. This traditional focus on the distant past and contemporary preliterate peoples, however, is currently undergoing rapid change as anthropologists increasingly turn to the study of people in industrialized settings. Anthropologists who focus on modern societies are practically indistinguishable from sociologists.

Psychology concentrates on processes occurring within the individual. Psychologists deal with what takes place within what they call the "skinbound organism." The psychologist is primarily concerned with processes which occur in what is sometimes referred to as the "mind." This term is still regularly used by the public, but it is used with increasing reservation by psychologists, probably, among other reasons, because no physical entity can be located which exactly corresponds to "mind." Psychologists typically study such phenomena as perception, attitudes, values, and their influences or determinants. They are also especially interested in personality and in how individuals cope with the problems they face.

Sociology is like history in that sociologists also attempt to establish the human context of what they are attempting to explain. Sociology is similar to political science in that sociologists are also extremely interested in how people govern one another, especially in the human consequences of various forms of government. Sociology is like economics in that sociologists are also highly interested in what happens to the goods and services of a society, especially the social consequences of production and distribution. Sociology is also similar to anthropology in that sociologists focus on the study of culture. Sociologists are particularly interested in the social consequences of artifacts, group structure, and belief systems, as well as how people communicate with one another. Sociology is like psychology in that sociologists are also very much concerned with how people adjust to the various contingencies they confront in life. With these overall similarities, where are the differences?

Unlike historians, sociologists are primarily concerned with events in the present. Unlike political scientists and economists, sociologists do not concentrate on a single social institution. Unlike anthropologists, sociologists primarily focus on industrialized societies. And unlike psychologists, sociologists deal primarily with variables external to the individual which influence behavior patterns and life styles.

Because all the social sciences focus on the study of human behavior, they differ from each other not so much in the content of what is being studied than in what social scientists look for when they conduct their studies. It is basically their approaches, their orientations, or their emphases which differentiate the social sciences. Accordingly, to make clearer the differences between them, it might be helpful to look at how different social scientists might approach the same subject or topic. To do this, we shall use juvenile delinquency as our example.

If a historian is interested in juvenile delinquency, he is apt to investigate juvenile delinquency in some particular historical epoch, such as New York City in the 1920s or Los Angeles in the 1950s. The historian would particularly examine the social context (or social milieu) of the era. If delinquent gangs in New York City in the 1920s were his focus, he would especially emphasize the social disruption of that period caused by World War I; the problems of unassimilated, recently arrived ethnic groups; competition and rivalry for social standing among ethnic groups; intergenerational conflict; the national, state, and local political and economic situation; and so on. The historian might also document the number of gangs, and ethnic participation in delinquent gangs. He would then produce a history of juvenile delinquency in New York City in the 1920s.

The political scientist would be less likely to be interested in juvenile delinquency. But if he were, he would be especially concerned to search for relationships between the political structure of the area and the existence of juvenile gangs. He might study the power structure within one particular gang by locating its varying levels or dimensions of power. The political scientist might also compare the political structure of one gang with another, perhaps even drawing analogies with the political structure of the local area, or perhaps even with the United States.

The economist also would not typically study delinquent gangs or juvenile delinquency. But if he did, he would emphasize the economic aspects of delinquent behavior. The economist might examine the differential allocation of material goods within a particular gang, to see who gets what. But he would be more inclined to focus on delinquency in general, emphasizing the relationship of delinquency to economic factors in the country. The economist would be especially interested in examining the effects of varying economic conditions, such as booms and recessions, on the formation of gangs or on the incidence or prevalence of delinquency. He might also be quite interested in determining the cost of juvenile delinquency to the economy of the nation in terms of property stolen and destroyed or in terms of lost man-hours in material production.

The anthropologist is likely to be highly interested in studying juvenile delinquency and the formation of juvenile gangs. If an anthropologist were to study a particular gang, he would probably examine the implements of delinquency, such as tools used in car theft or in burglary. The anthropologist would also focus on the social organization of the group's membership in terms of the structure of power or the various roles within the group. He would also study the belief system of the group to see how it fosters the group's delinquent activities. He would also concentrate on the ways in which group members communicate with one another, especially their *argot* or special language. The anthropologist would examine delinquency within a larger cultural context in order to see what cultural patterns lead to the existence of delinquency and gangs. He would then compare these findings with what anthropologists have discovered about other cultures. In making such a *cross-cultural comparison*, the anthropologist would probably indicate that juvenile delinquency is not a universal phenomenon but a characteristic of industrialized societies. He would point out that industrialized societies typically increase the length of expected or required formal education, especially for males. They thus postpone the age at which a male is allowed to assume the responsibilities of manhood, and it is during this "in-between status," this literal "no-man's-land," that delinquency occurs. The emphasis given by the anthropologist in such a study, then, would be true to his calling: That is, the anthropologist would be focusing on culture.

The psychologist also has a high interest in studying juvenile delinquency. When the psychologist approaches this subject, however, he tends to focus on what exists *within* the delinquent. He would perhaps make and test the assumption (or *hypothesis*) that gang leaders are characterized by more outgoing personality traits or that they are marked by personality patterns of greater hostility and aggressiveness than are their followers. The psychologist might also be concerned with testing for personality differences between adolescent males who join gangs and those in the general population who do not become gang members. He might perhaps run a series of personality tests to determine whether gang members are more insecure, hostile, or aggressive than nonmembers.

The sociologist is also interested in most of these aspects emphasized by the other social scientists. The sociologist, however, is ordinarily not concerned with a particular gang in a past time, as the historian might be, although he is interested in the same variables. The sociologist would probably focus on the power structure of the gang, as would the political scientist, and he is also interested in certain aspects of property, like the economist. But the sociologist would be more interested in the gang members' attitudes toward property, the types of property rights they violate, why they feel it is legitimate to violate them, and how they divide up the property they steal.

In studying juvenile delinquency, the sociologist would also approach the subject in a way quite similar to that of the anthropologist and be interested in the same sorts of things. But the sociologist would particularly focus on the roles within the group. He would want to know if there is greater likelihood that a person will join a delinquent gang if his parents have a particular level of education or how gang membership varies by level of income. If the sociologist found that delinquency varies with education, age, sex, religion, income, or race, he would want to know the reasons for it. Do the sons of workingmen have a greater chance of becoming juvenile delinquents than the sons of doctors and lawyers? If so, what factors lead to such differential recruitment into delinquency?

It is especially with regard to questions concerning *social class* membership (which is based on type of occupation, amount of income, and level of education) that the sociologist differs from the psychologist. The sociologist is not very interested in what are called personality differences. He is more inclined to look for determining variables according to characteristics of social class than is the psychologist. The sociologist also differs from the psychologist in other ways. For example, to determine the reasons that someone becomes the leader of a delinquent gang, the sociologist may want to observe *face-to-face interaction* among gang members (what they do in each other's presence) to see how leaders differ from followers. He would especially want to see whether the values of the group are upheld differently by leaders and followers, and how and why this is so. The sociologist would also want to determine whether leaders and followers act differently when it comes to suggesting activities and who does what when the activity is carried out, whether that activity be simply some form of recreation or a criminal act. For example, do leaders maintain their leadership by committing more acts of daring and bravery than their followers? The sociologist would look for recruitment into gang membership more on the basis of social class characteristics than would the psychologist and would focus more on the informal interaction between gang members to determine differences between leaders and followers.

Further aspects of delinquency that the sociologist would tend to emphasize more than other social scientists are those of police discretion, the judicial process, and changing norms. The police do not by any means arrest everyone who commits a crime. If they were to do so, there would not be enough jails to hold all of us. The police, rather, approach their job with preconceived ideas about who is likely to commit crimes and who is not. These ideas are based on their experiences "on the streets," as well as on a belief system nurtured within their occupation. They typically view some people (usually lower-class males living in a particular area of the city) to be more apt to commit delinquent acts than either females in general or males from other areas or from a higher social class. Moreover, the police are able to charge an offender with a variety of offenses, and they develop a working consensus concerning "appropriate" charges for "typical" acts. What is this consensus, how does it develop, and how is it applied to different offenders? The sociologist, in other words, is deeply interested in finding out how the police define people and human behavior, and how these definitions help to determine whom the police arrest and with what they charge them.

In addition to police discretion on the street, the sociologist is interested in what occurs following an arrest. Prosecutors also work within an area of discretion. For the same act they can charge an individual with a variety of offenses, such as first-degree or second-degree burglary, breaking and entering, or merely trespassing. The sociologist is interested in this process of decision-making as well as its effects on the lives of those charged with crimes. The sociologist also studies what happens when an individual comes before a judge; the types of trial; the outcomes of trials by the sex, age, or race of the offender, and by the type of offense. He also focuses on the effects of detention and incarceration on those who are brought before the bar of justice, as well as the reactions of others when an offender is released and is free to go back into his community.

Norms, the behaviors that people expect of others, obviously change over time. What was considered proper behavior a generation ago is certainly not the same as what is considered proper today. Because expectations of propriety can undergo marked change over time and because some of these expectations become written into law, acts considered to be law violations at one time are not necessarily considered criminal at another time. Similarly, acts not considered criminal at one time may be law violations at a later date. For example, drinking alcohol in public at age sixteen was within the law in some communities at one point in our history, but it would be an act of delinquency today. In the same way, a person under sixteen who is on the streets after 10 P.M. unaccompanied by an adult is breaking the law in some communities. But if the law is changed or if the sixteen-year-old goes to a different community, the same act is not a violation of the law. With marijuana the case is similar. Millions of Americans break the law when they smoke grass. But if the law is changed, legal violations for the same act disappear. The sociologist, more perhaps than any of the other social scientists, maintains a critical interest in the effects of changing legal definitions in determining what people are arrested for and charged with. In effect, the sociologist is interested in what juvenile delinquency is in the first place. He takes the definition of delinquency not as obvious, but as problematic, something to be studied in the context of lawmaking, lawbreaking, and the workaday world of the judicial system.

By means of this example of juvenile delinquency, it is easy to see that the social sciences greatly overlap one another. Sociology is an overarching social science, because sociologists are, for the most part, interested in the same things that other social scientists are interested in. Sociology, however, is not as limited in its scope or focus as are the other social sciences. Except for its traditional concerns with preliterate societies, anthropology is similarly broad in its treatment of human behavior.

Sociologists are interested in how people relate to one another. They focus on *patterned* relationships, that is, the recurring aspects of human behavior. In following this interest, sociologists examine two major aspects of life in society: (1) the *institutions* of society, that is, those patterned, established, or customary arrangements by which humans attempt to solve the perennial problems they face, such as the need for social order and dealing with sickness and death, and (2) *face-to-face interaction*, that is, the ways people interact with others when they are in one another's presence.

In the *first* major form of sociology, the institutional, the focus is on relationships between *social groups*, such as the relationship between membership in a particular religion or occupation and participation in political activities. The sociologist is interested in determining, for example, how participation in a religious group influences whether one votes or not and the stand one takes on social issues. Are there voting differences, for example, between Roman Catholics, Lutherans, Christian Scientists, and Methodists? Does the religion one belongs to influence how one votes—even and especially on issues not directly affecting one's religion? The sociologist, in just the single area of voting, would also be interested in determining how voting patterns change with age, with sex, with different occupations, by different income levels, by race, nationality or ethnicity, by level of education, and by geographical residence—both by region of the country and by urban or rural setting.

The sociologist, however, is interested in more than what we call the *correlates* (relationships) between groups. He is also interested in finding out the significance that membership in a social group at a particular time in history holds for people. The sociologist wants to know what difference it makes for someone's life whether he is a member of one group or another group. It is one thing, for example, to know the proportion of Roman Catholics who vote Democratic (or, in sociological jargon, "the correlation between religious-group membership and voting behavior"), but it is quite another thing to know what difference being a Roman Catholic makes in dating practices, in attitudes toward and participation in premarital sex, or in what one does for recreation, how one treats one's spouse, and how one raises children. The sociologist, unlike the political scientist, the his-

torian, and the others, is interested in all these aspects of life in society—
and more.

In the *second* major form of sociology, the interactional, sociologists
focus on what people do when they are in the presence of one another.
Sociologists observe the behavior of people wherever they meet. They record this behavior by means of note-taking, tape recordings, video taping,
and film. They survey people by means of questionnaires and interviews.
They read social records, from diaries and letters to court transcripts, as
well as memorabilia of pop culture such as *Playboy* and *Playgirl*, science
fiction and comic books. They systematically observe soap operas, children's cartoons, police dramas, and situation comedies. Sociologists then
develop ways of classifying what they have observed, read, recorded, or
been told. Out of their analyses of these various types of observations come
the information, or *data*, from which sociologists draw their conclusions.

Wherever and whenever people come into one another's physical
presence, there is potential data for the sociologist—whether that be on
the street, in the bar, in the classroom, or even in the bedroom—all provide material for sociologists to observe and analyze. Nothing is really taboo to them—in the sense that sociologists are probably right now raising
questions about most aspects of social behavior. Sociologists can whet their
curiosity simply by overhearing a conversation or by catching a glimpse
of an unusual happening. In following that curiosity, they can simply continue to "overhear" conversations, but this time purposely, or they can
conduct an elaborate study with a scientifically selected random sample
backed by huge fundings from some agency. What sociologists study can
be as socially significant as a race riot or as common but personally significant as two people parting with a kiss or greeting with a handshake.

In this sense, then, the world belongs to the sociologist—for to the
sociologist everything is fair game. This characteristic all-inclusiveness of
sociology, indeed, is what makes it so intrinsically fascinating for so many:
Sociology offers a framework that provides a penetrating perspective of
almost everything in which people are interested.

Some who are being introduced to sociology through this little essay
may find the sociological approach to understanding rewarding enough
to take other courses in sociology and, after college, to be attracted to
books of sociological interest. A few, perhaps, may even make sociology
their life's vocation and thus embark on a lifelong journey that takes them
to the far corners of human endeavor, as well as to the more familiar
pursuits in their own society. Certainly some of us, already tempted by
sociology's enchantment and seduction, have experienced an unfolding
panorama of intellectual delight in the midst of an intriguing exploration
of the social world. And, in this enticing process, we discover and rediscover ourselves.

3 The Promise

C. WRIGHT MILLS

The "sociological imagination" is seeing how the unique historical circumstances of a particular society affect people and, at the same time, seeing how people affect history. Every individual lives out his or her life in a particular society, with the historical circumstances of that society greatly influencing what that individual becomes. People who have been shaped by their society contribute, in turn, to the formation of that society and to the course of its history.

It is this quality of mind (termed the sociological imagination by Mills and the "sociological perspective" by others) that is presented for exploration in the readings of this book. As this intersection of biography and history becomes more apparent to you, your own sociological imagination will bring you a deepened and broadened understanding of social life.

NOWADAYS, MEN OFTEN FEEL that their private lives are a series of traps. They sense that, within their everyday worlds, they cannot overcome their troubles, and, in this feeling, they are quite correct: What ordinary men are directly aware of and what they try to do are bounded by the private orbits in which they live; their visions and their powers are limited to the close-up scenes of job, family, neighborhood; in other milieux, they move vicariously and remain spectators. And the more aware they become, however vaguely, of ambitions and of threats, that transcend their immediate locales, the more trapped they seem to feel.

Underlying this sense of being trapped are seemingly impersonal changes in the very structure of continent-wide societies. The facts of contemporary history are also facts about the success and the failure of individual men and women. When a society is industrialized, a peasant becomes a worker; a feudal lord is liquidated or becomes a businessman. When classes rise or fall, a man is employed or unemployed; when the rate of investment goes up or down, a man takes new heart or goes broke. When wars happen, an insurance salesman becomes a rocket launcher; a store clerk, a radar man; a wife lives alone; a child grows up without a father. Neither the life of an individual nor the history of a society can be understood without understanding both.

Yet, men do not usually define the troubles they endure in terms of

historical change and institutional contradiction. The well-being they enjoy, they do not usually impute to the big ups and downs of the societies
in which they live. Seldom aware of the intricate connection between the
patterns of their own lives and the course of world history, ordinary men
do not usually know what this connection means for the kinds of men they
are becoming and for the kinds of history-making in which they might
take part. They do not possess the quality of mind essential to grasp the
interplay of man and society, of biography and history, of self and world.
They cannot cope with their personal troubles in such ways as to control
the structural transformations that usually lie behind them.

Surely, it is no wonder. In what period have so many men been so
totally exposed at so fast a pace to such earthquakes of change? That
Americans have not known such catastrophic changes as have the men and
women of other societies is due to historical facts that are now quickly
becoming "merely history." The history that now affects every man is
world history. Within this scene and this period, in the course of a single
generation, one-sixth of mankind is transformed from all that is feudal
and backward into all that is modern, advanced, and fearful. Political
colonies are freed; new and less visible forms of imperialism, installed.
Revolutions occur; men feel the intimate grip of new kinds of authority. Totalitarian societies rise, and are smashed to bits—or succeed fab-
ulously. After two centuries of ascendancy, capitalism is shown up as only
one way to make society into an industrial apparatus. After two centuries
of hope, even formal democracy is restricted to a quite small portion of
mankind. Everywhere in the underdeveloped world, ancient ways of life
are broken up and vague expectations become urgent demands. Everywhere in the overdeveloped world, the means of authority and of violence
become total in scope and bureaucratic in form. Humanity itself now lies
before us, the supernation at either pole concentrating its most coordinated and massive efforts upon the preparation of World War III.

The very shaping of history now outpaces the ability of men to orient
themselves in accordance with cherished values. And which values? Even
when they do not panic, men often sense that older ways of feeling and
thinking have collapsed, and that newer beginnings are ambiguous to the
point of moral stasis. Is it any wonder that ordinary men feel they cannot
cope with the larger worlds with which they are so suddenly confronted?
That they cannot understand the meaning of their epoch for their own
lives? That—in defense of selfhood—they become morally insensible,
trying to remain altogether private men? Is it any wonder that they come
to be possessed by a sense of the trap?

It is not only information that they need—in this Age of Fact, information often dominates their attention and overwhelms their capacities
to assimilate it. It is not only the skills of reason that they need—although
their struggles to acquire these often exhaust their limited moral energy.

What they need, and what they feel they need, is a quality of mind that will help them to use information and to develop reason in order to achieve lucid summations of what is going on in the world and of what may be happening within themselves. It is this quality, I am going to contend, that journalists and scholars, artists and publics, scientists and editors are coming to expect of what may be called the sociological imagination.

The sociological imagination enables its possessor to understand the larger historical scene in terms of its meaning for the inner life and the external career of a variety of individuals. It enables him to take into account how individuals, in the welter of their daily experience, often become falsely conscious of their social positions. Within that welter, the framework of modern society is sought, and within that framework the psychologies of a variety of men and women are formulated. By such means, the personal uneasiness of individuals is focused upon explicit troubles, and the indifference of publics is transformed into involvement with public issues.

The first fruit of this imagination—and the first lesson of the social science that embodies it—is the idea that the individual can understand his own experience and gauge his own fate only by locating himself within his period, that he can know his own chances in life only by becoming aware of those of all individuals in his circumstances. In many ways, it is a terrible lesson; in many ways, a magnificent one. We do not know the limits of man's capacities for supreme effort or willing degradation, for agony or glee, for pleasurable brutality or the sweetness of reason. But in our time we have come to know that the limits of "human nature" are frighteningly broad. We have come to know that every individual lives, from one generation to the next, in some society; that he lives out a biography, and that he lives it out within some historical sequence. By the fact of his living he contributes, however minutely, to the shaping of this society and to the course of its history, even as he is made by society and by its historical push and shove.

The sociological imagination enables us to grasp history and biography and the relations between the two within society. That is its task and its promise. To recognize this task and this promise is the mark of the classic social analyst. It is characteristic of Herbert Spencer—turgid, polysyllabic, comprehensive; of E. A. Ross—graceful, muckraking, upright; of Auguste Comte and Emile Durkheim; of the intricate and subtle Karl Mannheim. It is the quality of all that is intellectually excellent in Karl Marx; it is the clue to Thorstein Veblen's brilliant and ironic insight, to Joseph Schumpeter's many-sided constructions of reality; it is the basis of the psychological sweep of W. E. H. Lecky no less than of the profundity and clarity of Max Weber. And it is the signal of what is best in contemporary studies of man and society.

No social study that does not come back to the problems of biography, of history, and of their intersections within a society has completed its intellectual journey. Whatever the specific problems of the classic social analysts, however limited or however broad the features of social reality they have examined, those who have been imaginatively aware of the promise of their work have consistently asked three sorts of questions:

1. What is the structure of this particular society as a whole? What are its essential components, and how are they related to one another? How does it differ from other varieties of social order? Within it, what is the meaning of any particular feature for its continuance and for its change?

2. Where does this society stand in human history? What are the mechanics by which it is changing? What is its place within, and its meaning for, the development of humanity as a whole? How does any particular feature we are examining affect, and how is it affected by, the historical period in which it moves? And this period—what are its essential features? How does it differ from other periods? What are its characteristic ways of history-making?

3. What varieties of men and women now prevail in this society and in this period? And what varieties are coming to prevail? In what ways are they selected and formed, liberated and repressed, made sensitive and blunted? What kinds of "human nature" are revealed in the conduct and character we observe in this society in this period? And what is the meaning for "human nature" of each and every feature of the society we are examining?

Whether the point of interest is a great power state or a minor literary mood, a family, a prison, a creed—these are the kinds of questions the best social analysts have asked. They are the intellectual pivots of classic studies of man in society—and they are the questions inevitably raised by any mind possessing the sociological imagination. For that imagination is the capacity to shift from one perspective to another—from the political to the psychological; from examination of a single family to comparative assessment of the national budgets of the world; from the theological school to the military establishment; from considerations of an oil industry to studies of contemporary poetry. It is the capacity to range from the most impersonal and remote transformations to the most intimate features of the human self—and to see the relations between the two. Back of its use, there is always the urge to know the social and historical meaning of the individual in the society and in the period in which he has his quality and his being.

That, in brief, is why it is by means of the sociological imagination that men now hope to grasp what is going on in the world, and to understand what is happening in themselves as minute points of the intersections of biography and history within society. In large part, contemporary man's self-conscious view of himself as at least an outsider, if not a permanent stranger, rests upon an absorbed realization of social relativity and of the transformative power of history. The sociological imagination is the most fruitful form of this self-consciousness. By its use, men whose mentalities have swept only a series of limited orbits often come to feel as if suddenly awakened in a house with which they had only supposed themselves to be familiar. Correctly or incorrectly, they often come to feel that they can now provide themselves with adequate summations, cohesive assessments, comprehensive orientations. Older decisions that once appeared sound now seem to them products of a mind unaccountably dense. Their capacity for astonishment is made lively again. They acquire a new way of thinking, they experience a transvaluation of values: In a word, by their reflection and by their sensibility, they realize the cultural meaning of the social sciences.

Perhaps the most fruitful distinction with which the sociological imagination works is between the "personal troubles of milieu" and the "public issues of social structure." This distinction is an essential tool of the sociological imagination and a feature of all classic work in social science.

Troubles occur within the character of the individual and within the range of his immediate relations with others; they have to do with his self and with those limited areas of social life of which he is directly and personally aware. Accordingly, the statement and the resolution of troubles properly lie within the individual as a biographical entity and within the scope of his immediate milieu—the social setting that is directly open to his personal experience and, to some extent, his willful activity. A trouble is a private matter: Values cherished by an individual are felt by him to be threatened.

Issues have to do with matters that transcend these local environments of the individual and the range of his inner life. They have to do with the organization of many such milieux into the institutions of a historical society as a whole, with the ways in which various milieux overlap and interpenetrate to form the larger structure of social and historical life. An issue is a public matter: Some value cherished by publics is felt to be threatened. Often, there is a debate about what that value really is and about what it is that really threatens it. This debate is often without focus, if only because it is the very nature of an issue, unlike even widespread trouble, that it cannot very well be defined in terms of the immediate and everyday environments of ordinary men. An issue, in fact, often involves a crisis in institutional arrangements, and often, too, it involves what Marxists call "contradictions" or "antagonisms."

In these terms, consider unemployment. When, in a city of 100,000, only one man is unemployed, that is his personal trouble, and for its relief we properly look to the character of the man, his skills, and his immediate opportunities. But when, in a nation of 50 million employees, 15 million men are unemployed, that is an issue, and we may not hope to find its solution within the range of opportunities open to any one individual. The very structure of opportunities has collapsed. Both the correct statement of the problem and range of possible solutions require us to consider the economic and political institutions of the society, and not merely the personal situation and character of a scatter of individuals.

Consider war. The personal problem of war, when it occurs, may be how to survive it or how to die in it with honor; how to make money out of it; how to climb into the higher safety of the military apparatus; or how to contribute to the war's termination. In short, according to one's values, to find a set of milieux and within it to survive the war or make one's death in it meaningful. But the structural issues of war have to do with its causes; with what types of men it throws up into command; with its effects upon economic and political, family and religious institutions, with the unorganized irresponsibility of a world of nation-states.

Consider marriage. Inside a marriage, a man and a woman may experience personal troubles; but, when the divorce rate during the first four years of marriage is 250 out of every 1,000 attempts, this is an indication of a structural issue having to do with the institutions of marriage and the family and other institutions that bear upon them.

Or consider the metropolis—the horrible, beautiful, ugly, magnificent sprawl of the great city. For many upper-class people, the personal solution to the problem of the city is to have an apartment with private garage under it in the heart of the city, and forty miles out, a house by Henry Hill, garden by Garrett Eckbo, on a hundred acres of private land. In these two controlled environments—with a small staff at each end and a private helicopter connection—most people could solve many of the problems of personal milieux caused by the facts of the city. But all this, however splendid, does not solve the public issues that the structural fact of the city poses. What should be done with this wonderful monstrosity? Break it all up into scattered units, combining residence and work? Refurbish it as it stands? Or, after evacuation, dynamite it and build new cities according to new plans in new places? What should those plans be? And who is to decide and to accomplish whatever choice is made? These are structural issues; to confront them and to solve them requires us to consider political and economic issues that affect innumerable milieux.

Insofar as an economy is so arranged that slumps occur, the problem of unemployment becomes incapable of personal solution. Insofar as war is inherent in the nation-state system and in the uneven industrialization of the world, the ordinary individual in his restricted milieu will be powerless—with or without psychiatric aid—to solve the troubles this system or lack of system imposes upon him. Insofar as the family as an institution turns women into darling little slaves and men into their chief providers and unweaned dependents, the problem of a satisfactory marriage remains incapable of purely private solution. Insofar as the overdeveloped megalopolis and the overdeveloped automobile are built-in features of the overdeveloped society, the issues of urban living will not be solved by personal ingenuity and private wealth.

What we experience in various and specific milieux, I have noted, is often caused by structural changes. Accordingly, to understand the changes of many personal milieux, we are required to look beyond them. And the number and variety of such structural changes increase as the institutions within which we live become more embracing and more intricately connected with one another. To be aware of the idea of social structure and to use it with sensibility is to be capable of tracing such linkages among a great variety of milieux. To be able to do that is to possess the sociological imagination.

What are the major issues for publics and the key troubles of private individuals in our time? To formulate issues and troubles, we must ask what values are cherished yet threatened, and what values are cherished and supported, by the characterizing trends of our period. In the case both of threat and of support, we must ask what salient contradictions of structure may be involved.

When people cherish some set of values and do not feel any threat to them, they experience *well-being*. When they cherish values but *do* feel them to be threatened, they experience a crisis—either as a personal trouble or as a public issue. And, if all their values seem involved, they feel the total threat of panic.

But suppose people are neither aware of any cherished values nor experience any threat? That is the experience of *indifference*, which, if it seems to involve all their values, becomes apathy. Suppose, finally, they are unaware of any cherished values, but still are very much aware of a threat? That is the experience of *uneasiness*, of anxiety, which, if it is total enough, becomes a deadly, unspecified malaise.

Ours is a time of uneasiness and indifference—not yet formulated in such ways as to permit the work of reason and the play of sensibility. Instead of troubles—defined in terms of values and threats—there is often the misery of vague uneasiness; instead of explicit issues, there is often merely the beat feeling that all is somehow not right. Neither the values threatened nor whatever threatens them has been stated; in short, they have not been carried to the point of decision. Much less have they been formulated as problems of social science.

In the 1930s, there was little doubt—except among certain deluded business circles—that there was an economic issue that was also a pack of personal troubles. In these arguments about the "crisis of capitalism," the formulations of Marx and the many unacknowledged reformulations of his work probably set the leading terms of the issue, and some men came to understand their personal troubles in these terms. The values threatened were plain to see and cherished by all; the structural contradictions that threatened them also seemed plain. Both were widely and deeply experienced. It was a political age.

But the values threatened in the era after World War II are often neither widely acknowledged as values nor widely felt to be threatened. Much private uneasiness goes unformulated; much public malaise and many decisions of enormous structural relevance never become public issues. For those who accept such inherited values as reason and freedom, it is the uneasiness itself that is the trouble; it is the indifference itself that is the issue. And it is the condition, of uneasiness and indifference, that is the signal feature of our period.

All this is so striking that it is often interpreted by observers as a shift in the very kinds of problems that need now to be formulated. We are frequently told that the problems of our decade, or even the crises of our period, have shifted from the external realm of economics and now have to do with the quality of individual life—in fact, with the question of whether there is soon going to be anything that can properly be called individual life. Not child labor but comic books, not poverty but mass leisure, are at the center of concern. Many great public issues as well as many private troubles are described in terms of "psychiatric"—often, it seems in a pathetic attempt to avoid the large issues and problems of modern society. Often, this statement seems to rest upon a provincial narrowing of interest to the Western societies, or even to the United States—thus ignoring two-thirds of mankind; often, too, it arbitrarily divorces the individual life from the larger institutions within which that life is enacted, and which on occasion bear upon it more grievously than do the intimate environments of childhood.

Problems of leisure, for example, cannot even be stated without considering problems of work. Family troubles over comic books cannot be formulated as problems without considering the plight of the contemporary family in its new relations with the newer institutions of the social structure. Neither leisure nor its debilitating uses can be understood as problems without recognition of the extent to which malaise and indifference now form the social and personal climate of contemporary American society. In this climate, no problems of the "private life" can be stated and solved without recognition of the crisis of ambition that is part of the very career of men at work in the incorporated economy.

It is true, as psychoanalysts continually point out, that people do often have the "increasing sense of being moved by obscure forces within themselves that they are unable to define." But it is *not* true, as Ernest Jones asserted, that "man's chief enemy and danger is his own unruly nature and the dark forces pent up within him." On the contrary: "Man's chief danger" today lies in the unruly forces of contemporary society itself, with its alienating methods of production, its enveloping techniques of political domination, its international anarchy—in a word, its pervasive transformations of the very "nature" of man and the conditions and aims of his life.

It is now the social scientist's foremost political and intellectual task— for here the two coincide—to make clear the elements of contemporary uneasiness and indifference. It is the central demand made upon him by other cultural workmen—by physical scientists and artists, by the intellectual community in general. It is because of this task and these demands, I believe, that the social sciences are becoming the common denominator of our cultural period, and the sociological imagination, our most needed quality of mind.

PART II

The Cultural Context of Social Life

WHAT IS CULTURE? The concept is sometimes easier to grasp by description than by definition. For example, when we meet someone from a different culture, that person's culture is immediately evident to us. We see it in his or her clothing, jewelry, mannerisms, language, beliefs expressed about the world, and opinions of what is valuable or worthwhile in life. These characteristics, which may contrast sharply with our own, alert us to broad differences in the way the person was raised—to that person's culture.

Culture consists of *material* things, such as art, weapons, utensils, machinery, or, from the above example, clothing and jewelry. Culture also has a *nonmaterial* aspect, the general beliefs and patterns of behavior common to a group of people. Nonmaterial culture is of primary interest to sociologists for it provides the broad framework within which people interpret life, the lens through which they see the world and perceive reality.

Understanding how culture affects people's lives is essential to attaining a sociological imagination. But while we may become aware of culture's pervasive influence when we meet someone from a different culture, our own culture is quite another matter. Our speech, our mannerisms, our beliefs, and our ways of doing things are usually taken for granted. We assume that they are normal or natural, and almost without exception we perform them ritually without question. As Ralph Linton said, "The last thing a fish would ever notice would be water." So it is with us; except for unusual circumstances, the effects of our own culture are generally imperceptible to us.

Yet culture's significance for our behavior, our orientation to life, and ultimately our very being is profound. Hardly an aspect of who and what we are is untouched by our culture. We came into this life without a language, without values, with no ideas about religion, education, war, money, friendship, love, economic necessity, family relationships, duties and privileges, rights and obligations, and so on. We had none of these fundamental orientations that we take for granted and that are so essential in determining the type of people we are. Yet at this point in our lives we all have them. That is culture *within* us.

These learned and shared ways of believing and of doing things (another way of defining *culture*) penetrate our beings at an early age and become part of our basic orientation to life. They become part of our assumptions of what normal is, the screen through which we perceive and evaluate what is going on around us. Seldom do we question these assumptions; a part of our framework for viewing life, they are themselves beyond our perception.

The rare instances in which they emerge, however, can be an upsetting experience. For example, if several Americans arrive at a ticket booth at the same time, they will usually line up, each taking a place behind the other on the basis of time of arrival. The ticket seller, a member of this culture, also assumes the normalcy of this behavior, and he or she sells tickets routinely on a "first come, first served" basis. To us, this seems most natural, and we engage in this behavior routinely.

But in northern Africa, where the ideas of space are quite different from ours, when several people want a ticket, each pushes his or her way noisily toward the ticket booth. With no conception similar to our "first come, first served" notion, the ticket seller first dispenses tickets to the noisiest, the pushiest, and, not incidentally, to those with the longest arms.

When I traveled in northern Africa, this part of their culture was most upsetting to me. It violated my basic expectations of "the way people ought to be"—expectations that I did not even know I had until they were so abruptly overturned. At that point I experienced *culture shock,* unable to depend on the basics of social interaction that I had learned in childhood. The fact that I was several inches taller than most Africans and that with my longer arms I was able to outreach almost everyone helped me, however, to adjust partially to this different way of doing things. I never did get used to the idea that this was "right," however, and always felt guilty using the accident of my size to receive preferential treatment.

It is to sensitize us to this aspect of life in society—to the role that fundamental cultural factors play in our lives—that these selections are directed. Ralph Linton, Horace Miner, the Halls, and Erving Goffman each introduce us to parts of our social lives that ordinarily go unquestioned and largely unnoticed. In his inimitable fashion, Linton indicates the critical dependence of modern life on material developments from present and past societies around the world. Miner, the Halls, and Goffman helps us to see more clearly our basic assumptions about taking care of the body, about our nonverbal communications, and about the intricate ways by which we continually try to manipulate the opinions others have of us. These analyses of culture can serve as beginning points from which we can start to analyze other assumptions of reality and gain a startlingly different perspective of social life.

4 One Hundred Per Cent American

RALPH LINTON

In every society of the world people are *ethnocentric;* that is, tending to see life from the framework of what is common in their own group, they generally evaluate the ways of other groups as inferior to their own. From the beginning of our history Americans have been no exception to this tendency, and with the extensive political and social dominance of the United States in recent decades we have become even more proudly ethnocentric. (As our dominance has come under severe challenge in some areas, however, as with Oriental production of automobiles and electronic products, our ethnocentrism has taken a blow, becoming somewhat less certain and more defensive.)

We tend to think of *cultural diffusion,* the spread of culture from one society to another, as a one-way street—others adopting our superior American "know-how." Almost invisible to us, however, is the amazing extent to which our way of life is vitally dependent on the contributions of other peoples. As Ralph Linton so compellingly points out in this selection, much of what we take for granted as being "American" has its origins elsewhere.

THERE CAN BE NO QUESTION ABOUT the average American's Americanism or his desire to preserve this precious heritage at all costs. Nevertheless, some insidious foreign ideas have already wormed their way into his civilization without his realizing what was going on. Thus dawn finds the unsuspecting patriot garbed in pajamas, a garment of East Indian origin; and lying in a bed built on a pattern which originated in either Persia or Asia Minor. He is muffled to the ears in unAmerican materials: cotton, first domesticated in India; linen, domesticated in the Near East; wool from an animal native to Asia Minor; or silk whose uses were first discovered by the Chinese. All these substances have been transformed into cloth by methods invented in Southwestern Asia. If the weather is cold enough he may even be sleeping under an eiderdown quilt invented in Scandinavia.

On awakening he glances at the clock, a medieval European invention, uses one potent Latin word in abbreviated form, rises in haste, and

33

goes to the bathroom. Here, if he stops to think about it, he must feel himself in the presence of a great American institution; he will have heard stories of both the quality and frequency of foreign plumbing and will know that in no other country does the average man perform his ablutions in the midst of such splendor. But the insidious foreign influence pursues him even here. Glass was invented by the ancient Egyptians, the use of glazed tiles for floors and walls in the Near East, porcelain in China, and the art of enameling on metal by Mediterranean artisans of the Bronze Age. Even his bathtub and toilet are but slightly modified copies of Roman originals. The only purely American contribution to the ensemble is the steam radiator, against which our patriot very briefly and unintentionally places his posterior.

In this bathroom the American washes with soap invented by the ancient Gauls. Next he cleans his teeth, a subversive European practice which did not invade America until the latter part of the eighteenth century. He then shaves, a masochistic rite first developed by the heathen priests of ancient Egypt and Sumer. The process is made less of a penance by the fact that his razor is of steel, an iron-carbon alloy discovered in either India or Turkestan. Lastly, he dries himself on a Turkish towel.

Returning to the bedroom, the unconscious victim of un-American practices removes his clothes from a chair, invented in the Near East, and proceeds to dress. He puts on close-fitting tailored garments whose form derives from the skin clothing of the ancient nomads of the Asiatic steppes and fastens them with buttons whose prototypes appeared in Europe at the close of the Stone Age. This costume is appropriate enough for outdoor exercise in a cold climate, but is quite unsuited to American summers, steam-heated houses, and Pullmans. Nevertheless, foreign ideas and habits hold the unfortunate man in thrall even when common sense tells him that the authentically American costume of gee string and moccasins would be far more comfortable. He puts on his feet stiff coverings made from hide prepared by a process invented in ancient Egypt and cut to a pattern which can be traced back to ancient Greece, and makes sure that they are properly polished, also a Greek idea. Lastly, he ties about his neck a strip of bright-colored cloth which is a vestigial survival of the shoulder shawls worn by seventeenth-century Croats. He gives himself a final appraisal in the mirror, an old Mediterranean invention, and goes downstairs to breakfast.

Here a whole new series of foreign things confronts him. His food and drink are placed before him in pottery vessels, the popular name of which—china—is sufficient evidence of their origin. His fork is a medieval Italian invention and his spoon a copy of a Roman original. He will usually begin the meal with coffee, an Abyssinian plant first discovered by the Arabs. The American is quite likely to need it to dispel the morning-after effects of overindulgence in fermented drinks, invented in the Near East;

or distilled ones, invented by the alchemists of medieval Europe. Whereas the Arabs took their coffee straight, he will probably sweeten it with sugar, discovered in India; and dilute it with cream, both the domestication of cattle and the technique of milking having originated in Asia Minor.

If our patriot is old-fashioned enough to adhere to the so-called American breakfast, his coffee will be accompanied by an orange, domesticated in the Mediterranean region, a cantaloupe domesticated in Persia, or grapes domesticated in Asia Minor. He will follow this with a bowl of cereal made from grain domesticated in the Near East and prepared by methods also invented there. From this he will go on to waffles, a Scandinavian invention, with plenty of butter, originally a Near-Eastern cosmetic. As a side dish he may have the egg of a bird domesticated in Southeastern Asia or strips of the flesh of an animal domesticated in the same region, which have been salted and smoked by a process invented in Northern Europe.

Breakfast over, he places upon his head a molded piece of felt, invented by the nomads of Eastern Asia, and, if it looks like rain, puts on outer shoes of rubber, discovered by the ancient Mexicans, and takes an umbrella, invented in India. He then sprints for his train—the train, not sprinting, being an English invention. At the station he pauses for a moment to buy a newspaper, paying for it with coins invented in ancient Lydia. Once on board he settles back to inhale the fumes of a cigarette invented in Mexico, or a cigar invented in Brazil. Meanwhile, he reads the news of the day, imprinted in characters invented by the ancient Semites by a process invented in Germany upon a material invented in China. As he scans the latest editorial pointing out the dire results to our institutions of accepting foreign ideas, he will not fail to thank a Hebrew God in an Indo-European language that he is a one hundred percent (decimal system invented by the Greeks) American (from Americus Vespucci, Italian geographer).

[From the time that this selection was written we have moved from origins of material culture to a much more extensive exchange of the items themselves. If Ralph Linton were alive today, he might add that his "typical American" is likely to watch a television made in Japan and drive a car that, if not made in another country, is likely to contain at least some parts from Japan or Germany, while it is fueled by products from Saudi Arabia and Mexico; wear shoes made in Brazil and a shirt or blouse manufactured in Taiwan or Formosa; and play computer games made in Hong Kong. With very recent changes, he or she may unknowingly shop in an "old name" American supermarket now owned by a British firm, paying for the groceries with a check drawn on a landmark bank controlled by Arabian financial interests.—Ed.]

5 Body Ritual Among the Nacirema

HORACE MINER

As part of their culture, all peoples develop ideas about proper ways to care for their bodies. The Nacirema, however, have developed these ideas to a phenomenal degree, spending a good deal of their time, energy, and income following the rituals prescribed by their culture. Taking care of the body in the prescribed manner is so important to these people that a good part of their childraising revolves around teaching their unquestioned cultural rituals. With intense and prolonged training, accompanied by punishing children who fail to conform and shunning nonconforming adults, it is no wonder that almost all members of Nacirema culture unquestioningly conform to their prescribed body rituals and pass them on dutifully to their own children.

A better understanding of the Nacirema culture might possibly shed some light on our own way of life.

THE ANTHROPOLOGIST HAS BECOME SO FAMILIAR with the diversity of ways in which different peoples behave in similar situations that he is not apt to be surprised by even the most exotic customs. In fact, if all of the logically possible combinations of behavior have not been found somewhere in the world, he is apt to suspect that they must be present in some yet undescribed tribe. This point has, in fact, been expressed with respect to clan organization by Murdock. In this light, the magical beliefs and practices of the Nacirema present such unusual aspects that it seems desirable to describe them as an example of the extremes to which human behavior can go.

Professor Linton first brought the ritual of the Nacirema to the attention of anthropologists twenty years ago, but the culture of this people is still very poorly understood. They are a North American group living in the territory between the Canadian Cree, the Yaqui and Tarahumare of Mexico, and the Carib and Arawak of the Antilles. Little is known of their origin, although tradition states that they came from the east. . . .

Nacirema culture is characterized by a highly developed market economy which has evolved in a rich natural habitat. While much of the people's time is devoted to economic pursuits, a large part of the fruits of these labors and a considerable portion of the day are spent in ritual activity. The focus of this activity is the human body, the appearance and health of which loom as a dominant concern in the ethos of the people. While such a concern is certainly not unusual, its ceremonial aspects and associated philosophy are unique.

The fundamental belief underlying the whole system appears to be that the human body is ugly and that its natural tendency is to debility and disease. Incarcerated in such a body, man's only hope is to avert these characteristics through the use of the powerful influences of ritual and ceremony. Every household has one or more shrines devoted to this purpose. The more powerful individuals in the society have several shrines in their houses and, in fact, the opulence of a house is often referred to in terms of the number of such ritual centers it possesses. Most houses are of wattle and daub construction, but the shrine rooms of the more wealthy are walled with stone. Poorer families imitate the rich by applying pottery plaques to their shrine walls.

While each family has at least one such shrine, the rituals associated with it are not family ceremonies but are private and secret. The rites are normally only discussed with children, and then only during the period when they are being initiated into these mysteries. I was able, however, to establish sufficient rapport with the natives to examine these shrines and to have the rituals described to me.

The focal point of the shrine is a box or chest which is built into the wall. In this chest are kept the many charms and magical potions without which no native believes he could live. These preparations are secured from a variety of specialized practitioners. The most powerful of these are the medicine men, whose assistance must be rewarded with substantial gifts. However, the medicine men do not provide the curative potions for their clients, but decide what the ingredients should be and then write them down in an ancient and secret language. This writing is understood only by the medicine men and by the herbalists who, for another gift, provide the required charm.

The charm is not disposed of after it has served its purpose, but is placed in the charmbox of the household shrine. As these magical materials are specific for certain ills, and the real or imagined maladies of the people are many, the charm-box is usually full to overflowing. The magical packets are so numerous that people forget what their purposes were and fear to use them again. While the natives are very vague on this point, we can only assume that the idea in retaining all the old magical materials is that their presence in the charm-box, before which the body rituals are conducted, will in some way protect the worshipper.

Beneath the charm-box is a small font. Each day every member of the family, in succession, enters the shrine room, bows his head before the charm-box, mingles different sorts of holy water in the font, and proceeds with a brief rite of ablution. The holy waters are secured from the Water Temple of the community, where the priests conduct elaborate ceremonies to make the liquid ritually pure.

In the hierarchy of magical practitioners, and below the medicine men in prestige, are specialists whose designation is best translated "holy-mouth-men." The Nacirema have an almost pathological horror of and fascination with the mouth, the condition of which is believed to have a supernatural influence on all social relationships. Were it not for the rituals of the mouth, they believe that their teeth would fall out, their gums bleed, their jaws shrink, their friends desert them, and their lovers reject them. They also believe that a strong relationship exists between oral and moral characteristics. For example, there is a ritual ablution of the mouth for children which is supposed to improve their moral fiber.

The daily body ritual performed by everyone includes a mouth-rite. Despite the fact that these people are so punctilious about care of the mouth, this rite involves a practice which strikes the uninitiated stranger as revolting. It was reported to me that the ritual consists of inserting a small bundle of hog hairs into the mouth, along with certain magical powders, and then moving the bundle in a highly formalized series of gestures.

In addition to the private mouth-rite, the people seek out a holy-mouth-man once or twice a year. These practitioners have an impressive set of paraphernalia, consisting of a variety of augers, awls, probes, and prods. The use of these objects in the exorcism of the evils of the mouth involves almost unbelievable ritual torture of the client. The holy-mouth-man opens the client's mouth and, using the above mentioned tools, enlarges any holes which decay may have created in the teeth. Magical materials are put into these holes. If there are no naturally occurring holes in the teeth, large sections of one or more teeth are gouged out so that the supernatural substance can be applied. In the client's view, the purpose of these ministrations is to arrest decay and to draw friends. The extremely sacred and traditional character of the rite is evident in the fact that the natives return to the holy-mouth-men year after year, despite the fact that their teeth continue to decay.

It is to be hoped that, when a thorough study of the Nacirema is made, there will be careful inquiry into the personality structure of these people. One has but to watch the gleam in the eye of a holy-mouth-man, as he jabs an awl into an exposed nerve, to suspect that a certain amount of sadism is involved. If this can be established, a very interesting pattern emerges, for most of the population shows definite masochistic tendencies. It was to these that Professor Linton referred in discussing a distinctive part of the daily body ritual which is performed only by men. This part of the rite involves scraping and lacerating the surface of the face with a sharp instrument. Special women's rites are performed only four times during each lunar month, but what they lack in frequency is made up in barbarity. As part of this ceremony, women bake their heads in small ovens for about an hour. The theoretically interesting point is that what seems to be a preponderantly masochistic people have developed sadistic specialists.

The medicine men have an imposing temple, or *latipso*, in every community of any size. The more elaborate ceremonies required to treat very sick patients can only be performed at this temple. These ceremonies involve not only the thaumaturge but a permanent group of vestal maidens who move sedately about the temple chambers in distinctive costume and headdress.

The *latipso* ceremonies are so harsh that it is phenomenal that a fair proportion of the really sick natives who enter the temple ever recover. Small children whose indoctrination is still incomplete have been known to resist attempts to take them to the temple because "that is where you go to die." Despite this fact, sick adults are not only willing but eager to undergo the protracted ritual purification, if they can afford to do so. No matter how ill the supplicant or how grave the emergency, the guardians of many temples will not admit a client if he cannot give a rich gift to the custodian. Even after one has gained admission and survived the ceremonies, the guardians will not permit the neophyte to leave until he makes still another gift.

The supplicant entering the temple is first stripped of all his or her clothes. In everyday life the Nacirema avoids exposure of his body and its natural functions. Bathing and excretory acts are performed only in the secrecy of the household shrine, where they are ritualized as part of the body-rites. Psychological shock results from the fact that body secrecy is suddenly lost upon entry into the *latipso*. A man whose own wife has never seen him in an excretory act, suddenly finds himself naked and assisted by a vestal maiden while he performs his natural functions into a sacred vessel. This sort of ceremonial treatment is necessitated by the fact that the excreta are used by a diviner to ascertain the course and nature of the client's sickness. Female clients, on the other hand, find their naked bodies are subjected to the scrutiny, manipulation and prodding of the medicine men.

Few supplicants in the temple are well enough to do anything but lie on their hard beds. The daily ceremonies, like the rites of the holy-mouth-men, involve discomfort and torture. With ritual precision, the vestals awaken their miserable charges each dawn and roll them about on their beds of pain while performing ablutions, in the formal movements of which the maidens are highly trained. At other times they insert magic wands in the supplicant's mouth or force him to eat substances which are supposed to be healing. From time to time the medicine men come to their clients and jab magically treated needles into their flesh. The fact that these temple ceremonies may not cure, and may even kill the neophyte, in no way decreases the people's faith in the medicine men.

There remains one other kind of practitioner, known as a "listener." This witchdoctor has the power to exorcise the devils that lodge in the heads of people who have been bewitched. The Nacirema believe that parents bewitch their own children. Mothers are particularly suspected of putting a curse on children while teaching them the secret body rituals. The counter-magic of the witchdoctor is unusual in its lack of ritual. The patient simply tells the "listener" all his troubles and fears, beginning with the earliest difficulties he can remember. The memory displayed by the Nacirema in these exorcism sessions is truly remarkable. It is not uncommon for the patient to bemoan the rejection he felt upon being weaned as a babe, and a few individuals even see their troubles going back to the traumatic effects of their own birth.

In conclusion, mention must be made of certain practices which have their base in native esthetics but which depend upon the pervasive aversion to the natural body and its functions. There are ritual fasts to make fat people thin and ceremonial feasts to make thin people fat. Still other rites are used to make women's breasts larger if they are small, and smaller if they are large. General dissatisfaction with breast shape is symbolized in the fact that the ideal form is virtually outside the range of human variation. A few women afflicted with almost inhuman hyper-mammary development are so idolized that they make a handsome living by simply going from village to village and permitting the natives to stare at them for a fee.

Reference has already been made to the fact that excretory functions are ritualized, routinized, and relegated to secrecy. Natural reproductive functions are similarly distorted. Intercourse is taboo as a topic and scheduled as an act. Efforts are made to avoid pregnancy by the use of magical materials or by limiting intercourse to certain phases of the moon. Conception is actually very infrequent. When pregnant, women dress so as to hide their condition. Parturition takes place in secret, without friends or relatives to assist, and the majority of women do not nurse their infants.

Our review of the ritual life of the Nacirema has certainly shown them to be a magic-ridden people. It is hard to understand how they have managed to exist so long under the burdens which they have imposed upon themselves. But even such exotic customs as these take on real meaning when they are viewed with the insight provided by Malinowski when he wrote:

"Looking from far and above, from our high places of safety in the developed civilization, it is easy to see all the crudity and irrelevance of magic. But without its power and guidance early man could not have mastered his practical difficulties as he has done, nor could man have advanced to the higher stages of civilization."

6 The Sounds of Silence

EDWARD T. HALL
MILDRED R. HALL

When two people are talking to each other, they communicate by much more than spoken words. They are constantly exchanging subtle meanings by their inflections, their pauses, and the rapidity and volume of their speech. And they are also communicating significant messages to one another by their gestures, expressions, mannerisms, and use of space.

We seldom think about our body language. We just "do what is natural" for us. Even though it appears natural to us, however, there is nothing "natural" about it. Our body language and other forms of communication are acquired; they are a part of our social heritage or culture. It is these forms of communication that the Halls explore in this selection.

BOB LEAVES HIS APARTMENT at 8:15 A.M. and stops at the corner drugstore for breakfast. Before he can speak; the counterman says, "The usual?" Bob nods yes. While he savors his Danish, a fat man pushes onto the adjoining stool and overflows into his space. Bob scowls, and the man pulls himself in as much as he can. Bob has sent two messages without speaking a syllable.

Henry has an appointment to meet Arthur at 11:00 A.M.; he arrives at 11:30. Their conversation is friendly, but Arthur retains a lingering hostility. Henry has unconsciously communicated that he doesn't think the appointment is very important or that Arthur is a person who needs to be treated with respect.

George is talking to Charley's wife at a party. Their conversation is entirely trivial, yet Charley glares at them suspiciously. Their physical proximity and the movements of their eyes reveal that they are powerfully attracted to each other.

José Ybarra and Sir Edmund Jones are at the same party, and it is important for them to establish a cordial relationship for business reasons. Each is trying to be warm and friendly, yet they will part with mutual distrust, and their business transaction will probably fall through. José, in Latin fashion, moves closer and closer to Sir Edmund as they speak, and this movement is being miscommunicated as pushiness to Sir Edmund, who keeps backing away from this intimacy, which in turn is being miscommunicated to José as coldness. The silent languages of Latin and English cultures are more difficult to learn than their spoken languages.

In each of these cases, we see the subtle power of nonverbal communication. The only language used throughout most of the history of humanity (in evolutionary terms, vocal communication is relatively recent), it is the first form of communication you learn. You use this preverbal language, consciously and unconsciously, every day to tell other people how you feel about yourself and them. This language includes your posture, gestures, facial expressions, costume, the way you walk, even your treatment of time and space and material things. All people communicate on several different levels at the same time but are usually aware of only the verbal dialogue and don't realize that they respond to nonverbal messages. But when a person says one thing and really believes something else, the discrepancy between the two can usually be sensed. Nonverbal communication systems are much less subject to the conscious deception that often occurs in verbal systems. When we find ourselves thinking, "I don't know what it is about him, but he doesn't seem sincere" it's usually this lack of congruity between a person's words and his behavior that makes us anxious and uncomfortable.

Few of us realize how much we all depend on body movement in our conversation or are aware of the hidden rules that govern listening behavior. But we know instantly whether or not the person we're talking to is "tuned in," and we're very sensitive to any breach in listening etiquette. In white middle-class American culture, when someone wants to show he is listening to someone else, he looks either at the other person's face or, specifically, at his eyes, shifting his gaze from one eye to the other.

If you observe a person conversing, you'll notice that he indicates he's listening by nodding his head. He also makes little "Hmm" noises. If he agrees with what's being said, he may give a vigorous nod. To show pleasure or affirmation, he smiles; if he has some reservations, he looks skeptical by raising an eyebrow or pulling down the corners of his mouth. If a participant wants to terminate the conversation, he may start shifting his body position, stretching his legs, crossing or uncrossing them, bobbing his foot, or diverting his gaze from the speaker. The more he fidgets, the more the speaker becomes aware that he has lost his audience. As a last measure, the listener may look at his watch to indicate the imminent end of the conversation.

Talking and listening are so intricately intertwined that a person cannot do one without the other. Even when one is alone and talking to oneself, there is part of the brain that speaks while another part listens. In all conversations, the listener is positively or negatively reinforcing the speaker all the time. He may even guide the conversation without knowing it, by laughing or frowning or dismissing the argument with a wave of his hand.

The language of the eyes—another age-old way of exchanging feelings—is both subtle and complex. Not only do men and women use their eyes differently, but there are class, generation, regional, ethnic, and national cultural differences. Americans often complain about the way foreigners stare at people or hold a glance too long. Most Americans look away from someone who is using his eyes in an unfamiliar way because it makes them self-conscious. If a man looks at another man's wife in a certain way, he's asking for trouble, as indicated earlier. But he might not be ill-mannered or seeking to challenge the husband. He might be a European in this country who hasn't learned our visual mores. Many American women visiting France or Italy are acutely embarrassed because, for the first time in their lives, men really look at them—their eyes, hair, nose, lips, breasts, hips, legs, thighs, knees, ankles, feet, clothes, hairdo, even their walk. These same women, once they have become used to being looked at often return to the United States and are overcome with the feeling that "No one ever really looks at me anymore."

Analyzing the mass of data on the eyes, it is possible to sort out at least three ways in which the eyes are used to communicate: dominance vs. submission, involvement vs. detachment, and positive vs. negative attitude. In addition, there are three levels of consciousness and control, which can be categorized as follows: (1) conscious use of the eyes to communicate, such as the flirting blink and the intimate nosewrinkling squint; (2) the very extensive category of unconscious but learned behavior governing where the eyes are directed and when (this unwritten set of rules dictates how and under what circumstances the sexes, as well as people of all status categories, look at each other); and (3) the response of the eye itself, which is completely outside both awareness and control—changes in the cast (sparkle) of the eye and the pupillary reflex.

The eye is unlike any other organ of the body for it is an extension of the brain. The unconscious pupillary reflex and the cast of the eye have been known by people of Middle Eastern origin for years—although most are unaware of their knowledge. Depending on the context, Arabs and others look directly at the eyes or deeply *into* the eyes of their interlocutor. We became aware of this in the Middle East several years ago while looking at jewelry. The merchant suddenly started to push a particular bracelet at a customer and said, "You buy this one." What interested us was that the bracelet was not the one that had been consciously selected by the purchaser. But the merchant, watching the pupils of the eyes, knew what the purchaser really wanted to buy. Whether he specifically knew *how* he knew is debatable.

A psychologist at the University of Chicago, Eckhard Hess, was the first to conduct systematic studies of the pupillary reflex. His wife remarked one evening, while watching him reading in bed, that he must be very interested in the text because his pupils were dilated. Following up on this, Hess slipped some pictures of nudes into a stack of photographs that he gave to his male assistant. Not looking at the photographs but watching his assistant's pupils, Hess was able to tell precisely when the assistant came to the nudes. In further experiments, Hess retouched the eyes in a photograph of a woman. In one print, he made the pupils small, in another, large; nothing else was changed. Subjects who were given the photographs found the woman with the dilated pupils much more attractive. Any man who has had the experience of seeing a woman look at him as her pupils widen with reflex speed knows that she's flashing him a message.

The eye-sparkle phenomenon frequently turns up in our interviews of couples in love. It's apparently one of the first reliable clues in the other person that love is genuine. To date, there is no scientific data to explain eye sparkle; no investigation of the pupil, the cornea, or even the white sclera of the eye shows how the sparkle originates. Yet we all know it when we see it.

One common situation for most people involves the use of the eyes in the street and in public. Although eye behavior follows a definite set of rules, the rules vary according to the place, the needs and feelings of the people, and their ethnic background. For urban whites, once they're within definite recognition distance (sixteen to thirty-two feet for people with average eyesight), there is mutual avoidance of eye contact—unless they want something specific: a pickup, a handout, or information of some kind. In the West and in small towns generally, however, people are much more likely to look and greet one another, even if they're strangers.

It's permissible to look at people if they're beyond recognition distance, but once inside this sacred zone, you can only steal a glance at strangers. You *must* greet friends, however; to fail to do so is insulting. Yet, to stare too fixedly even at them is considered rude and hostile. Of course, all of these rules are variable.

A great many blacks, for example, greet each other in public even if they don't know each other. To blacks, most eye behavior of whites has the effect of giving the impression that they aren't there, but this is due to white avoidance of eye contact with *anyone* in the street.

Another very basic difference between people of different ethnic backgrounds is their sense of territoriality and how they handle space. This is the silent communication, or miscommunication, that caused friction between Mr. Ybarra and Sir Edmund Jones in our earlier example. We know from the research that everyone has around himself an invisible bubble of space that contracts and expands depending on several factors: his emotional state, the activity he's performing at the time, and his cultural background. This bubble is a kind of mobile territory that he will defend against intrusion. If he is accustomed to close personal distance between himself and others, his bubble will be smaller than that of someone who's accustomed to greater personal distance. People of northern European heritage—English, Scandinavian, Swiss, and German—tend to avoid contact. Those whose heritage is Italian, French, Spanish, Russian, Latin American, or Middle Eastern like close personal contact.

People are very sensitive to any intrusion into their spatial bubble. If someone stands too close to you, your first instinct is to back up. If that's not possible, you lean away and pull yourself in, tensing your muscles. If the intruder doesn't respond to these body signals, you may then try to protect yourself, using a briefcase, umbrella, or raincoat. Women—especially when traveling alone—often plant their pocketbooks in such a way that no one can get very close to them. As a last resort, you may move to another spot and position yourself behind a desk or a chair that provides screening. Everyone tries to adjust the space around himself in a way that's comfortable for him; most often, he does this unconsciously.

Emotions also have a direct effect on the size of a person's territory. When you're angry or under stress, your bubble expands and you require more space. New York psychiatrist Augustus Kinzel found a difference in what he calls body-buffer zones between violent and nonviolent prison inmates. Dr. Kinzel conducted experiments in which each prisoner was placed in the center of a small room, and then Dr. Kinzel slowly walked toward him. Nonviolent prisoners allowed him to come quite close, while prisoners with a history of violent behavior couldn't tolerate his proximity and reacted with some vehemence.

Apparently, people under stress experience other people as looming larger and closer than they actually are. Studies of schizophrenic patients have indicated that they sometimes have a distorted perception of space, and several psychiatrists have reported patients who experience their body boundaries as filling up an entire room. For these patients, anyone who comes into the room is actually inside their body, and such an intrusion may trigger a violent outburst.

Unfortunately, there is little detailed information about normal people who live in highly congested urban areas. We do know, of course, that the noise, pollution, dirt, crowding, and confusion of our cities induce feelings of stress in most of us, and stress leads to a need for greater space. The man who's packed into a subway, jostled in the street, crowded into an elevator, and forced to work all day in a bull pen or in a small office without auditory or visual privacy is going to be very stressed at the end of his day. He needs places that provide relief from constant overstimulation of his nervous system. Stress from overcrowding is cumulative, and people can tolerate more crowding early in the day than later; note the increased bad temper during the evening rush hour as compared with the morning melee. Certainly one factor in people's desire to commute by car is the need for privacy and relief from crowding (except, often, from other cars); it may be the only time of the day when nobody can intrude.

In crowded public places, we tense our muscles and hold ourselves stiff, and thereby communicate to others our desire not to intrude on their space and, above all, not to touch them. We also avoid eye contact, and the total effect is that of someone who has "tuned out." Walking along the street, our bubble expands slightly as we move in a stream of strangers, taking care not to bump into them. In the office, at meetings, in restaurants, our bubble keeps changing as it adjusts to the activity at hand.

Most white middle-class Americans use four main distances in their business and social relations: intimate, personal, social, and public. Each of these distances has a near and a far phase and is accompanied by changes in the volume of the voice. Intimate distance varies from direct physical contact with another person to a distance of six to eighteen inches and is used for our most private activities—caressing another person or making love. At this distance, you are overwhelmed by sensory inputs from the skin, the fragrance of perfume, even the sound of breathing—all of which literally envelop you. Even at the far phase, you're still within easy touching distance. In general, the use of intimate distance in public between adults is frowned on. It's also much too close for strangers, except under conditions of extreme crowding.

In the second zone—personal distance—the close phase is one and a half to two and a half feet; it's at this distance that wives usually stand from their husbands in public. If another woman moves into this zone, the wife will most likely be disturbed. The far phase—two and a half to four feet—is the distance used to "keep someone at arm's length" and is the most common spacing used by people in conversation.

The third zone—social distance—is employed during business transactions or exchanges with a clerk or repairman. People who work together tend to use close social distance—four to seven feet. This is also the distance for conversation at social gatherings. To stand at this distance from someone who is seated has a dominating effect (e.g., teacher to pupil, boss to secretary). The far phase of the third zone—seven to twelve feet—is where people stand when someone says, "Stand back so I can look at you." This distance lends a formal tone to business or social discourse. In an executive office, the desk serves to keep people at this distance.

The fourth zone—public distance—is used by teachers in classrooms or speakers at public gatherings. At its farthest phase—twenty-five feet and beyond—it is used for important public figures. Violations of this distance can lead to serious complications. During his 1970 U.S. visit, the president of France, Georges Pompidou, was harassed by pickets in Chicago, who were permitted to get within touching distance. Since pickets in France are kept behind barricades a block or more away, the president was outraged by this insult to his person, and President Nixon was obliged to communicate his concern as well as offer his personal apologies.

It is interesting to note how American pitchmen and panhandlers exploit the unwritten, unspoken conventions of eye and distance. Both take advantage of the fact that once explicit eye contact is established, it is rude to look away, because to do so means to brusquely dismiss the other person and his needs. Once having caught the eye of his mark, the panhandler then locks on, not letting go until he moves through the public zone, the social zone, the personal zone and, finally, into the intimate sphere, where people are most vulnerable.

Touch also is an important part of the constant stream of communication that takes place between people. A light touch, a firm touch, a blow, a caress are all communications. In an effort to break down barriers among people, there's been a recent upsurge in group-encounter activities, in which strangers are encouraged to touch one another. In special situations such as these, the rules for not touching are broken with group approval, and people gradually lose some of their inhibitions.

Although most people don't realize it, space is perceived and distances are set not by vision alone but with all the senses. Auditory space is perceived with the ears, thermal space with the skin, kinesthetic space with the muscles of the body, and olfactory space with the nose. And, once again, it's one's culture that determines how his senses are programmed—which sensory information ranks highest and lowest. The important thing to remember is that culture is very persistent. In this country, we've noted the existence of culture patterns that determine distance between people in the third and fourth generations of some families, despite their prolonged contact with people of very different cultural heritages.

Whenever there is great cultural distance between two people, there are bound to be problems arising from differences in behavior and expectations. An example is the American couple who consulted a psychiatrist about their marital problems. The husband was from New England and had been brought up by reserved parents who taught him to control his emotions and to respect the need for privacy. His wife was from an Italian family and had been brought up in close contact with all the members of her large family, who were extremely warm, volatile, and demonstrative.

When the husband came home after a hard day at the office, dragging his feet and longing for peace and quiet, his wife would rush to him and smother him. Clasping his hands, rubbing his brow, crooning over his weary head, she never left him alone. But when the wife was upset or anxious about her day, the husband's response was to withdraw completely and leave her alone. No comforting, no affectionate embrace, no attention—just solitude. The woman became convinced her husband didn't love her, and in desperation she consulted a psychiatrist. Their problem wasn't basically psychological but cultural.

Why has man developed all these different ways of communicating messages without words? One reason is that people don't like to spell out certain kinds of messages. We prefer to find other ways of showing our feelings. This is especially true in relationships as sensitive as courtship. Men don't like to be rejected, and most women don't want to turn a man down bluntly. Instead, we work out subtle ways of encouraging or discouraging each other that save face and avoid confrontations.

How a person handles space in dating others is an obvious and very sensitive indicator of how he or she feels about the other person. On a first date, if a woman sits or stands so close to a man that he is acutely conscious of her physical presence—inside the intimate-distance zone—the man usually construes it to mean that she is encouraging him. However, before the man starts moving in on the woman, he should be sure what message she's really sending; otherwise, he risks bruising his ego. What is close to someone of northern European background may be neutral or distant to someone of Italian heritage. Also, women sometimes use space as a way of misleading a man, and there are few things that put men off more than women who communicate contradictory messages, such as women who cuddle up and then act insulted when a man takes the next step.

How does a woman communicate interest in a man? In addition to such familiar gambits as smiling at him, she may glance shyly at him, blush, and then look away. Or she may give him a real come-on look and move in very close when he approaches. She may touch his arm and ask for a light. As she leans forward to light her cigarette, she may brush him lightly, enveloping him in her perfume. She'll probably continue to smile at him, and she may use what ethologists call preening gestures—touching the back of her hair, thrusting her breasts forward, tilting her hips as she stands, or crossing her legs if she's seated, perhaps even exposing one thigh or putting a hand on her thigh and stroking it. She may also stroke her wrists as she converses or show the palm of her hand as a way of gaining his attention. Her skin may be unusually flushed or quite pale, her eyes brighter, the pupils larger.

If a man sees a woman whom he wants to attract, he tries to present himself by his posture and stance as someone who is self-assured. He moves briskly and confidently. When he catches the eye of the woman, he may hold her glance a little longer than normal. If he gets an encouraging smile, he'll move in close and engage her in small talk. As they converse, his glance shifts over her face and body. He, too, may make preening gestures—straightening his tie, smoothing his hair, or shooting his cuffs.

How do people learn body language? The same way they learn spoken language—by observing and imitating people around them as they're growing up. Little girls imitate their mothers or an older female. Little boys imitate their fathers or a respected uncle or a character on television. In this way, they learn the gender signals appropriate for their sex. Regional, class, and ethnic patterns of body behavior are also learned in childhood and persist throughout life. . . .

Nonverbal communications signal to members of your own group what kind of person you are, how you feel about others, how you'll fit into and work in a group, whether you're assured or anxious, the degree to which you feel comfortable with the standards of your own culture, as well as deeply significant feelings about the self, including the state of your own psyche. For most of us, it's difficult to accept the reality of another's behavioral system. And, of course, none of us will ever become fully knowledgeable of the importance of every nonverbal signal. But as long as each of us realizes the power of these signals, this society's diversity can be a source of great strength rather than a further—and subtly powerful— source of division.

7 The Presentation of Self in Everyday Life

ERVING GOFFMAN

All the world's a stage
And all the men and women merely players.
They have their exits and their entrances;
And one man in his time plays many parts . . .
      William Shakespeare
      As You Like It, Act 2, Scene 7

This quotation from Shakespeare could well serve as the keynote for the following selection. Taking Shakespeare's statement seriously, Goffman presents a dramaturgical model of human life and uses it as the conceptual framework for understanding life-in-society. In this view, people in everyday life are actors onstage, the audience consists of those persons who observe what others are doing, the parts are the roles that people play (whether occupational, familial, friendship roles, or whatever), the dialogue consists of ritualized conversational exchanges ("Hi. How ya doin'?," "Hey, bro', wha's happnin'?" the hellos, the goodbyes, and the inbetweens), while the costuming consists of whatever clothing happens to be in style.

Goffman's insightful analysis provides a framework from which we can gain a remarkably different perspective of the actions of both ourselves and others. When understood properly, however, you may find this approach to understanding human behavior disturbing. For example, if we are all actors playing roles on the stage of life, where is the "real me"? Is all of life merely a "put-on"? Does not this framework for understanding human interaction constitute an essentially manipulative approach to life, a sort of everyday Machiavellianism?

WHEN AN INDIVIDUAL ENTERS THE PRESENCE OF OTHERS, they commonly seek to acquire information about him or to bring into play information about him already possessed. They will be interested in his general socio-economic status, his conception of self, his attitude toward them, his competence, his trustworthiness, etc. Although some of this information seems to be sought almost as an end in itself, there are usually

Healthy Schools

Bohen @ss Decass (good morning)

Brenass Tadvs (good Aftoonoon)

Cómo se guana usted (
Whats your Name)

Tronqui por aqui cera
(where is the Nearist
Quiet Beach)

By

Sophie Mason

quite practical reasons for acquiring it. Information about the individual helps to define the situation, enabling others to know in advance what he will expect of them and what they may expect of him. Informed in these ways, the others will know how best to act in order to call forth a desired response from him.

For those present, many sources of information become accessible and many carriers (or "sign-vehicles") become available for conveying this information. If unacquainted with the individual, observers can glean clues from his conduct and appearance which allow them to apply their previous experience with individuals roughly similar to the one before them or, more important, to apply untested stereotypes to him. They can also assume from past experience that only individuals of a particular kind are likely to be found in a given social setting. They can rely on what the individual says about himself or on documentary evidence he provides as to who and what he is. If they know, or know of, the individual by virtue of experience prior to the interaction, they can rely on assumptions as to the persistence and generality of psychological traits as a means of predicting his present and future behavior.

However, during the period in which the individual is in the immediate presence of the others, few events may occur which directly provide the others with the conclusive information they will need if they are to direct wisely their own activity. Many crucial facts lie beyond the time and place of interaction or lie concealed within it. For example, the "true" or "real" attitudes, beliefs, and emotions of the individual can be ascertained only indirectly, through his avowals or through what appears to be involuntary expressive behavior. Similarly, if the individual offers the others a product or service, they will often find that during the interaction there will be no time and place immediately available for eating the pudding that the proof can be found in. They will be forced to accept some events as conventional or natural signs of something not directly available to the senses. In Ichheiser's terms,[1] the individual will have to act so that he intentionally or unintentionally *expresses* himself, and the others will in turn have to be *impressed* in some way by him.

The expressiveness of the individual (and therefore his capacity to give impressions) appears to involve two radically different kinds of sign activity: the expression that he *gives*, and the expression that he *gives off*. The first involves verbal symbols or their substitutes which he uses admittedly and solely to convey the information that he and the others are known to attach to these symbols. This is communication in the traditional and narrow sense. The second involves a wide range of action that others can treat as symptomatic of the actor, the expectation being that the action was performed for reasons other than the information conveyed in this way. As we shall have to see, this distinction has an only initial validity. The individual does of course intentionally convey misinformation by means of both of these types of communication, the first involving deceit, the second feigning.

Taking communication in both its narrow and broad sense, one finds that when the individual is in the immediate presence of others, his activity will have a promissory character. The others are likely to find that they must accept the individual on faith, offering him a just return while he is present before them in exchange for something whose true value will not be established until after he has left their presence. (Of course, the others also live by inference in their dealings with the physical world, but it is only in the world of social interaction that the objects about which they make inferences will purposely facilitate and hinder this inferential process.) The security that they justifiably feel in making inferences about the individual will vary, of course, depending on such factors as the amount of information they already possess about him, but no amount of such past evidence can entirely obviate the necessity of acting on the basis of inferences. As William I. Thomas suggested:

> It is also highly important for us to realize that we do not as a matter of fact lead our lives, make our decisions, and reach our goals in everyday life either statistically or scientifically. We live by inference. I am, let us say, your guest. You do not know, you cannot determine scientifically, that I will not steal your money or your spoons. But inferentially I will not, and inferentially you have me as a guest.[2]

Let us now turn from the others to the point of view of the individual who presents himself before them. He may wish them to think highly of him, or to think that he thinks highly of them, or to perceive how in fact he feels toward them, or to obtain no clearcut impression; he may wish to ensure sufficient harmony so that the interaction can be sustained, or to defraud, get rid of, confuse, mislead, antagonize, or insult them. Regardless of the particular objective which the individual has in mind and of his motive for having this objective, it will be in his interests to control the conduct of the others, especially their responsive treatment of him.[3] This control is achieved largely by influencing the definition of the situation which the others come to formulate, and he can influence this definition by expressing himself in such a way as to give them the kind of impression that will lead them to act voluntarily in accordance with his own plan. Thus, when an individual appears in the presence of others, there will usually be some reason for him to mobilize his activity so that it will convey an impression to others which it is in his interests to convey. Since a girl's dormitory mates will glean evidence of her popularity from the calls she receives on the phone, we can suspect that some girls will arrange for calls to be made, and Willard Waller's finding can be anticipated.

It has been reported by many observers that a girl who is called to the telephone in the dormitories will often allow herself to be called several times, in order to give all the other girls ample opportunity to hear her paged.[4]

Of the two kinds of communication—expressions given and expressions given off—this report will be primarily concerned with the latter, with the more theatrical and contextual kind, the non-verbal, presumably unintentional kind, whether this communication be purposely engineered or not. As an example of what we must try to examine, I would like to cite at length a novelistic incident in which Preedy, a vacationing Englishman, makes his first appearance on the beach of his summer hotel in Spain:

But in any case he took care to avoid catching anyone's eye. First of all, he had to make it clear to those potential companions of his holiday that they were of no concern to him whatsoever. He stared through them, round them, over them—eyes lost in space. The beach might have been empty. If by chance a ball was thrown his way, he looked surprised; then let a smile of amusement lighten his face (Kindly Preedy), looked round dazed to see that there *were* people on the beach, tossed it back with a smile to himself and not a smile *at* the people, and then resumed carelessly his nonchalant survey of space.

But it was time to institute a little parade, the parade of the Ideal Preedy. By devious handlings he gave any one who wanted to look a chance to see the title of his book—a Spanish translation of Homer, classic thus, but not daring, cosmopolitan too—and then gathered together his beachwrap and bag into a neat sand-resistant pile (Methodical and Sensible Preedy), rose slowly to stretch at ease his huge frame (Big-Cat Preedy), and tossed aside his sandals (Carefree Preedy, after all).

The marriage of Preedy and the sea! There were alternate rituals. The first involved the stroll that turns into a run and a dive straight into the water, thereafter smoothing into a strong splashless crawl towards the horizon. But of course not really to the horizon. Quite suddenly he would turn on to his back and thrash great white splashes with his legs, somehow thus showing that he could have swum further had he wanted to, and then would stand up a quarter out of water for all to see who it was.

The alternative course was simpler, it avoided the cold-water shock and it avoided the risk of appearing too high-spirited. The point was to appear to be so used to the sea, the Mediterranean, and this particular beach, that one might as well be in the sea as out of it. It involved a slow stroll down and into the edge of the water—not even noticing his toes were wet, land and water all the same to *him!*—with his eyes up at the sky gravely surveying portents, invisible to others, of the weather (Local Fisherman Preedy).[5]

The novelist means us to see that Preedy is improperly concerned with the extensive impressions he feels his sheer bodily action is giving off to those around him. We can malign Preedy further by assuming that he has acted merely in order to give a particular impression, that this is a false impression, and that the others present receive either no impression at all, or, worse still, the impression that Preedy is affectedly trying to cause them to receive this particular impression. But the important point for us here is that the kind of impression Preedy thinks he is making is in fact the kind of impression that others correctly and incorrectly glean from someone in their midst.

I have said that when an individual appears before others his actions will influence the definition of the situation which they come to have. Sometimes the individual will act in a thoroughly calculating manner, expressing himself in a given way solely in order to give the kind of impression to others that is likely to evoke from them a specific response he is concerned to obtain. Sometimes the individual will be calculating in his activity but be relatively unaware that this is the case. Sometimes he will intentionally and consciously express himself in a particular way, but chiefly because the tradition of his group or social status require this kind of expression and not because of any particular response (other than vague acceptance or approval) that is likely to be evoked from those impressed by the expression. Sometimes the traditions of an individual's role will lead him to give a well-designed impression of a particular kind and yet he may be neither consciously nor unconsciously disposed to create such an impression. The others, in their turn, may be suitably impressed by the individual's efforts to convey something, or may misunderstand the situation and come to conclusions that are warranted neither by the individual's intent nor by the facts. In any case, in so far as the others act *as if* the individual had conveyed a particular impression, we may take a functional or pragmatic view and say that the individual has "effectively" projected a given definition of the situation and "effectively" fostered the understanding that a given state of affairs obtains.

There is one aspect of the others' response that bears special comment here. Knowing that the individual is likely to present himself in a light that is favorable to him, the others may divide what they witness into two parts: a part that is relatively easy for the individual to manipulate at will, being chiefly his verbal assertions, and a part in regard to which he seems to have little concern or control, being chiefly derived from the expressions he gives off. The others may then use what are considered to be the ungovernable aspects of his expressive behavior as a check upon the validity of what is conveyed by the governable aspects. In this a fundamental asymmetry is demonstrated in the communication process, the individual presumably being aware of only one stream of his communication, the witness of this stream and one other. For example, in Shetland Isle one crofter's wife, in serving native dishes to a visitor from the mainland of Britain, would listen with a polite smile to his polite claims of liking what he was eating; at the same time she would take note of the rapidity with which the visitor lifted his fork or spoon to his mouth, the eagerness with which he passed food into his mouth, and the gusto expressed in chewing the food, using these signs as a check on the stated feelings of the eater. The same woman, in order to discover what one acquaintance (A) "actually" thought of another acquaintance (B), would wait until B was in the presence of A but engaged in conversation with still another person (C). She would then covertly examine the facial expressions of A as he regarded B in conversation with C. Not being in coversation with B, and not being directly observed by him, A would sometimes relax usual constraints and tactful deceptions, and freely express what he was "actually" feeling about B. This Shetlander, in short, would observe the unobserved observer.

Now given the fact that others are likely to check up on the more controllable aspects of behavior by means of the less controllable, one can expect that sometimes the individual will try to exploit this very possibility, guiding the impression he makes through behavior felt to be reliably informing.[6] For example, in gaining admission to a tight social circle, the participant observer may not only wear an accepting look while listening to an informant, but may also be careful to wear the same look when observing the informant talking to others; observers of the observer will then not as easily discover where he actually stands. A specific illustration may be cited from Shetland Isle. When a neighbor dropped in to have a cup of tea, he would ordinarily wear at least a hint of an expectant warm smile as he passed through the door into the cottage. Since lack of physical obstructions outside the cottage and lack of light within it usually made it possible to observe the visitor unobserved as he approached the house, islanders sometimes took pleasure in watching the visitor drop whatever expression he was manifesting and replace it with a sociable one just before reaching the door. However, some visitors, in appreciating that this examination was occurring, would blindly adopt a social face a long distance from the house, thus ensuring the projection of a constant image.

This kind of control upon the part of the individual reinstates the symmetry of the communication process, and sets the stage for a kind of information game—a potentially infinite cycle of concealment, discovery, false revelation, and rediscovery. It should be added that since the others are likely to be relatively unsuspicious of the presumably unguided aspect of the individual's conduct, he can gain much by controlling it. The others of course may sense that the individual is manipulating the presumably spontaneous aspects of his behavior, and seek in this very act of manipulation some shading of conduct that the individual has not managed to control. This again provides a check upon the individual's behavior, this time his presumably uncalculated behavior, thus re-establishing the asymmetry of the communication process. Here I would like only to add the suggestion that the arts of piercing an individual's effort at calculated un-intentionality seem better developed than our capacity to manipulate our own behavior, so that regardless of how many steps have occurred in the information game, the witness is likely to have the advantage over the actor, and the initial asymmetry of the communication process is likely to be retained.

When we allow that the individual projects a definition of the situation when he appears before others, we must also see that the others, however passive their role may seem to be, will themselves effectively project a definition of the situation by virtue of their response to the individual and by virtue of any lines of action they initiate to him. Ordinarily the definitions of the situation projected by the several different participants are sufficiently attuned to one another so that open contradiction will not occur. I do not mean that there will be the kind of consensus that arises when each individual present candidly expresses what he really feels and honestly agrees with the expressed feelings of the others present. This kind of harmony is an optimistic ideal and in any case not necessary for the smooth working of society. Rather, each participant is expected to suppress his immediate heartfelt feelings, conveying a view of the situation which he feels the others will be able to find at least temporarily acceptable. The maintenance of this surface of agreement, this veneer of consensus, is facilitated by each participant concealing his own wants behind statements which assert values to which everyone present feels obliged to give lip service. Further, there is usually a kind of division of definitional labor. Each participant is allowed to establish the tentative official ruling regarding matters which are vital to him but not immediately important to others, e.g., the rationalizations and justifications by which he accounts for his past activity. In exchange for this courtesy he remains silent or noncommittal on matters important to others but not immediately important to him. We have then a kind of interactional *modus vivendi*. Together, the participants contribute to a single over-all definition of the situation which involves not so much a real argument as to what exists but rather a real agreement as to whose claims concerning what issues will be temporarily honored. Real agreement will also exist concerning the desirability of avoiding an open conflict of definitions of the situation.[7] I will refer to this level of agreement as a "working consensus." It is to be understood that the working consensus established in one interaction setting will be quite different in content from the working consensus established in a different type of setting. Thus, between two friends at lunch, a reciprocal show of affection, respect, and concern for the other is maintained. In service occupations, on the other hand, the specialist often maintains an image of disinterested involvement in the problem of the client, while the client responds with a show of respect for the competence and integrity of the specialist. Regardless of such differences in content, however, the general form of these working arrangements is the same.

In noting the tendency for a participant to accept the definitional claims made by the others present, we can appreciate the crucial importance of the information that the individual *initially* possesses or acquires concerning his fellow participants, for it is on the basis of this initial information that the individual starts to define the situation and starts to build up lines of responsive action. The individual's initial projection commits him to what he is proposing to be and requires him to drop all pretenses of being other things. As the interaction among the participants progresses, additions and modifications in this initial informational state will of course occur, but it is essential that these later developments be related without contradiction to, and even built up from, the initial positions taken by the several participants. It would seem that an individual can more easily make a choice as to what line of treatment to demand from and extend to the others present at the beginning of an encounter than he can alter the line of treatment that is being pursued once the interaction is under way.

In everyday life, of course, there is a clear understanding that first impressions are important. Thus, the work adjustment of those in service occupations will often hinge upon a capacity to seize and hold the initiative in the service relation, a capacity that will require subtle aggressiveness on the part of the server when he is of lower socio-economic status than his client. W. F. Whyte suggests the waitress as an example:

> The first point that stands out is that the waitress who bears up under pressure does not simply respond to her customers. She acts with some skill to control their behavior. The first question to ask when we look at the customer relationship is, "Does the waitress get the jump on the customer, or does the customer get the jump on the waitress?" The skilled waitress realizes the crucial nature of this question. . . .
>
> The skilled waitress tackles the customer with confidence and without hesitation. For example, she may find that a new customer has seated himself before she could clear off the dirty dishes and change the cloth. He is now leaning on the table studying the menu. She greets him, says, "May I change the cover, please?" and, without waiting for an answer, takes his menu away from him so that he moves back from the table, and she goes about her work. The relationship is handled politely but firmly, and there is never any question as to who is in charge.[8]

When the interaction that is initiated by "first impressions" is itself merely the initial interaction in an extended series of interactions involving the same participants, we speak of "getting off on the right foot" and feel that it is crucial that we do so. Thus, one learns that some teachers take the following view:

> You can't ever let them get the upper hand on you or you're through. So I start out tough. The first day I get a new class in, I let them know who's boss . . . You've got to start off tough, then you can ease up as you go along. If you start out easy-going, when you try to be tough, they'll just look at you and laugh.[9]

Similarly, attendants in mental institutions may feel that if the new patient is sharply put in his place the first day on the ward and made to see who is boss, much future difficulty will be prevented.[10]

Given the fact that the individual effectively projects a definition of the situation when he enters the presence of others, we can assume that events may occur within the interaction which contradict, discredit, or otherwise throw doubt upon this projection. When these disruptive events occur, the interaction itself may come to a confused and embarrassed halt. Some of the assumptions upon which the responses of the participants had been predicted become untenable, and the participants find themselves lodged in an interaction for which the situation has been wrongly defined and is now no longer defined. At such moments the individual whose presentation has been discredited may feel ashamed while the others present may feel hostile, and all the participants may come to feel ill at ease, nonplussed, out of countenance, embarrassed, experiencing the kind of anomy that is generated when the minute social system of face-to-face interaction breaks down.

In stressing the fact that the initial definition of the situation projected by an individual tends to provide a plan for the cooperative activity that follows—in stressing this action point of view—we must not overlook the crucial fact that any projected definition of the situation also has a distinctive moral character. It is this moral character of projections that will chiefly concern us in this report. Society is organized on the principle that any individual who possesses certain social characteristics has a moral right to expect that others will value and treat him in an appropriate way. Connected with this principle is a second, namely that an individual who implicitly or explicitly signifies that he has certain social characteristics ought in fact to be what he claims he is. In consequence, when an individual projects a definition of the situation and thereby makes an implicit or explicit claim to be a person of a particular kind, he automatically exerts a moral demand upon the others, obliging them to value and treat him in the manner that persons of his kind have a right to expect. He also implicitly forgoes all claims to be things he does not appear to be[11] and hence forgoes the treatment that would be appropriate for such individuals. The others find, then, that the individual has informed them as to what is and as to what they *ought* to see as the "is."

One cannot judge the importance of definitional disruptions by the frequency with which they occur, for apparently they would occur more frequently were not constant precautions taken. We find that preventive practices are constantly employed to avoid these embarrassments and that corrective practices are constantly employed to compensate for discrediting occurrences that have not been successfully avoided. When the individual employs these strategies and tactics to protect his own projections, we may refer to them as "defensive practices"; when a participant employs them to save the definition of the situation projected by another, we speak of "protective practices" or "tact." Together, defensive and protective practices comprise the techniques employed to safeguard the impression fostered by an individual during his presence before others. It should be added that while we may be ready to see that no fostered impression would survive if defensive practices were not employed, we are less ready perhaps to see that few impressions could survive if those who received the impression did not exert tact in their reception of it.

In addition to the fact that precautions are taken to prevent disruption of projected definitions, we may also note that an intense interest in these disruptions comes to play a significant role in the social life of the group. Practical jokes and social games are played in which embarrassments which are to be taken unseriously are purposely engineered.[12] Fantasies are created in which devastating exposures occur. Anecdotes from the past—real, embroidered, or fictitious—are told and retold, detailing disruptions which occurred, almost occurred, or occurred and were admirably resolved. There seems to be no grouping which does not have a ready supply of these games, reveries, and cautionary tales, to be used as a source of humor, a catharsis for anxieties, and a sanction for inducing individuals to be modest in their claims and reasonable in their projected expectations. The individual may tell himself through dreams of getting into impossible positions. Families tell of the time a guest got his dates mixed and arrived when neither the house nor anyone in it was ready for him. Journalists tell of times when an all-too-meaningful misprint occurred, and the paper's assumption of objectivity or decorum was humorously discredited. Public servants tell of times a client ridiculously misunderstood form instructions, giving answers which implied an unanticipated and bizarre definition of the situation.[13] Seamen, whose home away from home is rigorously he-man, tell stories of coming back home and inadvertently asking mother to "pass the fucking butter."[14] Diplomats tell of the time a near-sighted queen asked a republican ambassador about the health of his king.[15]

To summarize, then, I assume that when an individual appears before others he will have many motives for trying to control the impression they receive of the situation.

Notes

1. Gustav Ichheiser, "Misunderstandings in Human Relations," Supplement to *The American Journal of Sociology*, 55 (September, 1949): 6–7.

2. Quoted in E. H. Volkart, editor, *Social Behavior and Personality*, Contributions of W. I. Thomas to Theory and Social Research (New York: Social Science Research Council, 1951), p. 5.

3. Here I owe much to an unpublished paper by Tom Burns of the University of Edinburgh. He presents the argument that in all interaction a basic underlying theme is the desire of each participant to guide and control the responses made by the others present. A similar argument has been advanced by Jay Haley in a recent unpublished paper, but in regard to a special kind of control, that having to do with defining the nature of the relationship of those involved in the interaction.

4. Willard Waller, "The Rating and Dating Complex," *American Sociological Review*, 2: 730.

5. William Sansom, *A Contest of Ladies* (London: Hogarth, 1956), pp. 230–32.

6. The widely read and rather sound writings of Stephen Potter are concerned in part with signs that can be engineered to give a shrewd observer the apparently incidental cues he needs to discover concealed virtues the gamesman does not in fact possess.

7. An interaction can be purposely set up as a time and place for voicing differences in opinion, but in such cases participants must be careful to agree not to disagree on the proper tone of voice, vocabulary, and degree of seriousness in which all arguments are to be phrased, and upon the mutual respect which disagreeing participants must carefully continue to express toward one another. This debaters' or academic definition of the situation may also be invoked suddenly and judiciously as a way of translating a serious conflict of views into one that can be handled within a framework acceptable to all present.

8. W. F. Whyte, "When Workers and Customers Meet," Chap. VII, *Industry and Society*, ed. W. F. Whyte (New York: McGraw-Hill, 1946), pp. 132–33.

9. Teacher interview quoted by Howard S. Becker, "Social Class Variations in the Teacher-Pupil Relationship," *Journal of Educational Sociology*, 25: 459.

10. Harold Taxel, "Authority Structure in a Mental Hospital Ward" (unpublished Master's thesis, Department of Sociology, University of Chicago, 1953).

11. This role of the witness in limiting what it is the individual can be has been stressed by Existentialists, who see it as a basic threat to individual freedom. See Jean-Paul Sartre, *Being and Nothingness*, trans. by Hazel E. Barnes (New York: Philosophical Library, 1956), p. 365 ff.

12. Erving Goffman, "Communication Conduct in an Island Community" (unpublished Ph.D. dissertation, Department of Sociology, University of Chicago, 1953), pp. 319–27.

13. Peter Blau, *Dynamics of Bureaucracy; A Study of Interpersonal Relationships in Two Government Agencies*, 2nd ed. (Chicago; University of Chicago Press, 1963).

14. Walter M. Beattie, Jr., "The Merchant Seaman" (unpublished M. A. Report, Department of Sociology, University of Chicago, 1950), p. 35.

15. Sir Frederick Ponsonby, *Recollections of Three Reigns* (New York: Dutton, 1952), p. 46.

PART III Socialization and Sex Roles

Essential to our survival following birth is *socialization*, learning to become full-fledged members of a group. As we covered in Part II, this learning involves all the fundamental aspects of group life that we take for granted, including communication—not just the standard words of a language but also the many nuances of nonverbal communication.

In addition to communication, socialization involves learning rules (what we should and should not do under different circumstances), values (what is considered good or bad), knowledge (such as the "facts" taught in school), as well as expectations about how we should present the self in different social settings (as Goffman and the Halls analyzed in the preceding Part). The agents of socialization include our parents, brothers and sisters and other relatives, friends, and neighbors, as well as clergy and school teachers. They also include people we do not know and never will know, such as clerks and shoppers who, by their very presence—and the expectations we know they have of us—help to bring our behavior under control at that moment and thereby shape it for similar situations in the future. Through this process of socialization each of us develops a particular *personality*, the tendency to behave in a certain manner that carries over from one situation to another.

Essential to this identity formation is socialization into sexuality. That is, a large part of learning who we are (*personal identity*) and what others expect of us (*public identity*) lies in learning our sex roles. Although we come into this world with the biological equipment of a male or female, these physical organs do not determine what we shall be like as a male or a female. Whether or not we defer to members of the opposite sex, for example, is not an automatic result of our particular sexual equipment but is due to what we learn is proper for us because of the particular biological equipment we possess. This learning process is called *sex role socialization*.

The sex roles that we learn extend into almost every area of our lives, even into situations for which they may be quite irrelevant. Whatever we do, we generally do as a male or as a female. For example, if we are grocery clerks, through the mannerisms we express while doing our work, we communicate expectations attached to our sex. By means of clothing, language, and gestures, we communicate to others that we are *male* or *female* clerks. Because sex roles cut across most other aspects of social life, they are sometimes referred to as a *master trait*.

Challenged for generations (the Women's Movement was active before our grandparents were born), the traditional expectations attached to sex roles have undergone substantial modification in recent years. One can no longer safely assume particular behavior on the part of another simply because of that person's sex. As alternate models of behavior are developing, our social institutions are undergoing modification. In spite of such changes, however, most Americans appear to follow rather traditional lines as they socialize their children. The changes take place slowly, and male dominance remains a fact of social life.

How are males and females socialized for the roles they will later play? Memories of childhood may surface while reading James M. Henslin's analysis of some of the processes by which males are socialized into dominance. By focusing on childhood, he examines experiences that lead men to think of themselves as superior, that direct them into a world drastically separated from the female world, and that later cause them difficulty communicating in depth with women and in maintaining "significant relationships" with the opposite sex. Ann Oakley then examines the situation that females face as they grow up in a male-dominated society. As she examines controlling mechanisms by which females are socialized to fit into a more constraining role in society, she presents broad historical/cultural materials that illustrate the pervasive nature of male dominance. The final two articles discuss how sex roles affect adult interaction. Pepper Schwartz and Janet Lever focus on how sex roles are played out in college dating, while Mimi Rodin examines interaction among what she calls "young, never-married, urban apartment dwellers."

Taken together, these articles ought to provide considerable insight into your own socialization into sexuality—how you became a male or female in today's world and, once propelled into that role, how social constraints continue to operate to control your behavior.

8 On Becoming Male: Reflections of a Sociologist on Childhood and Early Socialization

JAMES M. HENSLIN

Although this area of social life is enveloped in social change, men still dominate the social institutions of the Western world: law, politics, business, religion, education, the military, medicine, science, and in many ways, even the family. In spite of far-reaching change, as women participate in our social institutions they are generally in a position of subservience to men. Women are usually found in more backstage, nurturing, and supportive roles—and those roles are generally supportive of the more dominant roles men play.

Why? Is this a fact of genetic heritage, or is it due to culture, because males are socialized into dominance? While there is considerable debate on this matter, sociologists side almost unanimously with the proponents of socialization. In this article, Henslin analyzes some of the socialization experiences that place males in a distinctive social world and prepare them for dominance. It is an attempt to penetrate the taken for granted behind-the-scenes aspects of socialization into masculine sexuality. You might find it useful to contrast your experiences in growing up with those the author describes.

ACCORDING TO THE PREVAILING SOCIOLOGICAL PERSPECTIVE, our masculinity or femininity is not biologically determined. Although each of us receives from our biological inheritance certain genetic characteristics that determine whether we possess the sex organs of a male or female, how our "maleness" or "femaleness" is expressed depends on what we learn. Our masculinity or femininity, that is, what we are like as sexual beings—our orientations and how we behave as a male or female—does not depend on biology but on social learning. It can be said that while our gender is part of our biological inheritance, our sexuality (or masculinity or femininity) is part of our social inheritance.

If this sociological position on sexuality is correct, how do we become the "way we are"? What factors shape or influence us into becoming masculine or feminine? If our characteristic behaviors do not come from our biology, how do we end up having those that we do have? What is the *process* by which we come to possess behaviors typically associated with our gender? How do the expectations of other people influence these behaviors and characteristics? If they *are* learned, how do behaviors, attitudes, and other orientations come to be felt by us as the natural and essential part of our identity? (And indeed, they are essential to our identity.) In what way is the "becoming process" related to the social structure of a society?

Not only would it take volumes to answer these questions fully, but it would also be impossible, since the answers are only now slowly being unraveled by researchers. In this short and rather informal article, I will be able only to indicate some of the basics underlying this learning. I will focus exclusively on being socialized into masculinity, and will do this by reflecting on: (1) my own experience in "becoming"; (2) my observations as a sociologist of the experiences of others; and (3) what students have shared with me concerning their own experiences. The reader should keep in mind that this article is not meant to be definitive or exhaustive, but is designed to demonstrate major areas of male socialization and thereby to provide insight into the learning of masculinity in our culture.

In the Beginning . . .

Except for a few rare instances,[1] each of us arrives in this world with a clearly definable physical characteristic that sets us apart from about half the rest of the world. This characteristic makes a literal world of difference. Our parents become excited about whether we have a penis or a vagina. They are usually either happy or disappointed about which organ we possess, seldom feeling neutral about the matter. They announce it to friends, relatives, and often to complete strangers ("It's a boy!" "It's a girl!"). Regardless of how they feel about it, on the basis of our possessing a particular physical organ they purposely, but both consciously and subconsciously, separate us into one of two worlds. Wittingly and unwittingly, they thereby launch us on a career that will emcompass almost every aspect of our lives—and will remain with us until death.

COLORS, CLOTHING, AND TOYS

While it is no more masculine or feminine than red, yellow, purple, orange, white, or black, the color blue has become arbitrarily associated with *infantile masculinity*. After what is usually a proud realization that the neonate possesses a penis (which destines him to become one of the overlords of his universe), the inheritor of dominance is wrapped in blue. This color is merely an arbitrary choice, as originally any other would have done as well. But now that the association is made, no other will do. The colors maintain this meaning for only a fairly short period, gradually becoming sexually neutralized.[2] Pink, however, retains at least part of its meaning of sexuality, for males tend to shy away from it.

Our parents gently and sometimes not so gently push us onto a predetermined course. First they provide clothing designated appropriate to our masculine status. Even as infants our clothing has sexual significance, and our parents are extremely careful that we never are clothed in either dresses or ruffles. While our plastic panties, for example, are designed to keep mothers (primarily) and furniture (secondarily) and fathers (only tertiarily) dry, our parents make absolutely certain that ours are never pink with white ruffles. Even if our Mom had run out of all other plastic panties, she would rather stay home than take us out in public wearing ruffled pinkies. Mom would be likely to feel a tinge of guilt to do such cross-dressing even in private.[3]

So both Mom and Dad are extremely careful about our clothing. Generally plain, often simple, and usually sturdy, our clothing is designed to take the greater "rough and tumble" that they know boys are going to give it. They also choose clothing to help groom us into future adult roles; depending on the style of the period, they dress us in little sailor suits, miniature jogging togs, or two-piece suits with matching ties. Although at this early age we could care less about such things, and their significance is at least consciously invisible to us, our parents' concern is always present. If even a stranger during a supermarket expedition mistakes our sexual identity, an upsetting consternation immediately penetrates our parents' awareness of their responsibility in maintaining the reality-ordering structure of the sex worlds. Such a mistaken identification forces them to rethink their role in proper sex typing, in making certain that their offspring is receiving the right start in life. They will either ascribe the mistake to the stupidity of the stranger or immediately foreswear some particular piece of clothing.

Our parents' "gentle nudging" into masculinity does not overlook our toys. These represent both current activities thought sexually appropriate and those symbolic of our future masculine activities involving courage, danger, and daring. We are given trucks, tanks, and guns. Although our mother might caution us about breaking them, it is apparent by her tone and facial expressions that she does not mean what she says. We can continue banging them together roughly, and she merely looks at us—sometimes quite uncomprehendingly, occasionally muttering something to the effect that boys will be boys. We somehow perceive her sense of confirmation and we bang them all the more, laughing gleefully at the approval we know it is bringing.

PLAY AND THE SEXUAL BOUNDARIES OF TOLERANCE

We can make all sorts of expressive sounds as we play. We can shout, grunt, groan, and roll around in the sandbox. As she shoves us out the door, Mom always cautions us not to get dirty, but when we come in filthy her verbal and gestural disapproval is only mild. From holistic perception, of which by now we have become young masters, we have learned that no matter what her words say they do not represent the entirety of her feelings.

When we are "dressed up" before going someplace, or before company comes, Mom acts differently. We learn that at those times she means what she says about not getting dirty, and if we do not want "fire in our pants" we had better remain clean—at least for a while, for we also learn that after company has come and has had a glimpse of the neat and clean little boy (or, as they say, "the nice little gentleman" or the "fine young man"), we can go about our rough and tumble games. Pushing, shouting, running, climbing, and other expressions of competition, glee, and freedom then become permissible. We learn that the appearance required at the beginning of a visit is quite different from that which is passable at the end of the visit.

Our more boisterous and rougher play continues to help us learn the bounds of our parents' tolerance limits. As we continuously test those limits, somewhat to our dismay we occasionally find ourselves having gone beyond them. Through what is at times painful trial and error, we learn both the boundaries and how they vary with changed circumstance. We eventually learn those limits extremely well and know, for example, precisely how much more we can "get away with" when company comes than when only the immediate family is present, when Mom and Dad are tired, or when they are arguing.

As highly rational beings, who are seldom adequately credited by adults for our keen cunning, we learn to calculate those boundaries exceedingly carefully. We eventually come to the point where we know that one more word of back talk, one more quarrel with our brother, sister, or friend, even a small one, or even one more whine will move our parents from words to deeds, and their wrath will fall upon us with full force. Depending on our parents' orientation to child rearing (or on their predilection of the moment), this will result in either excruciating humiliation in front of our friends and horrible (though momentary) physical pain, or excruciating humiliation in front of our friends and the horrifying (and longer) deprivation of a privilege (which of course we know is really a "right" and is being unjustifiably withheld from us).

ON FREEDOM AND BEING

As we calculate those boundaries of tolerance (or in the vernacular used by our parents and well understood by us, find out how much they can "stand"), we also learn something about our world vis-à-vis that of those strange female creatures who coinhabit our space. We learn that we can get dirtier, play rougher, speak louder and more crudely, wander farther from home, stay away longer, and talk back more.

We see girls living in a different world, one that is foreign to us. It is quieter, neater, daintier, and in general more subdued. Sometimes our worlds touch, but usually only briefly. We learn, for example, that while little sisters might be all right to spend an occasional hour or so with on a rainy afternoon, they are, after all, "only girls." They really cannot enter our world, and we certainly do not want to become a part of theirs, with its greater restrictions and fewer challenges. Occasionally, we even find ourselves delighting in this difference and taunting them about not being able to do something because they are "only girls."

If we sometimes wonder about the reason for the differences between our worlds, our curiosity quickly runs its course, as we realize that these differences are proper. They are *girls* and, as our parents have told us over and over, we are *NOT* girls. We have learned the appropriateness of our worlds, what is right for us and what is right for them. Seldom are we sorry for the tighter reins placed on girls. We are just glad that we are not one of "them." We stick with "our own kind," and immensely enjoy our greater freedom. Rather than losing ourselves in philosophical reflections about the inequalities of this world (greatly beyond our mental capacities at this point anyway), we lose ourselves in the exultation of our greater freedom and the good fortune that made us a boy instead of a girl.

This greater freedom becomes the most prized aspect of our existence. Before we are old enough to go to school (and later, during summer, weekends, and any other nonschool days), when we awaken in the morning we can hardly wait to get our clothes on. Awaiting us is a world of adventure. If we are up before Mom, we can go outside and play in the yard. Before venturing beyond voice distance, however, we have to have our "wholesome" breakfast, one that somehow is always in the process of "making a man" out of us. After this man-producing breakfast, which might well consist of little more than cereal, we are free to roam, to discover, to experience. There are no dishes to do, no dusting, sweeping, or cleaning. Those things are for sisters, mothers and other females.

Certainly we have spatial and associational restrictions placed on us— but they are much more generous than those imposed on girls of our age. We know how many blocks we can go and who we are allowed to see. But just as significant, we know how to go beyond that distance without getting caught and how to play with the "bad boys" and the "too big boys" without Mom ever being the wiser. So long as we are home within a certain time limit, in spite of verbal restrictions we really are free to come and go.

We do learn to accept limited responsibility in order to guard our freedom, and we are always pestering other mothers for the time or, when we are able, arranging for them to tell us when it is "just about noon" so we can make our brief appearance for lunch—and then quickly move back into the exciting world of boy activity. But we also learn to lie a lot, finding out that it is better to say anything plausible rather than to admit that you violated the boundaries and be "grounded," practically the worse form of punishment a boy can receive. Consequently, we learn to deny, to avoid, to deceive, to tell half-truths, and to involve ourselves in other sorts of subterfuge rather than admit to violations that can restrict our freedom of movement.

Our freedom is infinitely precious to us, for whether it is cops and robbers or space bandits, the Lone Ranger or Darth Vader, ours is an imaginary world filled with daring and danger. Whether it is sixshooters and bullets or space missiles and laser disintegrators, we are always shooting or getting shot. There are always the good guys and the bad guys. There is always a moral victory to be won. We are continuously running, shouting, hiding, and discovering. The world is filled with danger, and the inopportune and unexpected are always lurking just around the corner. As the enemy stalks, the suddenness of discovery and the sweet joys of being undiscovered are unsurpassable. Nothing in adulthood, in spite of its great allure, its challenges and victories yet to be experienced, will ever be greater than this intense bliss of innocence—and part of the joy of this period is being entirely unaware of this savage fact of life.

. . . And the Twain Shall Never Meet

None of us is thinking about being masculine. We are just being. The radical social differences that separate us from girls have not gone unnoticed. Rather, they have resulted in essential differences in life-orientations that not only have penetrated our consciousness but have saturated our very beings. Our initial indifference to things male and female has turned to violent tastes and distastes. We have learned our lessons so well that we sometimes end up teaching our own mothers lessons in sexuality. For example, we would rather be caught dead than wear sissy clothing, and our tantrums will not cease until our mother comes to her senses and relents concerning putting something on us that we consider sissified.

We know there are two worlds, and we are glad for the one we are in. Ours is superior. The evidence surrounds us, and we exult in masculine privilege. We also protect our sexual boundaries from encroachment and erosion. The encroachment comes from tomboys who want to become part of our world. We tolerate them—up to a point. But by excluding them from certain activities, we let them know that there are irrevocable differences that forever separate us.

Erosion comes from sissies. Although we are unaware that they pose a threat to our masculine identity, we know that we dislike them intensely. To be a sissy is to be a traitor to one's very being. It is to be "like a girl," that which we are not—and that which we definitely never will be like.

Sissies are to be either pitied or hated. While they are not girls, neither are they real boys. They look like us, but they bring shame on us because they do not represent anything we are. We are everything they are not. Consequently, we separate ourselves from them in the most direct manner possible. While we may be brutal about this separation, it is necessary, for we must define the boundaries of our own existence, and one way that we know who we are is by knowing what we are not.

So we shame sissies. We make fun of anyone who is not the way he "ought" to be. If he hangs around the teacher or girls during recess instead of playing our rough and tumble games, if he will not play sports because he is afraid of getting dirty or being hurt, if he backs off from a fight, if he cries, or even if he gets too many A's, we put him through a ridicule process. We gather around him in a circle. We call him a sissy. We say, "Shame! Shame!" We call him gay and queer. We tell him he is a girl and not fit for us.

And as far as we are concerned, he never will be fit for us. He belongs to some strange status, not quite a girl and not quite a boy. Whatever he is, he certainly is not one of us. We don't cry when we are punished or hurt. We don't hang around girls. We are proud of our average grades. We play rough games. We are not afraid of getting hurt. (Or if we are, we would never let it show.) We are not afraid of sassing the teacher, or at least of calling the teacher names when his or her back is turned. We know who we are. We are boys.

THE PUBERTY SHOCK

We never know, of course, how precarious our sexual identity is. We have been sharply differentiated from females, and we have sharply differentiated ourselves both from females and from those who do not match up to the masculine ideal. Our world of masculinity seems sound, with distinct boundaries that clearly define "us" from "them." We know who we are, and we are cocky about it.

Things are solid. Our existence is well defined. By the end of grade school the pecking order is clear. For good or ill, each of us is locked in it somewhere, our destiny determined.

But then comes puberty, and overnight the world undergoes radical metamorphosis. Girls suddenly change. Right before our eyes the flat chests we have always taken for granted begin to protrude. Two little bumps magically appear, and while we are off playing our games, once in a while we cast quizzical glances in the direction of the girls. Right before us is a haunting change, but we shrug it off and go back to our games.

Then the change hits us. We feel something happening within our own bodies. At first the feeling is vague, undefined. There is no form to it. We just know that something is different. Then we begin to feel strange stirrings within us. These stirrings come on abruptly, and that abruptness begins to shake everything loose in our secure world. Until this time our penis has never given us any particular trouble. It has just "been there," like a finger or a toenail. It has been a fact of life, something that "we" had and "they" didn't. But now it literally springs to life, taking on an existence of its own and doing things that we previously could not even imagine would ever take place. It creates various sorts of embarrassment, and there are even times when we are called to the blackboard to work out some problem and we must play dumb about knowing the answer because of the bulge that we never willed.

It is a new game. The girls in our class are different. And we are different. We will never be the same.

We have to learn new concepts of masculinity. This is upsetting, but fortunately we do not have to begin from scratch. We can build on our past. Mostly, the change involves just one area of our lives, girls, and the rest is able to remain intact. We can still swagger, curse, get dirty, and bloody ourselves. While the girls still watch us admiringly from the sidelines as we "do our manly thing," we also now watch them as they "do their womanly thing" and strut before us in tight sweaters.

While the girls still admire our toughness, a change is now demanded. At times we must now show gentleness. We must be cleaner and watch our language more than before. We must even show consideration. These shifting requirements are not easy to master, but we have the older, more experienced boys to count on—and they are more than happy to initiate us into this new world and, while doing so, demonstrate their (always) greater knowledge and skills in traversing the social world.

THE TRANSITION INTO ARTIFICIALITY

And we make the transition. But with difficulty. A new sexuality must come into being, and that can never be easy. What we really learn, however, is to be extremely adept role players. We learn one way of behaving when we are with the guys. This is the "natural" way, the way we feel. It is relaxed and easy. And we learn a different way of acting while we are around the girls, much more contrived and artificial, a way of being that requires greater politeness, consideration, and gentleness. In other words, it is a way that is contrary to all that we have previously learned. Consequently we become actors, putting on expected performances. Actually, we always have been actors; it is just that our earlier role was more comfortable. We behave more or less as expected while we are around females, when we must enter their world temporarily. But this never becomes a part of our being. It always consists of superficial behaviors added on to what is truly and, by this time, "naturally" us.

This artificiality forces us to become manipulators. We learn that to get what we want, whether it is an approving smile, or more, that we must meet the expectations of the one from whom we desire something. We are no strangers to this fact of life, of course, but the faces we must wear in these situations, our gestures and the expected words, make us appear as strangers to ourselves. We wonder why we must be in situations that require this constant posing and posturing.

But uncomfortable or not (and as we learn to play the game better, most of the initial discomfort leaves), we always come back for more. By now sports and games with the fellows are no longer enough. Females now appear to hold the key to our happiness. They can withhold or grant as they see fit. And for favors to be granted, a particular game must be played.

The Continuing Masculine World—And Marriage

We become highly adept at the intersexual game, even though its hypocrisies and deceits make us feel uncomfortable at times. Manly activities provide us refuge from this discomfort, activities in which we truly understand one another, where we share the same world of aspiration, conflict, and competition. Here we can laugh at the same things and talk the way we really feel without having to worry about the words we choose. We know that among men our interests, activities, and desires are understood and accepted because they are shared, are part of a mutual, self-enclosing world.

We must, of course, leave our comfortable world of manliness occasionally to penetrate the conjoint world occupied by our feminine counterparts. But this is temporary, and never a "real" part of us. Always waiting for us are the "real" conversations that reflect the "real" world, that exciting world worth living in because it is filled with challenge, creativity, competition, and conflict.

And we are fortunate in having a socially constructed semi-imaginary masculine world into which we can retreat. This world of televised football, basketball, wrestling, boxing, and car racing is part of the domain of men. At least here is a world, manly and comfortable, that we can enter at will and avoid confronting that feminine world that both is threatening with its strangeness and appears ready to suffocate us with its outrageous demands. This semi-imaginary world is also so attractive (and never to be adequately understood by the females of our species) because it brings back so many unconscious feelings from our childhood, our adolescence, and eventually as we grow older, our early manhood.

Many of us would not deny that the characteristics we males learn or, if you prefer, the persons we tend to become are not the best for the development of solid intersexual relationships. But those characteristics, while underlying what is often the shallowness of our relationships with females, are indeed us. They are the logical consequence of our years of experience. We have become what we have been painstakingly shaped to become. Although willing participants in our social destiny, we have merely received our social inheritance. Some of us, only with great difficulty, have overcome our masculine socialization into intersexual superficiality and have developed relationships with wives and girlfriends that transcend this cultural learning. But such relearning inevitably is painful and leaves in its wake much hurt and brokenness.

Hardly any of this process of becoming a man in our society augurs well for marriage. The separateness of the world that we males join at birth signals our embarkation on an intricate process whereby we become a different type of being. Our world differs in almost all aspects from the world of females. Not only do we look different, not only do we talk differently and act differently, but our fundamental orientation to life sharply contrasts with theirs. This basic divergence is so difficult for females to grasp and, when grasped, is often accompanied by a shudder of disbelief and distaste at the reveletory insight into such a contrasting reality. Yet we are expected to unite permanently with someone from the contradispositional world and, in spite of these basic and essential differences, share not only a life space, but also bring together our goals, hopes, dreams, aspirations, and other "stuff" of which life is made.

Is it any wonder that in perhaps the typical case men remain strangers to women and women to men? . . .

Notes

1. Of about one in every 30,000 births, the sex of a baby is unclear. A genetic disorder called congenital adrenal hyperplasis results in the newborn having parts of both male and female genitals (*St. Louis Globe-Democrat*, March 10–11, 1979: 3D).

2. When people (almost exclusively women) are invited to a baby shower and the expectant mother has not yet given birth (or if they wish to take advantage of a sale and buy a gift in advance of the delivery), they find themselves in a quandary. What has become the institutionalized solution to this problem of not knowing the sex of the child (at least in the Midwest) is to purchase either a "sex neutral" item or clothing of yellow color.

3. The historical arbitrariness and relativity of the gender designation of clothing is, of course, duly noted. Ruffles and other stylistic variations can very well have different significance in other historical periods.

9 Childhood Lessons

ANN OAKLEY

Now that we have examined how broader cultural expectations are played out in the case of male socialization into sex roles, we shall turn to the social context within which females learn the part they are expected to play in society. Oakley focuses on the "messages" given to female children, which result in their adopting a feminine identity. Her comparison of the feminine and masculine roles should help you gain insight into how society has given shape to your own sexual identity, into the social bases that underlie your display of sexual behaviors and attitudes.

Taking this selection conjointly with the one preceding, you might ask yourself what you like and do not like about current socialization into sex roles in American society. How do you think you could change what you do not like? What obstacles would you have to overcome? Finally, assuming the continuance of society along more or less its present lines, how do you think you could make things more to your liking for your own children?

DOCTOR: *Come on junior. Only a lady could cause so much trouble.*
 Come on, little one [baby is delivered].
MOTHER: *A girl!*
DOCTOR: *Well, it's got the right plumbing.*
MOTHER: *Oh, I'm sorry, darling.*
FATHER: *(laughs)*
DOCTOR: *What are you sorry about?*
MOTHER: *He wanted a boy.*

          —Macfarlane (1977, p. 63)

CONVERSATIONS OF THIS KIND SET THE SCENE for a lifetime's lessons. Gender is in most situations the most salient social fact about an individual, both because of its presumed relationship to eroticism and because in the culture of capitalist societies social differences between females and males are a basic structural theme.

Gender is assigned at birth when parents and medical staff view a baby's external genitals. They bring to this occasion all their own preconceptions about the social content and psychic meaning of boyhood/girlhood and manhood/womanhood, matching their categorization of the newborn's genitals with this determination of gender. It is therefore long before she reaches adulthood that a female experiences the full extent of her cultural definition as a secondary feminine being. . . .

Let us look at some of those factors known to be responsible for the development of gender identity. Few parents, in the first place, are indifferent to the sex of their child. In my own study of London women having their first babies in 1975–76, three-quarters said in pregnancy they had a definite sex preference and many of those who said they "didn't mind" added after the child was born that they had minded, but hadn't wanted to voice a preference for fear of being disappointed, or because to do so is regarded superstitiously as bringing bad luck. Table 9.1 shows how many women wanted boys and girls and what their reactions were: 93 per cent of those who had boys were pleased; 44 per cent who had daughters were not (as in the delivery room scene above). Whatever treatment girls receive in childhood to point them in the direction of femininity, it is clear that they are more likely to start off as a disappointment to their parents. Dana Breen (1975) found more cases of postnatal depression occurring among mothers of girls than mothers of boys. . . .

TABLE 9.1. Sex Preferences and Reactions

Wanted girl	22%
Wanted boy	54%
Didn't mind	25%
Had girl: pleased	56%
Had boy: pleased	93%
Had girl: disappointed	44%
Had boy: disappointed	7%

Source: Oakley (1979) p. 118.

Sex preferences are conscious; gender-differentiated treatment of children often is not. Lake (1975) gave five young mothers Beth, a six-month-old in a pink frilly dress, for a period of observed interaction; five others were given Adam, a six-month-old in blue overalls. Compared to Adam Beth was smiled at more, offered a doll to play with more often and described as "sweet" with a "soft cry." Adam and Beth were the same child.

Conceiving Gender

. . . But the question is: How do women come to think of themselves as feminine people?

Money and Ehrhardt (1972) have suggested that a relevant analogy for the development of gender identity is that of bilingualism. A child growing up in a bilingual environment is presented with two languages that require two different sets of behavioural responses. So with gender: There are two sets of stimuli to be programmed by the brain into two different complexes of behaviour. The child's task is to identify with one and reject the other; the parents' conscious or unconscious duty is to provide the means whereby little girls identify with the feminine model and little boys with the masculine one.

"Identification" is the key concept. Most theories of gender-identity development reserve an important place for it. Because it implies the idea of a "model" with whom identification can take place, most theories also stress the importance of parents as the primary teachers of gender. The three main theories are the cognitive-developmental, the social learning, and the psychoanalytic.

The first of these builds on the work of Piaget (1952) and says that gender is based on genital sex and so is a physical property of people that has to be learnt in the same way as other unchanging physical properties. Children below the age of 4 or 5 years cannot appreciate the unchangeable character of physical objects: cats can become dogs at will, water poured into different-sized glasses has changed its volume; girls can become boys. Thus a little girl first of all develops the idea that she is a girl and later (by the age of 5 or 6) appreciates that gender is invariant, that everyone has a gender and that gender is primarily a question of physical sex differences. Once the idea of a stable feminine gender identity is developed, she begins actively to prefer feminine activities and objects. The thinking is: I am a girl; therefore I like girl things; therefore doing girl things is rewarding (Kohlberg, 1967; Kohlberg and Ullian, 1974).

The second theory, that of social learning, contends that the development of gender identity involves a learning process that is essentially the same as other learning processes. A little girl observes her parents performing feminine and masculine roles, but when she imitates the various behaviours she sees, she is only rewarded for those considered appropriate to her gender. Through such differential reinforcement, feminine behaviours come to be positively evaluated and masculine ones rejected: I want rewards; I am rewarded for doing girl things; therefore I want to be (am) a girl. The results is a generalized tendency to imitate all same-gendered "models" (Mischel, 1967, 1970).

Thirdly, we have the psychoanalytic view of gender-identity development. . . . In this, awareness of genital difference comes first and paves the way for an identification with the parent who has a similar set of genitals. The formula runs: I do not have a penis; therefore I am a girl. . . . Because women rear children, the love of both girls and boys is originally centered on the mother. This, combined with an early unawareness in small children of the genital difference, means that at first the psychological development of females and males is the same. But when the girl discovers that she has no penis she also recognizes that her mother shares the same fate and blames her for her disadvantaged condition. This leads to a rejection of the mother as a love object; the girl turns to her father instead, a move that lays the foundation for her adult sexual attraction to males and her desire to bear male children. When she realizes the futility of seeing her father as a love object and its threat to her mother's attitude towards her, she is again inclined to a maternal identification. The discovery of the missing penis is thus the event that, in a complex series of stages, determines the feminine character with its three special qualities of masochism (a permanent sense of being castrated), passivity (the reluctant acceptance of the clitoris as an inadequate analogue of the penis), and narcissism (women's overvaluation of their superficial physical charms as compensation for their inferior genital equipment).

All three theories—the cognitive-developmental, the social-learning and the psychoanalytic—take the actual processes that are involved in the emergence of adult femininity and masculinity as in need of explanation. All assume that some identification with the same-sexed parent has to take place and is the main precursor of the desire to be seen as feminine or masculine. This "motivational consequence" is not only a necessary element in the continuing gender socialization of children ('self-socialization'), but is, of course, an absolutely central means for the cultural transmission of gender concepts from one generation to another. Lessons learnt in childhood become the lessons that parents want their own children to learn. . . .

Penis and Other Envies

It is significant that feminist descriptions of the imprisonment of women in a feminine mould blame "society" in general for their captivity. Particular individuals are not usually identified as the teachers of femininity; it is the wide range of cultural pressures all acting in the same direction—the "overdetermination" of gender—that is implicated. In Simone de Beauvoir's words,

> One is not born, but rather becomes, a woman. No biological, psychological, or economic fate determines the figure that the human female presents in society; it is *civilisation as a whole* that produces this creature, intermediate between male and eunuch, which is described as feminine. [De Beauvoir, 1960, p. 8; italics added]

"Civilization" is not feminine; it is "a man's world." Of all the lessons girls learn, this is the most important one. Freud, from his enviable position of masculine hegemony, called it penis envy, but it is not the penis that women want. Clara Thompson, one of the small band of female analysts who challenged Freud's thinking, wrote

> one can say the term penis envy is a symbolic representation of the attitude of women in this culture . . . the penis is the sign of the person in power in

one particular competitive set-up in this culture, that between man and woman. The attitude of the woman in this situation is not qualitatively different from that found in any minority group in a competitive culture. So, the attitude called penis envy is similar to the attitude of any underprivileged group toward those in power. . . . [Thompson, 1974, pp. 53–54]

Women envy men their power. Small children learn effortlessly about masculine power within the asymmetrical nuclear family. Father leaves the house each day as the family's representative in the public world and returns with proof (money) of the valuation of his labour; his status in the household and in society is clearly different from that of mother. But in fact, and paradoxically, dominance and nurturance are the two adult qualities that most attract children to identify with parents (Bandura and Huston, 1961; Hetherington, 1965; Hetherington and Frankie, 1967). Such an inherent contradiction throws light on many of the difficulties men and women have in adjusting their identities to fit the standard gender formulae.

When Florence Nightingale was born, she was the second daughter, intended to be a son, of ill-matched parents. Fanny Nightingale was six years older than her husband, a dedicated hostess married to an indolent and charming dilettante. Florence's biographer, Cecil Woodham-Smith, comments:

> She did not attach herself to her mother. The companion of her childhood was W.E.N. [as her father was known].
> W.E.N. was a man to enchant a child. He loved the curious and the odd, and he loved jokes; he had a mind stored with information and the leisure to impart it. He had great patience, and he was never patronising. Partly as a result of marrying Fanny, partly by temperament, he was a lonely man, and it was with intense pleasure he discovered intellectual companionship in his daughters. Both were quick; both were unusually responsive; both learned easily, but the more intelligent, just as she was the prettier, was Flo. [Woodham-Smith, 1952, pp. 7–8]

He educated both Florence and her elder sister Parthenope (Parthe) himself, teaching them Greek, Latin, German, French, Italian, history and philosophy. Parthe rebelled and joined her mother in domestic activities. Florence and her father "were deeply in sympathy. Both had the same regard for accuracy, the same cast of mind at once humorous and gloomy, the same passion for abstract speculation." Affection for her father and resentment of her mother (and her sister) were the dominating passions of her life.

Florence found the life of a Victorian lady boring, debilitating and depressing; her two havens were her father, who had some understanding of his daughter's need to find an outlet for her energy, and her father's sister, with whom she conspired to learn mathematics "instead of doing worsted work and practising quadrilles." Her difficulties were multiplied by the fact that she was evidently a success at the feminine role: "very gay . . . Her demure exterior concealed wit. She danced beautifully." For this success she reproached herself: "All I do is done to win admiration" she wrote in a private note. When she was 16, Florence received her first call from God. "On February 7, 1837, God spoke to me and called me to His service." The voice reappeared three more times: in 1853, just before she took up her first post at the Hospital for Poor Gentlewomen in Harley Street; before the Crimean War in 1854; and after the death of her friend and "Master," Lord Sidney Herbert in 1861. Seven years after the first call, and after an intense inner struggle, Florence became certain that her vocation was to nurse the sick. It took nine more years to convince her family that this was what she should be allowed to do. Her mother was "terrified" and "angry," her sister "hysterical." Her father was disappointed that his education of Florence had led to this unsuitable wilfulness, but he did eventually grant her an allowance of £500 a year, and later bought her a house. In his last years, they were completely reconciled and had "long talks on metaphysics" together.

Such closeness between father and daughter allows the model of a masculine life-style to filter through the barrier of feminine socialization pressures. A study of women enrolled in the Harvard Business school in the mid-1960s picked up this theme in the childhood histories of "managerial" women. Most were first children, and "all had extremely close relationships with their fathers and had been involved in an unusually wide range of traditionally masculine activities in the company of their fathers, beginning when they were very young" (Hennig and Jardim, 1978, p. 99). While the *absence* of a father appears to endanger the learning of masculinity in boys (Tiller, 1967), his presence would therefore seem to encourage androgynous development in girls.

The role played by fathers as powerful and affectionate representatives of non-domestic culture can, of course, be taken by mothers as well. Daughters of working mothers have less rigid conceptions of gender roles than daughters of "non-working" mothers (Morantz and Mansfield, 1977; Hansson *et al.*, 1977). They tend to have less "feminine" identities, stressing such masculine qualities as independence and self-reliance (Hoffman and Nye, 1974).

In a very different society, that of the !Kung bush people of the Kalahari desert, the same general importance of women's socially valued productivity is seen. Among the !Kung, women's agricultural work is crucial to everyone's physical survival. Women have a great deal of autonomy and influence over the economic resources of the community as well as its ceremonial and power relations:

> A common sight in the late afternoon is clusters of children standing on the edge of camp, scanning the bush with shaded eyes to see if the returning women are visible. When the slow-moving file of women is finally discerned

in the distance, the children leap and exclaim. As the women draw closer, the children speculate as to which figure is whose mother and what the women are carrying in their karosses. [Draper, 1975, p.82]

Women's work is part of their childhood games, of female socialization:

We . . . played at being hunters and we went out tracking animals and when we saw one we struck it with our make-believe arrows. We took some leaves and hung them over a stick and pretended it was meat. Then we carried it back to our village. When we got back, we stayed there and ate the meat and then the meat was gone. We went out again, found another animal and killed it. We again threw leaves over a stick, put other leaves in our karosses, and brought it back. We played at living in the bush like that. [Interview with !Kung woman, *Spare Rib*, October 1975, pp. 15–16]

In a society where small children of both sexes are brought up by women but expected to learn to be different genders, it is also true to say that girls have an obvious built-in advantage. There is no room for doubt as to who they are expected to be like—whereas boys have the problem of working out what masculinity is and switching from an early identification with their mothers to a later and more enduring one with their fathers. . . .

Artifacts of Gender

Parental work in the area of teaching gender also takes place within the broad context of cultural artifacts that separate the world of girls from the world of boys.

Gender-appropriate toys are both the cause and the proof of correct gender identification. In the case of the boy whose penis was accidentally removed and who was reassigned as a girl at the age of 17 months:

The mother reported: "I started dressing her not in dresses but, you know, in little pink slacks and frilly blouses . . . and letting her hair grow." A year and six months later, the mother wrote that she had made a special effort at keeping her girl in dresses, almost exclusively, changing any item of clothes into something that was clearly feminine. "I even made all her nightwear into granny gowns and she wears bracelets and hair ribbons." The effects of emphasizing feminine clothing became clearly noticeable in the girl's attitude towards clothes and hairdo another year later, when she was observed to have a clear preference for dresses over slacks. [Money and Erhardt, 1972, p. 119]

The girl asked for dolls, a dolls' house and a dolls' pram for Christmas; her [twin] brother, a toy garage with cars.

Walum (1977, p. 49) did an analysis of the 1972 edition of the Sears Roebuck Christmas toy catalogue. Her base unit was each half page of the catalogue showing a different toy with a picture of the child (female, male, both genders) for whom it was promoted. She found that 84 per cent of the toys portrayed as suitable for girls fell under the heading of "preparatory for spousehood and parenthood," whereas none of those portrayed for males did so; 75 per cent of male toys were "manipulatory" in character, and 25 per cent related to male occupational roles. As Alice Rossi once remarked, a girl may spend more time playing with her dolls than a mother will ever spend with her children (Rossi, 1964, p. 105), and the message is clearly that girls play house and do not play the kinds of games with the kinds of toys that would prepare them for other occupational roles. . . .

The child's own space within the home is full of gender signals. In a middle-class area of a university community, "a locale that would presumably be on the less differentiated end of the sex role socialization spectrum" (Weitz, 1977, p. 61), the bedrooms of boys and girls were instantly identifiable. Boys' rooms "contained more animal furnishings, more educational art materials, more spatial-temporal toys, more sports equipment and more toy animals. The rooms of girls contained more dolls, more floral furnishings and more 'ruffles' " (Rheingold and Cook, 1975, p. 461). The 48 girls' rooms boasted 17 toy vehicles—the 48 boys', 375; 26 of the girls' rooms had dolls, compared with 3 of the boys'. . . .

Another potent source of gender messages is children's literature. . . . Weitzman et al.'s (1976) survey of [pre-school picture books] begins by noting the fact that women are barely visible in most of them. In their sample of prizewinning books, the male: female sex ratio in pictures of people was 11:1 (for animals it was 95:1). Most of the plots centered on some form of male adventure and females figured chiefly in their traditional service function or in the more imaginative, but ultimately no less restrictive, roles of fairy, fairy godmother and underwater maiden. In the duo *What Girls Can Be* and *What Boys Can Be* (Walley, n.d.), the pinnacle of achievement for a boy is to be President of the nation and for a girl it is motherhood. . . .

Although much of the early analysis of sexism in children's literature was done in the United States, similar studies in Britain have shown no substantive differences, except perhaps that British material lags behind American in revising the stereotypes it presents to children. Glenys Lobban (1976) looked at six popular British reading schemes: *Janet and John, Happy Venture, Ready to Read, Ladybird, Nipper* and *Breakthrough to Literacy.* Table 9.2 gives some of her findings. It shows the same definition of girls and women as relatively passive, indoor creatures, the same glorification of masculine adventurousness as the American research.

TABLE 9.2. Sex Roles Occurring in Three or More of Six British Reading Schemes.*

	CONTENT OF CHILDREN'S ROLES				
SEX FOR WHICH ROLE IS PRESCRIBED	Toys and Pets	Activities	Taking Lead in Both-Sex Activities	Learning New Skill	Adult Roles Presented
Girls only	Doll Skipping rope Doll's pram	Preparing tea Playing with dolls Taking care of younger siblings	Hopping Shopping with parents Skipping	Taking care of younger siblings	Mother Aunt Grandmother
Boys only	Car Train Aeroplane Boat Football	Playing with cars Playing with trains Playing football Lifting/pulling heavy objects Playing cricket Watching adult males in occupational roles Heavy gardening	Going exploring alone Climbing trees Building things Taking care of pets Flying kites Washing and polishing Dad's car	Taking care of pets Making/building Saving/rescuing people or pets Playing sport	Father Uncle Grandfather Postman Farmer Fisherman Shop or business owner Policeman Builder Bus driver Bus conductor Train driver Railway porter
Both sexes	Book Ball Paints Bucket & spade Dog Cat Shop	Playing with pets Writing Reading Going to seaside Going on family outing			Teacher Shop assistant

*Janet and John, Happy Venture, Ready to Read, Ladybird, Nipper, Breakthrough to Literacy. [The term "Reading Schemes" refers to a programmed series of reading lessons.—Ed.]

. . . [As] Belotti observes in her retelling of some traditional fables, [women are often portrayed as pervasively stupid]:

> "Little Red Riding Hood" is the story of a girl, bordering on mental deficiency, who is sent out by an irresponsible mother through dark wolf-infested woods to take a little basket full to the brim with cakes, to her sick grandmother. Given these circumstances her end is hardly surprising. But such foolishness, which would never have been attributed to a male, depends on the assurance that one will always find at the right moment and in the right place a brave huntsman ready to save grandmother and granddaughter from the wolf. [Belotti, 1975, p. 102]

It is sadly true that female figures in fairy tales and in children's fiction generally belong to two alternative categories: the good but useless, and the wicked. It has been calculated that 80 per cent of the negative characters in comics and fairy tales are female (d'Ascia, 1971), and the myth of feminine evil is a pervasive cultural theme with which women still have to contend.

Lastly, children's television provides no relief from the relentless feminine message. Even such "liberal" programmes as Sesame Street do not place girls and women in prominent or seriously powerful positions. It is relevant to observe that most of the controversy about the effects of television on children is about the prevalence of male aggression in programmes directed at children. It is also important that children spend more of their lives watching television than they do at school, and that much of what they watch from an early age is adult television: they are thus exposed to the general range and effect of media representations of women.

All cultures have a division of labour by gender, but some are more divided than others. The need to differentiate children's roles and identities by sex is therefore immensely variable. Such variation must be borne in mind when viewing our own arrangements, which are one, not the only, way of grouping children in readiness for their adult life. . . .

References

Bandura, A., and A. C. Huston (1961). "Identification as a process of incidental learning," *Journal of Abnormal and Social Psychology*, 63: 311–18.

Belotti, E. G. (1975). *Little Girls*. London, Writers and Readers Publishing Co-operative.

Breen, D. (1975). *The Birth of a First Child*. London, Tavistock.

D'Ascia, U. (1971). "Onorevolmente Cative," *Noi Donne* no. 50, 19 December. Cited in Belotti (1975).

De Beauvoir, S. (1960). *The Second Sex*. London, Four Square Books.

Draper, P. (1975). "!Kung women: Contrasts in sexual egalitarianism in foraging and sedentary contexts," in Reiter (ed.) (1975).

Friedman, R. C.; R. M. Richart; and R. L. Vande Weile (eds.) (1978). *Sex Differences in Behavior*. New York, John Wiley.

Hansson, R. E.; M. E. Chernovetz; and H. Jones (1977) "Maternal employment and androgyny," *Psychology of Women Quarterly*, 2: 76–78.

Hennig, M., and A. Jardim (1978). *The Managerial Woman*. New York, Pocket Books.

Hetherington, E. M. (1965). "A developmental study of the effects of sex of the dominant parent on sex-role preference, identification and imitation in children," *Journal of Personality and Social Psychology*, 2: 188–94.

Hetherington, E. M., and G. Frankie (1967). "Effects of parental dominance, warmth and conflict on imitation in children," *Journal of Personality and Social Psychology*, 6: 119–25.

Hoffman, L. W., and F. I. Nye (eds.) (1974). *Working Mothers: An Evaluative Review of the Consequences for Wife, Husband and Child*. San Francisco, Jossey-Bass.

Kohlberg, L. (1967). "A cognitive-developmental analysis of children's sex-role concepts and attitudes," in Maccoby (ed.).

Kohlberg, L., and D. Z. Ullian (1974). "Stages in the development of psychosexual concepts and attitudes," in Friedman et al. (eds.) (1978).

Lake, A. (1975). "Are we born into our sex roles or programmed into them?" *Woman's Day*, January, pp. 24–25.

Lobban, G. (1976). "Sex roles in reading schemes," in Children's Rights Workshop.

Maccoby, E. E. (ed.) (1967). *The Development of Sex Differences*. London, Tavistock.

Macfarlane, A. (1977). *The Psychology of Childbirth*. London, Fontana.

Mischel, W. (1967). "A social-learning view of sex differences in behaviour," in Maccoby (ed.) (1967).

Mischel, W. (1970). "Sex-typing and socialization," in Mussen (ed.) (1970).

Money, J., and A. E. Ehrhardt (1972). *Man and Woman, Boy and Girl*. Baltimore, Johns Hopkins Press.

Morantz, S., and A. Mansfield (1977). "Maternal employment and the development of sex role stereotyping in five to eleven year olds," *Child Development*, 48: 668–73.

Mussen, P. H. (ed.) (1970). *Carmichael's Manual of Child Psychology*. New York, John Wiley.

Oakley, A. (1979). *Becoming a Mother*. Oxford, Martin Robertson.

Piaget, J. (1952). *The Origins of Intelligence in Children*. New York, International Universities Press.

Reiter, R. R. (ed.) (1975). *Toward an Anthropology of Women*. New York, Monthly Review Press.

Rheingold, H. L., and K. V. Cook (1975). "The content of boys' and girls' rooms as an index of parents' behaviour," *Child Development*, 46, no. 2: 459–63.

Rossi, A. (1964). "Equality between the sexes," in R. J. Lifton (ed.), *The Woman in America*. Boston, Houghton Mifflin.

Thompson, C. (1974). "Penis envy in women," in J. B. Miller (ed.), *Psychoanalysis and Women*. Harmondsworth, Penguin. (First published 1943.)

Tiller, P. O. (1967). "Parental role division and the child's personality development," in E. Dahlstrom (ed.), *The Changing Roles of Men and Women.* London, Duckworth.

Walley, D. (n.d.). *What Boys Can Be* and *What Girls Can Be.* Kansas City, Mo., Hallmark.

Walum, C. R. (1977). *The Dynamics of Sex and Gender: A Sociological Perspective.* Chicago, Rand McNally.

Weitz, S. (1977). *Sex Roles: Biological, Psychological and Social Foundations.* Oxford, Oxford University Press.

Weitzman, L. J.; D. Eifler; E. Hokada; and C. Ross (1976). "Sex-role socialization in picture books for pre-school children," in Children's Rights Workshop.

Woodham-Smith, C. (1952). *Florence Nightingale 1820–1910.* London, The Reprint Society.

10 Fear and Loathing at a College Mixer

PEPPER SCHWARTZ
JANET LEVER

Learning the sex role society assigns us is not a "once and for all" type of thing. It is not as though we learn our maleness or femaleness in childhood and then simply act accordingly the rest of our lives. Rather, all sorts of mechanisms come into play to "nudge" us into acting in ways appropriate to our assigned sex role. As we conform to these expectations, successfully passing each test, so to speak, we become more confident in our assignments, more at ease in the role, and more certain that it reflects the "real me."

Dating is one of those aspects of society that refines the nuances of our sex role. Dating is both a test and a teaching device—and rather effective at both. Schwartz and Lever analyze a form of college dating that forces its participants into acting in ways many find distasteful. Your own experiences with dating may differ somewhat, but this analysis should provide a good comparative base for examining your own sex role in dating.

THE PREDOMINANT VIEW EXPRESSED in the sociological literature on dating is that the social events and interactions are "fun" for the participants. An adult observer of adolescents at a social gathering would see them dressed up for the occasion, flirting with one another, dancing to loud music, engaging in light conversation, and generally seeming to be enjoying themselves. . . .

Our study of social patterns on a college campus leads us to believe that the moves and countermoves of dating carry great meaning for the individual and for the group and that the process of finding a balance between self-protection and self-exposure is anything but pure play. The participant, while supposedly in a "light" environment of introduction to

Authors' Note: The authors are grateful to Wendell Bell, Philip Blumstein, Louis Wolf Goodman, R. Stephen Warner, and Stanton Wheeler for their helpful comments on an earlier draft of this paper. We also wish to thank J. A. Gilboy and Erving Goffman for the constructive criticism they offered at the 66th Annual Meeting of the American Sociological Association.

peers, is at the same time in a situation where his or her desirability as a partner is being tested. The rating and ranking of the individual may be apparent and stressful. As the individual seeks to be both vulnerable (open to meeting an attractive other) and self-protective (invulnerable to rejection), the social world becomes fraught with tension, anxiety, and implications for the individual's sense of self. . . .

The mixer is a dance sponsored for the express purpose of meeting members of the opposite sex. Mixers have always been an integral part of the formal social system in most high schools, colleges, and universities. The ideal-type is represented by the schoolwide dance which ends freshman orientation week each fall. But graduate student "happy hours," sorority-fraternity exchanges, and dorm dances are variations on the same theme. . . .

These data were collected as part of a larger study chronicling the first year of coeducation at Yale (Lever and Schwartz, 1971). We conducted 96 in-depth interviews with Yale undergraduates.[1] Sixty-five percent of the women in our sample had transferred to Yale from Eastern women's colleges and had been long acquainted with the mixer system. Ninety percent of the men and the women in the sample had attended at least one mixer during their college career. In addition, the authors were participant observers at five mixer dances during the academic year.

The Mixer

Heterosexual encounters are universal features of the social world, but their forms vary according to the structural constraints of the environment. The physical location of monosexual schools place severe strains on the natural development of heterosexual relationships.[2] Yale is approximately 80 miles from Vassar, Smith, and Mt. Holyoke—the closest of the prestigious Seven Sister schools. The scheduling of classes forces monosexual institutions to endorse a weekend dating system, encouraging their students to study for five days and play for the remaining two. Even with the beginning of coeducation at Yale, the sex ratio remained weighted with eight men to every woman. Clearly, the men were forced to take steps to increase the recruitment pool of available women if they wanted to participate in heterosexual dating activities.

The mixer has long been the solution to this structural problem. Each of Yale's twelve residential colleges sponsors its own dances several times during the year. The social committees at the women's colleges charter buses for the trip and sell low-cost tickets on a first-come-first-serve basis. The less prestigious schools from the immediate vicinity also send small envoys, but the main purpose of mixers is to attract women of comparable social status and educational attainment, i.e., potential future mates, not just sex partners for an evening. In this sense, mixers perform the same endogamous screening services of the sorority-fraternity system described by Scott (1965: 12).[3] Although the monosexual mixer bears important similarities to institutions on coeducated campuses, it also has special properties that cause strained relations between the sexes that we wish to explore.

Before the women arrive, the men take their positions in the college dining hall where the dance will take place. The dining room, like high school gymnasiums decked out for a prom, is suitably changed. The tables have been cleared away, the lights are low, and a stage has been marked off at one end of the room for the band. A beer table is set up, usually in the common room outside the dancing hall. Here the lights are brighter and groups of men stand around talking. This beer table will serve as a prop for them throughout the dance. Getting a beer gives people something to do when they need to look busy, provides an avenue of escape ("Pardon me, I think I'll go get a beer"), and allows people to get drunk to loosen inhibitions and numb sensitivities for the personal tests that are to come.

The typical mixer at Yale starts around 8:30 P.M., when the buses from surrounding women's colleges begin to arrive. These same buses leave promptly at midnight. So time pressure exists. In fact, the element of time points to one major difference between the mixer and other kinds of formal dating. The mixer is not like a Saturday night dance on a coeducated campus. The girl will not be there throughout the week. Both male and female are aware that they have approximately two hours to find out if they want to get to know each other better.

People must quickly evaluate each other and attempt to make contact with those they have decided are desirable partners for the evening. Some are mutually attracted, but many more get rebuffed or end up with someone they do not really care for. All night long people are being approved or discarded on the basis of one characteristic that is hard, or at least painful, to discount—their appearance.

When persons are asked to dance, their names are exchanged and often some light conversation occurs but the rating and ranking that goes on is still primarily by personal appearance. The music level is deafening. As one woman said, "How can you expect to really meet anyone at 400 decibels?" Since conversation is difficult and people have just met one another, physical appearance is the only criterion of selection. There is little chance to talk, to be clever or interesting or simply flattering. Therefore, if the other person is not interested, that fact cannot be rationalized as a lack of things in common, a fundamental difference in world views, or dissimilar kinds of temperament. Only one criterion exists, so the situation is bound to be more tense. When rejection is obvious and even recurrent within the same four-hour period, it makes inroads on one's self-image.

Students reported feelings of "ugliness," "fatness," "clumsiness," and so forth during and after the mixer situation.[4]

Thus, there is a strong approach-avoidance tension in the air. Some women stand slightly apart so that they are more approachable; some stand close together and look indifferent. The general strategy of both sexes seems to be a question of how to achieve the maximum exposure with the least possible risk. That is, one wants to be seen and appreciated and asked for a dance (or be given the cue that someone would like you to ask her for a dance) without being seen as alone and needing someone. Erving Goffman (1967: 43) maintains that social life is orderly because people voluntarily stay away from places where they might be disparaged for going. The monosexual arena is different from the coeducated one precisely because the opportunities to meet others of the opposite sex in "safer" situations where one can protect his or her "face" have been minimized. Defensive maneuvers available in the mixer are few, difficult to manage, and, as we shall see, can be self-defeating.

The men first ask pretty women or those with good figures to dance; women usually prefer handsome men or men with some sort of "cool." Being "cool" is not necessarily based on looks for a man. It means that somebody "puts himself together" well, that he walks or talks with some authority, or that he looks "interesting" or at ease. The participants know that the appearance criterion is inadequate and demeaning, but they use it. People are very conscious about how their partner will reflect on their own desirability. A male junior was very frank about the situation:

> There have been times when I've seen a girl and, you know, I imagined I might not get along too well with her just from talking with her, but she was so good-looking that I just wanted to be seen walking into the dining hall with her or something like that, something prestigious.

Since there is only one "prestigious" criterion, meeting the standard becomes more and more consuming. You try to better your own game. One man put it this way:

> It's such a superficial thing. You judge a girl there strictly by her looks. So you talk to a pretty girl while your eyes scan the floor for another pretty girl. . . . It's like looking at an object in the window. It's probably mutual.

Women *are* under the same sort of pressures. Besides appearance, a man's age influences his overall rating. A sophomore man testified to this fact bitterly:

> Sophomore and freshman girls really have a thing. It's very important to them that they be dating an upperclassman. Like last year when I would be at a dance and it would come out that I was a freshman, that was it.

. . . [N]one of the women we interviewed, and only one of the men, claimed personally to like mixers. They referred to mixers as "body exchanges" and "meat markets." The women reacted most strongly against the mixer system. A junior transfer described her feelings:

> I generally think mixers are grotesque. There you are, a piece of meat lined up along a wall in this herd of ugly females. You try to stand casually as guys walk back and forth and you know you're on display. You just want to crawl up the wall. Then you're asked to dance by these really gross creatures. I'm so revolted by the whole thing.

. . . Throughout the evening men and women are conscious of being constantly evaluated, desired, or disregarded. But they don't leave the mixer even though they feel uncomfortable there. The women are captive until their buses leave at midnight; the men stay because the mixer is the place to secure names for the year's dating events. Because everyone's ego is threatened, people devise ways to protect themselves. Verbal patter and social maneuvering are used in this instance to avoid being too vulnerable. Fear of ridicule and rejection is so great that methods of ego preservation (be they cruel, clever, even ultimately self-defeating) are seen as essential. . . . The three protective devices we saw and heard about most frequently were "eye messages," the "ritualistic brush-off," and the "offensive-defensive" tactic.

"Eye messages" are part of the more general category of body language. If someone undesirable is approaching, the uninterested party allows her eyes to glaze over; she looks past the individual and concentrates on some other direction. Or the person finds "something to do." A man becomes engrossed in the beer stand; a woman can be totally preoccupied in a hitherto trivial conversation with a friend. The eyes are straight—locked into the diversion—never once glancing in the direction of the person to be avoided. The intent is usually obvious: by denying eye contact, one is refusing to acknowledge the other's presence or claim on one's attentions. If eye contact is achieved, then the individuals are forced to interact, if only to the extent that now they must acknowledge ignoring one another.

On the other hand, eye contact can be used for the opposite effect. If the individual wishes to engage someone in an encounter, eye contact is used to grab attention. A really aggressive person may lock eyes with someone, but many just glance at one another. The meaning is clear, that is "I consider you very attractive. Come over." (Or, "Can I come over?") One senior described the technique which had served him well during his four years at Yale:

> You try to meet eyes with a girl who doesn't look happy with the person she's with, in the hope that she'll say she has to go to the bathroom. Then you pick her up on the return trip. It's a big game, obviously.

The woman who changes partners in the manner described above is employing what we call the "ritualistic brush-off." Excuses and lines that would be embarrassing to use elsewhere are used with great frequency during a mixer to get out of an unpleasant mismatch with the least amount of trauma and embarrassment for all concerned. Unfortunately, because they have become ritualized, they only mute the surface blow. Everyone recognizes them for what they are, and the rejection still hurts. The favorite line used by men, as we have mentioned, is "Pardon me, I think I'll go get a beer." At a mixer the ladies' room is to women what the beer table is to men. Leaving for the bathroom, as indicated in the quotation above, serves as an excuse for the woman to get out of an uncomfortable match and to reenter the room in a different area and meet new partners. Of course, she is bound to see the man she has "temporarily" left, but they usually avert eyes. It is an effective "good-bye."

Sometimes the rituals are only recognizable to one partner in the interaction. This way of ending further contact is even less benign. One woman related common practices among her friends at Wellesley:

> At Wellesley, I heard stories about how to brush off a guy you don't like. Like one thing you do is give him your phone number and when he calls he gets "Dial-A-Prayer." Or you tell him it's your number and it's really a guy's.

Instead of lines, some people merely say "thank you" with a final-sounding air. After the dance is over there are a couple of seconds of undefined meaning. The girl is undecided whether she is going to be asked to dance again, and the boy may be unsure whether the girl would like to stay with him. A "thank you" and exit often end the suspense—sometimes precipitously. Afraid to be the one who is turned down, people protect themselves by terminating the interaction first. We call this the "offensive-defensive" tactic. No matter what the original likelihood was that the couple would not get along, by "jumping the gun" the individual has made the outcome virtually guaranteed. This protective device often condemns the innocent before any act has been committed and nurtures the type of interaction that the individuals say they are trying to escape. . . .

People at a mixer, or in a mixer-like situation, describe members of the opposite sex as the "enemy." They act as though their chosen roles are conflicting, not complementary. They assess the risks of "winning" and "losing," net outcomes, and maintenance of face. Winning means a date, self-enhancement, status in the eyes of others. Losing means letting someone feel superior to you and perhaps accepting their definition of your unworthy status. It means being seen as less attractive than you had previously thought and having that verified in front of your peers. It means for some very vulnerable people, taking on an identity as a social maladept or Unattractive Person. This identity is one that most people will avoid even if avoidance means "cutting off one's nose to spite one's face."

Thus, a situation forces these kinds of choices [see Figure 10.1]: if the

Figure 10.1.

| | | MALE | |
		Continues	*Terminates*
FEMALE	*Continues*	opportunity for new relationship	loss of face for female
	Terminates	loss of face for male	no loss of face but loss of opportunity for relationship

person terminates the encounter quickly, s/he has saved face, but s/he loses the opportunity to establish a new relationship. On the other hand, if the initiator (always the male) waits and tries to engage his partner for another dance, the woman may terminate the encounter and the man will consequently lose face. Again, the opportunity for a successful relationship—which is one's motive for risking "face" in the first place—is lost. Or if both the man and woman trust each other, there is a possibility that both will win what they are seeking. Unfortunately, since both have been to a mixer or similar event before, or heard about mixer norms, they do not expect that the other person will "cooperate" and openly court their attention; therefore, they minimize risk-taking by showing a low level of affect. The individuals have saved face, but in so doing they have undermined their initial goals.

Of course, some do play the game cooperatively, and risk face while allowing the other person to decide whether to continue the relationship or break it off. If the other person takes a similar risk, the couple will most likely remain together for the duration of the evening. Sometimes such unions are immediately romanticized by both persons as part of what we call the "pit or the pedestal" syndrome. That is, the boy then treats the girl as a "one-nighter" or as a "dream girl," and the girl makes a similar judgment. Because the mixer is experienced as unpleasant, both men and women are searching for someone they can date so that they [can] minimize the number of mixers they must attend during the year. Because they live so far apart, there is encouragement for an immediate, intense experience that will justify a weekend together in the future.

For the majority, however, it is clear that the effects of the mixer are seen as personally destructive. To take a symbolic interactionist perspective, one's image of self grows out of interaction with significant others. Repeated failures can cause people to doubt their attractiveness to the opposite sex. A junior transfer reflected back on her three years in the mixer system:

> I always ended up with someone I was very unhappy with. I used to wonder why I attracted that type. Very few people ever found anyone decent. Most people came back from those things feeling negatively about the experience and feeling negatively about themselves.

Mixers had long-term effects on the self-images of the successful as well; many of those individuals had come to see their worth mostly in terms of their surface qualities. For everyone involved, the mixer situation encourages a calculating approach to heterosexual contact that is more starkly visible than in settings which do not limit such encounters to specific times and places. . . .

Notes

1. We drew a stratified sample which included an equal number of males and females, randomly selected from the student body of approximately 4,000 men and 500 women. According to all available indicators, the sample well represented the Yale undergraduate population, except for the deliberate over-representation of females. All grade levels were represented equally, as were all twelve residential colleges. The percentage of students in our sample (1) from public high schools versus private schools, (2) from the Eastern seaboard versus other regions of the country, and (3) from alumni families, mirrored the percentages for the entire student population.

2. We are primarily speaking of those institutions not affiliated with a co-ordinate college for the opposite sex.

3. Although the singles' bar and the mixer share structural similarities they are functionally distinct in that the former does not perform the endogamous screening services of the latter. The customers in a singles' bar will vary with respect to age, educational attainment, and social class background (and often marital status as well).

4. During participant observation at mixers, the authors never grew accustomed to the role of "coeds." Considering that we as "researchers" had little personally at stake, we found that our egos were, nevertheless, involved. No matter how peripheral one is to this kind of situation, it is never easy to disregard completely someone else's estimation of one's attractiveness.

References

Goffman, E. (1967). *Interaction Ritual: Essays on Face-to-Face Behavior.* New York: Anchor.

Lever, J., and P. Schwartz (1971). *Women at Yale: Liberating a College Campus.* Indianapolis: Bobbs-Merrill.

Scott, J. R. (1965). "Sororities and husbands." *Transaction* 2 (Sept./Oct.): 10–14.

11 The World of Singles

MIMI RODIN

Between 90 and 95 percent of Americans marry at least once. For a period of time before "settling down," many work at some job and live away from either parents or dormitory. This "single" period is the subject of Mimi Rodin's analysis. What is the off-the-job life of these singles like? How do they arrange their time? How do they avoid "entanglements" or "getting serious" if they do not want marriage at this point in their lives? And, especially for the purposes we are examining in this section, how do single men and women play out their sex roles? Do singles, with neither commitments nor obligations to one another, treat one another with idealistic equality? That is, are traditional sex roles mostly irrelevant at this point in their lives? As Rodin discovered, the world of singles is quite the contrary, for early sex role socialization continues its powerful presence in this setting also.

THE PURPOSE OF THIS STUDY is to provide a description of the social and domestic organization of young, never-married, urban, American apartment dwellers, whose lifestyles have never been studied by anthropologists or sociologists. . . .

Gatherings are often occasioned by culturally determined holiday seasons. Over the last Christmas-New Year holiday, one person organized a reunion of his high-school graduating class. Another attempted to organize a week-end reunion of several college friends, now married, in their old college town. Both reunions failed. A third donated his apartment for a highly successful office Christmas party.

Two examples illustrate the consequences of violating the discreteness of sectors of one's networks. One woman stated that whenever she had invited her boyfriend, whom she had met at work, to gatherings of her college friends, he sulked in a corner. Another told of inviting friends from work and friends from a voluntary association to a party. The party broke up into two groups along the lines of prior acquaintance, and she spent the evening moving back and forth between them.

Membership in any of the above categories differentially calls into play informal social pressures to communicate with others. As greater social and geographical distances arise between members, due to marriage and job changes, the pressures on people to reaffirm these relationships decreases. This is especially true of some relatives, old friends and college friends. Ultimately, the relationships are terminated or reduced to networks of letters, occasional telephone calls, or symbolic exchanges of Christmas cards. . . .

Members of "the gang" were predominantly single, and predominantly male, although the office employed about equal numbers of men and women. Several women carried the burden of entertaining. When informants were asked who had been present at parties, they noted that several people had dropped out of the party circuit after marriage. These married individuals no longer gave parties for "the gang," although they occasionally invited individuals from it home to dinner. Subsequently, two informants observed that acquaintances from their college and voluntary association sectors also became socially detached from them after marriage.

I have labeled this phenomenon the "dropping out through marriage phenomenon." It effectively functions to keep social networks distinct on the basis of marital status. It is interpreted as a sign of marital problems for a married man to appear on the single's party circuit.

Perhaps the least easily explainable feature of singles' networks is the predominantly male composition, although it appears to be related to the "dropping out through marriage phenomenon." When women were asked to account for how they met people, they included in their list of acquaintances that the connecting individuals were usually men. I was not able to confirm this for men, but the following generalizations appear to be true. Single men meet single women at work and through other men in their job and voluntary association networks. Women meet men through the same sectors of their networks, which are predominantly male by actual count. Same-sex acquaintances are recruited the same way. This would appear to indicate that men have more acquaintances than women and that men are the active links through which both men and women extend their networks.

The discussion suggests a process by which singles prune their networks of past associations based on kinship and childhood, propelling themselves into a world rooted firmly in the present. After marriage, former singles drift away from their single acquaintances. The remaining singles operate, as they grow older, in a world that is progressively more oriented around their place of work and more masculine in composition. . . .

In the personal networks I studied, the men were usually several years older than the women with whom they associated. This is consistent with census data that show that the median age at marriage for men is slightly higher than for women. Only a small percentage of adults over the age of thirty-four have never married. Functionally this means that men are marrying women who are several years their juniors. There are indications then that singles' networks function to bring potentially marriageable people into contact with each other. . . .

Singles move often. During the period of study, I documented four moving parties demonstrating how sectors of personal networks can become cooperative labor groups. "Saturday at my place. Free beer for anyone who helps load the van. Bring a muscle-bound friend." There are apartment-painting parties, "booze and brushes provided by the management." Another singles-set mailed out engraved invitations to "a gala fete in honour of D. D., on his natal date." Friends look in on each other when they are ill. They stay up all night with emotionally distressed friends and call in sick at work while bringing a friend down from a bad drug experience.

The following example illustrates the extent to which singles' networks provide support for their members:

> Nan moved to Chicago, found an apartment on the near-north side and a job at the firm. She met Sara at work and they found they both lived in the same apartment building. Every now and then they had dinner together at home or went out. A couple of times a week they went singly or together to Mother's. Mother's is a bar, one of about two dozen such establishments located within three blocks of each other on North Lincoln Avenue. Like the others, it caters to singles. Nan says: "I don't like bars, but I like Mother's. If you've gotta get out, there's always someone there you know. And if some guy starts hassling you, Andy throws them out." Andy is the bartender and part-owner of Mother's. He is a former roommate of Sara's boyfriend. Meredith was one of Sara's friends from Mother's. She was out of work for two months until Sara and Nan found an opening for her at the firm. During those two months she crashed with Sara. Andy gave Meredith a free steak sandwich and fries every night at Mother's until her first paycheck. "He says it's good for business." After that, Nan loaned Meredith her car to go apartment hunting.

Organization of Time, Space, and Property

The diaries [that the author had her informants keep on their personal relationships—Ed.] indicated that people who live alone actually spend very little time alone. Time alone was always punctuated by telephone calls from others who lived alone. Informants said that if they felt lonely or were suffering from "cabin fever" that they phoned friends to talk or to arrange to meet them. Women met other women for a drink, shopping, or a movie. Men went to bars, played pool or golf, visited female friends, or found card games. If none of these activities were possible, all resorted to television or going to sleep. Most of the time that singles spent alone at home was accompanied by noisemaking devices such as radio, stereo, or television.

There was a noticeable tendency for men to spend less time alone at home or even at home than women. Men were less likely to answer the telephone than women when they were alone. This is apparently related to several of the findings previously discussed under social networks. Men are the active links in arranging social meetings. It appears that women will remain alone rather than violate that norm. It has also been suggested that women simply have a greater tolerance for solitude, which may or may not be biologically based, but it is not my purpose here to discuss such notions. It is clear, however, that single men and women do structure their solitude in ways that are generally characteristic of their sex, as it is socially defined.

"Cabin fever" was mentioned only by women and was brought on not so much by being alone as by self-imposed solitary confinement during periods of nervousness, depression, or embarrassment. Such feelings were termed "the blue funk." Women were also more likely than men to mediate solitude with nonhuman companionship (such as pets) or by using the telephone.

Singles' time is relatively loosely scheduled, and this characteristic is carried over into the way they organize their living space. American houses are designed to provide for the privacy of their residents by partitioning of internal space by function. Living rooms and dining rooms are public and social gathering places. Bedrooms and bathrooms are private.

Although singles differ from members of family households in their organization of property and time, their usage of space maintains many of the same features. They have few possessions, but, as one woman observed, these possessions spread out to fill the available space, besides, "Why buy it? I'd only have to move it." After a moment's reflection, she observed that her activities also spread out to fill the available space.

All of the singles lived in at least two- or three-room apartments. Several had four or more rooms. Though they felt free about states of undress and rarely closed doors, even to the bathroom, they observed a discreteness of function for the areas of their apartments.

There was an air of impermanence to their apartments, a lack of investment in time or money. Furniture was sparse, provided by the landlord, obviously secondhand or collapsible. Steamer trunks were left packed. Luggage was shoved in a corner not stowed out of sight in a closet. Laundry in its wrapping paper lay on, not in, chests of drawers. Dishes, silverware, and linens were rarely of matched sets. A few maintained office addresses or post office boxes in lieu of home mail delivery.

This pattern is rather different from that of older singles who were less eager or likely to marry or remarry. Their residence histories indicated that they moved less often. The older singles to whom I talked placed their first purchases of furniture soon after their decisions to remain single, at least for the time being. Older singles (over thirty) had acquired matched sets of linens, dishes and silverware, draperies, carpets, life insurance and annuity policies, and home mortgages.

This is especially instructive if we notice that in American society a permanent home, furniture, and matching housewares are expectably acquired by newlyweds. These things are a material representation of the stability of married life. The distinction seems to be the difference between "my place" of the young single, who regards himself as going through a stage of independence before settling into marriage, and "my home" of the older single whose complete residence expresses his personal completeness. . . .

Quasi-Conjugal Households

Earlier in the discussion, it was shown that singles can mobilize sectors of their social networks as cooperative labor groups to assist for special purposes, such as moving and house-painting. Individuals exchange domestic services as well. Such a reciprocal relationship can become routinized between a single man and a single woman, while each continues to maintain a separate residence. I have termed this a quasi-conjugal household.

All eight of the original group of informants are currently, or have recently been, members of one or more quasi-conjugal households. Some of the households were regarded as preliminary to living together in a marriagelike joint household, either as a preface to marriage or not. Other households were regarded as satisfactory without the likelihood of eventual marriage.

Although all of the singles in the original sample expressed the desire to marry "sometime" in the future, they had many reservations about immediate marriage, even with the people they planned to marry "eventually." The following passage is quite typical in giving reasons for not marrying, and for maintaining separate residences.

> Right after college I got very uptight about not being married. But then I decided I had my own life to lead. No, I'm not in any rush to get married. Children seem like an awfully heavy responsibility. After that (getting together again after breaking up) Mike decided we should live together. He said it would be cheaper since we did everything together anyway. But I decided not to because if we broke up then I would be the one to move out and there wouldn't be anywhere to go home to. It's security. (Anne, age twenty-five)

The division of labor in quasi-conjugal households is nearly identical to that described by Blood and Wolfe for nuclear families. Women provided shopping, cooking, and housekeeping services for their boyfriends. Men sometimes assisted them in this, and usually offered to share expenses for the running of both households. This kind of division of labor developed after the establishment of a sexual relationship in all cases.

One woman said that she regularly kept house for her boyfriend but never initiated such activities until he asked her to or offered some sort of trade in the form of a "heavy date." She said that once he had offered cash payment for a particularly thorough job, which she accepted rather than be "pushy." She felt that if she kept house for free, that the man might "take her for granted" or suspect that she was escalating the relationship to marriage. By not permitting him to reciprocate immediately, she felt she would have endangered the relationship.

Some tasks are highly indicative markers of the degree of commitment by partners to a relationship. Men and women agreed that washing dishes was not a loaded service. But one man added, "You've got to watch out when they start wanting to do your laundry." Sometimes women will attempt to force reciprocation on men who are not willing.

> I'd just like to find a nice girl to call up and go out for a beer. Just to have fun. But the first thing they do when you bring them home, like the first thing they do when they come in, is start picking up your socks. (Hal, age twenty-six)

The degree of commitment to a quasi-conjugal household and the relationship it symbolizes is measurable along two axes: the number and kind of domestic services traded and shared and the degree of routinization and coordination of scheduling between members. Scheduling increases with the intensity of the relationship. Activities, especially meals, become increasingly routinized into predictable time slots, unlike the timetables we saw for unattached singles.

In more fragile relationships, the exchange of services is carefully negotiated and casually scheduled. Several stable couples in the sample, both during and prior to the study, reciprocated services easily and spent three or more evenings a week together. Because they spent so much time in each others' apartments, they frequently kept toothbrushes, changes of clothing, and other personal items in both apartments, thus symbolically staking out a joint territory.

In each of the quasi-conjugal households I found, there seemed to be no routinized pattern of sleeping arrangements. The sexual business of the household was conducted about equally under both roofs. Singles felt that if they stayed away from their own apartments too regularly their independence would be challenged. Men especially felt that women should not spend "too much" time in their apartments.

[I]n American culture, kinship is traced through the children of the married couples. Some social scientists consider marriage no more than legitimate sexual relations. They do not take into account the legal standing of such relations and especially the prescriptions in law pertaining to the maintenance of a joint residence by married couples. In some states joint residence acquires jural standing in definitions of common-law marriages and provisions for the legitimation of the children of couples who have not legally married.

The conjugal nature of quasi-conjugal households derives from the fact that the sexual aspect of the relationship is routinely conducted within the homes of its members. Sexual encounters of brief duration, such as "one-night stands" or encounters situated in borrowed apartments, hotels, and motels, are not accorded the same aura of legitimacy.

It is important to recognize that quasi-conjugal relationships are further routinized to the degree that partners reciprocate domestic services. The relationship has no jural content, however. There are no enforceable sanctions for failure to reciprocate. The relationship is based rather on mutual expectations. When expectations on the part of either or both parties no longer coincide and negotiation fails to restore agreement on the content of the relationship, the quasi-conjugal household is dissolved.

> Anne told me that Laura's boyfriend, Jack, was a real SOB because he had started seeing Carol even though Laura continued to do his laundry, as she had for nearly six months. Anne said that Laura was being a real idiot for letting Jack "use" her that way. But Laura kept on doing Jack's wash. Later Jack defended his actions to Don, who worked in the same office as Jack, Laura and Anne. Jack said that he had no intention of marrying her. But despite his protests, Laura insisted on helping him.

As single men and women form intense, personal relationships, women extend their housekeeping to more than one residence. To a much lesser degree, men extend domestic services to women. Since most of these services are given by women and taken by men, we may say that a woman establishes sexual rights in a man to the degree to which she keeps his house. A single man validates her claim to the extent that he permits and publicly encourages her in this.

Sexual relationships between single men and women are mediated through this exchange of domestic services. Either party can symbolically assert the right to other sexual partners by refusing to accept or to perform domestic services. The giving and taking of some services are more obligating than others.

Not every quasi-conjugal household leads to marriage, but an individual's willingness to escalate its conjugal nature indicates a willingness to marry. By following the career of a quasi-conjugal household, and by seeing whether reciprocity is increasing or decreasing, it is possible to tell whether it is a transitional stage to living together or marriage. A quasi-conjugal household can also be a steady and ambiguous state in which each member remains self-sufficient and nominally head of his or her own household.

Summary

This study is not intended to account for all possible singles' lifestyles. Thus, such subjects as "the singles' bar complex" and the "swinging-singles" lifestyle have not been considered here. Instead, I have focused on a limited sample of semiprofessional singles in a small midwestern city, where the possibility of developing the kind of lifestyle that is alleged to be characteristic of big-city singles' life is less likely to develop because of the lack of the appropriate facilities (such as singles bars) and conditions (such as the anonymity of urban housing and settings). For these reasons it would be inappropriate to draw broad general conclusions from this research. Thus, the following statements are offered more as tentative hypotheses for further testing than as conclusions.

Urban singles operate as autonomous individuals in a social milieu devoid of kin or conjugal ties. Few of their interpersonal relationships are invested with jural rights and duties. That is to say, their personal relationships are not formed or sanctioned in terms of extrapersonal rules or norms other than those applicable throughout the society. Concomitantly, singles are free of enforceable obligations to others. Their freedom from such restriction is expressed in their high degree of job and residence mobility. Thus, the majority of personal relationships among singles lack the time depth and the complexity of overlapping identities that are characteristic of married people.

Young urban singles, however, develop strategies for building a modicum of stability and predictable reciprocity into their relationships. Through processes of social selection, singles form personal relationships primarily with other singles. The resulting personal networks provide the basis for various kinds of cooperative and supportive activities and exchanges. The shared knowledge that they all lack other sorts of support groups draws them together. . . .

As the personal relationship between a man and a woman approaches the conjugal form and becomes more or less stable, the man begins to perform the traditionally male tasks involved in maintaining both of their residences, thus approximating the form of the conjugal family in terms of the division of labor. An alternate pattern may also develop as the man assumes or shares some of the traditionally female tasks, such as shopping or laundry, creating a division of domestic labor in which men and women are structurally and functionally equivalent.

PART IV Social Groups and Social Structure

NO ONE IS ONLY A MEMBER OF HUMANITY IN GENERAL; each of us is also a member of particular social groups. We live in certain neighborhoods of particular countries. We belong to families and are members of ethnic groups. Most of us work at some job and have friends, and many of us belong to churches, clubs, and organizations. The social world is not a random collection of its components, but, rather, the various social groups making up our lives are interrelated. This relationship between social groups is referred to as *social structure*.

When the term is used to refer to a particular society, social structure indicates several levels. On the broadest level social structure refers to the interrelationships of the social institutions of a society, such as how economic interests and political decisions affect families, schools, the practice of medicine, and the like. On a smaller scale this term refers to the relationships between particular social groups, such as the relationship between McDonald's and other firms in the fast-food business. On an even smaller level, social structure refers to how people are organized within some social group, such as an individual's role as either a leader or a follower in a gang of juvenile delinquents; the privileges business managers have that are denied other employees; or parents' authority over their young children that empowers them to determine what the children will eat, where they will live, and how they are disciplined.

The term also has an international dimension. On the broadest level, social structure refers to the interrelationships among groups of nations, such as the West's dependence on the Mideast for much of its oil and the ever-freezing/ever-thawing relationships between the West and the Communist bloc nations. On the next broadest level social structure refers to

103

the interrelationships between particular nations, such as India's dependence on the United States for much of its grain and the extensive role the United States plays in the Canadian economy. This international dimension of social structure especially sensitizes us to relationships based on past historical events and current balances of power and resources.

Social structure, then, refers to the social organization that underlies people's lives and that determines their relationships to one another. The foregoing examples illustrate that the term demarcates at least five levels. The first three are *intra*societal, referring to relationships within a particular society: (1) on the largest scale, the relationships between social institutions; (2) on a medium level, the relationships between smaller social groups; and (3) on the smallest scale, how positions within some particular social group are interrelated. The other two are *inter*societal, referring to (1) the relationships between blocs of nations and (2) the relationships between individual nations.

By referring to these organized aspects of social life, social structure pinpoints major influences on people's behavior. The articles in this section are meant to sensitize us to some of the far-reaching effects of social structure on our own lives. Whenever we belong to a group we yield to others the right to make certain decisions about our behavior, while assuming obligations to act according to those expectations. This is illustrated by a parent saying to a teenaged daughter: "As long as you are living under my roof, you had better be home by midnight." As a member of the family, the daughter is expected to conform to her parents' expectations, and in this instance the parents are saying that as long as the daughter wants to remain a member of the social group known as the household her behavior must conform to their expectations.

So it is with all the social groups to which we belong. By our membership and participation in them we relinquish to others at least some control over our own lives. Those social groups that provide little option to belong or not are called *involuntary* memberships or associations. These include our family and the sexual, ethnic, and racial groups into which we are born. With other types of social groups, we may choose whether or not to belong and in certain instances we willingly, sometimes even gladly, conform to the rules and expectations of others in order to become members. Such examples of *voluntary* memberships or associations include the Boy and Girl Scouts, professional associations, church groups, clubs, and work groups. We deliberately alter some of our behaviors in order to belong and to remain members. Not all membership in voluntary associations, of course, involves the same degree of willingness to give others a measure of control over our lives and there are even occasions, as in some occupational situations, when we can hardly bear to be a member of the group but feel that under the circumstances we have no choice.

Both types of membership vitally affect our lives, for our participation in specific social groups shapes our ideas and orientations to life. In this Part we focus on various social groups and examine some of those influences. First, James M. Henslin looks at an occupational group. By analyzing how trust works in the cab-driving situation, he reveals some of the basics of this essential component that underlies almost all human interaction. Barry Schwartz then turns the sociological focus onto the social patterning of time, analyzing how waiting is related to the ways in which power is distributed in the human group. James M. Henslin and Mae A. Biggs then use Goffman's dramaturgical model to uncover the means by which nonsexuality is sustained during the vaginal examination. William Foote Whyte examines a broader aspect of social structure—how ethnic and neighborhood solidarity affects people's behaviors and orientations to life. Elaine Fox and George E. Arquitt, using the case of the VFW, then analyze how power in voluntary associations tends to become concentrated in the hands of a select few. Finally, William E. Thompson returns our focus to the work setting, in this instance looking at how workers experience the assembly line in the meat packing industry.

Participant observation—directly observing what is going on in a social setting—is the method these authors used to gain their information. Henslin drove cabs, Schwartz observed people waiting in lines and for appointments, Biggs worked as a gynecological nurse, Whyte took up residence in an Italian-American community, Fox and Arquitt frequented the local VFW, and Thompson took a job in a meat packing plant. As these researchers *participated* in the lives of the people they were studying, they *observed* what was happening (hence the name *participant observation*), and these selections are reports on what they observed. Largely because of their research method (sometimes supplemented by interviews) these authors provide rich, detailed descriptions that, by retaining some of the flavor of the settings, bring the reader close to the events that occurred.

While this is not the place to detail the differences between types of participant observation, more sensitive readers may perceive that observing people waiting in different social settings is different from driving cabs, working as a gynecological nurse, living in a particular social environment, hanging around VFW clubs, and working on an assembly line. In some instances social researchers place much emphasis on observing and do little actual participation. Regardless of whether participation or observation receives the greater emphasis, when a researcher enters a social setting to observe what is occurring, the term participant observation is generally used to describe this method of studying social life.

12 What Makes for Trust?

JAMES M. HENSLIN

Behind almost everything we do is trust. When you walk down the hall between classes you are trusting hundreds of people. The same is true in a crowded subway or on a street filled with strangers. You may know no one and think that you trust none of them, but, in reality, you trust them all at least to some degree. For example, you trust that they will not suddenly lunge out and rob, rape, or murder you. Even though you would not trust many of these same people under different circumstances, such as in a deserted school building or a dark back alley, you trust that in these circumstances, with others present, at this moment, they will not do such things. Among other factors, you trust that the presence of others is sufficient to restrain anyone who might be disposed to do such things.

How can you trust strangers? If someone asks you for directions, how do you know you can trust that person? Even though we have no way of knowing for certain, each of us routinely makes such decisions of trust. Within the social context of uncertainty and lack of knowledge, we all try to insert certainty and knowledge. As we strive to traverse this risky ground, we all rely on "social cues." In this article, Henslin analyzes some of the cues that cab drivers use to make their decisions of trust—decisions that for them can be matters of life and death.

What social cues do you use? How did you learn to depend on those cues? How well do they serve you?

TRUST IS A FUNDAMENTAL ASPECT of anyday/everyday-life-in-society.[1] We all deal with trust all the time. It is with us each day as we go about our regular routines, but it is one of those taken-for-granted aspects of life-in-society that we seldom analyze. At times we may be sharply aware of our distrust of others and be quite verbal in specifying why. At other times we may be only vaguely aware that we are uneasy and distrustful in the presence of a certain person, being unable even to specify the factors that have led to our distrust. There are also occasions when we are very trusting and comfortable in the presence of others, but when we would be "hard put" to explain just why this was so.

We usually miss the subtlety of our own perceptions when it comes to trust. The probable reason is that most of the behavioral cues by which we are judging the "trustability" of others are finely honed characteristics about which we have been socialized since we were children. Although these variables are continually affecting our lives, and we routinely make both important and trivial decisions on the basis of them, they are ordinarily below the threshold of our awareness.

As such, if we are asked why we didn't trust a particular person, rather than being able to specify the relevant variables, we might more likely say something like, "I just didn't like the looks of him." And it is true that we *didn't* like the looks of him. But what are the variables that go into determining whether we like or do not like the looks of someone? What determines whether we will trust or distrust someone? To move in the direction of an answer to this question, we shall examine what trust means for the cab driver, looking specifically at what determines whether a cab driver will accept someone as his passenger.

Definition

Erving Goffman[2] has developed useful concepts concerning the *front* of performers (the expressive equipment that serves to define the situation for the observer) that can be utilized as a conceptual framework in analyzing how a cab driver determines whether an individual can be trusted to become his passenger or not. Goffman states that there are three standard parts to front: a general aspect, (1) the *setting* (the background items which supply scenery and props for the performance, e.g., furniture, decor, and physical layout), and two personal aspects, (2) the *appearance* of the performer (the stimuli that tell the observer the social statuses of the performer, e.g., clothing), and (3) the *manner* of the performer (the stimuli that tell the observer the role that the performer will play on a particular occasion or the way in which he will play his role, e.g., being meek or haughty). Goffman adds that the audience ordinarily expects a "fit" or coherence among these standard parts of the front.

Actors are continually offering definitions of themselves to audiences. The audience, by checking the fit of the parts that compose the front of the actor, determines whether it will accept or reject the offered definition. *Trust consists of an actor offering a definition of himself and an audience being willing to interact with the actor on the basis of that definition.* If the audience does not accept the definition of the actor and is not willing to interact with the actor on the basis of his proffered definition, the situation is characterized by *distrust*.

Thus trust, more fully, is conceptualized for our purposes as consisting of:

1. The offering of a definition of self by an actor;
2. Such that when the audience perceives fit between the parts of the front of the actor;

3. And accepts this definition as valid;
4. The audience is willing, without coercion, to engage in interaction with the actor;
5. The interaction being based on the accepted definition of the actor, and;
6. The continuance of this interaction being dependent on the continued acceptance of this definition, or the substitution of a different definition that is also satisfactory to the audience.

Trust and Accepting Someone as a Passenger

The major definition people offer of themselves that cab drivers are concerned with is that of "passenger." In trying to hire a cab, an individual is in effect saying to the cab driver, "I am (or more accurately, I want to be) a passenger," that is, I will fulfill the role obligations of a passenger. In the driver's view the role obligations of "passenger" include having a destination, being willing to go to a destination for an agreed upon rate, being able and willing to pay the fare, and not robbing or harming the cab driver. If a cab driver accepts someone as a passenger—is interacting with him on the basis of this definition—it means, according to our conceptualization, that trust is present.

How does the cab driver know whether he can accept someone's definition of himself as a passenger and interact with him on the basis of that definition, that is, how does he know whether he can trust him? This is our major concern here. We shall now try to explicate what enters into such a decision by the cab driver. The table [on the next page] diagrams the variables we shall examine.

The cab driver typically accepts as passengers those to whom he has been dispatched, especially when he is sent to a middle- or upper-class residential area during daylight hours. He is progressively less likely to do so as the time becomes later in hour or as he enters lower-class or black neighborhoods. When these three conditions of time, social class, and race are combined, he is least likely to accept someone who wants to become a passenger.

From his past experiences a driver assumes that he is safer as the *neighborhood* becomes "better." This is even more the case when the passenger emerges from the residence to which the driver has been dispatched. Hence the driver assumes that there is a connection between such a caller and his point of departure. Responsible people whom one can trust to be "good passengers" live in neighborhoods like these. If a caller lives in such an area, he *is* a good passenger; if the caller doesn't actually live there, then he must be known by those who do live in the location from which he is now emerging, so it is unlikely that this individual would be

The Variables That, in the Cab Driver's View, Lead to Greater or Lesser Trust of One Who Wants To Be (or Has Become) a Passenger

TRUST	TYPE OF ORDER		TIME
HI	Dispatched order	Regular rider or charge customer	Day
LO	Flag load	Stranger	Night

TRUST	CHARACTERISTICS OF LOCATION				
	Match with Physical Reality	Social Class	Racial Make-up	Driver's Knowledge of	Illumination and Habitation
HI	Matches (a location)	(a) Upper class (b) Middle class	White	Known to driver	Light, inhabited area
LO	Doesn't match (a non-location)	Lower class (poverty area)	Black (ghetto area)	Strange to driver	Dark, deserted area

TRUST	CHARACTERISTICS OF PASSENGER				
	Social Class	Sex	Race	Age	Sobriety
HI	(a) Upper class (a) Middle class	Female	White	(a) Very old (b) Very young	(a) Sober (b) "High" (c) Drunk (d) Very drunk
LO	Lower class (poverty)	Male	Black	Ages between above	(a) Sober (b) "High" (c) Drunk

TRUST	BEHAVIOR OF PASSENGER			
	Emergent Behavior	Sitting Behavior Where	Sitting Behavior How	Rationality of Behavior
HI	Seen emerging from primary location	(a) In rear, diagonal from driver (b) In front	"Open sitting"	Acts rationally
LO	Not seen emerging from primary location	In rear, behind driver	Sitting that seems to conceal passenger	Acts irrationally

TRUST	BEHAVIOR OF DISPATCHER	THE CAB DRIVER'S PREVIOUS EXPERIENCE WITH A GIVEN VARIABLE	SUMMARY OF THE VARIABLES OF THIS TABLE
HI	(a) Dispatches order without comment (b) Offers assurance	Positive experience: "Known that can be trusted"	Matches any stereotype the driver has of a trusted category
LO	Dispatches order with a warning	(a) Negative experience: "Known that cannot be trusted" (b) No experience: "Not known whether can be trusted"	Matches any stereotype the driver has of a distrusted category

anything other than a good passenger. This latter case illustrates "track-ability," that is, the rider can be traced back to his point of origin and his association with the residence or with the people who live in that residence. Those who possess the greatest amount of trackability, and in whom the drivers place the greatest trust, are *regular riders* who routinely use cabs in their activities and who consequently become known to the drivers. (In many of these cases the interaction between cab drivers and regular riders moves into the personal sphere.)[3]

However, this is not the case when a driver is dispatched to a potential passenger in a neighborhood where, in the driver's view, less responsible types of people live, people who are not as financially established, who do not own their own homes, and whose trackability is low. The drivers view poor or black neighborhoods as an indication of correspondingly less responsibility and trackability on the part of potential passengers. Accordingly, they trust persons from these origins less, and the likelihood increases that they will be rejected as passengers.

The same is true of *time of day*. A driver feels that daylight provides greater trackability, because it is possible to get a better look at a potential passenger and to observe much more about him than he is able to at night. This means that he can notice any discrepancies or lack of fit among the parts of the front of the individual, especially in terms of his appearance and manner. Thus, in a lower-class or black neighborhood the cab driver can "look over good" any potential passenger, whether the individual either has phoned for a cab or is trying to flag down the driver. He can observe quickly and well any discrepancies about the potential passenger's manner, and in the case of a flag load, determine whether to stop or not. When it is night, the driver simply cannot see as well, so that with the lateness of the hour he is progressively less likely to stop for people in such areas.

Night and trust work out in practice the following way. A driver will always enter certain neighborhoods at any time of the night or day, for a dispatched order to a residence. These are the upper- and middle-class neighborhoods of the city. He is, however, less likely to accept as a passenger someone who is calling from a phone booth in this area because the trackability is lower, and because the connection between the caller and the residents of that neighborhood becomes more tenuous, that is, it could be anyone calling from a public phone booth, including, and more likely, someone who doesn't belong there.

Drivers will enter some neighborhoods during the day for a dispatched order and also stop for a flag load, yet at night they will enter only for dispatched orders. That is, the drivers assume that one can trust people at night in this neighborhood if there is a call from an apartment for a cab, but not if a person is flagging from the street. In this type of neighborhood, veteran drivers frequently exhort novice drivers to be very careful to observe that their passenger is actually coming from the house to which they were dispatched, and not from an area nearby the house. If the house has a light on inside, then so much the better. (If there is no light on inside, it becomes difficult to tell whether or not the person is actually coming from within the house.)

Finally, there are neighborhoods that drivers will enter for a dispatched order during the day, and perhaps reluctantly stop for flag loads during the day, but that they will not enter at night to pick up any passengers, dispatched or otherwise. This is true of the hard core ghetto of the city studied, St. Louis. The demand for cabs from this area is serviced by a cab firm run by blacks.

Sex is another variable used by drivers to size up a potential passenger. Under almost all circumstances a driver will exhibit greater trust for a female than for a male.[4] The following comment by a driver illustrates this trust of the female:

> I was driving down Union and Delmar about two o'clock this morning, and this woman hollered "Taxi." I wouldn't have stopped at that time in the morning, but I saw it was a woman, so I stopped for her. At least I thought it was a woman. And she gets into the cab, and she turns out to be a guy all dressed up like a woman.

Aside from the humor present in this case, the driver furnishes us with an excellent illustration of the differential trust cab drivers place in the female. Union and Delmar is on the fringe of the ghetto, and drivers would ordinarily stop for flag loads during the day there, but not at this time of night. This driver, however, typically stops for a woman in this area at a time when, according to his own statement, he would not think of stopping for a male who was trying to flag him down.

Another determinant of trust is *age*. If a passenger is quite aged, the driver will trust him. I was unaware of the influence of this variable until the following took place:

> About midnight I was dispatched to an apartment building where I picked up two men who appeared to be in their seventies or eighties. As we drove along I started to count the money that was in my pocket. Ordinarily every time I accumulated five dollars over enough to make change for a ten I would put the excess away to make certain that it would be safe in case of robbery. I thought to myself, "I should put this away," but then I thought, "No, these guys aren't going to rob me." It was at this point that I realized that I felt safe from robbery because of their ages. These men were not too spry; they walked with the aid of canes; and they didn't look as though they were physically able to rob me.[5]

The same applies at the other end of the age continuum; children are more trusted than adults. Very young children, at least, are physically incapable of carrying out a robbery or of harming the driver, and as they become older, until they reach a certain age or size, can do so only with difficulty.

Another relevant personal characteristic is the *degree of sobriety* of the passenger. This variable does not operate by itself, however; it operates rather as a "potentiator."[6] The passenger's degree of sobriety takes on meaning for the driver only in conjunction with other variables. Thus sobriety allows the other variables to retain their meaning, but different levels of intoxication intensify the meaning of the other variables. When a passenger reaches a level of intoxication that is described by drivers as "He is high," then he is more trusted. Such passengers are more likely to increase their tips or be amenable to the driver's suggestions. At the same time, this level of intoxication makes those who do not normally meet the criteria of a passenger even less trusted. The driver views such individuals, when they are "high," as being even more likely than when sober to "try something funny."

When intoxication is greater than "high," and the passenger could be called "drunk," drivers have less trust, regardless of whether he meets the criteria of a good passenger or not. This is because of the basic unpredictability of a drunk, or as the drivers say, "Ya don't know what a drunk is gonna do." Yet when intoxication is to the point where the passenger has little control over his actions (close to being "dead drunk" or "passed out"), trust again increases. Such persons become defined by drivers as being unable to carry out evil intentions even if they wanted to. The person inebriated to this degree, of course, easily becomes prey for the cab driver.[7]

The *secondary location*, the destination to which the passenger is going, is another variable that determines trust for the cab driver. In the driver's view, the passenger's destination is frequently considered to be a part of the passenger himself. Thus, if a passenger is going to an area that the driver distrusts, his distrust of the area can be transferred to the passenger whom he otherwise trusted. That is, if this same passenger were going to a location that the driver trusted, the driver would not give a second thought about this passenger. If everything else is the same—except that the passenger wants to go to an area that the driver doesn't trust—the driver will begin to wonder about the trustworthiness of his passenger, and he will begin to question the correctness of his original decision to trust this individual as a passenger. He will wonder why his passenger is going into that area, an area that the driver himself doesn't like to enter.[8] Usually the reason becomes apparent: Sometimes the driver elicits the information, either directly or indirectly, and sometimes the passenger, aware of the driver's concerns, volunteers the information. Usual reasons for this discrepancy involve such things as the passenger's place of residence versus his place of work (e.g., a black domestic returning by cab to the ghetto), or continuing relationships with friends and relatives who have not moved out of the ghetto, or "slumming" by persons who are out for kicks that they can't receive in their usual haunts.

Another way that the passenger's destination can communicate distrust to the driver is the driver's perception of the destination as a *non-location*, that is, there is no "match" between the location given and a corresponding location in physical reality. For example, a street address is given, but the street does not run as far as the number indicates. In this case, too, the driver will seek an explanation for the discrepancy, and many times a plausible explanation exists, for example, the person has read the number incorrectly. If a plausible explanation is not readily available, or if the individual is one for whom low trust exists, this fiction will lead to distrust.

If no specific destination is given, this too can lead to distrust. A passenger telling a driver to "just drive around" is suspect unless there is a satisfactory explanation for this lack of a specific destination, for example, a tourist who wants to see various parts of the city or a woman who wants to be driven around the park because it is a beautiful day. Where the explanation is not available, the driver is likely to suspect that the passenger might be setting him up for robbery.

The secondary location also communicates trust. A passenger who gives as his destination a "good" part of town, or an area that the driver already trusts, is less likely to be under the driver's suspicion than in the above case. In some instances, the secondary location can even mitigate distrust that has developed for other reasons. For example:

> It was about 1:00 A.M. I had taken a practical nurse home after her work shift and ended up in part of the ghetto. Since I was next to a stand, I decided to park there. As I was pulling into the space, I saw a man standing at the bus stop which was next to the stand, with his arm held out horizontally and wagging his finger a bit. He was a large black male wearing a dark blue overcoat. He opened the back door of the cab, and my first thought was, "Well, here goes! I'm going to be robbed. I'd better turn on the tape recorder and get this on tape!" After he got into the cab, he said, "I want to go to Richmond Heights. You know where Richmond Heights is?"

Although there was originally a high level of distrust of this passenger, when he gave his destination I was much reassured. My perception at that time of the black community in Richmond Heights was that of a small community of blacks in the midst of middle-class whites, a black community that was "solid," composed of black professional and working people. His destination was "paired" with him, and I figured if he was going to where this class of blacks live, that I did not have to worry about being robbed.

Many variables affect trust that are not as easily analyzable as the above variables. Many of these are subtle interactional cues that communicate much to the driver but that are difficult to explicate. Such a variable is the *sitting behavior* of the passenger. It is possible for the passenger to sit in such a way that he communicates "evil intention" to the driver in that his manner doesn't fit the rest of his front or his definition of himself as a trustworthy passenger. In the above case, for example:

> After I was reassured about this passenger because of his destination, I noticed by means of the mirror that he was sitting in a slumped-over position in the extreme right-hand side of the back seat. It seemed that he could be sitting this way to hide his face from me. I decided to turn around and get a good look at him. I turned around and made some innocuous comment about directions, and as I did I noticed that he was sleeping. When he heard my question his eyes popped open, and he began to respond. It was then obvious that his manner of sitting was due to his sleepiness, and I was again reassured.

Another type of sitting behavior that lessens a driver's trust of his passenger concerns single passengers. A single passenger will almost invariably sit on the right-hand side of the back seat (the side diagonal from the driver), or, at times, in the front seat next to the driver. The driver views either of these positions as being appropriate for his passenger. Occasionally, however, a passenger will sit directly behind the driver in the back seat. This ordinarily makes the driver uncomfortable and wary of the passenger; he begins to wonder why the passenger is sitting there. Interaction between the driver and passenger is more difficult in this position, and the cab driver cannot easily keep tabs on what his passenger is doing.

There are additional subtle interaction cues that affect a driver's trust of his passenger. They range from the looks of somebody (e.g., "sneaky, slitty eyes") to body language—and beyond. Cab drivers interpret and react to others in stereotypical ways on the basis of the symbols to which they have been socialized. It is obvious that there are any number of such cues, gestures, or symbols that lead to trust or distrust. Most of these are beyond the scope of this analysis except to state the obvious: When the driver deals with symbols to which he has feelings of distrust attached, he will distrust the bearer of the symbol, the passenger.

An example of something to which the meaning of distrust has become attached is the sound of one's voice. This was the manifest variable leading to distrust in the following case:

> DISPATCHER: Twenty-third and Choteau. . . .
> DRIVER: ((not broadcast))
> DISPATCHER: It's fine if you can't. Don't take any chances. . . .
> DRIVER: ((not broadcast))
> DISPATCHER: I don't like the order myself. *I don't like the sound of the man's voice.* . . .

This order is given at 1:10 A.M., and the dispatcher himself was answering incoming calls. According to his statement, there was something about the caller's voice that made him reluctant to dispatch a cab. But what was it about the caller's voice that led to this reaction? It is this type of variable, though both interesting and important in determining trust, to which our data unfortunately do not lend themselves for analysis.

Because the dispatcher is essential in the communication process of dispatching drivers to passengers, he plays a vital role in determining whether or not a driver will trust a potential passenger to become an actual passenger. The above taped conversation concluded with:

> DISPATCHER: No. It is not a Missouri Boiler order! It is not a Missouri Boiler order! It's a terminal railroad man on Twenty-third and Choteau, or Twenty-third street north of Choteau. . . .
> DRIVER: ((not broadcast))
> DISPATCHER: Let me know if you get the man or if you do not get him. . . .

The driver, who wants and needs the order at this slack period of his shift, tries to tie the order in with the known and trusted. That is, workers getting off the swing shift at Missouri Boiler sometimes take cabs, and they can be trusted. Perhaps this is such an order. But the dispatcher, showing his impatience with the driver's lack of knowledge that the address he gave is not that of Missouri Boiler, tells him that it is not that kind of order and the caller should be carefully approached if the driver is going to take the order. This dispatcher then does an unusual thing, he makes the dispatched order optional at the discretion of the driver. Ordinarily a dispatched order becomes a sacred thing to the driver, not an option. It is a responsibility for which the driver assumes completion and for which he can be fired if he fails to complete. Yet here in the view of both the cab driver and the dispatcher, the driver need not accept the responsibility for completing an order when the passenger cannot be trusted.[9]

The dispatcher, when he is able, offers assurance to drivers who do not have enough cues to know whether or not they can trust a passenger. The following example illustrates this:

> DISPATCHER: You have to go in the rear of the court to get in there, Driver. We had that last night, so it's all right. . . .

The dispatcher is assuring the driver that the people waiting are acceptable as passengers, that is, that although the driver must drive where he is reluctant to go, in the back where it is perhaps dark, it is all right to do so: this is not a set-up for a robbery. How can the dispatcher give such an assurance? As he states, there had been an order from that location the night before and it turned out to be an acceptable passenger. In this case, the setting, "in the rear of the court at night," did not fit the driver's estimation of acceptability for trusting someone to become a passenger, but, because the dispatcher has had a previous rewarding experience with this lack of fit, he knows that it is all right, and he is able to assure the driver.

The passenger of mine who best incorporated most of the above variables of distrust within a single case and who illustrates other variables that have not been explicated was the following:

> About 2:00 A.M. I was dispatched to just within the ghetto, to a hotel which also serves as a house of prostitution. My passenger turned out to be a drunk, elderly, black male, who chose to sit next to me in the front seat. He ordered me to take him to East St. Louis and said "We're going to a rough neighborhood. Lock your doors. Roll up your windows."
>
> The passenger then began talking to himself. As he did so, I thought he was talking to me, and I said, "What did you say?" He looked up and said, "None of your business!" He then continued talking to himself. As we passed the Atlas Hotel in the 4200 block of Delmar, he made the comment that he should have stopped there and seen someone, but that since we had already passed it I should go on. I said, "No, that's all right. I'll take you there," and I drove around the block to the hotel. He got out and was about to leave when I said, "I'll wait for you, but you'll have to pay what's on the meter." He became rather angry, gave me some money, and then urinated against the side of the cab.
>
> I drove on without him.

This man was distrusted because he was a stranger, a male, a black, at night, had been drinking, was coming from the edge of the ghetto, going to a ghetto area, which area was "unknown" to the driver, and acted irrationally by speaking aloud to himself.

The driver has less trust for someone who acts irrationally, just as most members of society would have less trust for someone who exhibited this type of behavior. Because the individual is irrational, predictability of his behavior decreases, while to trust someone means that one can predict his behavior on the basis of acceptance of his identity. This is what cannot be done with someone who does not act as we have learned that "ordinary" persons act.

The driver has less trust for an area that he does not know, that is, an area whose layout he is unfamiliar with, because he cannot easily maneuver his cab or plan and carry out routes in such areas. Control in such situations passes from the driver to the passenger who possesses such knowledge. To enter an interaction with someone who possesses the greater control requires trust that the other individual will not use this control to his advantage and to one's own disadvantage, in this case such things as robbery or not paying the fare.

Conclusion

Cabbies will usually accept an actor's definition of himself as belonging to the category "passenger," and they almost without exception will do so when they are dispatched to an order. However, under some circumstances, especially flag loads, the cab driver will refuse to allow a potential passenger to become his passenger. In examining how the cab driver differentiates between those he allows to become his passengers and those he does not, we have attempted to delineate the variables that go into this foundational aspect of our life-in-society—trust.

Although the specific interaction situation in which trust has been analyzed is that of the cab driver as he goes about his daily routines, the import of this analysis extends beyond the cab driver-passenger interaction situation to all life-in-society. The specific variables that lead to trust and distrust change with each situation, but the fundamental principles of evaluating others are the same. Your world is also composed of situations in which people are continually offering you a definition of themselves, and you must, and do, evaluate that definition on the basis of your perception of the fit or misfit among the parts presented that you have learned to associate with that particular front. Your evaluation, as it does with the cabbie, although perhaps based on differing expectations of parts to be associated with particular fronts, leads to a reaction of trust or distrust. By examining the way trust operates in the cabbie's life, we can gain both a clearer perception of the principles underlying trust in our own social world and a more complete understanding of our reactions to others within that world.

Notes

1. This article is a version of Chapter VI of *The Cab Driver: An Interactional Analysis of An Occupational Culture*, unpublished dissertation, Washington University, 1967, pp. 214–250. A different version has appeared in *Sociology and Everyday Life*, Marcello Truzzi, ed., Englewood Cliffs, N. J.: Prentice Hall, Inc., 1968, pp. 138–58.

2. Erving Goffman, *The Presentation of Self in Everyday Life*, Garden City, N.Y.: Doubleday Anchor Books, 1959, pp. 22–30.

3. This is true for Metro Cab even though it does not allow "personals," i.e., a passenger who is allowed to phone the company and ask for "his" driver, regardless of spatial rules. Where this is allowed, we would be a step closer to "maximum trust." Personals would be more common in smaller towns, but they also exist in St. Louis with some of the smaller cab companies. A specific type of regular rider is the "charge customer," the passenger who has a charge account with Metro,

who, instead of paying cash, fills out and signs a charge slip. Like many other charge accounts in our society, he is billed monthly by the company.

4. This was evidenced by the incredulity and shock Metro drivers expressed when during the Christmas season of 1964 it was learned that a female passenger had robbed a cab driver.

5. I assume that the health of an individual would be another such variable; that is, if an individual were sick or weak, the driver would have fewer reservations about accepting him as a passenger. One's perception of health could, of course, be erroneous. The individual could be faking his illness or even be forced into robbery due to needs caused by his illness. He could, of course, also be faking his sex (see quotation above), his residence, his social class, and his agedness. But we are here speaking of the driver's perceptions as they relate to trust and the acceptance of a passenger, not the accuracy of those perceptions.

6. "Potentiate" or "potentiator" is a term used by chemists to refer to a substance that makes the action of the other chemicals more powerful or effective or active. It is different from a catalyst because it is consumed in the reaction. I am indebted to Elliott G. Mishler for this analogy.

7. For an analysis of extortive practices of cabbies, see, James M. Henslin, "Sex and Cabbies," in *Studies in The Sociology of Sex*, James M. Henslin, ed., N. Y.: Appleton-Century-Crofts, 1971, pp. 193–223. For those directed against cabbies, see James M. Henslin, "The Underlife of Cabdriving: A Study in Exploitation and Punishment," in *Varieties of Work Experience: The Social Control of Occupational Groups and Roles*, New York: John Wiley and Sons, 1974: 67–79.

8. In addition to the ghetto and other lower-class "tough neighborhoods," other areas of the city that will elicit distrust, unless there is an adequate "account" given, are areas of the city that are relatively deserted, especially at night, such as a small back street or a dead-end street with few or no lights, or a warehouse or riverfront section of town.

9. It is again, of course, irrelevant whether the passenger can, in fact, be trusted. It is the driver's perception of trust that matters.

13 Waiting, Exchange, and Power: The Distribution of Time in Social Systems[1]

BARRY SCHWARTZ

One of the most common features of life in society is waiting. We all wait, at least occasionally. We wait to be seated in a restaurant, then to be served; we wait in a doctor's outer office, then in the inner office; we wait for buses, trains, and planes; and we wait for an instructor to get our papers and tests graded and returned.

We already know about waiting, for all of us have experienced much of it—from our early lives until now. So what could be so significant about waiting that it deserves a place in this book? Or your time in reading it? And could waiting really be important enough for sociologists to spend their time studying it?

It is precisely because waiting is so readily familiar—having become a part of our unexamined background expectancies of social life—that it is worth analyzing. Waiting, as Schwartz shows, is much more than simply passing time prior to participating in some event. Waiting is an integral part of the social order: It is part and parcel of the basics on which our society is constructed. By examining the social significance of waiting, we gain insight into many aspects of life in society, even into *power* (the ability that some have to get their way) and *social stratification* (the divisions, or inequalities, that are built into a society).

After reading this article, it may be difficult for you ever again to see waiting as "simply waiting," for this selection examines the social bases that determine who waits for whom, making you aware—perhaps painfully so—of the power dimensions of waiting.

Waiting, Scarcity, and Power

STRATIFICATION OF WAITING

... TYPICAL RELATIONSHIPS OBTAIN between the individual's position within a social system and the extent to which he waits for and is waited for by other members of the system. In general, the more powerful and important a person is, the more others' access to him must be regulated. Thus, the least powerful may almost always be approached at will; the most powerful are seen only "by appointment." Moreover, because of heavy demands on their time, important people are most likely to violate the terms of appointments and keep their clients waiting. It is also true that the powerful tend not to ask for appointments with their own subordinates; rather, the lowly are summoned—which is grounds for them to cancel their own arrangements so as not to "keep the boss waiting."

The lowly must not only wait for their appointments with superiors; they may also be called upon to wait during the appointment itself. This may be confirmed in innumerable ways. For one, consider everyday life in bureaucracies. When, in their offices, superordinates find themselves in the company of a subordinate, they may interrupt the business at hand to, say, take a phone call, causing the inferior to wait until the conversation is finished. Such interruption may be extremely discomforting for the latter, who may wish not to be privy to the content of the conversation but, having no materials with which to express alternative involvement, must wait in this exposed state until his superior is ready to reengage him. The event becomes doubly disturbing when the superior is unable to recover from the distraction, loses his train of thought, and is unable to properly devote himself to the moment's business. Of course, the subordinate is demeaned not only by the objective features of this scene but also by his realization that for more important clients the superior would have placed an embargo on all incoming calls or visitors. He would have made others wait. The assumption that the client correctly makes is that his own worth is not sufficient to permit the superior to renounce other engagements; being unworthy of full engagement, he is seen, so to speak, between the superior's other appointments. In this way, the client is compelled to bear witness to the mortification of his own worthiness for proper social interaction.

While the derogatory implications for self are clear when the person must repeatedly step aside and wait until the superordinate decides that the granting of his time will not be excessively costly, debasement of self may be attenuated by the client's own consideration that his superior is, after all, in a position of responsibility and assailed by demands over which he may not exercise as much control as he would like. But even this comforting account may be unavailable when the server himself initiates the interruption. It is possible for him to make a call, for example, or to continue his work after the client enters, perhaps with the announcement that he will "be through in a minute."

It is especially mortifying when the superior initiates a wait when an engagement is in progress. Thus, a subordinate, while strolling along a corridor in conversation with his superior, may find himself utterly alone when the latter encounters a colleague and breaks off the ongoing relationship in his favor. The subordinate (who may not do the same when encountering one of his peers) is compelled to defer by standing aside and waiting until the unanticipated conversation is finished. Nothing less is expected by his superior, who, finding himself gaining less from the engagement than his inferior, assumes the right to delay or interrupt it at will if more profitable opportunities should arise.

The Immunity of the Privileged. . . . Powerful clients are relatively immune from waiting. This remark accords with Tawney's (1931) emphasis on the asymmetry of power relations. "Power," he writes, "may be defined as the capacity of an individual, or group of individuals, to modify the conduct of other individuals or groups in the manner which he desires, *and to prevent his own conduct being modified in the manner in which he does not"* (p. 229; emphasis added).

The relative immunity from waiting which the powerful enjoy is guaranteed because they have the resources to refuse to wait; that is, because they can often afford to go elsewhere for faster service or cause others, such as servants or employees, to wait in their places. Thus, while the relationship between privilege and the necessity of waiting cannot be generalized in any deterministic way, there appears nevertheless to be a relationship between the two, with the least-privileged clients compelled to do the most waiting. . . .

It is noticeable, for one example, that in the "best" of urban department stores a customer is met by a salesperson as soon as he enters; the customer makes a selection under his guidance and makes payment to him. In establishments which are a grade below the best, customers may have difficulty finding someone to serve them during busy periods but, when they do, are accompanied by him, that is, "waited on," until the transaction is consummated by payment. The lowest-grade stores, however, provide few servers; as a result, customers must for the most part wait on themselves, then line up behind others at a cashier counter in order to make payment. . . .

In general, it may be said that establishments which cater to a relatively wealthy clientele must serve them quickly (if the clients desire) not only because of the objective or assumed value of clients' time but also because they have the means to take their business elsewhere if it is not respected. Commercial places which service the less wealthy are less constrained in this respect because they tend to deal with a larger and/or less independent clientele. Within organizations, clients who promise to bring the most profit to a server enjoy a competitive advantage; they wait the least, to the disadvantage of their lesser endowed brethren who can find no one to honor the value of their time.[2]

WAITING AND THE MONOPOLIZATION OF SERVICES

The above rule, however, rests on the assumption that faster alternative services are available to those who want and can pay for them. In fact, the availability of such alternatives is itself variable. Waiting is therefore affected not only by clients' resources and consequent ability to go elsewhere for service but also by the opportunity to do so.

It follows that establishments with many competitors are most likely to be concerned about the amount of time they keep clients waiting. Chicago Loop banks are among such organizations. In the words of one banking consultant, "The industry is too competitive to allow a dozen people waiting in line when they could just as easily take their business across the street where there is a teller at every window, a customer at every teller and waiting time is less than one minute" (*Chicago Tribune*, September 28, 1971, p. 7). However, organizations with few or no competitors are less obliged to reduce the waiting time of clients. (This condition makes waiting a national pastime in the Soviet Union, where most services are rendered by government-run establishments that are not subject to market forces.) . . .

We now turn to public services which by their very nature admit of no alternatives and which at the same time are so organized as to constitute the most radical instance of the principle we are now discussing.

A Day in Court. Discrepancy between demand for and supply of "authoritative judgment" is perhaps the most notorious source of waiting for both rich and poor. In fact, those who look forward to their "day in court," whether civil, criminal, or juvenile, very often find themselves spending their day in the courthouse corridor (many courts do not provide waiting rooms). In some courts, in fact, all parties whose cases are scheduled to be heard on a particular day are instructed to be present at its beginning when the judge arrives.[3] This . . . ensures that the judge (whose bench is separated from his office or working area) will not be left with idle time that cannot be put to productive use—a consideration which may help us understand the seemingly irrational practice of assembling together at the beginning of the day those who are to be served during its course. While this tactic guarantees that the judge's valuable time will not be wasted, it also ensures that most parties will be kept waiting for a substantial period of time; some, all day long. Indeed, because they have no means to retaliate against the judge's own tardiness or excessive lunch breaks, some individuals may not be served at all and must return on the next day to wait further. Clients' attorneys, incidentally, keep them company during much of this time—a service for which the former pay dearly. . . .

Some persons and groups are relatively exempt from waiting. . . . In making up the docket, for example, resources are taken into account. Defendants who are represented by an attorney are very often scheduled before those who are not (in Chicago traffic courts, at least). And cases involving important and powerful contestants, witnesses, and/or lawyers may be scheduled at their convenience and not be delayed for long periods of time. Similarly, attorneys who enjoy favor with the court clerk are also able to avoid long waits because they are allowed to schedule their case early. Thus, while waiting time may be maximized by persons or in organizations which enjoy full or near monopoly on the services they offer, the relationship between the power and waiting time of their clients is probably attenuated rather than negated. For, while the powerful may lack the opportunity to take their business elsewhere, they nevertheless possess the resources to ensure that their needs will be accommodated before the needs of those with fewer means. . . .

Social Psychological Aspects of Delay

MAKING OTHERS WAIT

Because the worth of a person is not independent of the amount of time others must wait for him, that person can maintain and dramatize his worth by purposely causing another to wait.

Of course, the imposition of a waiting period does not in itself make a person or his services valuable; it can only magnify existing positive evaluations or transform neutral feelings into positive ones. If these initial feelings are not favorable, or at least neutral, the waiting caused by a server may lower clients' estimations of his worth. Instead of a sought-after and important man, the server becomes an incompetent who cannot perform his job properly; thus is his initial inferiority confirmed. (This is why subordinates who know where they stand do not like to keep their superiors waiting.) Generally, the dramatization of ascendency by keeping another waiting will do a server the most good when his social rank exceeds that of his client or when the difference beween their ranks is ambiguous. In the latter case, ascendency accrues to him who can best dramatize it; in the former, ascendency may be dramatized by him to whom it already accrues.

Thus, just as authority is affirmed by the placement of social distance between super and subordinate, so temporal distance subserves the ascendency of the person who imposes it. More precisely, the restriction of access to oneself by forcing another to "cool his heels" is instrumental to the cultivation of social distance. . . .

THE IMPOSITION OF WAITING AS AN AGGRESSIVE ACT

If the temporal aspect of relationships between those occupying different social positions may be stated in terms of who waits for whom, then we would expect to find a reversal of the waiting-delaying pattern when persons "switch" positions. Furthermore, this reversal may be accentuated through retaliation by the one who suffered under the initial arrangement. A former president furnishes us with an example:

Ken Hechler, who was director of research at the White House from 1948 to 1952, recalled the day Mr. Truman kept Winthrop Aldrich, president of the Chase Manhattan Bank, waiting outside the White House office for 30 minutes. Hechler quoted Mr. Truman as saying:

"When I was a United States senator and headed the war investigation committee, I had to go to New York to see this fella Aldrich. Even though I had an appointment he had me cool my heels for an hour and a half. So just relax. He's got a little while to go yet." [*Chicago Daily News*, December 27, 1972, p. 4]

Punitive sanctioning through the imposition of waiting is met in its most extreme forms when a person is not only kept waiting but is also kept ignorant as to how long he must wait, or even of what he is waiting for. One manifestation of the latter form is depicted by Solzhenitsyn (1968):

Having met the man (or telephoned him or even specially summoned him), he might say: "Please step into my office tomorrow morning at ten." "Can't I drop in now?" the individual would be sure to ask, since he would be eager to know what he was being summoned for and get it over with. "No, not now," Rusanov would gently, but strictly admonish. He would not say that he was busy at the moment or had to go to a conference. He would on no account offer a clear, simple reason, something that could reassure the man being summoned (for that was the crux of this device). He would pronounce the words "not now" in a tone allowing many interpretations—not all of them favorable. "About what?" the employee might ask, out of boldness or inexperience. "You'll find out tomorrow," Pavel Nikolaevich would answer in a velvet voice, bypassing the tactless question. But what a long time it is until tomorrow. [p. 222]

. . . This kind of strategy can only be employed by superordinates who have power over a client in the first place. The effect on the client is to further subordinate him, regardless of a server's initial attractiveness or a client's realization that the delay has been deliberately imposed. Furthermore, this practice leaves the client in a psychologically as well as a ritually unsatisfactory state. The two presumably act back on each other in a mutually subversive way, for by causing his client to become tense or nervous the server undermines the self-confidence necessary for him to maintain proper composure. This tendency, incidentally, is routinely applied by skillful police interrogators who deliberately ignore a suspect waiting to be questioned, assuming that a long, uncertain wait will "rattle him" sufficiently to disorganize the kinds of defenses he could use to protect himself (Arthur and Caputo 1959, p. 31).

RITUAL WAITING AND AUTONOMY

. . . While the imposition of delay allows a superordinate to give expression to his authority, waiting may also be imposed in protest against that authority. The latter achievement is valued, naturally, among those of despised status and low rank. Because they lack the wherewithal to do so in most of their other relations, the powerless, in their capacity as servers, delight in keeping their superiors waiting. The deliberately sluggish movements of many store clerks, telephone operators, cashiers, toll collectors, and the like, testify to the ability of the lowly as well as the lofty to dramatize their autonomy. This accords with Meerloo's (1966) assertion that "the strategy of delay is an ambivalent attack on those who command us" (p. 249). This kind of aggression is perhaps most pronounced under sociologically ambivalent conditions: as the legitimacy of the existing distribution of status honor ceases to be taken for granted, prescribed deference patterns give way to institutionalized rudeness, which may be expressed by appearing late for appointments with a superordinate as well as by dillydallying while he waits for his needs to be serviced. . . .

Summary

. . . The broader implication of this essay is that it finds . . . time itself a generalized resource whose distribution affects life chances with regard to the attainment of other, more specific kinds of rewards. This is true in a number of respects. Time, like money, is valuable because it is necessary for the achievement of productive purposes; ends cannot be reached unless an appropriate amount of it is "spent" or "invested" on their behalf. On the other hand, the power that a time surplus makes possible may be protected and/or expanded by depriving others of their time. By creating queues to reduce idle periods, for example, a server exploits clients by converting their time to his own use. A server does the same by "overcharging" in the sense of deliberately causing a particular client to wait longer than necessary.

The monetary analogies we have used are not without some justification. Just as money possesses no substantive value independent of its use as a means of exchange, time can only be of value if put to substantive use in an exchange relationship. Both time and money may be regarded as generalized means because of the infinity of possibilities for their utilization: both are possessed in finite quantities; both may be counted, saved, spent, lost, wasted, or invested. . . . Accordingly, while the powerful can allocate monetary means to their own desired ends by controlling the *budget*, they also regulate the distribution of time—rewarding themselves, depriving others—through their control of the *schedule*. What is at stake in the first instance is the *amount* of resources to which different parts of a system are entitled; in the second, it is the *priority* of their entitlements. Far from being a coincidental by-product of power, then, control of time comes into view as one of its essential properties.

Notes

1. This paper was supported by grant 1-5690-00-4335 from the Ford Foundation and by the Center for Health Administration Studies, University of Chicago. The writer wishes to acknowledge the very useful comments made on this paper by Peter Blau and Morris Janowitz.

2. Even when circumstances make it necessary for the resourceful to wait, they suffer less than their inferiors. As a general rule, the wealthier the clientele, the more adequate the waiting accommodations. Thus, persons who can afford bail can await their trial (or, far more frequently, attorneys' bargaining on their behalf) in the free community. The poor must wait in jail. The same is true of facilities. In airports, for example, those who can afford it may simultaneously avoid contamination by the masses and engross themselves in a variety of activities, including fabulous eating and drinking, in "VIP lounges." The term "lounge" instead of the vulgar "waiting area" or "gate" is also applied to facilities set aside for those who travel a specified number of miles with (and pay a substantial sum of money to) a particular airline. In this as in many other settings, waiting locales for the poor and less rich lack the elaborate involvement supplies, pleasant decor, and other physical and psychological comforts that diminish the pain of waiting among those who are better off.

3. A functional equivalent is found in the Soviet Union. "Aleksandr Y. Kabalkin and Vadim M. Khinchuk . . . describe what they termed 'classic cases' in everyday life in the Soviet Union, in which customers wait for the television repairman or for a messenger delivering a train or plane ticket that had been ordered by phone. To the question 'About what time can I expect you?' the stereotyped reply is, 'It can be any time during the day.' And people have to excuse themselves from work and wait—there is no other way out" (*New York Times*, November 7, 1971, p. 5).

References

Arthur, R., and R. Caputo (1959). *Interrogation for Investigators.* New York: Copp.

Meerloo, Joost (1966). "The Time Sense in Psychiatry." In *The Voices of Time*, edited by J. T. Fraser. New York: Braziller.

Solzhenitsyn, Aleksandr (1968). *The Cancer Ward.* New York: Dial.

Tawney, R. H. (1931). *Equality.* London: Allen & Unwin.

14 The Sociology of the Vaginal Examination*

JAMES M. HENSLIN
MAE A. BIGGS

All of us depend on others for the successful completion of the roles we play. In many ways, this makes cooperation the essence of social life (with due apologies to my conflict theorist friends). Dependence on the cooperation of others is no less true of the specialist, the individual whose role (occupational or otherwise) is highly focused. Without cooperative teamwork, performances fall apart, people become disillusioned, jobs don't get done, and society is threatened. Accordingly, much of our socialization centers on learning to be good team players.

The work setting lends itself well to examine cooperative interaction and the socially acceptable handling of differences—"working arrangements" that defuse threats to fragile social patterns. For example, instructors often accept from students excuses that they know do not "match reality." For their part, students often accept what instructors teach even though they privately disagree with their interpretations. Confrontation is not only unpleasant, and therefore preferable to avoid, but confrontation also threatens the continuity of the interaction. Thus both instructors and students generally allow one another enough leeway to "get on with business" (which some might say is education but others, more cynical, might say is one earning a living and the other a degree).

In any event, underlying our basic interactions in most social settings are such implicit understandings about how to handle differences. One can gain much insight into the nature of society by trying to identify the rules under which we interact with one another—and the definitions that the interaction is designed to maintain. In this selection, Henslin and Biggs draw heavily on Goffman's dramaturgical framework as they focus on the vaginal examination. Note the teamwork that this requires, especially in making the definition stick that nothing sexual is occurring.

What areas of your life are based on teamwork in the interest of trying to "get the show on the road," that is, to make desired definitions stick and allow the action to unfold? (Actually, it might be easier to try to determine what parts of social life do not require teamwork.)

*Our thanks to Erving Goffman for commenting on this paper while it was in manuscript form. We have resisted the temptation to use his suggested title, "Behavior in Pubic Places."

GENITAL BEHAVIOR is problematic in American society. Americans in our society are socialized at a very early age into society's dictates concerning the situations, circumstances, and purposes of allowable and unallowable genital exposure.

After an American female has been socialized into rigorous norms concerning society's expectations in the covering and privacy of specified areas of her body, especially her vagina, exposure of her pubic area becomes something that is extremely problematic for her. Even for a woman who has overcome this particular problem when it comes to sexual relations and is no longer bothered by genital exposure in the presence of her sexual partner, the problem frequently recurs when she is expected to expose her vagina in a nonsexual manner to a male. Such is the case with the vaginal examination. The vaginal examination can become so threatening, in fact, that for many women it not only represents a threat to their feelings of modesty but also threatens their person and their feelings of who they are.

Because emotions are associated with the genital area through the learning of taboos, the vaginal examination becomes an interesting process; it represents a structured interaction situation in which the "privates" no longer remain private. From a sociological point of view, what happens during such interaction? Since a (if not *the*) primary concern of the persons involved is that all the interaction be defined as nonsexual, with even the hint of sexuality being avoided, what structural restraints on behavior operate? How does the patient cooperate in maintaining this definition of nonsexuality? In what ways are the roles of doctor, nurse, and patient performed such that they conjointly contribute to the maintenance of this definition?

This analysis is based on a sample of 12,000 to 14,000 vaginal examinations. The female author served as an obstetrical nurse in hospital settings and as an office nurse for general practitioners for fourteen years, giving us access to this area of human behavior which is ordinarily not sociologically accessible. Based on these observations, we have divided the interaction of the vaginal examination into five major scenes. We shall now examine each of these bounded interactions.

The setting for the vaginal examination may be divided into two areas (see Figure 14.1). Although there are no physical boundaries employed to demarcate the two areas, highly differentiated interaction occurs in each. Area 1, where Scenes I and V are played, includes that portion of the "office-examination" room which is furnished with a desk and three chairs. Area 2, where Scenes II, III, and IV take place, is furnished with an examination table, a swivel stool, a gooseneck lamp, a table for instruments, and a sink with a mirror above it.

AREA 1
Patient as Person
(Scenes I and V)

AREA 2
Patient as Pelvic
Transitional Area of Depersonalization and
Repersonalization (Scenes II, III, IV)

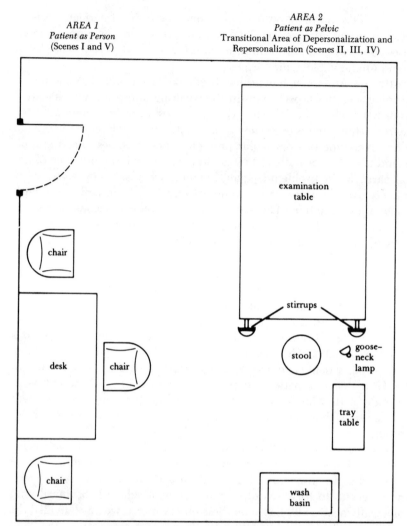

Figure 14.1. The Doctor's Office-Examination Room

Scene I: The Personalized Stage: The Patient as Person

The interaction flow of Scene I is as follows: (a) the doctor enters the "office-examination" room; (b) greets the patient; (c) sits down; (d) asks the patient why she is there; (e) questions her on specifics; (f) decides on a course of action, specifically whether a pelvic examination is needed or not; (g) if he thinks a pelvic is needed, he signals the nurse on the intercom and says, "I want a pelvic in room (X)"; (h) he gets up, and (i) leaves the room.

During this scene the patient is treated as a full person, that is, the courtesies of middle-class verbal exchange are followed, and, in addition to gathering medical information, if the doctor knows the patient well he may intersperse his medical questions with questions about her personal life. The following interaction that occurred during Scene I demonstrates the doctor's treatment of his patient as a full person:

> DOCTOR (upon entering the room): Hello, Joyce, I hear you're going to Southern Illinois University.
> PATIENT: Yes, I am. I've been accepted, and I have to have my health record completed.
>
> The doctor then seated himself at his desk and began filling out the health record that the patient gave him. He interspersed his questions concerning the record form with questions about the patient's teaching, about the area of study she was pursuing, about her children, their health and their schooling. He then said, "Well, we have to do this right. We'll do a pelvic on you." He then announced via the intercom, "I want to do a pelvic on Joyce in room 1." At that point he left the room.

This interaction sequence is typical of the interaction that occurs in Scene I between a doctor and a patient he knows well. When the doctor does not know the patient well, he does not include his patient's name, either her first or last name, in his announcement to the nurse that she should come into the room. In such a case, he simply says, "I want to do a pelvic in room 1," or, "Pelvic in room 1." The doctor then leaves the room, marking the end of this scene.

Scene II: The Depersonalizing Stage: Transition from Person to Pelvic

When at the close of Scene I the doctor says, "Pelvic in room (X)," he is in effect announcing the transition of the person to a pelvic. It is a sort of advance announcement, however, of a coming event, because the transition has not yet been effected. The doctor's signal for the nurse to come in is, in fact, a signal that the nurse should now help with the transition of the patient from a person to a pelvic. Additionally, it also serves as an announcement to the patient that she is about to undergo this metamorphosis.

The interaction flow which accomplishes the transition from person to pelvic is as follows: Upon entering the room, the nurse, without preliminaries, tells the patient, "The doctor wants to do a vaginal examination on you. Will you please remove your panties?" While the patient is undressing, the nurse prepares the props, positioning the stirrups of the examination table, arranging the glove, the lubricant, and the speculum (the instrument which, when inserted into the vagina, allows visual examination of the vaginal tract). She then removes the drape sheet from a drawer and directs the patient onto the table, covers the patient with the drape sheet, assists her in placing her feet into the stirrups, and positions her hips, putting her into the lithotomy position (lying on her back with knees flexed and out).

MEANING OF THE DOCTOR'S ABSENCE

The doctor's exiting from this scene means that the patient will be undressing in his absence. This is not accidental. In many cases, it is true, the doctor leaves because another patient is waiting, but even when there are no waiting patients, the doctor always exits at the end of Scene I. His leaving means that he will not witness the patient undressing, thereby successfully removing any suggestion whatsoever that a striptease is being performed. From the patient's point of view, the problem of undressing is lessened since a strange male is not present. Thus sexuality is removed from the undressing, and when the doctor returns, only a particularized portion of her body will be exposed for the ensuing interaction. As we shall see, the doctor is no longer dealing with a person, but he is, rather, confronted by a "pelvic."

THE PROBLEM OF UNDERCLOTHING

Undressing and nudity are problematic for the patient since she has been socialized into not undressing before strangers.[1] Almost without exception, when the woman undresses in Scene II, she turns away from the nurse and the door, even though the door is closed. She removes only her panties in the typical case, but a small number of the patients also remove their shoes.

After the patient has removed her panties and/or girdle, the problem for her is what to do with them. Panties and girdles do not have the same meaning as other items of clothing, such as a sweater, that can be casually draped around the body or strewn on furniture. Clothing is considered to be an extension of the self (Gross and Stone 1964), and in some cases the clothing comes to represent the particular part of the body that it covers. In this case, this means that panties represent to women their "private area." Comments made by patients that illustrate the problematics of panty exposure include: "The doctor doesn't want to look at these," "I want to get rid of these before he comes in," and, "I don't want the doctor to see these old things."

Some patients seem to be at a loss in solving this problem and turn to the nurse for guidance, asking her directly what they should do with their underclothing. Most patients, however, do not ask for directions, but hide their panties in some way. The favorite hiding or covering seems to be in or under the purse.[2] Other women put their panties in the pocket of their coat or in the folds of a coat or sweater, some cover them with a magazine, and some cover them with their own body on the examination table. It is rare that a woman leaves her panties exposed somewhere in the room.

THE DRAPE SHEET

Another problematic area in the vaginal examination is what being undressed can signify. Disrobing for others frequently indicates preparation for sexual relations. Since sexuality is the very thing that this scene is oriented toward removing, a mechanism is put into effect to eliminate sexuality—the drape sheet. After the patient is seated on the table, the nurse places a drape sheet from just below her breasts (she still has her blouse on) to over her legs. Although the patient is draped by the sheet, when she is positioned on the table with her legs in the stirrups, her pubic region is exposed. Usually it is not necessary for the doctor even to raise a fold in the sheet in order to examine her genitals.

Since the drape sheet does not cover the genital area, but, rather, leaves it exposed, what is its purpose? The drape sheet depersonalizes the patient. It sets the pubic area apart, letting the doctor view the pubic area in isolation, separating the pubic area from the person. The pubic area or female genitalia becomes an object isolated from the rest of the body. With the drape sheet, the doctor, in his position on the low stool, does not even see the patient's head. He no longer sees or need deal with a person, just the exposed genitalia marked off by the drape sheet. Yet, from the patient's point of view in her prone position, her genitals are covered! When she looks down at her body, she does not see exposed genitalia. The drape sheet effectively hides her pubic area *from herself* while exposing it to the doctor.

THIGH BEHAVIOR

American girls are given early and continued socialization in "limb discipline," being taught at a very early age to keep their legs close together while they are sitting or while they are retrieving articles from the ground. They receive such cautions from their mothers as, "Keep your dress down,"

"Put your legs together," and "Nice girls don't let their panties show."
Evidence of socialization into "acceptable" thigh behavior shows up in the
vaginal examination while the women are positioned on the examination
table and waiting for the doctor to arrive. They do not let their thighs fall
outwards in a relaxed position, but they try to hold their upper or mid-
thighs together until the doctor arrives. They do this even in cases where
it is very difficult for them to do so, such as when the patient is in her late
months of pregnancy.

Although the scene has been played such that desexualization is taking place, and although the patient is being depersonalized such that when
the doctor returns he primarily has a pelvic to deal with and not a person,
at this point in the interaction sequence the patient is still holding onto
her sexuality and "personality" as demonstrated by her "proper" thigh behavior. Only later, when the doctor reenters the scene will she fully consent to the desexualized and depersonalized role and let her thighs fall
outwards.

After the props are ready and the patient is positioned, the nurse
announces to the doctor via intercom that the stage is set for the third
scene, saying "We're ready in room (X)."

Scene III: The Depersonalized Stage: The Person as Pelvic

FACE-TO-PUBIC INTERACTION

The interaction to this point, as well as the use of props, has been structured to project a singular definition of the situation—that of legitimate
doctor–patient interaction and, specifically, the nonsexual examination of
a woman's vaginal region by a male. In support of this definition, a team
performance is given in this scene (Goffman 1959: 104). Although the previous interaction has been part of an ongoing team performance, it has
been sequential, leading to the peak of the performance, the vaginal examination itself. At this time, the team goes into a tandem cooperative
act, utilizing its resources to maintain and continue the legitimation of the
examination, and by its combined performance reinforcing the act of each
team member. The doctor, while standing, places a plastic glove on his
right hand, again symbolizing the depersonalized nature of the action—
by using the glove he is saying that he will not himself be actually touching
the "private area" since the glove will serve as an insulator. It is at this
point that he directs related questions to the patient regarding such things
as her bowels or bladder. Then, while he is still in this standing position,
the nurse in synchronization actively joins the performance by squeezing
a lubricant onto his outstretched gloved fingers, and the doctor inserts the
index and middle fingers of his right hand into the patient's vagina while

externally palpating (feeling) the uterus. He then withdraws his fingers from the vagina, seats himself on the stool, inserts a speculum, and while the nurse positions the gooseneck lamp behind him, he visually examines the cervix.

Prior to this third scene, the interaction has been dyadic only, consisting of nurse and patient in Scene II and doctor and patient in Scene I. In this scene, however, the interaction becomes triadic in the sense that the doctor, nurse, and patient are simultaneously involved in the performance. The term triadic, however, does not even come close to accurately describing the role-playing of this scene. Since the patient has essentially undergone a metamorphosis from a person to an object—having been objectified or depersonalized, the focus of the interaction is now on a specific part of her body. The positioning of her legs and the use of the drape sheet have effectively made her pubic region the interaction focus, not only demarcating the pubic region as the focus of interaction but also blocking out the "talklines" between the doctor and patient, physically obstructing their exchange of glances (Goffman 1963: 161). Interaction between the doctor and the patient is no longer "face-to-face," being perhaps now more accurately described as "face-to-pubic" interaction.

BREASTS AS NONSEXUAL OBJECTS

Projecting and maintaining the definition of nonsexuality in the vaginal examination applies also to other parts of the body that are attributed to have sexual meaning in our culture, specifically the breasts. When the breasts are to be examined in conjunction with a vaginal examination, a rather interesting ritual is regularly employed in order to maintain the projected definition of nonsexuality. This ritual tries to objectify the breasts by isolating them from the rest of the body, permitting the doctor to see the breasts apart from the person. In this ritual, after the patient has removed her upper clothing, a towel is placed across her breasts, and the drape sheet is then placed on top of the towel. Since the towel in and of itself more than sufficiently covers the breasts, we can only conclude that the purpose of the drape sheet is to further the definition of nonsexual interaction. Additionally, the doctor first removes the sheet from the breasts and exposes the towel. He then lifts the towel from *one* breast, makes his examination, and *replaces* the towel over that breast. He then examines the other breast in exactly the same way, again replacing the towel after the examination.

THE NURSE AS CHAPERONE

That interaction in Scene III is triadic is not accidental, nor is it instrumentally necessary. It is, rather, purposely designed, being another means of desexualizing the vaginal examination. Instrumentally, the nurse functions merely to lubricate the doctor's fingers and to hand him the speculum. These acts obviously could be handled without the nurse's presence. It becomes apparent, then, that the nurse plays an entirely different role in this scene, that of chaperone, the person assigned to be present in a male–female role relationship to give assurance to interested persons that no untoward sexual acts take place. Although the patient has been depersonalized, or at least this is the definition that has been offered throughout the performance and is the definition that the team has been attempting to maintain, the possibility exists that the vaginal examination can erupt into a sexual scene. Because of this possibility (or the possible imputation or accusation of sexual behavior having taken place), the nurse is always present.[3] Thus even the possibility of sexual content in the vaginal examination is ordinarily denied by all the role-players. It would appear that such denial serves as a mechanism to avoid apprehension and suspicion concerning the motivations and behaviors of the role-players, allowing the performance to be initiated and to continue smoothly to its logical conclusion.[4]

THE PATIENT AS A NONPERSON TEAM MEMBER

With this definition of objectification and desexualization, the patient represents a vagina disassociated from a person. She has been dramaturgically transformed for the duration of this scene into a nonperson (Goffman 1959: 152). This means that while he is seated and performing the vaginal examination, the doctor need not interact with the patient as a person, being, for example, constrained neither to carry on a conversation nor to maintain eye contact with her. Furthermore, this means that he is now permitted to carry on a "side conversation" with the person with whom he does maintain eye contact, his nurse. For example, during one examination the doctor looked up at the nurse and said: "Hank and I really caught some good-sized fish while we were on vacation. He really enjoyed himself." He then looked at his "work" and announced, "Cervix looks good; no inflammation—everything appears fine down here." Such ignoring of the presence of a third person would ordinarily constitute a breach of etiquette for middle-class interactions, but *in this case there really isn't a third person present.* The patient has been "depersonalized," and, correspondingly, the rules of conversation change, and no breach of etiquette has taken place.[5]

The patient, although defined as an object, is actually the third member of the team in the vaginal examination. Her role is to "play the role of being an object"; that is, she contributes her part to the flow of the interaction by acting as an object and not as a person. She contributes to the definition of herself as an object through studied alienation from the interaction, demonstrating what is known as dramaturgical discipline (Goffman 1959: 216–218). She studiously gazes at the ceiling or wall, only occasionally allowing herself the luxury (or is it the danger?) of fleeting eye contact with the nurse. Eye contact with the doctor is, of course, prevented by the position of her legs and the drape sheet.

After the doctor tells the patient to get dressed, he leaves the room, and the fourth scene is ready to unfold.

Scene IV: The Repersonalizing Stage: The Transition from Pelvic to Person

During this stage of the interaction the patient undergoes a demetamorphosis, dramaturgically changing from vaginal object to person. Immediately after the doctor leaves, the nurse assists the patient into a sitting position, and she gets off the table. The nurse then asks the patient if she would like to use a towel to cleanse her genital area, and about 80 percent of the patients accept the offer. In this scene, it is not uncommon for patients to make some statement concerning their relief that the examination is over. Statements such as "I'm glad that's over with" seem to indicate the patient's overt recognition of the changing scene, to acknowledge that she is now entering a different scene in the vaginal drama.

During this repersonalizing stage the patient is concerned with regrooming and recostuming. Patients frequently ask if they look all right, and the common question, "My dress isn't too wrinkled, is it?" appears to indicate the patient's awareness of and desire to be ready for the resumption of roles other than vaginal object. Her dress isn't too wrinkled for what? It must be that she is asking whether it is too wrinkled (1) for her resumption of the role of (patient as) person and (2) her resumption of nonpatient roles.

Modesty continues to operate during this scene, and it is interesting that patients who have just had their genital area thoroughly examined both visually and tactually by the doctor are concerned that this same man will see their underclothing. ("He won't be in before I get my underwear on, will he?") They are now desiring and preparing for the return to the feminine role. They apparently fear that the doctor will reenter the room as they literally have one foot in and one foot out of their panties. They want to have their personal front reestablished to their own satisfaction before the return of this male and the onset of the next scene. For this, they strive for the poise and composure that they deem fitting the person role for which they are now preparing, frequently using either their own pocket-mirror or the mirror above the sink to check their personal front.

During this transitional role patients indicate by their comments to the nurse that they are to again be treated as persons. While they are dressing, they frequently speak about their medical problems, their aches and pains, their fight against gaining weight, or feelings about their pregnancy. In such ways they are reasserting the self and are indicating that they are again entering "personhood."

The patient who best illustrates awareness that she had undergone a process of repersonalization is the woman who, after putting on her panties, said, "There! Just like new again." She had indeed moved out of her necessary but uncomfortable role as object, and her appearance or personal front once again matched her self-concept.

After the patient has recostumed and regroomed, the nurse directs the patient to the chair alongside the doctor's desk, and she then announces via intercom to the doctor, "The patient is dressed," or, "The patient is waiting." It is significant that at this point the woman is referred to as "patient" in the announcement to the doctor and not as "pelvic" as she was at the end of second scene. Sometimes the patient is also referred to by name in this announcement. The patient has completed her demetamorphosis at this point, and the nurse, by the way she refers to her, is officially acknowledging the transition.

The nurse then leaves the room, and her interaction with the patient ceases.

Scene V: The Repersonalized Stage: The Patient as Person Once More

When the doctor makes his third entrance, the patient has again resumed the role of person and is interacted with on this basis. She is both spoken to and receives replies from the doctor, with her whole personal front being visible in the interaction. During this fifth scene the doctor informs the patient of the results of her examination, he prescribes necessary medications, and, wherever indicated, he suggests further care. He also tells the patient whether or not she need see him again.

The significance of the interaction of Scene V for us is that the patient is again allowed to interact *as a person within the role of patient*. The doctor allows room for questions that the patient might have about the results of the examination, and he also gives her the opportunity to ask about other medical problems that she might be experiencing.

Interaction between the doctor and patient terminates as the doctor gets up from his chair and moves toward the door.

Conclusion: Desexualization of the Sacred

In concluding this analysis, we shall briefly indicate that conceptualizing the vagina as a sacred object yields a perspective that appears to be of value in analyzing the vaginal examination. Sacred objects are surrounded by rules protecting the object from being profaned, rules governing who may approach the "sacred," under what circumstances it may be approached, and what may and may not be done during such an approach (Durkheim 1965: 51–59). If these rules are followed, the "sacred" will lose none of its "sacredness," but if they are violated, there is danger of the sacred being profaned.

In conceptualizing the vagina in this way, we find, for example, that who may and who may not approach the vagina is highly circumscribed, with the primary person so allowed being one who is ritually related to the possessor of the vagina, the husband. Apart from the husband (with contemporary changes duly noted),[6] except in a medical setting and by the actors about whom we are speaking, no one else may approach the vagina other than the self and still have it retain its sacred character.[7]

Because of this, the medical profession has taken great pains to establish a routine and ritual that will ensure the continued sacredness of the vaginas of its female patients, one that will avoid even the imputation of taboo violation. Accordingly, as we have herein analyzed, this ritual of the vaginal examination allows the doctor to approach the sacred without profaning it or violating taboos by dramaturgically defining the vagina as just another organ of the body, disassociating the vagina from the person, while desexualizing the person into a cooperative object.

Notes

1. With a society that is as clothing conscious and bodily conscious as is ours, undressing and nudity are probably problematic for almost everyone in our society from a very eary age. It is, however, probably more problematic for females than for males since males ordinarily experience structured situations in which they undress and are nude before others, such as showering after high school physical education classes, while females in the same situation are afforded a greater degree of privacy with, for example, private shower stalls in place of the mass showers of the males. Jim Hayes has given us a corroborating example. In the high school of 4,000 students that he attended in Brooklyn, swimming classes were segregated by sex. Male students swam nude in their physical education classes, but female students wore one-piece black bathing suits provided by the school. One can also think of the frequently traumatic, but required, en masse nudity experiences of males in military induction centers; such experiences are not forced upon our female population.

2. From a psychiatric orientation this association of the panties with the purse is fascinating, given the Freudian interpretation that the purse signifies the female genitalia.

In some examination rooms, the problem of where to put the undergarments is solved by the provision of a special drawer for them located beneath the examination table.

3. It is interesting to note that even the corpse of a female is defined as being

in need of such chaperonage. Erving Goffman, on reading this paper in manuscript form, commented that hospital etiquette dictates that "when a male attendant moves a female stiff from the room to the morgue he be accompanied by a female nurse."

4. Compare what Goffman (1959: 104) has to say about secrets shared by team members. Remember that the patient in this interaction is not simply a member of the audience. She is a team member, being also vitally interested in projecting and maintaining the definition of nonsexuality. Another reader of this paper, who wishes to remain anonymous, reports that during one of her pregnancies she had a handsome, young, and unmarried Hungarian doctor and that during vaginal examinations with him she would "concentrate on the instruments being used and the uncomfortableness of the situation" so as not to become sexually aroused.

5. In this situation a patient is "playing the role" of an object, but she is still able to hear verbal exchange, and she could enter the interaction if she so desired. As such, side comments between doctor and nurse must be limited. In certain other doctor–patient situations, however, the patient completely leaves the "person role," such as when the patient is anesthetized, which allows much freer banter. In delivery rooms of hospitals, for example, it is not uncommon for the obstetrician to comment while stitching the episiotomy, "She's like a new bride now," or, when putting in the final stitches, to say, "This is for the old man." Additionally, while medical students are stitching their first episiotomy, instructing doctors have been known to say, "It's not tight enough. Put one more in for the husband."

6. Consensual approaches by boyfriends certainly run less risk of violating the sacred than at earlier periods in our history, but this depends a good deal on religion, education, age, and social class membership.

7. It is perhaps for this reason that prostitutes ordinarily lack respect: They have profaned the sacred. And in doing so, not only have they failed to limit vaginal access to culturally prescribed individuals, but they have added further violation by allowing vaginal access on a pecuniary basis. They have, in effect, sold the sacred.

References

Durkheim, Emile (1965). *The Elementary Forms of the Religious Life.* New York: The Free Press (1915 copyright by George Allen and Unwin Ltd.)

Goffman, Erving (1959). *The Presentation of Self in Everyday Life.* Garden City, N.Y.: Doubleday, Anchor Books.

Goffman, Erving (1963). *Behavior in Public Places: Notes on the Social Organization of Gatherings.* New York: The Free Press.

Gross, Edward, and Gregory Stone (1964). "Embarrassment and the Analysis of Role Requirements," *American Journal of Sociology* 70:1–15.

15 Street Corner Society: The Social Structure of an Italian Slum

WILLIAM FOOTE WHYTE

To many Americans ethnicity is relatively unimportant. ("My great grandparents came from Germany. So what?") To others, ethnicity is a central feature of their lives. This is especially the case for many poor Americans who are now clustered together in relatively homogeneous areas variously known as ghettos, barrios, and slums. Here they share with other residents many customs not readily understood by people living elsewhere in that they are based on different experiences and sometimes contrasting values. They have developed institutions and expectations of one another that have helped them adapt to their impoverished life circumstances. With their common culture, they often form an in-group, looking outward at a larger society that they do not understand, while those in the larger society look at them, equally uncomprehending.

It is the inside story of such a group, with close boundaries drawn around themselves to separate them from others, that William Foote Whyte set out to get. He lived for three and a half years in what he calls Cornerville, observing and analyzing how people interact with one another. We can conclude from this selection, as well as from the previous ones, that one cannot understand the behavior of others until one can see things from their perspective.

You might wish to grapple with the question of how you can overcome your own perspectives (biases, socialization into particular views) in order to grasp the perspective of others.

THIS IS A REPORT UPON a three-and-a-half-year study of "Cornerville." My aim was to gain an intimate view of Cornerville life. My first problem, therefore, was to establish myself as a participant in the society so that I would have a position from which to observe. I began by going to live in Cornerville, finding a room with an Italian family. Since the mother and father of the family spoke no English, I began studying Italian. Conversations with them and practice with the Linguaphone enabled me to learn enough to talk fairly fluently with the older generation.

As I became largely concerned with the second-generation men, who conducted their activities in English, Italian was not essential to me; but the fact that I made the effort to learn the language was important, since it gave the impression that I had a sincere and sympathetic interest in Cornerville people.

Staying with an Italian family gave me a view of family life and also provided important contacts with the community. Through the family I met a cousin of State Senator George Ravello's secretary. Through the cousin I met the secretary, and through the secretary I met Ravello. In this way I was able to establish myself in the politician's office at a time when he was running for Congress. He had no opposition from within Cornerville in his campaign, which made it possible for me to work for him without losing standing with other local groups. During the campaign I did various odd jobs which were of no particular significance for the organization but which gave me an excuse for being around when things were happening. It was in this way that I found most of my material on politics.

I made my first contacts with the "corner boys" known as the Nortons through the Norton Street Settlement House. I subsequently learned that too close identification with the settlement would prevent me from becoming intimate with the rank and file of the people, but at this time I was fortunate in meeting corner boys who, while they had some contact with the settlement, also had a recognized position outside of it. Through the Nortons I came to know the college men of the Italian Community Club.

After I had lived eighteen months with the Italian family, I married, and my wife and I moved into a flat on Shelby Street. This opened for me a new field of contacts. One evening I went with the son of my Italian family to a banquet in honor of the local police lieutenant. There were three main groups of people present: policemen, politicians, and racketeers. My companion had met Tony Cataldo, a prominent local racketeer, and Tony had seen me around his district. We became acquainted in this way, and shortly thereafter Tony invited my wife and me to dinner at his house. We spent a number of evenings with the Cataldos and also came to know other members of the family. In order to study the influence of the racketeer upon a specific group of people, I joined the Cornerville Social and Athletic Club. Since the organization was located on Shelby Street, my contacts made it quite natural for me to join.

It was not enough simply to make the acquaintance of various groups of people. The sort of information that I sought required that I establish intimate social relations, and that presented special problems. Since illegal activities are prevalent in Cornerville, every newcomer is under suspicion. So that I would not be taken for a "G-man," I had to have some way of explaining my presence. I began by telling people that I was studying the history of Cornerville since the beginning of the Italian immigration, but

I used this story only a few times. I found that in each group I met there was one man who directed the activities of his fellows and whose word carried authority. Without his support, I was excluded from the group; with his support, I was accepted. Since he had to take the responsibility of vouching for me, I made a practice of talking with him quite frankly about the questions in which I was interested. When his friends questioned him, he knew much more about me than they did, and he was therefore in a position to reassure them. In the course of my stay in Cornerville, several of these men came to have a very clear and detailed idea of the nature of my research, and this knowledge made it possible for them to help me by observing and discussing with me the sort of situations in which I was interested. . . .

It is customary for the sociologist to study the slum district in terms of "social disorganization" and to neglect to see that an area such as Cornerville has a complex and well-established organization of its own. I was interested in that organization. I found that in every group there was a hierarchical structure of social relations binding the individuals to one another and that the groups were also related hierarchically to one another. Where the group was formally organized into a political club, this was immediately apparent, but for informal groups it was no less true. While the relations in such groups were not formally prescribed, they could be clearly observed in the interactions of individuals. To determine the relative standing of members of the group, I paid particular attention to the origination of action. When the group or several of its members engaged in some common activity, I wanted to know who suggested what was to be done and whose agreement was necessary before the action could be carried out. . . .

The corner boys do not explicitly recognize the structure of the gang, but it is implicit in all their actions. When, toward the end of my study, I discussed these matters with my informants, I made them conscious of the nature of their unreflective behavior. To that extent I changed the situation: the men talked to me about things that they had never formulated before. This did not mean that they were enabled to act more effectively. Doc, my chief informant, once told me:

> You've slowed me up plenty since you've been down here. Now when I do something, I have to think what Bill Whyte would want to know about it and how I can explain it. . . . Before I used to do these things by instinct.

This awareness, however, contributed toward building up a systematic picture of the corner gang. . . .

The life of the corner boy proceeds along regular and narrowly circumscribed channels. As Doc said to me:

> Fellows around here don't know what to do except within a radius of about three hundred yards. That's the truth, Bill. They come home from work,

hang on the corner, go up to eat, back on the corner, up a show, and they come back to hang on the corner. If they're not on the corner, it's likely the boys there will know where you can find them. Most of them stick to one corner. It's only rarely that a fellow will change his corner.

The stable composition of the group and the lack of social assurance on the part of its members contribute toward producing a very high rate of social interaction within the group. The group structure is a product of these interactions.

Out of such interaction there arises a system of mutual obligations which is fundamental to group cohesion. If the men are to carry on their activities as a unit, there are many occasions when they must do favors for one another. The code of the corner boy requires him to help his friends when he can and to refrain from doing anything to harm them. When life in the group runs smoothly, the obligations binding members to one another are not explicitly recognized. Once Doc asked me to do something for him, and I said that he had done so much for me that I welcomed the chance to reciprocate. He objected: "I don't want it that way. I want you to do this for me because you're my friend. That's all."

It is only when the relationship breaks down that the underlying obligations are brought to light. While Alec and Frank were friends, I never heard either one of them discuss the services he was performing for the other, but when they had a falling-out over the group activities with the Aphrodite Club, each man complained to Doc that the other was not acting as he should in view of the services that had been done him. In other words, actions which were performed explicitly for the sake of friendship were revealed as being part of a system of mutual obligations.

Not all the corner boys live up to their obligations equally well, and this factor partly accounts for the differentiation in status among them. The man with a low status may violate his obligations without much change in his position. His fellows know that he has failed to discharge certain obligations in the past, and his position reflects his past performances. On the other hand, the leader is depended upon by all the members to meet his personal obligations. He cannot fail to do so without causing confusion and endangering his position. . . .

A man with a low position in the group is less flexible in his adjustments than the leader, who customarily deals with groups outside of his own. . . . However, no matter what the corner boy's position, he suffers when the manner of his interaction must undergo drastic changes. This is clearly illustrated in the case of . . . Doc's dizzy spells. . . .

Doc's dizzy spells came upon him when he was unemployed and had no spending money. He considered his unemployment the cause of his difficulties, and, in a sense, it was, but in order to understand the case it is necessary to inquire into the changes which unemployment necessitated in the activity of the individual. While no one enjoys being unemployed and without money, there are many Cornerville men who could adjust themselves to that situation without serious difficulties. Why was Doc so different? To say that he was a particularly sensitive person simply gives a name to the phenomenon and provides no answer. The observation of interactions provides the answer. Doc was accustomed to a high frequency of interaction with the members of his group and to frequent contacts with members of other groups. While he sometimes directly originated action in set events for the group, it was customary for one of the other members to originate action for him in a pair event, and then he would originate action in a set event. That is, someone would suggest a course of action, and then Doc would get the boys together and organize group activity. The events of Doc's political campaign indicate that this pattern had broken down. Mike was continually telling Doc what to do about the campaign, and I was telling him what to do about seeing Mr. Smith and others to get a job. While we originated action for him with increasing frequency, he was not able to originate action in set events. Lacking money, he could not participate in group activities without accepting the support of others and letting them determine his course of action. Therefore, on many occasions he avoided associating with his friends—that is, his frequency of interaction was drastically reduced. At a time when he should have been going out to make contacts with other groups, he was unable to act according to the political pattern even with the groups that he knew, and he saw less and less of those outside his circle of closest friends. When he was alone, he did not get dizzy, but, when he was with a group of people and was unable to act in his customary manner, he fell prey to the dizzy spells. . . .

The type of explanation suggested to account for the difficulties of . . . Doc has the advantage that it rests upon the objective study of actions. A man's attitudes cannot be observed but instead must be inferred from his behavior. Since actions are directly subject to observation and may be recorded like other scientific data, it seems wise to try to understand man through studying his actions. This approach not only provides information upon the nature of informal group relations but it also offers a framework for the understanding of the individual's adjustment to his society. . . .

According to Cornerville people, society is made up of big people and little people—with intermediaries serving to bridge the gaps between them. The masses of Cornerville people are little people. They cannot approach the big people directly but must have an intermediary to intercede for them. They gain this intercession by establishing connections with the intermediary, by performing services for him, and thus making him obligated to them. The intermediary performs the same functions for the big man. The interactions of big shots, intermediaries, and little guys build up a hierarchy of personal relations based upon a system of reciprocal obligations.

Corner gangs such as the Nortons and the cliques of the Cornerville Social and Athletic Club fit in at the bottom of the hierarchy, although certain social distinctions are made between them. Corner-boy leaders like Doc, Dom Romano, and Carlo Tedesco served as intermediaries, representing the interests of their followers to the higher-ups. Chick and his college boys ranked above the corner boys, but they stood at the bottom of another hierarchy, which was controlled from outside the district. There are, of course, wide differences in rank between big shots. Viewed from the street corner of Shelby Street, Tony Cataldo was a big shot, and the relations of the corner-boy followers to him were regulated by their leaders. On the other hand, he served as an intermediary, dealing with big shots for the corner boys and trying to control the corner boys for the big shots. T. S., the racket boss, and George Ravello, the state senator, were the biggest men in Cornerville. T. S. handled those below him through his immediate subordinates. While Ravello refused to allow any formal distinctions to come between himself and the corner boys, the man at the bottom fared better when he approached the politician through an intermediary who had a connection than when he tried to bridge the gap alone.

The corner gang, the racket and police organizations, the political organization, and now the social structure have all been described and analyzed in terms of a hierarchy of personal relations based upon a system of reciprocal obligations. These are the fundamental elements of which all Cornerville institutions are constructed. . . .

16 The VFW and the "Iron Law of Oligarchy"

ELAINE FOX

GEORGE E. ARQUITT

In the introduction to Part IV I stressed that membership in voluntary associations requires us to relinquish to others some degree of control over our lives. Something that often surprises people is how democratic many such organizations seem or claim to be, but how concentrated the power in those organizations really is. The more familiar we become with the organization, in fact, the more likely we are to observe that power not only is unevenly distributed but, in fact, tends to be passed from one leader to another.

Although the organization's constitution and by-laws say one thing, the reality is usually something different. Why should this be? Are there characteristics of human organizations that encourage the concentration of power? Fox and Arquitt's look behind the scenes at the local VFW helps explain this phenomenon—and in so doing may help you account for what you have experienced in many situations, from high school leadership to scouts and fraternal and religious organizations. Again, what things look like is not necessarily the way they are; that is, appearance is often—indeed usually—not the reality.

ROBERT MICHELS (1915) WAS ONE OF THE FIRST sociologists to identify organizational inconsistencies when he analyzed and interpreted what was happening in the development of the German Social Democratic Party. He made a number of generalizations concerning what he saw as the inevitable results of large scale organization. Michels (1915:393–409) argued that every organization, no matter how egalitarian its roots or how democratic its governing procedures, will inevitably become an oligarchy, that is, an organization controlled by a small self-perpetuating elite group. He refers to this tendency of large membership organizations to become controlled by an elite few as the "iron law of oligarchy." Michels indicates that the basis of this inevitable tendency toward oligarchy in democratic organization ". . . is to be found in the technical indispensability of leadership. This process . . . is completed by a complex of qualities which the leaders acquire through their detachment from the mass. At the outset, leaders arise spontaneously; their functions are accessory and gratuitous. Soon, however, they become professional leaders, and in this second stage of development they are stable and ir-removable" (Michels, 1915: 417–418).

He saw this tendency as the result of "organic necessity" and therefore as present in every large organization. This tendency toward oligarchy is inevitable due simply to the fact that large size and an elaborate division of labor require centralization and regulation for effective action (Michels, 1915: 421).

Further, Michels (1915: 417) points out that there is a tendency for leaders to organize themselves and to consolidate their interests, for the masses to develop a sense of gratitude towards the leaders and for the masses to be generally immobile, passive, and immature. . . .

Finally, Michels suggests that the overall objectives of the organization might change. The essence of this is "the domination of the elected over the electors" (Michels, 1915: 418). The ultimate result of this is often a total restructuring of the major goals of the organization. It is not un-usual for new goals to be in direct opposition to initial goals with a limited awareness of this on the part of the masses. The "power of the elected leaders over the electing masses is almost unlimited" (Michels, 1915: 418).

Olsen (1968: 310) has interpreted and identified the following major points made by Michels:

1. Large size and an elaborate division of labor necessitate centralized coordination and regulation for effective action.
2. Collective decisions on complex organizational matters can be made speedily and efficiently only by a few elites.
3. Incumbents of leadership positions become indispensable as they develop special skills and experience in running the organization, so that other members cannot afford to deprive them of power.
4. Over time, leaders build up a legitimate right to high office, as well as an extensive web of personal influence, which further increases their power.
5. Leaders acquire dominant control over organizational finances, communications, disciplinary agencies, and so on, all of which they can use to their own advantage.
6. Leaders are normally more unified than other members, and hence they can effectively thwart or absorb (coopt) potential challengers.
7. Most rank-and-file members tend to be indifferent and apathetic toward the organization and its problems, and are only too happy to leave the problems of leadership to those who are willing to assume them. . . .

The purpose of our study was to look at the organizational characteristics of the Veterans of Foreign Wars Association from the theoretical perspective suggested by Michels. This, we hope, will further our understanding of the organizational behavior of the VFW and large democratic organizations in general. . . .

Research data for this paper were secured over a three-month period using participant observation and interviews at three VFW posts in Oklahoma. Initially one of the researchers joined the VFW and utilized club facilities, as a member, at least twice weekly for over two months prior to initiating interviews. Thus, the researcher was acquainted with or at least familiar to most of the respondents, having first established rapport and credibility as a participating member of the organization. . . .

Interviews were loosely structured and allowed for open-ended responses. . . . An attempt was made to insure that respondents interviewed varied with respect to length of membership and age. Interviews generally lasted no more than forty-five minutes and were tape-recorded except in those cases where the respondent objected to the procedure. This occurred only three times out of fifty interviews. . . .

The Veterans of Foreign Wars

The VFW was established in 1913 by combining three existing organizations: the Army of the Philippines, American Veterans of Foreign Service, and the Army of the Philippines, Cuba and Puerto Rico. After an initial slow start of several decades, this organization, like many other militarily inspired organizations, enjoyed an increase in membership during the years following World War I and continuing well into the late 1930s. Its membership is open to any serviceman who has honorably served in any foreign war, insurrection, or expedition for which service has been recognized as "campaign-medal service" and governed by the government of the United States (Constitution and Bylaws of the VFW).

A local VFW post may be formed by the authority of the Commander-in-Chief on the application of not less than twenty-five persons eligible for membership. From this point on, the organizational make up of the VFW is similar to that of all other clubs having local, state and national chapters. Each member of the local post has the right to vote on all local business. Delegates are elected from each post to represent their constituency at the district, state and national levels. Every member of the organization has the right to be elected to positions of leadership within the organization based on democratic procedures. . . . Local chapters are under the domain of national headquarters (Constitution and Bylaws of the VFW). . . .

. . . In the three VFW posts visited by the researchers, participants were generally employed in blue-collar occupations. Of those respondents interviewed, most listed jobs in such areas as cab driving, janitorial services, automobile repair, or some types of skilled or semi-skilled labor. Very few members interviewed over the three-month time span identified themselves as college graduates; however, those who did usually had completed their degrees using the GI bill after retiring from active service. Those members with some college or holding degrees generally were in positions of leadership within the organization. . . .

Within the three VFW posts included in this research, there appear to be three distinct categories of members. The first of these categories is the "silent majority," or those individuals holding membership but who rarely participate in any of the local post meetings. These individuals occasionally visit the post facilities with the primary intention of playing bingo, dancing, or utilizing the bar. They are not generally known by the more devoted members and appear to have little effect on the organizational proceedings. The other two categories of members are clearly visible, frequent the local posts with great regularity, and know each other by name. These remaining categories include "leaders" and "rank and file members." . . .

Comparison of Leaders and Rank and File Members

DRINKERS AND WORKERS

VFW members label themselves as "drinking or social" members and "working members," with much respect being awarded the "working" or leadership group by the drinking members. This respect is not necessarily reciprocal and the leaders of the organization interact with the "drinking members" by exercising considerable tolerance on frequent occasions. The leaders are skillful at concealing their contempt for the drinking membership while interacting with them. However, during interviews they often expressed contempt for the "old boozers" who impeded the growth and operation of the organization.

The "working members" are generally those persons who presently hold some position of authority in the organization. These leaders attend business meetings at the local, state and, occasionally, national level; are knowledgeable with regard to the organizational make-up of the post; appear to be on intimate terms with other leaders; and, with few exceptions, are the most articulate, educated, and informed members of the organization. Most leaders give a history of having served within the noncommissioned officer ranks while in military service. In short, those individuals best suited for presenting a dignified and businesslike appearance to the public are the individuals who represent the organization in the form of elected officials.

In contrast, in the interview situation, "drinking members" were seldom articulate, at ease socially or very well informed. Aside from differences in personal appearance and interactional skills, the clearest distinction between leaders and rank and file members was the way in which they perceived the VFW as a national organization. The leaders tended to view the VFW on a macro level. The term VFW represented to the leadership the entire body of 1.8 million members and even when questioned regarding any aspect of the local VFW post they tended to respond in terms of the national organization. Rank and file members seldom, even under direct prodding, focused attention beyond the local level.

Drinking members were concerned only with local club activity and quickly identified themselves as such to the interviewer. Common responses from drinking members included such statements as: "I don't know much about that. I just come to enjoy the bar" or "I'm just a social member. I don't keep up with the business part."

All drinking members were quick to point out various leaders within the post and frequently referred the interviewer to those persons. "Ask Sam those questions. He knows about that stuff." All referrals were to leaders of the post and never to another rank and file member. The differentiation between leaders and rank and file members was clearly recognized and accepted by all members. Leadership positions are legitimated by the membership based on an assumption of superior knowledge on the part of those in authority. This is in accordance with Michels's observations regarding leadership positions within large organizations in contrast with the masses.

PASSING AROUND POWER

There appears to be a circulation of positions of leadership within the organization. Leaders pass the various authority positions around among themselves. An example of this was demonstrated on several occasions during referrals to working members. "You need to meet Jim. He's the next post commander after Sam does his time." Although the constitution of the organization clearly outlines a democratic election procedure which guarantees each member having the opportunity to be elected to a leadership role, most individuals in the organization could identify the next individual destined to hold the title of post commander. "Well, Jim will be the next commander. He's service officer now." Service officer is an appointed position and appears to be a step in the hierarchy of leadership positions one must assume before gaining the post commander position. It appears that there exists a clear ordering of leadership positions and post commanders work their way up the leadership ladder by serving time in various positions of authority, although this arrangement is informal. Since a large portion of leadership roles are appointed, leaders are able to maintain control by appointing members of the inner circle to these positions.

This rotation of elites through the positions of authority is justified in the perceptions of those who hold authority status, as is evidenced by an observation offered by a post commander. "Certainly everyone has the same rights within this organization but, let's face it, many people don't care, particularly the 'lushes'. If we want to grow and become stronger we need to ensure that individuals who are aware and willing to work are those who are elected." And most assuredly, those who are aware and willing to work are those who become elected to positions of leadership. Again, this is clear evidence for the tendency of the majority of the rank and file to abdicate power.

According to Michels, over time, leaders aid in the legitimation of their positions through development of an extensive web of personal influence. This appears to be valid in the case of the VFW. Many leaders of various posts were acquainted with each other. The interviewer was entrusted with messages to leaders of other posts. "When you go to interview in Ponca City, say hello to Joe [post commander of Ponca City VFW] for me and tell him to come down deer hunting soon." This informal or "old boy" network was extensive and included leaders not only in other posts but also leaders at the state level. This network of personal influence was lacking among the rank and file to the extent that many drinking members were unaware of various other posts within the region, much less familiar with the leaders of other posts.

IDEOLOGICAL SPLITS

The differing ideologies expressed by leaders and rank and file members serve to reinforce Michels's view that leaders develop values which are at odds with those of the membership body. This is best evidenced by the responses of both groups with regard to the perceived purpose and function of the VFW. All of the interviewed leaders saw the organization as an activist group working for the protection of veterans' rights. When pressed for secondary functions, such responses as concern with national defense, promotion of patriotism and charitable works were common. For the rank and file membership, the generic response involved concern with maintenance of a congenial bar atmosphere. When pressed for further detail, drinking members cited obscure functions such as "help the veteran" although most were unsure of exactly how this was accomplished within the organizational framework.

An interesting aspect of the opposing ideologies was observed when the term "political group" was utilized during interviews. Leaders of the organization readily acknowledged that the VFW is indeed a political group and expressed hope that more political power would soon be realized. Rank and file members were adamant in their positions that the VFW could not be conceptualized as a political organization. As one drinking member explained, "We are a bipartisan party. We don't support any special group. We are not political at all. We're just for America and not any man." Contrast that viewpoint with one offered by a leader; "Yes, we must necessarily consider ourselves a political group. Government is politics and in order to have a voice in our government we must play ball in a political ballfield." . . .

For the rank and file member of the post, the local VFW offered not an opportunity to participate politically but rather an environment which produced a sense of *gemeinschaft*. Many of these drinking members had no family and appeared to have few ties with persons outside the organization. As one member explained, "I have no family except these people here. I know I can come and drink and not get into a fight and will be taken care of. These are my people." And to a large extent this is true. On several occasions members were observed drinking to the point of intoxication and incapacitation. When this occurred it was the responsibility of the bartender to place the drunken member in a cab and direct it to the patron's home.

Although the large numbers of drinking members were held frequently in contempt by the leadership, the practice of controlling the consumption of alcohol for members was not enforced nor did leaders interfere with the practice of bartenders assuming responsibility for intoxicated members. In view of the contempt the leaders held for their drinking compatriots, the tolerance of drinking members is an interesting point. Several leaders commented on the apparent lack of commitment to organizational goals these drinking members displayed although one post commander explained, "We hope to eventually turn these people around and make them understand the importance of the fight for veterans rights. Some of them we can, but for those we can't—they still represent membership and large membership means more power."

Within the VFW posts included in this research, a demarcation between leaders and rank and file members was clearly demonstrated time and again to fit the typology laid out by Michels with regard to power networks and ideological differences.

Goal Reorganization over Time

As stated earlier, Michels noted the tendency for large organizations to change their objectives over time. Garner (1977) refers to this tendency as goal displacement. MacIver and Page (1971) attribute this change to the necessity for the organization to insure its continuation. As they explain

> Organizations of people, like the individuals themselves, are tenacious of life. They refuse to die when their day is past. New interests are thus sought within them which will justify their existence in a continuing purpose. This organizational "Will to live" centers in the officials, in the occupants of the "Bureaucratic structure."

The VFW can be seen as having altered its expressed purpose over time in order to ensure its survival. In the period from the 1930s through the 1950s, the VFW was considered to be primarily concerned with anti-communist oriented goals. The concentration of the organization on communist hunts died with the McCarthy era. While the promotion of patriotism is viewed as lying within the realm of the organizational purpose, it has decreased in importance compared with the concern for veterans' rights. The VFW leaders therefore changed the objectives of the organization as a means of maintaining the organization and its oligarchic structure.

The perceived purposes of the organization, particularly those views expressed by the leadership, give credibility to those who have observed the tendency of goals to change within large organizations, inasmuch as the constitution of the organization clearly states the purpose of the organization to be that of a fraternal group primarily concerned with charitable acts and remembrance of the war dead with inherent patriotic philosophies. Thus, since its establishment, the purpose of the organization has become altered in the perceptions of its member to such a degree that leaders quote such purposes only secondarily and then only upon prompting. Presently, retention of veterans rights is of foremost concern to members. . . .

Conclusion

We have attempted to present an analysis of the VFW utilizing Michels's "iron law of oligarchy." A clear distinction between leaders and rank and file members is evidenced by the research. Michels posits that inherent in all large membership organizations is the tendency of those organizations to become bureaucratic in nature. We have found this to be so in the VFW as demonstrated by the elite leadership segments, as opposed to the rank and file membership, and the alteration of the VFW goals over time. . . . It is indeed possible that the area of veterans rights may be the mobilizing focus for renewed spirit in this organization. There is little reason to believe, however, that this change will have a significant impact on the organizational structure itself. It will function to strengthen and, therefore, maintain the developed oligarchy.

References

Garner, Roberta Ash (1977). *Social Change.* Chicago: Rand McNally College Publishing Company.

MacIver, R. M., and C. H. Page (1971). "On Associations and Interests." In M. Truzzi (ed.), *The Classic Statements.* New York: Random House.

Michels, Robert (1915). *Political Parties.* Glencoe, Ill.: The Free Press.

Olsen, Marvin E. (1968). *The Process of Social Organization.* New York: Holt, Rinehart and Winston, Inc.

17 Hanging Tongues: A Sociological Encounter with the Assembly Line

WILLIAM E. THOMPSON

Few of us are born so wealthy—or so deprived—that we do not have to work for a living. Some jobs seem to be of little importance, as with those in high school and college. We simply take what is available and look at it as a temporary activity to help us get by for the time being. When its time is up, we discard it as we would worn-out clothing. In contrast, the jobs we take after we have completed our education—those full-time, more or less permanent endeavors at which we labor so long and hard—in these we invest much of ourselves. In turn, as our schedules come to revolve around their demands, we become aware of how central these jobs are to our lives.

All jobs, however, whether full-time and permanent or temporary, expedient, and discarded, are significant to our lives. Each contributes in its own way to our thinking and attitudes, becoming a part of the general stockpile of experiences that culminates in our basic orientation to life. Because of the significance of work for our lives, then, sociologists pay a great deal of attention to the work setting. They focus on interaction in that setting, as well as the consequences of the work (including its organization, constraints, benefits, and other outcomes).

Of all jobs, one of the most demanding, demeaning, and demoralizing is that of the assembly line. Those of us who have worked on an assembly line have shared a work experience unlike any other, and for many of us education was the way by which we escaped this form of modern slavery. As Thompson examines the assembly line in the meat packing industry, he makes evident how this job affects all aspects of the workers' lives. It provides a good framework for you to use in reflecting on your own work experiences.

THIS QUALITATIVE SOCIOLOGICAL STUDY analyzes the experience of working on a modern assembly line in a large beef plant. It explores and examines a special type of assembly line work which involves the slaughtering and processing of cattle into a variety of products intended for human consumption and other uses.

Working in the beef plant is "dirty work," not only in the literal sense of being drenched with perspiration and beef blood, but also in the figurative sense of performing a low status, routine, and demeaning job. Although the work is honest and necessary in a society which consumes beef, slaughtering and butchering cattle is generally viewed as an undesirable and repugnant job. In that sense, workers at the beef plant share some of the same experiences as other workers in similarly regarded occupations (for example, ditchdiggers, garbage collectors, and other types of assembly line workers). . . .

The Setting

The setting for the field work was a major beef processing plant in the Midwest. At the time of the study, the plant was the third largest branch of a corporation which operated ten such plants in the United States. . . .

The beef plant was organizationally separated into two divisions: Slaughter and Processing. This study focused on the Slaughter division in the area of the plant known as the *kill floor*. A dominant feature of the kill floor was the machinery of the assembly line itself. The line was comprised of an overhead stainless steel rail which began at the slaughter chute and curved its way around every work station in the plant. Every work station contained specialized machinery for the job performed at that place on the line. Dangling from the rail were hundreds of stainless steel hooks pulled by a motorized chain. Virtually every part of the line and all of the implements (tubs, racks, knives, etc.) were made of stainless steel. The walls were covered with a ceramic tile and the floor was made of sealed cement. There were floor drains located at every work station, so that at the end of each work segment (at breaks, lunch, and shift's end) the entire kill floor could be hosed down and cleaned for the next work period.

Another dominant feature of the kill floor was the smell. Extremely difficult to describe, yet impossible to forget, this smell combined the smells of live cattle, manure, fresh beef blood, and internal organs and their contents. This smell not only permeated the interior of the plant, but was combined on the outside with the smell of smoke from various waste products being burned and could be smelled throughout much of the community. This smell contributed greatly to the general negative feelings about work at the beef plant, as it served as the most distinguishable symbol of the beef plant to the rest of the community. The single most often asked question of me during the research by those outside the beef plant was, "How do you stand the smell?" In typical line workers' fashion, I always responded, "What smell? All I smell at the beef plant is money."
. . .

Method

The method of this study was nine weeks of full-time participant observation as outlined by Schatzman and Strauss (1973) and Spradley (1979; 1980). To enter the setting, the researcher went through the standard application process for a summer job. No mention of the research intent was made, though it was made clear that I was a university sociology professor. After initial screening, a thorough physical examination, and a helpful reference from a former student and part-time employee of the plant, the author was hired to work on the *Offal* crew in the Slaughter division of the plant. . . .

The Work

. . . The line speed on the kill floor was 187. That means that 187 head of cattle were slaughtered per hour. At any particular work station, each worker was required to work at that speed. Thus, at my work station, in the period of one hour, 187 beef tongues were mechanically pulled from their hooks; dropped into a large tub filled with water; had to be taken from the tub and hung on a large stainless steel rack full of hooks; branded with a "hot brand" indicating they had been inspected by a USDA inspector; and then covered with a small plastic bag. The rack was taken to the cooler, replaced with an empty one, and the process began again.

It would be logical to assume that if a person worked at a steady, continuous pace of handling 187 tongues per hour, everything would go smoothly; not so. In addition to hanging, branding, and bagging tongues, the worker at that particular station also cleaned the racks and cleaned out a variety of empty stainless steel tubs used to hold hearts, kidneys, and other beef organs. Thus, in order to be free to clean the tubs when necessary, the "tongue-hanger" had to work at a slightly faster pace than the line moved. Then, upon returning from cleaning the tubs, the worker would be behind the line (*in a hole*) and had to work much faster to catch up with the line. Further, one fifteen minute break and a thirty minute lunch break were scheduled for an eight-hour shift. Before the "tongue-hanger" could leave his post for one of these, all tongues were required to be properly disposed of, all tubs washed and stored, and the work area cleaned.

The first two nights on the job, I discovered the consequences of working at the line speed (hanging, branding, and bagging each tongue as it fell in the tub). At the end of the work period when everybody else was leaving the work floor for break or lunch, I was furiously trying to wash all the tubs and clean the work area. Consequently, I missed the entire fifteen minute break and had only about ten minutes for lunch. By observing other workers, I soon caught on to the system. Rather than attempting to work at a steady pace consistent with the line speed, the norm was to work sporadically at a very frenzied pace, actually running ahead of the line and plucking tongues from the hooks before they got to the station. With practice, I learned to hang two or three tongues at a time, perform all the required tasks, and then take an unscheduled two or three minute break until the line caught up with me. Near break and lunch everybody worked at a frantic pace, got ahead of the line, cleaned the work areas, and even managed to add a couple of minutes to the scheduled break or lunch.

Working ahead of the line seems to have served as more than merely a way of gaining a few minutes of extra break time. It also seemed to take on a symbolic meaning. The company controlled the speed of the line. Seemingly, that took all element of control over the work process away from the workers. . . . However, when the workers refused to work at line speed and actually worked faster than the line, they not only added a few minutes of relaxation from the work while the line caught up, but they symbolically regained an element of control over the pace of their own work. . . .

Coping

One of the difficulties of work at the beef plant was coping with three aspects of the work: monotony, danger, and dehumanization. While individual workers undoubtedly coped in a variety of ways, some distinguishable patterns emerged.

MONOTONY

The monotony of the line was almost unbearable. At my work station, a worker would hang, brand, and bag between 1,350 and 1,500 beef tongues in an eight-hour shift. With the exception of the scheduled 15 minute break and a 30 minute lunch period (and sporadic brief gaps in the line), the work was mundane, routine, and continuous. As in most assembly line work, one inevitably drifted into daydreams (e.g., Garson, 1975; King, 1978; Linhart, 1981). It was not unusual to look up or down the line and see workers at various stations singing to themselves, tapping their feet to imaginary music, or carrying on conversations with themselves. I found that I could work with virtually no attention paid to the job, with my hands and arms almost automatically performing their tasks. In the meantime, my mind was free to wander over a variety of topics, including taking mental notes. In visiting with other workers, I found that daydreaming was the norm. Some would think about their families, while others fantasized about sexual escapades, fishing, or anything unrelated to the job. One individual who was rebuilding an antique car at home in his spare time would meticulously mentally rehearse the procedures he was going to perform on the car the next day.

Daydreaming was not inconsequential, however. During these periods, items were most likely to be dropped, jobs improperly performed, and accidents incurred. Inattention to detail around moving equipment, stainless steel hooks, and sharp knives invariably leads to dangerous consequences. Although I heard rumors of drug use to help fight the monotony, I never saw any workers take any drugs nor saw any drugs in any workers' possession. It is certainly conceivable that some workers might have taken something to help them escape the reality of the line, but the nature of the work demanded enough attention that such a practice could be ominous.

DANGER

The danger of working in the beef plant was well known. Safety was top priority (at least in theory) and management took pride in the fact that only three employee on-the-job deaths had occurred in 12 years. Although deaths were uncommon, serious injuries were not. The beef plant employed over 1,800 people. Approximately three-fourths of those employed had jobs which demanded the use of a knife honed to razor-sharpness. Despite the use of wire-mesh aprons and gloves, serious cuts were almost a daily occurrence. Since workers constantly handled beef blood, danger of infection was ever present. As one walked along the assembly line, a wide assortment of bandages on fingers, hands, arms, necks, and faces could always be seen.

In addition to the problem of cuts, workers who cut meat continuously sometimes suffered muscle and ligament damage to their fingers and hands. In one severe case, I was told of a woman who worked in processing for several years who had to wear splints on her fingers while away from the job to hold them straight. Otherwise, the muscles in her hand would constrict her fingers into the grip position, as if holding a knife. . . .

When I spoke with fellow workers about the dangers of working in the plant, I noticed interesting defense mechanisms. . . . After a serious accident, or when telling about an accident or death which occurred in years past, the workers would almost immediately disassociate themselves from the event and its victim. Workers tended to view those who suffered major accidents or death on the job in much the same way that non-victims of crime often view crime victims as either partially responsible for the event, or at least as very different from themselves (Barlow, 1981).

"Only a part-timer," "stupid," "careless" or something similar was used, seemingly to reassure the worker describing the accident that it could not happen to him. The reality of the situation was that virtually all the jobs on the kill floor were dangerous, and any worker could have experienced a serious injury at any time. . . .

DEHUMANIZATION

Perhaps the most devastating aspect of working at the beef plant (worse than the monotony and the danger) was the dehumanizing and demeaning elements of the job. In a sense, the assembly line worker became a part of the assembly line. The assembly line is not a tool used by the worker, but a machine which controls him/her. A tool can only be productive in the hands of somebody skilled in its use, and hence becomes an extension of the person using it. A machine, on the other hand, performs specific tasks, thus its operator becomes an extension of it in the production process. . . . When workers are viewed as mere extensions of the machines with which they work, their human needs become secondary in importance to the smooth mechanical functioning of the production process. In a bureaucratic structure, when "human needs collide with systems needs the individual suffers" (Hummel, 1977:65).

Workers on the assembly line are seen as interchangeable as the parts of the product on the line itself. An example of one worker's perception of this phenomenon at the beef plant was demonstrated the day after a fatal accident occurred. I asked the men in the our crew what the company did in the case of an employee death (I wondered if there was a fund for flowers, or if the shift was given time off to go to the funeral, etc.). One worker's response was: "They drag off the body, take the hard hat and boots and check 'em out to some other poor sucker, and throw him in the guy's place." While employee death on the job was not viewed quite that coldly by the company, the statement fairly accurately summarized the overall result of a fatal accident, and importance of any individual worker to the overall operation of the production process. It accurately summarized the workers' perceptions about management's attitudes toward them. . . .

Sabotage

It is fairly common knowledge that assembly line work situations often lead to employee sabotage or destruction of the product or equipment used in the production process (Garson, 1975; Balzer, 1976; Shostak, 1980). This is the classic experience of alienation as described by Marx (1964a,b). . . . At the beef plant I quickly learned that there was an art to effective sabotage. Subtlety appeared to be the key. "The art lies in sabotaging in a way that is not immediately discovered," as a Ford worker put it (King, 1978:202). This seemed to hold true at the beef plant as well. . . .

The greatest factor influencing the handling of beef plant products was its status as a food product intended for human consumption. . . . Though not an explicitly altruistic group, the workers realized that the product would be consumed by people (even family, relatives, and friends), so consequently, they rarely did anything to actually contaminate the product.

Despite formal norms against sabotage, some did occur. It was not uncommon for workers to deliberately cut chunks out of pieces of meat for no reason (or for throwing at other employees). While regulations required that anything that touched the floor had to be put in tubs marked "inedible," the informal procedural norms were otherwise. When something was dropped, one usually looked around to see if an inspector or foreman noticed. If not, the item was quickly picked up and put back on the line.

Several explanations might be offered for this type of occurrence. First, since the company utilized a profit-sharing plan, when workers damaged the product, or had to throw edible pieces into inedible tubs (which sold for pet food at much lower prices), profits were decreased. A decrease in profits to the company ultimately led to decreased dividend checks to employees. Consequently, workers were fairly careful not to actually ruin anything. Second, when something was dropped or mishandled and had to be rerouted to "inedible", it was more time-consuming than if the product had been handled properly and kept on the regular line. In other words, if no inspector noticed, it was easier to let it go through on the line. There was a third, and seemingly more meaningful explanation for this behavior, however. It was against the rules to do it, it was a challenge to do it, and thus it was fun to do it.

The workers practically made a game out of doing forbidden things simply to see if they could get away with it. . . . New workers were routinely socialized into the subtle art of rulebreaking as approved by the line workers. At my particular work station, it was a fairly common practice for other workers who were covered with beef blood to come over to the tub of swirling water designed to clean the tongues, and as soon as the inspector looked away, wash their hands, arms, and knives in the tub. This procedure was strictly forbidden by the rules. If witnessed by a foreman or inspector, the tub had to be emptied, cleaned, and refilled, and all the tongues in the tub at the time had to be put in the "inedible" tub. All of that would be a time-consuming and costly procedure, yet the workers seemed to absolutely delight in successfully pulling off the act. As Balzer (1976:90) indicates:

Since a worker often feels that much if not all of what he does is done in places designated by the company, under company control, finding ways to express personal freedom from this institutional regimentation is important.

Thus, artful sabotage served as a symbolic way in which the workers could express a sense of individuality, and hence, self-worth.

The Financial Trap

Given the preceding description and analysis of work at the beef plant, why did people work at such jobs? Obviously, there are a multitude of plausible answers to that question. Without doubt, however, the key is money. The current economic situation, the lack of steady employment opportunities (especially for the untrained and poorly educated), combined with the fact that the beef plant's starting wage exceeded the minimum wage by approximately $5.50 per hour emerge as the most important reasons people went to work there.

Despite the high hourly wage and fringe benefits, however, the monotony, danger, and hard physical work drove many workers away in less than a week. During my study, I observed much worker turnover. Those who stayed displayed an interesting pattern which helps explain why they did not leave. Every member of my work crew answered similarly my questions about why they stayed at the beef plant. Each of them took the job directly after high school, because it was the highest paying job available. Each of them had intended to work through the summer and then look for a better job in the fall. During that first summer on the job they fell victim to what I label the "financial trap."

The "financial trap" was a spending pattern which demanded the constant weekly income provided by the beef plant job. This scenario was first told to me by an employee who had worked at the plant for over nine years. He began the week after his high school graduation, intending only to work that summer in order to earn enough money to attend college in the fall. After about four weeks' work he purchased a new car. He figured he could pay off the car that summer and still save enough money for tuition. Shortly after the car purchase, he added a new stereo sound system to his debt; next came a motorcycle; then the decision to postpone school for one year in order to continue working at the beef plant and pay off his debts. A few months later he married; within a year purchased a house; had a child; and bought another new car. Nine years later, he was still working at the beef plant, hated every minute of it, but in his own words "could not afford to quit." His case was not unique. Over and over again, I heard stories about the same process of falling into the "financial trap."

The youngest and newest of our crew had just graduated high school and took the job for the summer in order to earn enough money to attend welding school the following fall. During my brief tenure at the beef plant, he purchased a new motorcycle, a new stereo, and a house trailer. When I left, he told me he had decided to postpone welding school for one year in order "to get everything paid for." I saw the financial trap closing in on him fast; he did too. . . .

Summary and Conclusions

There are at least three interwoven phenomena in this study which deserve further comment and research.

First is the subtle sense of unity which existed among the line workers. . . . The line both symbolically and literally linked every job, and consequently every worker, to each other. . . . A system of "uncooperative teamwork" seemed to combine simultaneously a feeling of "one-for-all, all-for-one, and every man for himself." Once a line worker made it past the first three or four days on the job which "weeded out" many new workers, his status as a *beefer* was assured and the sense of unity was felt as much by the worker of nine weeks as it was by the veteran of nine years. Because the workers maintained largely secondary relationships, this feeling of unification is not the same as the unity typically found on athletic teams, in fraternities, or among various primary groups. Yet it was a significant social force which bound the workers together and provided a sense of meaning and worth. Although their occupation might not be highly respected by outsiders, they derived mutual self-respect from their sense of belonging.

A second important phenomenon was the various coping methods . . . the beef plant line workers developed and practiced . . . for retaining their humanness. Daydreaming, horseplay and occasional sabotage protected their sense of self. Further, the prevailing attitude among workers that it was "us" against "them" served as a reminder that, while the nature of the job might demand subjugation to bosses, machines, and even beef parts, they were still human beings. . . .

A third significant finding was that consumer spending patterns among the beefers seemed to "seal their fate" and make leaving the beef plant almost impossible. A reasonable interpretation of the spending patterns of the beefers is that having a high income/low status job encourages a person to consume conspicuously. The prevailing attitude seemed to be "I may not have a nice job, but I have a nice home, a nice car, etc." This conspicuous consumption enabled workers to take indirect pride in their occupations. One of the ways of overcoming drudgery and humiliation on the job was to surround oneself with as many desirable material things as possible off the job. These items (cars, boats, motorcycles, etc.) became tangible rewards for the sacrifices endured at work.

The problem, of course, is that the possession of these expensive items required the continual income of a substantial paycheck which most of these men could only obtain by staying at the beef plant. These spending patterns were further complicated by the fact that they were seemingly "contagious." Workers talked to each other on breaks about recent purchases, thus reinforcing the norm of immediate gratification. A common activity of a group of workers on break or lunch was to run to the parking lot to see a fellow worker's new truck, van, car or motorcycle. Even the seemingly more financially conservative were usually caught up in this activity and often could not wait to display their own latest acquisitions. Ironically, as the workers cursed their jobs, these expensive possessions virtually destroyed any chance of leaving them.

Working at the beef plant was indeed "dirty work." It was monotonous, difficult, dangerous, and demeaning. Despite this, the workers at the beef plant worked hard to fulfill employer expectations in order to obtain financial rewards. Through a variety of symbolic techniques, they managed to overcome the many negative aspects of their work and maintain a sense of self respect about how they earned their living.

References

Balzer, Richard (1976). *Clockwork: Life In and Outside an American Factory*. Garden City, N.Y.: Doubleday.

Barlow, Hugh (1981). *Introduction to Criminology*. 2d ed. Boston: Little, Brown.

Garson, Barbara (1975). *All the Livelong Day: The Meaning and Demeaning of Routine Work*. Garden City, N.Y.: Doubleday.

Hummel, Ralph P. (1977). *The Bureaucratic Experience*. New York: St. Martin's Press.

King, Rick (1978). "In the sanding booth at ford." Pp. 199–205 in John and Erna Perry (eds.), *Social Problems in Today's World*. Boston: Little, Brown.

Linhart, Robert (translated by Margaret Crosland) (1981). *The Assembly Line*. Amherst: University of Massachusetts Press.

Marx, Karl (1964a). *Economic and Philosophical Manuscripts of 1844*. New York: International Publishing (1844).

—— (1964b). *The Communist Manifesto*. New York: Washington Square Press (1848).

Schatzman, Leonard, and Anselm L. Strauss (1973). *Field Research*. Englewood Cliffs, N.J.: Prentice-Hall.

Shostak, Arthur (1980). *Blue Collar Stress*. Reading, Mass.: Addison-Wesley.

Spradley, James P. (1979). *The Ethnographic Interview*. New York: Holt, Rinehart, and Winston.

—— (1980). *Participant Observation*. New York: Holt, Rinehart, and Winston.

Deviance and Social Control

F OR SOCIETY TO EXIST, PEOPLE MUST BE ABLE TO KNOW what to expect of others. If they could not, the world would be in chaos. Because the behavior of humans is not controlled by instincts, people have developed *norms* (rules and expectations) that provide regularity or patterns to social life. Norms provide a high degree of certainty in what would be a chaotic world if everyone followed his or her own inclinations and no one knew what to expect of others.

The confidence we can place in what others will do is only relative, however, because not everyone follows all the rules all the time. In fact *deviance*, the violation of rules and expectations, is universal. Some members of every social group in every society violate some of the expectations that others have of them.

The norms that people develop to control one another cover a fascinating variety of human behavior. They include rules and expectations concerning our appearance, manner, and conduct.

1. *Appearance* (what we look like): the norms concerning clothing, make-up, hairstyle, and other such presentational aspects of our body, including its cleanliness and smells. These rules also cover the *social extensions of the person*, those objects thought to represent the individual in some way, such as one's home, car, and pet.
2. *Manner* (our style of doing things): the usually informal expectations concerning the way we express ourselves, such as our mannerisms, gestures, and other body language. They include *personal style*, the expectations others have of an individual because of the

way he or she has acted in the past (personality, "the way he or she is"), as well as *group style*, the expectations attached to a social group (racial, sexual, occupational, age, and so on—"the way they are.") Rules or expectations of manner are held by the individual who is a member of a particular group, by the other group's members, and by persons who are not members of the group. These three sources are not necessarily in agreement with one another.

3. *Conduct* (what we say and do): rules covering the rest of human behavior, specifying what one can and cannot do and say under various circumstances. They include rules of authority (who has the right to give what orders to whom), rules of responsibility (who has the obligation to do what for whom), and rules of account-giving (what one is expected to say when called upon for explanations, including the degree to which one is expected to be honest or to go into detail).

These everyday rules of appearance, manner, and conduct cover what we can say or do to whom and when, and what we cannot do or say to whom and when, as well as how we must look and how we must phrase what we say with varying requisite degrees of respect or informality. In other words, hardly a single aspect of our lives is untouched by rules made by others. We are all immersed in these expectations. We are not free agents, able to do as we please. Rather, *social control* is a basic fact of social life as the behavior of all of us is brought under the control of rules, norms, and expectations.

The rules are extremely complex. They vary for the same person under different circumstances, dictating things such as proper attire in a university classroom, at a formal dance, or at the beach. They also differ according to people's social identity—that is, according to the group to which people are thought to belong. For example, the rules of conduct, appearance, and manner differ for convicts, presidents, students, children, and old people, that is, according to age, occupation, wealth, prestige, reputation, and, in some instances, they may vary according to race.

The rules also change depending on the audience for whom one is performing. For example, as teenagers know so well, their parents' expectations markedly differ from their friends' expectations. Similarly people are often expected to act one way when they are with members of their own racial or ethnic group but differently when they are with others.

These complex expectations define in and define out; that is, those who conform to the norms are accorded the status of members-in-good-standing while those who deviate are usually defined as outsiders of some sort. Viewed with suspicion, deviants are reacted to in a number of ways. They may be given more attention in order to bring them back into line or they may be ostracized or kicked out of the group. In extreme cases, they are tried and imprisoned. In less extreme cases they are simply stared at, or they may be shunned or physically attacked; people gossip about them, divorce them, strike their names off guests lists, fire and demote them.

This list of some of the social reactions to deviance indicates that people are extremely concerned with rule-following or rule-breaking behaviors. Deviance challenges fundamental expectations about the way social life is run and affects people's welfare. With such a stake in the conformity of others, people react to deviants—sharply and negatively if they consider the deviance threatening, tolerantly and with amusement if they believe it is mild.

As the word is used in sociology, deviance is not a term of negative judgment, as it often is when used by nonsociologists. To sociologists, the term is meant simply to be descriptive, referring to activities that violate the expectations of others, passing judgment neither on the merit of the rules nor on those who violate them.

In this Part, we focus on deviants (those who violate the rules) and deviance (what they do). Nanette J. Davis examines prostitution, interviewing women in order to discover the processes by which they became prostitutes. William J. Chambliss examines different reactions to lower-class and middle-class delinquents and the significance of those reactions for the later lives of the delinquents. Diane E. Taub and Robert G. Leger look at two specialized roles ("drag queen" and "fag hag") within a highly developed deviant subculture. Fred H. Goldner then focuses on another remarkable deviance, being blind to negative information about the self. Gresham M. Sykes and David Matza examine the broader question of how people escape social control, looking at how delinquents rationalize their lawbreaking activities. Through interviews with muggers, Robert Lejeune provides an inside account of one of the most feared and detested of all groups in American society. In the final selection we turn the focus onto institutions and processes of social control, as Philip G. Zimbardo examines the complex relationships and dynamics between prisoners and prison guards.

18 Becoming a Prostitute

NANETTE J. DAVIS

Would you ever consider becoming a prostitute? If someone were to ask you that question, chances are that you would be grievously offended. Such a question challenges fundamental self-expectations concerning proper, right, and moral sex roles. You probably would feel like punching the person in the nose. "I am not like that—and I never could be," is what you might reply. "Revolting and disgusting" are probably thoughts you would be having.

If you are male, you might be even more offended—as male prostitutes who solicit other males break even more rules than the rule that forbids the indiscriminate selling of sex. Males who thought the question referred to selling sex to females, however, might react in a much more positive manner, for to many males such a question implies inflated sexual capacities, exalting the expectations usually attached to the male sex role.

Why does someone become a prostitute? In order to ferret out the answer to this question, Nanette J. Davis interviewed prostitutes, and she came away with more than an answer to this question. Investigating the slide from promiscuity to prostitution, she also uncovered ways by which prostitutes evade social control, ways they think about themselves and what they are doing that help them continue in prostitution.

THE SOURCE OF DATA FOR THIS STUDY is provided by a jail sample of thirty prostitutes from three correctional institutions (reformatory, workhouse, and training school) in Minnesota. Included are seventeen white women, twelve black women, and one Indian woman. The age range was fifteen to thirty-four, with an average age of twenty-one. All of the thirty women were legally classified as "common prostitute," although only twenty-four of the thirty informants reported that they were

This study is based on an unpublished Master's thesis, "Prostitution and Social Control: An Empirical Inquiry Into the Socialization Process of Deviant Behavior," (1967) University of Minnesota, under the direction of Professor David A. Ward.

The writer wishes to express appreciation to James M. Henslin, Peter K. Manning, Bernard N. Meltzer, John Petras, and Ira Reiss for their helpful comments.

The selection is a condensed version of the author's more detailed analysis appearing in *Studies in the Sociology of Sex*, James M. Henslin, ed., New York: Appleton-Century-Crofts, 1971, 297–322.

professional prostitutes. The women operated at the "streetwalker" level of prostitution, that is, lounging in bars or on streetcorners and openly soliciting clients. High levels of spatial mobility were typical patterns for this group. Data were elicited through structured interviews, with emphasis, however, on the informants' verbalized statements. The interviews averaged one and one-half to two hours in length. Official records also were used. Further, informal data were gained through participant observation. . . .

The Process of Drift from Promiscuity to the First Act of Prostitution

AGE AT FIRST SEXUAL EXPERIENCE

The women in this sample were initiated into sexual experiences at an early age. The mean age at which they first had sexual intercourse was 13.6, with a range of seven to eighteen. Rape experiences, reported by two women, account for the lower age level (seven and nine years, respectively). Three other informants noted traumatic sexual experiences with brothers, step-father, or father, at age twelve or under. Nineteen of the thirty women report they had sexual intercourse by age thirteen, although almost one-half of the white girls had experienced intercourse by age twelve. The most characteristic pattern was coitus with a boyfriend, who was typically five or six years older than the girl was. Four informants were sexually initiated by another girl with heterosexual relations occurring within a year after such lesbian contacts. . . . First sexual contacts typically involved sexual intercourse, with only one girl reporting an initial petting experience.

Preconditions for those characterized by "early sexuality" are: (1) high levels of familial permissiveness led to association with older males at parties, neighboring houses, or street pickups, (2) familial social control was often lacking or inconsistent, (3) peer group norms encouraged early sexuality, and (4) sexuality was associated with freedom (a movement away from a disliked family) or, conversely, security (the certainty of male companionship). Three girls, on the other hand, did not experience their first sexual intercourse until age seventeen or eighteen. Those having this "late sexuality" experienced these typical conditions: (1) sexual matters were taboo areas in the family, (2) the mother was highly protective, exerting strong religious and familial controls with consequent little freedom of opportunity in early adolescence, and (3) a rebellion pattern eventually developed in opposition to the rigidity of the controls.

Almost all of the women (twenty-eight of thirty) report that their first sex experience was either meaningless or distasteful, for example, "It was nothing," "I did it just to please him," "I really didn't like it," "I disliked it," "It was awful," "I was scared," "It made me sick." A need for conformity seems to be the most salient motive for this first sexuality, as:

> I did it just to belong. Everybody was doing it.
>
> I was the only virgin in the crowd (age fifteen). Five of my girlfriends had kids at sixteen. . . .

The promiscuous pattern which developed for most girls (three women had early pregnancies which were followed by marriage, with promiscuity and prostitution occurring *after* these events) seems to reflect associates' expectations, the desire to attract males ("The boys were always hot after me"), and an opportunity structure which facilitated the behavior.

PERCEPTION OF CHILDHOOD AND ADOLESCENT YEARS

The promiscuous pattern may provide one condition which can lead to informal labeling ("bad" girl, "easy mark") and subsequent stigmatization by parents, teachers, and conventional associates. But other circumstances may arise, prior to or following this sexual behavior. . . . These women perceived their childhood and adolescent years as marked by negative or degrading interactions with society, as the following data indicate:

1. Familial instability was typical for almost all of the white girls (sixteen of seventeen) and two-thirds of the blacks (eight of twelve). Such instability included a drunken, violent or absentee parent (usually the father), extreme poverty, or families larger than the parents could cope with. Conditions within the family were eventually brought to the attention of neighbors, welfare board, or court. Such attention was defined as humiliating or demoralizing.

2. More than half of the informants (eighteen of thirty) have spent one year or more of their childhood (under twelve) in foster homes, living with relatives, or in other separations from the nuclear family.

3. Almost all of the informants (twenty-eight) report that parents, neighbors, and/or teachers considered them "troublemakers," "slow learners," or generally inadequate in relation to expectations.

4. The black women (nine of twelve) especially, reported "unfair" treatment by white teachers or students, inability to gain and/or hold a job, and frustration in cases where self-improvement was attempted.

5. *Twenty-three of the thirty* informants reported that they had been sentenced to a juvenile home or training school as adolescents for truancy, incorrigibility, or sex delinquency. . . .

In the interactional processes with significant others (parents, teachers, neighbors, and friends), the girl [is seen as] "different." She is a person who is expected to behave in unconventional ways. Absenteeism from school, chronic disobedience at home, and later, promiscuity, categorize the girl as difficult, if not impossible to control. Low family cohesion with consequent weak affectional ties between parents and daughter leads the girl to seek street associates. . . .

[T]he rationale for promiscuity, and initially for prostitution, is a hedonistic concern for fun, new experiences, excitement, and a response to peer group expectations. Sex as a status tool is exploited to gain male attention. The adolescent urge for liberation from the confines of the family and controls of school and job leads to involvement in drinking parties or hustler groups, wherein differential identification with sophisticated delinquents occurs.

THE DRIFT FROM PROMISCUITY TO FIRST ACT OF PROSTITUTION

Regardless of the age at which the girl first experienced intercourse, there then followed a *"drift"* or *"slide"* *process from promiscuity to prostitution*, with the girl first prostituting herself in late adolescence (mean = 17.3 years). There was a range, however, of fourteen to twenty-five years. The early age of prostitution was facilitated by a definition of the deviant situation as similar to sexual promiscuity—excitement and desire for male attention: . . .

> It was either jump in bed, and go with every Tom, Dick, and Harry, and just give it away, so I decided to turn tricks instead. . . . The money was so easy to get. . . .

My data strongly suggest that the movement from casual delinquency to the first phase of [prostitution] is facilitated by the policy of confining deviants to correctional institutions. The adolescent girl who is labeled a sex offender for promiscuity or "mixing" (white girls associating with black males) may initially experience a conflict about her identity. Intimate association with sophisticated deviants, however, may provide an incentive to learn the hustler role ("The girls told me about it—I was such an avid listener."), and thus resolve the status anxiety by gaining prestige through association with deviants, and later, experimentation in the deviant role. Frequent and predictable escapes from the open institution are common. Lines of communication between urban vice neighborhoods and training school inmates assures the escapee of finding accommodations during a "run."

As an outlaw, the girl cannot seek the security of parents or the home neighborhood. Thus, isolated from conventional associates or activities, and dependent on deviant contacts for financial and social support, the girl may come to define the situation as one that inevitably leads her into enacting the deviant role, as:

I ran away from the institution. I went and visited my girlfriends. I was out of the institution about a month, just loafing around. I talked to some friends of mine who were hustlers. Someone suggested I try it. I had been sponging off everybody. I got sick of sponging. I'd sleep here one night, and there another. . . .

I had run away (from the training school). I had no money or anything. I went walking the street. The older girls (institutionalized associates) told me about it.

ROADS TO RECRUITMENT

Adolescent institutionalization, then, often prior to the actual commission of a deviant act, may act as a structural condition which facilitates the learning of a deviant role. Induction into the career, on the other hand, proceeds through alternative routes, chief of which are: (1) response to peer group expectations, (2) involvement in a pimp-manager relationship, and (3) adolescent rebellion.

Response to *peer group expectations* undoubtedly provides the major avenue to recruitment ("It's the environment. Everyone is doing it.") Associating with hustlers, "party girls," or pimps, while viewed as prestigious, can only be maintained by "trying out" the behavior. Clearly, for twenty-eight of the thirty informants, differential identification with deviant associates accounts, in part, for the movement into prostitution.

I was on run . . . I didn't get up until 3 P.M. I was staying with my boyfriend. He was unemployed. He was planning to set me up [for prostitution]. We had been talking about it. I took long precautions. . . . A friend helped me out. Everything happened so fast. It was kind of like prearranged for me. Crazy! We were staying in a hotel with lots of pimps, prostitutes and faggots living there. The first time was at the World's Series. I was dressed like a normal teenager. . . .

Involvement in a *pimp-manager relationship* provides a typical method of entrance for some under-age girls (eight informants.) In other instances, the pimp may not have initially arranged the first contact, but he typically appears relatively early on the scene to direct the girl's activities. The uninitiated girl views the pimp relationship as a means of security in an otherwise rejecting world.

I always had a need to belong. . . . A pimp moves in, and he sees you're attractive, and he sees you want to belong. Pimps are the most understanding. They're the least educated persons, though. I thought my pimp was my knight in shining armor. . . .

The pimp's ability to "set the girl up" by arranging clients is a measure of the girl's arrival on the deviant scene. One informant, whose first experience was such an arrangement, recalled how the system operated.

> I was living with a girlfriend. . . . She wasn't a hustler—and started going
> with this one boy. He introduced me to this pimp. He asked me if I would
> [hustle]. I was against it, but they all said how easy it was. I went to this
> pimp's house. I was a call girl. There were three of us [hustlers]. The pimps
> would come in. They got all the contacts, and they'd say to the tricks,
> "Lookee here, I got these girls, see," and he'd line up the tricks. Then he'd
> say to the girls that there was a trick in this hotel, and you'd go to a room
> number.

Another girl commented that the pimp used alternate techniques of
violence ("He hit me on the head when I said no") and persuasion: "He
told me, 'I can put you in big business. You won't have to hustle hard.' I
saw the girls and how they did it. It was like a dream."

Adolescent rebellion operates for girls who have experienced oppressive familial controls (six women), forming another typical pattern.

> Well, I started hustling, I suppose, because the party group I ran around
> with were always talking about it. My mother had always picked my friends.
> She wouldn't allow any bad influences—the square friends only, the goody-
> goody club activities at church. My parents were very old-fashioned. They
> didn't drink or smoke, and were very church-going. But when I got in with
> this group, it was really different, man! . . .

DOMINANT MOTIVES DURING THE FIRST STAGE

Underlying these main roads to recruitment into prostitution are curiosity
and a desire for new experience, defined idleness, identification with hustler norms, and a strong present-time orientation.

Curiosity and access to new experiences (or "kicks") acts as a dominant motive to the naive girl who seeks esteem from the hustler group. "I
was unemployed at the time, just hanging around with a group. I wanted
some excitement—kicks, you know."

Remarks such as, "It was the glamour and game of it," "I did it just
for the fun of it," "There's a lot of excitement to that—the cops on you
and everything," indicate a perception of deviance as part of the excitement and risk of street life. . . .

Defined idleness is the typical pattern for most [of the] women
(twenty-three of thirty). Separations from family, school, job, or other
conventional activities characterize this first deviant phase. For the run-
away training school girl, prostitution may relieve the dullness of an otherwise undirected existence.

> I was sixteen and on the run, just loafing around my girlfriend's house. One
> of my girlfriends gave me the pointers, so I decided to try it.
> I had run away—like I was lost or something. I had been walking the streets
> all day, and at 6 P.M. I met this guy. I was really looking for love and at-
> tention, but not necessarily the men.

Identification with hustler norms undoubtedly accounts for the frequently expressed (twenty-seven of thirty) money rationale. However, economic deprivation is not the dominant element for most girls. Only two women, for instance, expressed intense financial need because of child support. Independence, isolation from conventional supports, and the lure of "easy" money, were major considerations.

> I was on run—no job or anything. I was by myself. It was about 8. I went out, went downtown. My boyfriend worked in the _____ Hotel. He called me up to say that he had a man who had fifty dollars to get a girl, and there it was. I got forty-five dollars the first night—for four men. Everyone was doing it, anyway. Then I walked back downtown, and had three more, and then went back to my apartment.

A strong present-time orientation characterizes the younger girl particularly, who conceives of the act as satisfying immediate needs only, without considering long-range implications.

> The first time I did it was to buy a present for my boyfriend. The next time just to have some spending money. I've been asked to hustle lots of times. I know all the gimmicks, and how to do it . . . all that stuff.
>
> I was going to school and I wanted to go to this dance the night after. I needed new clothes. I went out at ten o'clock and home at twelve. I had three tricks the first time, and fifteen dollars for every trick.

Whatever the mode of recruitment, or the dominant motives involved, this study shows certain common elements present at this state of deviant involvement. These generally include: informal labeling which early categorizes the girl as unconventional or "troublemaker"; isolation from conventional family, friends, or associates; response to deviant associates' expectations; and expressed need for economic self-sufficiency while "on run" or probation. Such motives indicate that: (1) episodic involvement, or a *drift into deviance*, is characteristic of prostitutes and is related to hedonistic and short-term concerns; and (2) stigmatized persons may respond to a morally degraded status by seeking associates who may reward the deviant behavior.

Transitional Deviance [and Professionalization]

Twenty-one of the thirty women interviewed experienced an "occasional" or "transitional" stage of deviance. Of the nine other labeled prostitutes, four repudiated the role after three or more deviant episodes, while five women moved directly into full-time deviance. The transitional stage lasted an average of six months (with a range from two weeks to four years). It could be viewed as an on-the-job learning period. . . .

Motivational ambivalence during the transitional phase creates a zigzag pattern of deviance for most prostitutes. They vacillate between conventionality and deviance. The conventional life, for instance, is not yet denied. Some girls make verbal commitments to stop, or even attempt to return to home, school, job or to set themselves up in an apartment with conventional associates. Conventional motives involve expressed reluctance to move into the act because of fear of discovery, interracial contacts, or belief that such conduct is immoral. ("It's not the right thing to do. I would get a bad reputation.") . . .

During this phase they indicate indecision and confusion regarding their role. By hustling only occasionally, not more than two or three times a week, or engaging in prostitution "only when I wanted to," or "sometimes when I'm lonesome," or for "just something to do," the individual perceives that she is in control of the situation. . . .

[T]he drift into deviance . . . occurs through *normalization of the act*. [This] may occur through rationalizations appropriate for promiscuity—the desire for male attention. . . .

> I'm a person who likes to walk. There's nothing wrong with picking somebody up while you're walking. I always like walking around at night, and girls will be tempted. Girls like the offer. They like to see what the guy is going to say.

The "gaming" element, which revolves around the excitement of the "pickup" and independence on the street, is also linked to a promiscuous, rather than deviant, orientation. The promiscuous girl with conventional in-group supports may not define herself as a prostitute at this point.

In certain cases role ambivalence may even lead to repudiation of the "trial" role after a few experiences (four informants). Negative experiences with a client, pimp, or policeman, for instance, may lead her to reject the role. Inadequate motivation is a typical condition leading to role failure in many areas of life. It was expressed by one seventeen-year-old informant who had hustled on-and-off for about a month before her career had been interrupted by jail:

> Hustling—I don't get no kicks from it. I wouldn't go out and do it for a living. There are better ways to make money. I couldn't go through everything a prostitute goes through. I really don't have the guts for it. A prostitute picks up anyone off the street, and gets money for it. The tricks I had it with I did it just for sex, but not for me—not the whole self. I knew I couldn't make a career out of it. When you don't care about the guy, sex isn't for that.

Sex with affection, uncontaminated by money, still operates as a norm for the deviant dropout.

Their continuation in this sexually deviant behavior, on the other hand, is contingent on strong economic motivation (twenty-one women), loneliness (three), and/or expressed entrapment because of pimp control (six). For two girls, drug addiction acted as an inducement for continuation of the deviant role. Continuation in the deviant role is further contingent on an adequate learning period uninterrupted by police harassment or jail sentencing. . . .

Delayed definitions of the act as immoral, degrading or repulsive (fifteen women report intense dissatisfaction or disgust with the situation) can no longer be postponed if situations occur that force unequivocal perception of a deviant self. Self-discovery, for instance, may be inevitable for some prostitutes when the pimp's behavior shifts from lover to exploiter, and for example, nightly money quotas become the primary condition for the relationship ("I was just another one of his hustlers"). . . . Another typical experience is contact with the police, court, or jail, where the label "common prostitute" is assigned. After the legal confrontation, public exposure proceeds in rapid order. Listing the girl's name in the paper, or passing the information to parents from "inside" sources, implies that, as a consequence, the girl soon renounces the pretense of conventional commitments. At this point, she may cut herself off from family and conventional others' support. Informants report such responses to the labeling procedure:

> They sent me up for something I didn't do, so I might as well do it. I wasn't afraid of anything.
>
> Society is really uninformed. They don't put themselves to the trouble to understand. There are lots worse things besides prostitution that happen. Society isn't helping at all. There's not a chance to be decent. Society has put the brand on us.

Personal integrity at earlier phases of the career had been maintained by secrecy regarding the deviant behavior. Role segmentation breaks down, however, if the woman has internalized the streetwalker's myth—"once a girl is on the streets, everyone knows what she is." For example,

> At first I was scared. The news gets out so fast. Everyone knows when a girl's on the streets a couple of nights. I thought about stopping, you know, but I just went on. . . .

In-service training for this streetwalker group during the transitional period includes: (1) willingness to satisfy a broad range of client requests, requiring certain social and sexual skills; (2) elimination of fears regarding clients who are defined as "odd" (sadomasochists); (3) adaptation to police surveillance and entrapment procedures; (4) avoidance of drunken clients, or those unable or unwilling to pay; and (5) substitution of a "business" ethic for the earlier one of "gaming" or excitement. . . .

[Having gone through this process of learning and of making the required adjustment in her identity, the woman has *become* a prostitute. Sex has become her vocation.]

19 The Saints and the Roughnecks

WILLIAM J. CHAMBLISS

When people deviate from expectations, other people react. But on what do their reactions depend? Do they depend simply on the nature of the deviance itself, or is more involved? If so, what sorts of things?

It is these fascinating questions that William J. Chambliss examines in this study of two groups of delinquents in the same high school. He found that although both groups were involved in serious delinquent acts, while one was perceived as a group of saints, the other was viewed as a bunch of roughnecks. After analyzing what influenced people's perceptions, and hence their reactions to the boys, Chambliss examines the far-reaching effects of those reactions. He indicates that in the case of the roughnecks, people's reactions helped lock the boys into behaviors that continued after high school, eventually leading to prison or to low-paying jobs, while social reaction to the saints set them on a life-course that not only meant staying out of prison but entering well-paying positions of prestige.

EIGHT PROMISING YOUNG MEN—children of good, stable, white upper-middle-class families, active in school affairs, good pre-college students—were some of the most delinquent boys at Hanibal High School. While community residents knew that these boys occasionally sowed a few wild oats, they were totally unaware that sowing wild oats completely occupied the daily routine of these young men. The Saints were constantly occupied with truancy, drinking, wild driving, petty theft and vandalism. Yet no one was officially arrested for any misdeed during the two years I observed them.

This record was particularly surprising in light of my observations during the same two years of another gang of Hanibal High School students, six lower-class white boys known as the Roughnecks. The Roughnecks were constantly in trouble with police and community even though their rate of delinquency was about equal with that of the Saints. What was the cause of this disparity? the result? The following consideration of the activities, social class and community perceptions of both gangs may provide some answers.

The Saints from Monday to Friday

The Saint's principal daily concern was with getting out of school as early as possible. The boys managed to get out of school with minimum danger that they would be accused of playing hookey through an elaborate procedure for obtaining "legitimate" release from class. The most common procedure was for one boy to obtain the release of another by fabricating a meeting of some committee, program or recognized club. Charles might raise his hand in his 9:00 chemistry class and ask to be excused—a euphemism for going to the bathroom. Charles would go to Ed's math class and inform the teacher that Ed was needed for a 9:30 rehearsal of the drama club play. The math teacher would recognize Ed and Charles as "good students" involved in numerous school activities and would permit Ed to leave at 9:30. Charles would return to his class, and Ed would go to Tom's English class to obtain his release. Tom would engineer Charles' escape. The strategy would continue until as many of the Saints as possible were freed. After a stealthy trip to the car (which had been parked in a strategic spot), the boys were off for a day of fun.

Over the two years I observed the Saints, this pattern was repeated nearly every day. There were variations on the theme, but in one form or another, the boys used this procedure for getting out of class and then off the school grounds. Rarely did all eight of the Saints manage to leave school at the same time. The average number avoiding school on the days I observed them was five.

Having escaped from the concrete corridors the boys usually went either to a pool hall on the other (lower-class) side of town or to a cafe in the suburbs. Both places were out of the way of people the boys were likely to know (family or school officials), and both provided a source of entertainment. The pool hall entertainment was the generally rough atmosphere, the occasional hustler, the sometimes drunk proprietor and, of course, the game of pool. The cafe's entertainment was provided by the owner. The boys would "accidentally" knock a glass on the floor or spill cola on the counter—not all the time, but enough to be sporting. They would also bend spoons, put salt in sugar bowls and generally tease whoever was working in the cafe. The owner had opened the cafe recently and was dependent on the boys' business which was, in fact, substantial since between the horsing around and the teasing they bought food and drinks.

The Saints on Weekends

On weekends the automobile was even more critical than during the week, for on weekends the Saints went to Big Town—a large city with a population of over a million 25 miles from Hanibal. Every Friday and Saturday night most of the Saints would meet between 8:00 and 8:30 and would go into Big Town. Big Town activities included drinking heavily in taverns or nightclubs, driving drunkenly through the streets, and committing acts of vandalism and playing pranks.

By midnight on Fridays and Saturdays the Saints were usually thoroughly high, and one or two of them were often so drunk they had to be carried to the cars. Then the boys drove around town, calling obscenities to women and girls; occasionally trying (unsuccessfully so far as I could tell) to pick girls up; and driving recklessly through red lights and at high speeds with their lights out. Occasionally they played "chicken." One boy would climb out the back window of the car and across the roof to the driver's side of the car while the car was moving at high speed (between 40 and 50 miles an hour); then the driver would move over and the boy who had just crawled across the car roof would take the driver's seat.

Searching for "fair game" for a prank was the boys principal activity after they left the tavern. The boys would drive alongside a foot patrolman and ask directions to some street. If the policeman leaned on the car in the course of answering the question, the driver would speed away, causing him to lose his balance. The Saints were careful to play this prank only in an area where they were not going to spend much time and where they could quickly disappear around a corner to avoid having their license plate number taken.

Construction sites and road repair areas were the special province of the Saints' mischief. A soon-to-be-repaired hole in the road inevitably invited the Saints to remove lanterns and wooden barricades and put them in the car, leaving the hole unprotected. The boys would find a safe vantage point and wait for an unsuspecting motorist to drive into the hole. Often, though not always, the boys would go up to the motorist and commiserate with him about the dreadful way the city protected its citizenry.

Leaving the scene of the open hole and the motorist, the boys would then go searching for an appropriate place to erect the stolen barricade. An "appropriate place" was often a spot on a highway near a curve in the road where the barricade would not be seen by an oncoming motorist. The boys would wait to watch an unsuspecting motorist attempt to stop and (usually) crash into the wooden barricade. With saintly bearing the boys might offer help and understanding.

A stolen lantern might well find its way onto the back of a police car or hang from a street lamp. Once a lantern served as a prop for a reenactment of the "midnight ride of Paul Revere" until the "play," which was taking place at 2:00 A.M. in the center of a main street of Big Town, was interrupted by a police car several blocks away. The boys ran, leaving the lanterns on the street, and managed to avoid being apprehended.

Abandoned houses, especially if they were located in out-of-the-way places, were fair game for destruction and spontaneouse vandalism. The boys would break windows, remove furniture to the yard and tear it apart, urinate on the walls and scrawl obscenities inside.

Through all the pranks, drinking and reckless driving the boys managed miraculously to avoid being stopped by police. Only twice in two years was I aware that they had been stopped by a Big City policeman. Once was for speeding (which they did every time they drove whether they were drunk or sober), and the driver managed to convince the policeman that it was simply an error. The second time they were stopped they had just left a nightclub and were walking through an alley. Aaron stopped to urinate and the boys began making obscene remarks. A foot patrolman came into the alley, lectured the boys and sent them home. Before the boys got to the car one began talking in a loud voice again. The policeman, who had followed them down the alley, arrested this boy for disturbing the peace and took him to the police station where the other Saints gathered. After paying a $5.00 fine, and with the assurance that there would be no permanent record of the arrest, the boy was released.

The boys had a spirit of frivolity and fun about their escapades. They did not view what they were engaged in as "delinquency," though it surely was by any reasonable definition of that word. They simply viewed themselves as having a little fun and who, they would ask, was really hurt by it? The answer had to be no one, although this fact remains one of the most difficult things to explain about the gang's behavior. Unlikely though it seems, in two years of drinking, driving, carousing and vandalism no one was seriously injured as a result of the Saints' activities.

The Saints in School

The Saints were highly successful in school. The average grade for the group was "B", with two of the boys having close to a straight "A" average. Almost all of the boys were popular and many of them held offices in the school. One of the boys was vice-president of the student body one year. Six of the boys played on athletic teams.

At the end of their senior year, the student body selected ten seniors for special recognition as the "school wheels"; four of the ten were Saints. Teachers and school officials saw no problem with any of these boys and anticipated that they would all "make something of themselves."

How the boys managed to maintain this impression is surprising in view of their actual behavior while in school. Their technique for covering truancy was so successful that teachers did not even realize that the boys were absent from school much of the time. Occasionally, of course, the system would backfire and then the boy was on his own. A boy who was caught would be most contrite, would plead guilty and ask for mercy. He inevitably got the mercy he sought.

Cheating on examinations was rampant, even to the point of orally communicating answers to exams as well as looking at one another's papers. Since none of the group studied, and since they were primarily dependent on one another for help, it is surprising that grades were so high. Teachers contributed to the deception in their admitted inclination to give these boys (and presumably others like them) the benefit of the doubt. When asked how the boys did in school, and when pressed on specific examinations, teachers might admit that they were disappointed in John's performance, but would quickly add that they "knew that he was capable of doing better," so John was given a higher grade than he had actually earned. How often this happened is impossible to know. During the time that I observed the group, I never saw any of the boys take homework home. Teachers may have been "understanding" very regularly.

One exception to the gang's generally good performance was Jerry, who had a "C" average in his junior year, experienced disaster the next year and failed to graduate. Jerry had always been a little more nonchalant than the others about the liberties he took in school. Rather than wait for someone to come get him from class, he would offer his own excuse and leave. Although he probably did not miss any more class than most of the others in the group, he did not take the requisite pains to cover his absences. Jerry was the only Saint whom I ever heard talk back to a teacher. Although teachers often called him a "cut up" or a "smart kid," they never referred to him as a troublemaker or as a kid headed for trouble. It seems likely, then, that Jerry's failure his senior year and his mediocre performance his junior year were consequences of his not playing the game the proper way (possibly because he was disturbed by his parents' divorce). His teachers regarded him as "immature" and not quite ready to get out of high school.

The Police and the Saints

The local police saw the Saints as good boys who were among the leaders of the youth in the community. Rarely, the boys might be stopped in town for speeding or for running a stop sign. When this happened the boys were always polite, contrite and pled for mercy. As in school, they received the mercy they asked for. None ever received a ticket or was taken into the precinct by the local police.

The situation in Big City, where the boys engaged in most of their delinquency, was only slightly different. The police there did not know the boys at all, although occasionally the boys were stopped by a patrolman. Once they were caught taking a lantern from a construction site. Another time they were stopped for running a stop sign, and on several occasions they were stopped for speeding. Their behavior was as before: contrite, polite and penitent. The urban police, like the local police, accepted their demeanor as sincere. More important, the urban police were convinced that these were good boys just out for a lark.

The Roughnecks

Hanibal townspeople never perceived the Saints' high level of delinquency. The Saints were good boys who just went in for an occasional prank. After all, they were well dressed, well mannered and had nice cars. The Roughnecks were a different story. Although the two gangs of boys were the same age, and both groups engaged in an equal amount of wild-oat sowing, everyone agreed that the not-so-well-dressed, not-so-well-mannered, not-so-rich boys were heading for trouble. Townspeople would say, "You can see the gang members at the drugstore, night after night, leaning against the storefront (sometimes drunk) or slouching around inside buying cokes, reading magazines, and probably stealing old Mr. Wall blind. When they are outside and girls walk by, even respectable girls, these boys make suggestive remarks. Sometimes their remarks are downright lewd."

From the community's viewpoint, the real indication that these kids were in trouble was that they were constantly involved with the police. Some of them had been picked up for stealing, mostly small stuff, of course, "but still it's stealing small stuff that leads to big time crimes." "Too bad," people said. "Too bad that these boys couldn't behave like the other kids in town; stay out of trouble, be polite to adults, and look to their future."

The community's impression of the degrees to which this group of six boys (ranging in age from 16 to 19) engaged in delinquency was somewhat distorted. In some ways the gang was more delinquent than the community thought; in other ways they were less.

The fighting activities of the group were fairly readily and accurately perceived by almost everyone. At least once a month, the boys would get into some sort of fight, although most fights were scraps between members of the group or involved only one member of the group and some peripheral hanger-on. Only three times in the period of observation did the group fight together: once against a gang from across town, once against two blacks and once against a group of boys from another school. For the first two fights the group went out "looking for trouble"—and they found it both times. The third fight followed a football game and began spontaneously with an argument on the football field between one of the Roughnecks and a member of the opposition's football team.

Jack had a particular propensity for fighting and was involved in most of the brawls. He was a prime mover of the escalation of arguments into fights.

More serious than fighting, had the community been aware of it, was theft. Although almost everyone was aware that the boys occasionally stole things, they did not realize the extent of the activity. Petty stealing was a frequent event for the Roughnecks. Sometimes they stole as a group and coordinated their efforts; other things they stole in pairs. Rarely did they steal alone.

The thefts ranged from very small things like paperback books, comics and ballpoint pens to expensive items like watches. The nature of the thefts varied from time to time. The gang would go through a period of systematically shoplifting items from automobiles or school lockers. Types of thievery varied with the whim of the gang. Some forms of thievery were more profitable than others, but all thefts were for profit, not just thrills.

Roughnecks siphoned gasoline from cars as often as they had access to an automobile, which was not very often. Unlike the Saints, who owned their own cars, the Roughnecks would have to borrow their parents' cars, an event which occurred only eight or nine times a year. The boys claimed to have stolen cars for joy rides from time to time.

Ron committed the most serious of the group's offenses. With an unidentified associate the boy attempted to burglarize a gasoline station. Although this station had been robbed twice previously in the same month, Ron denied any involvement in either of the other thefts. When Ron and his accomplice approached the station, the owner was hiding in the bushes beside the station. He fired both barrels of a double-barreled shotgun at the boys. Ron was severely injured; the other boy ran away and was never caught. Though he remained in critical condition for several months, Ron finally recovered and served six months of the following year in reform school. Upon release from reform school, Ron was put back a grade in school, and began running around with a different gang of boys. The Roughnecks considered the new gang less delinquent than themselves, and during the following year Ron had no more trouble with the police.

The Roughnecks, then, engaged mainly in three types of delinquency: theft, drinking and fighting. Although community members perceived that this gang of kids was delinquent, they mistakenly believed that their illegal activities were primarily drinking, fighting and being a nuisance to passersby. Drinking was limited among the gang members, although it did occur, and theft was much more prevalent than anyone realized.

Drinking would doubtless have been more prevalent had the boys had ready access to liquor. Since they rarely had automobiles at their disposal, they could not travel very far, and the bars in town would not serve them. Most of the boys had little money, and this, too, inhibited their purchase of alcohol. Their major source of liquor was a local drunk who would buy them a fifth if they would give him enough extra to buy himself a pint of whiskey or a bottle of wine.

The community's perception of drinking as prevalent stemmed from the fact that it was the most obvious delinquency the boys engaged in. When one of the boys had been drinking, even a casual observer seeing him on the corner would suspect that he was high.

There was a high level of mutual distrust and dislike between the Roughnecks and the police. The boys felt very strongly that the police were unfair and corrupt. Some evidence existed that the boys were correct in their perception.

The main source of the boys' dislike for the police undoubtedly stemmed from the fact that the police would sporadically harass the group. From the standpoint of the boys, these acts of occasional enforcement of the law were whimsical and uncalled for. It made no sense to them, for example, that the police would come to the corner occasionally and threaten them with arrest for loitering when the night before the boys had been out siphoning gasoline from cars and the police had been nowhere in sight. To the boys, the police were stupid on the one hand, for not being where they should have been and catching the boys in a serious offense, and unfair on the other hand, for trumping up "loitering" charges against them.

From the viewpoint of the police, the situation was quite different. They knew, with all the confidence necessary to be a policeman, that these boys were engaged in criminal activities. They knew this partly from occasionally catching them, mostly from circumstantial evidence ("the boys were around when those tires were slashed"), and partly because the police shared the view of the community in general that this was a bad bunch of boys. The best the police could hope to do was to be sensitive to the fact that these boys were engaged in illegal acts and arrest them whenever there was some evidence that they had been involved. Whether or not the boys had in fact committed a particular act in a particular way was not especially important. The police had a broader view: their job was to stamp out these kids' crimes; the tactics were not as important as the end result.

Over the period that the group was under observation, each member was arrested at least once. Several of the boys were arrested a number of times and spent at least one night in jail. While most were never taken to court, two of the boys were sentenced to six months' incarceration in boys' schools.

The Roughnecks in School

The Roughnecks' behavior in school was not particularly disruptive. During school hours they did not all hang around together, but tended instead to spend most of their time with one or two other members of the gang who were their special buddies. Although every member of the gang attempted to avoid school as much as possible, they were not particularly successful and most of them attended school with surprising regularity. They considered school a burden—something to be gotten through with a minimum of conflict. If they were "bugged" by a particular teacher, it could lead to trouble. One of the boys, Al, once threatened to beat up a teacher and, according to the other boys, the teacher hid under a desk to escape him.

Teachers saw the boys the way the general community did, as heading for trouble, as being uninterested in making something of themselves. Some were also seen as being incapable of meeting the academic standards of the school. Most of the teachers expressed concern for this group of boys and were willing to pass them despite poor performance, in the belief that failing them would only aggravate the problem.

The group of boys had a grade point average just slightly above "C". No one in the group failed either grade, and no one had better than a "C" average. They were very consistent in their achievement or, at least, the teachers were consistent in their perception of the boys' achievement.

Two of the boys were good football players. Herb was acknowledged to be the best player in the school and Jack was almost as good. Both boys were criticized for their failure to abide by training rules, for refusing to come to practice as often as they should, and for not playing their best during practice. What they lacked in sportsmanship they made up for in skill, apparently, and played every game no matter how poorly they had performed in practice or how many practice sessions they had missed.

Two Questions

Why did the community, the school and the police react to the Saints as though they were good, upstanding, nondelinquent youths with bright futures but to the Roughnecks as though they were tough, young criminals who were headed for trouble? Why did the Roughnecks and the Saints in fact have quite different careers after high school—careers which, by and large, lived up to the expectations of the community?

The most obvious explanation for the differences in the community's and law enforcement agencies' reactions to the two gangs is that one group of boys was "more delinquent" than the other. Which group was more delinquent? The answer to this question will determine in part how we explain the differential responses to these groups by the members of the community and, particularly, by law enforcement and school officials.

In sheer number of illegal acts, the Saints were the more delinquent. They were truant from school for at least part of the day almost every day of the week. In addition, their drinking and vandalism occurred with surprising regularity. The Roughnecks, in contrast, engaged sporadically in delinquent episodes. While these episodes were frequent, they certainly did not occur on a daily or even a weekly basis.

The difference in frequency of offenses was probably caused by the Roughnecks' inability to obtain liquor and to manipulate legitimate excuses from school. Since the Roughnecks had less money than the Saints, and teachers carefully supervised their school activities, the Roughnecks' hearts may have been as black as the Saints', but their misdeeds were not nearly as frequent.

There are really no clear-cut criteria by which to measure qualitative differences in antisocial behavior. The most important dimension is generally referred to as the "seriousness" of the offenses.

If seriousness encompasses the relative economic costs of delinquent acts, then some assessment can be made. The Roughnecks probably stole an average of about $5.00 worth of goods a week. Some weeks the figure was considerably higher, but these times must be balanced against long periods when almost nothing was stolen.

The Saints were more continuously engaged in delinquency but their acts were not for the most part costly to property. Only their vandalism and occasional theft of gasoline would so qualify. Perhaps once or twice a month they would siphon a tankful of gas. The other costly items were street signs, construction lanterns and the like. All of these acts combined probably did not quite average $5.00 a week, partly because much of the stolen equipment was abandoned and presumably could be recovered. The difference in cost of stolen property between the two groups was trivial, but the Roughnecks probably had a slightly more expensive set of activities than did the Saints.

Another meaning of seriousness is the potential threat of physical harm to members of the community and to the boys themselves. The Roughnecks were more prone to physical violence; they not only welcomed an opportunity to fight; they went seeking it. In addition, they fought among themselves frequently. Although the fighting never included deadly weapons, it was still a menace, however minor, to the physical safety of those involved.

The Saints never fought. They avoided physical conflict both inside and outside the group. At the same time, though, the Saints frequently endangered their own and other people's lives. They did so almost every time they drove a car, especially if they had been drinking. Sober, their driving was risky; under the influence of alcohol it was horrendous. In addition, the Saints endangered the lives of others with their pranks. Street excavations left unmarked were a very serious hazard.

Evaluating the relative seriousness of the two gangs' activities is difficult. The community reacted as though the behavior of the Roughnecks was a problem, and they reacted as though the behavior of the Saints was not. But the members of the community were ignorant of the array of delinquent acts that characterized the Saints' behavior. Although concerned citizens were unaware of much of the Roughnecks' behavior as well, they were much better informed about the Roughnecks' involvement in delinquency than they were about the Saints'.

Visibility

Differential treatment of the two gangs resulted in part because one gang was infinitely more visible than the other. This differential visibility was a direct function of the economic standing of the families. The Saints had access to automobiles and were able to remove themselves from the sight of the community. In as routine a decision as to where to go to have a milkshake after school, the Saints stayed away from the mainstream of community life. Lacking transportation, the Roughnecks could not make it to the edge of town. The center of town was the only practical place for them to meet since their homes were scattered throughout the town and any noncentral meeting place put an undue hardship on some members. Through necessity the Roughnecks congregated in a crowded area where everyone in the community passed frequently, including teachers and law enforcement officers. They could easily see the Roughnecks hanging around the drugstore.

The Roughnecks, of course, made themselves even more visible by making remarks to passersby and by occasionally getting into fights on the corner. Meanwhile, just as regularly, the Saints were either at the cafe on one edge of town or in the pool hall at the other edge of town. Without any particular realization that they were making themselves inconspicuous, the Saints were able to hide their time-wasting. Not only were they removed from the mainstream of traffic, but they were almost always inside a building.

On their escapades the Saints were also relatively invisible, since they left Hanibal and traveled to Big City. Here, too, they were mobile, roaming the city, rarely going to the same area twice.

Demeanor

To the notion of visibility must be added the difference in the responses of group members to outside intervention with their activities. If one of the Saints was confronted with an accusing policeman, even if he felt he was truly innocent of a wrongdoing, his demeanor was apologetic and penitent. A Roughneck's attitude was almost the polar opposite. When confronted with a threatening adult authority, even one who tried to be pleasant, the Roughneck's hostility and disdain were clearly observable. Sometimes he might attempt to put up a veneer of respect, but it was thin and was not accepted as sincere by the authority.

School was no different from the community at large. The Saints could manipulate the system by feigning compliance with the school norms. The availability of cars at school meant that once free from the immediate sight of the teacher, the boys could disappear rapidly. And this escape was well enough planned that no administrator or teacher was nearby when the boys left. A Roughneck who wished to escape for a few hours was in a bind. If it were possible to get free from class, downtown was still a mile away, and even if he arrived there, he was still very visible. Truancy for the Roughnecks meant almost certain detection, while the Saints enjoyed almost complete immunity from sanctions.

Bias

Community members were not aware of the transgressions of the Saints. Even if the Saints had been less discreet, their favorite delinquencies would have been perceived as less serious than those of the Roughnecks.

In the eyes of the police and school officials, a boy who drinks in an alley and stands intoxicated on the street corner is committing a more serious offense than is a boy who drinks to inebriation in a nightclub or a tavern and drives around afterwards in a car. Similarly, a boy who steals a wallet from a store will be viewed as having committed a more serious offense than a boy who steals a lantern from a construction site.

Perceptual bias also operates with respect to the demeanor of the boys in the two groups when they are confronted by adults. It is not simply that adults dislike the posture affected by boys of the Roughneck ilk; more important is the conviction that the posture adopted by the Roughnecks is an indication of their devotion and commitment to deviance as a way of life. The posture becomes a cue, just as the type of the offense is a cue, to the degree to which the known transgressions are indicators of the youths' potential for other problems.

Visibility, demeanor and bias are surface variables which explain the day-to-day operations of the police. Why do these surface variables operate as they do? Why did the police choose to disregard the Saints' delinquencies while breathing down the backs of the Roughnecks?

The answer lies in the class structure of American society and the control of legal institutions by those at the top of the class structure. Obviously, no representative of the upper class drew up the operational chart for the police which led them to look in the ghettos and on streetcorners—which led them to see the demeanor of lower-class youth as troublesome and that of upper-middle-class youth as tolerable. Rather, the procedures simply developed from experience—experience with irate and influential upper-middle-class parents insisting that their son's vandalism was simply a prank and his drunkenness only a momentary "sowing of wild oats"—experience with cooperative or indifferent, powerless, lower-class parents who acquiesced to the laws' definition of their son's behavior.

Adult Careers of the Saints and the Roughnecks

The community's confidence in the potential of the Saints and the Roughnecks apparently was justified. If anything, the community members underestimated the degree to which these youngsters would turn out "good" or "bad."

Seven of the eight members of the Saints went on to college immediately after high school. Five of the boys graduated from college in four years. The sixth one finished college after two years in the army, and the seventh spent four years in the air force before returning to college and receiving a B.A. degree. Of these seven college graduates, three went on for advanced degrees. One finished law school and is now active in state politics, one finished medical school and is practicing near Hanibal, and one boy is now working for a Ph.D. The other four college graduates entered submanagerial, managerial or executive training positions with larger firms.

The only Saint who did not complete college was Jerry. Jerry had failed to graduate from high school with the other Saints. During his second senior year, after the other Saints had gone on to college, Jerry began to hang around with what several teachers described as a "rough crowd"—the gang that was heir apparent to the Roughnecks. At the end of his second senior year, when he did graduate from high school, Jerry took a job as a used-car salesman, got married and quickly had a child. Although he made several abortive attempts to go to college by attending night school, when I last saw him (ten years after high school) Jerry was unemployed and had been living on unemployment for almost a year. His wife worked as a waitress.

Some of the Roughnecks have lived up to community expectations. A number of them were headed for trouble. A few were not.

Jack and Herb were the athletes among the Roughnecks and their athletic prowess paid off handsomely. Both boys received unsolicited athletic scholarships to college. After Herb received his scholarship (near the end of his senior year), he apparently did an about-face. His demeanor became very similar to that of the Saints. Although he remained a member in good standing of the Roughnecks, he stopped participating in most activities and did not hang on the corner as often.

Jack did not change. If anything, he became more prone to fighting. He even made excuses for accepting the scholarship. He told the other gang members that the school had guaranteed him a "C" average if he would come to play football—an idea that seems far-fetched, even in this day of highly competitive recruiting.

During the summer after graduation from high school, Jack attempted suicide by jumping from a tall building. The jump would certainly have killed most people trying it, but Jack survived. He entered college in the fall and played four years of football. He and Herb graduated in four years, and both are teaching and coaching in high schools. They are married and have stable families. If anything, Jack appears to have a more prestigious position in the community than does Herb, though both are well respected and secure in their positions.

Two of the boys never finished high school. Tommy left at the end of his junior year and went to another state. That summer he was arrested and placed on probation on a manslaughter charge. Three years later he was arrested for murder; he pleaded guilty to second degree murder and is serving a 30-year sentence in the state penitentiary.

Al, the other boy who did not finish high school, also left the state in his senior year. He is serving a life sentence in a state penitentiary for first degree murder.

Wes is a small-time gambler. He finished high school and "bummed around." After several years he made contact with a bookmaker who employed him as a runner. Later he acquired his own area and has been working it ever since. His position among the bookmakers is almost identical to the position he had in the gang; he is always around but no one is really aware of him. He makes no trouble and he does not get into any. Steady, reliable, capable of keeping his mouth closed, he plays the game by the rules, even though the game is an illegal one.

That leaves only Ron. Some of his former friends reported that they had heard he was "driving a truck up north," but no one could provide any concrete information.

Reinforcement

The community responded to the Roughnecks as boys in trouble, and the boys agreed with that perception. Their pattern of deviancy was reinforced, and breaking away from it became increasingly unlikely. Once the boys acquired an image of themselves as deviants, they selected new friends who affirmed that self-image. As that self-conception became more firmly entrenched, they also became willing to try new and more extreme deviances. With their growing alienation came freer expression of disrespect and hostility for representatives of the legitimate society. This disrespect increased the community's negativism, perpetuating the entire process of commitment to deviance. Lack of a commitment to deviance works the same way. In either case, the process will perpetuate itself unless some event (like a scholarship to college or a sudden failure) external to the established relationship intervenes. For two of the Roughnecks (Herb and Jack), receiving college athletic scholarships created new relations and culminated in a break with the established pattern of deviance. In the case of one of the Saints (Jerry), his parents' divorce and his failing to graduate from high school changed some of his other relations. Being held back in school for a year and losing his place among the Saints had sufficient impact on Jerry to alter his self-image and virtually to assure that he would not go on to college as his peers did. Although the experiments of life can rarely be reversed, it seems likely in view of the behavior of the other boys who did not enjoy this special treatment by the school that Jerry, too, would have "become something" had he graduated as anticipated. For Herb and Jack outside intervention worked to their advantage; for Jerry it was his undoing.

Selective perception and labeling—finding, processing and punishing some kinds of criminality and not others—means that visible, poor, non-mobile, outspoken, undiplomatic "tough" kids will be noticed, whether their actions are seriously delinquent or not. Other kids, who have established a reputation for being bright (even though underachieving), disciplined and involved in respectable activities, who are mobile and monied, will be invisible when they deviate from sanctioned activities. They'll sow their wild oats—perhaps even wider and thicker than their lower-class cohorts—but they won't be noticed. When it's time to leave adolescence most will follow the expected path, settling into the ways of the middle class, remembering fondly the delinquent but unnoticed fling of their youth. The Roughnecks and others like them may turn around, too. It is more likely that their noticeable deviance will have been so reinforced by police and community that their lives will be effectively channeled into careers consistent with their adolescent background.

20 "Drag Queens" and "Fag Hags"

DIANE E. TAUB
ROBERT G. LEGER

As should be apparent from some of the selections in earlier Parts of the book, by closely examining social life sociologists help make the familiar unfamiliar; that is, they cause us to look at familiar aspects of our world in a new light. Similarly, as in this selection, sociologists also examine the unfamiliar and help make them familiar; that is, their analyses help us to understand human behavior that might otherwise be incomprehensible.

The sexual preference of homosexuals, by setting them apart from the majority, isolates them in one way or another. Consequently, most heterosexuals have little direct contact with homosexuals—at least not knowingly. The negative attitudes that heterosexuals form come largely from cultural dictates, the mass media, and isolated instances of knowing, direct contact.

Not all heterosexuals have such limited contact with homosexuals, however, and Taub and Leger turn the sociological lens to one such exception. The "fag hag," (usually) a heterosexual female, skirts the edge of the male homosexual subculture, regularly participating in its social life and seldom crossing the line into homosexual behavior. This social role, incomprehensible to most heterosexuals, should become more understandable through this article. As Taub and Leger examine a second role, the "drag queen," and focus on leadership and rivalry, some of the complexities of the homosexual subculture should become evident. This is one benefit of an "insider's" approach to understanding social life.

. . . MOST HETEROSEXUALS HOLD RATHER DISTORTED IMAGES about the social identities of homosexuals. Contrary to popular belief homosexuals are not all alike. There are numerous social roles that have relevance for social identities within the homosexual community. This paper will focus on two important social identities related to the male homosexual scene. Although the vast majority of people in the male homosexual

195

community are not "drag queens" or "fag hags," our knowledge is increased by examining these identities in a college-aged population. These specific identities serve as important integrating influences within the male homosexual community. . . .

Since the most important public place for the young male homosexual subculture is often the local gay bar, the amateur entertainers or "drag queens" perform an important function. These individuals are focal points of interaction. Each clique has its own drag queens who serve to give the clique a particular identity and sense of exclusiveness. Another important social identity that has been virtually ignored is the "fag hag." The fag hag is a female who prefers the company of male gays. They are seen as nonstigmatizing by gays and serve an important friendship function.

The community studied maintains a value structure different from most values held by members of the older middle-class gay communities examined by Warren (1974) and Hooker (1967). An important value set of this community revolves around overtness and gay pride—an acceptance of one's sexual orientation as summarized in the phrase "gay is great." Beyond overtness, these young gays share many values with heterosexual young people, values that distinctly separate the old from the young in our society.

For example, one set of values centers around hedonistic activity that is a central aspect of sociability in some gay and heterosexual communities, that is, sexual relations without any emotional commitments coupled with high drug use. The lack of emotional involvement and an attitude of emotional indifference toward people and events are characteristic of many young people today. Young people often feel they are not responsible for making the world the mess it is today. They also feel they are not able to make it any better. The result is an escape into one's self—"partying," altered states of consciousness through drugs, and increased emphasis on the physical side of sex.

In addition, there is a pronounced tendency among some young people (both gay and straight) to forgo a pursuit of the success goal. Instead, the desire is either to prolong their student career or to get a limited-future type of job that provides a reasonably comfortable existence and allows people to "do their own thing." Thus, establishing one's personal identity is more important than pursuing the goals of society.

Data reported in this paper are part of an eighteen-month study of college-aged gays. The focal point of the gay community is a gay bar, located in close proximity to the local university. It is the only gay bar within a 100-mile radius of an area containing three cities: Johnson City, Bristol, and Kingsport, Tennessee. During the period of observation, the researchers employed ethnographic methodological techniques (see Warren, 1974). The researchers interacted with dozens of young gays, attended social functions, and were invited to the homes of several respondents. One researcher served as judge in two beauty pageants (drag contests). In general, the researchers were accepted as nonthreatening by most members of this gay community. To supplement the period of observation, interviews were conducted with six drag queens, six fag hags, and eight other members of the four cliques that share the use of the bar.

Social Groupings and the Gay Bar

Before the opening of the local gay bar, younger gays had no public places where they could meet, much less interact. When the *Connection* was turned into a gay bar, it quickly became the focal point not only for the local gay community, but also for attracting gays from around the region.

The opening of the gay bar led to the formation of a *bona fide* gay community. In fact, the community exists primarily *because* of the presence of the bar. This is because many of the gays are young (17-24 age group) and live with their parents. The parents are generally quite intolerant of homosexuality. Also, the few individuals who did maintain apartments either attended college or were just beginning a profession and were not in a position, financially, to have parties or other social events.

Initially, most gays were thrilled to have their own bar and there was much solidarity, a "family" feeling. Soon, however, cliques began forming around "reigning" individuals, the royalty at the bar, extremely popular and respected people such as financially endowed fag hags or performers (drag queens). Gays were attracted to reigning individuals from their own city. Of the four cliques, three formed around drag queens while the fourth coalesced around an affluent fag hag.

The basic unit of social organization in this community is the friendship clique. Within the bar, each clique always sat at a particular table that was publicly acknowledged as their home territory. Nongroup members did not sit at these tables unless invited (if nonmembers did sit at these tables they were met with silence or rudeness). On the rare occasions when clique members were not at the bar, their tables would remain empty even when the bar was fairly crowded.

While the bar featured a disco-type format, the main entertainment on the weekends consisted of drag shows. Because these shows were thoroughly enjoyed by young gays, the entertainers or drag queens received a great deal of prestige for their performances. In addition, young gays defined interaction with the queens as prestigious and "cool," resulting in the drag queens becoming major focal points of interaction at the bar.

The drag queen symbolizes a basic value orientation—overtness or the belief that one should accept the fact of one's gayness without any concern as to what others think. In contrast, however, Newton (1972:103) reports that gays in her sample avoided interaction with drag queens because these individuals symbolize "the stigma" of homosexuality. This resulted in the performer occupying an "ambivalent" position in that community. While amateur queens (like their professional counterparts) often represent "the stigma" of homosexuality, for younger gays interaction was appropriate because of their gay pride orientation toward their sexual preference.

When questioned as to why "she" is continuously surrounded by a lot of people, one drag queen replied:

> They're all my friends and they want to sit over at the front table, because they can see the shows better. I don't know, they just like to sit over there because our table gets crazy; we just love it. And that's why they come there—to have a good time. And then, I don't know, it makes them feel good if they know somebody personally that's up there on the stage. I mean, that's what they've said.

Each clique has its own drag performers, and the clique revolves around these individuals. Group members would show support for their particular drag queens by tipping them during performances.

Tipping is an integral part of the drag show. Tipping involves approaching the drag queen during the performance and placing money in her brassiere. In return, the performer may either kiss or hug the tipper. Sometimes, however, besides money, some members of the audience have given flowers, drinks, and *snorts* of amyl nitrite.

The ritual of tipping serves several useful functions. First, it is the only source of income for the performers since amateur queens are not paid by the bar. Second, tipping reinforces a clique's cohesiveness and identity by tipping a performer associated with one's particular group. Third, tipping provides higher status to the individuals who are seen giving the tip.

A major source of solidarity and identity for cliques, then, is the presence within the group of such reigning individuals as drag queens or affluent fag hags. Below, these two social identities will be examined in detail, focusing initially on specific characteristics of the roles in question. Then, where appropriate, the discussion will establish specifically the functionality of the role vis-à-vis the homosexual group.

Drag Queens

Drag queens are males who systematically wear female attire and, in this community, perform as female impersonators who pantomime to songs. While there is inherent within the role the desire to appear as feminine as possible both physically and mentally, drag queens go beyond simply imitating women to almost theatrically adopting as exquisite and "ladylike" an appearance as possible.

Most drag queens not only appear at the bar in drag, but also wear female attire to various public places. Some felt this was a test of their competence as a drag queen—if they can pass for straight women in heterosexual society, this is the ultimate compliment. One drag queen said:

> If you look good, you know, and you're coming across looking good, in the back of your mind you're thinking "Ha, ha, I've got all these people fooled, they all think I'm a woman, and I'm a man." The fact of fooling people is very satisfying.

Some, however, are discovered as female impersonators. Several of the drag queens stated that when heterosexuals or straights laugh or make fun of them in drag, they will proceed to act out the straights' expectations and stereotype of a "queer," that is, being as effeminate or "nelly" and flamboyant as possible. This behavior functions as a way of outraging straights because, "They have asked for it."

While going in drag is interpreted as "fun" by most gays (Warren, 1974:106), cross-dressing as a female for drag queens is taken quite seriously, to the extent that role incumbents imitate women not only behaviorally but attitudinally. They adopt most of the stereotypical characteristics that society attributes to the female role. A central aspect of the stereotypical female role, for example, is jealousy. One drag queen, the winner of the Ms. Gay Tri-Cities Pageant, reported that it was months before any of the other drag queens at the bar would speak to her. Drag queens are extremely jealous of one another as to the amount of money received through tipping, amount of applause, and general appearance.
. . .

Interestingly, drag queens could evidence a "we-feeling" in certain situations. For example, occasionally professional, out-of-town drag queens performed at the bar and for a while were given responsibility for running the shows. The presence of these individuals promoted hostility from area queens as the locals considered the professionals as "outsiders invading the territory." This produced the unusual situation of seeing Ms. Lovely (drag queen stage name) standing up and leading applause for another local drag queen, Ms. Smith, when, in fact, informants reported these two individuals could not stand one another under ordinary circumstances. Ms. Smith subsequently tipped Ms. Lovely after one of the latter's numbers. Again, this was highly unusual. Also, only when professionals perform will the amateur queens circulate among the crowd acting as hostesses, thereby showing the professionals how close they are to the crowd. In actuality, they are close only to their particular group.

The solidarity or "we-feeling" that develops in particular situations has been termed *calculated solidarity* (Giallombardo, 1966:15). . . . As calculated solidarity is based on the self-interests of the individuals involved, it can readily be seen that area queens were supportive of one another only when it was in their interests to do so in the first place. Perceiving a common threat, area drag queens exhibited solidarity to support one another and to give the professionals a false impression of unity.

Because the drag queens emulate women not only with respect to appearance but also with regard to stereotypical attitudes, we investigated the extent to which they have internalized an *actual* feminine identity. Except for a single respondent, all drag queens interviewed indicated experiencing desires to actually be women at one time or another in their lives. One drag queen said: .

> I would love to be a woman. I don't know if I could really go through a sex change, I think that would take so much—it would just be hard, you know. I've said so many times I'd just love to be able to have a baby.

All drag queens at least fantasized about various aspects of the female role such as having a baby or dreaming of being pregnant. The fantasies of pregnancy and the passionate longing for a maternal role in transsexuals have also been noted by Walinder (1967:3).

When considering homosexuality and gender identity, rather than classifying gays as possessing either a purely masculine identity or a purely feminine identity, a more valid approach is to think of male gays being ordered along a *continuum*, the polar extremes of which are masculinity and transsexuality or femininity. When interviewing drag queens on gender identity, a majority expressed similar opinions to the effect that one can be a certain percentage male and a certain percentage female. In fact, the fear of male characteristics reemerging is a major reason why many drag queens will not consider sex-change surgery. One respondent indicated that even if one were 90 percent female and 10 percent male

> that 10 percent male comes out quite often and I was afraid because if I ever have that change, I want to be pure woman. I don't want any male back here (points to his head). And I've seen people who are 60–40 and they—it drives them insane. You can understand how that would be. Here you are with the body of a man and the mind of a woman, yet you're thinking like a man. It's strange.

Fag Hags

A fag hag is a heterosexual woman who prefers to associate with gay males, usually platonically or maternally. A stereotypical fag hag is someone who is overweight (sometimes excessively so), is not especially attractive, and is a social outcast from the straight world. Some women often described themselves as "fag hags." When this label is used by heterosexuals, however, it is interpreted by gays as having a negative connotation.

In the literature there is but one study (Warren, 1976) that analyzes the role of women in the world of the gay male. However, Warren's sample was older and more conservative, predominantly lesbian, and was superficially functional in a passive sense within the gay community. For example, women were used by the gays to provide a straight "front" to members of conventional society and as a means of social control at gay social gatherings to prevent the occurrence of such events as orgies (Warren, 1976:161).

In our research, fag hags were very young, corresponding in age to the gay males with whom they associated. Also, the women interviewed were predominately heterosexual, although most respondents did report engaging in homosexual behavior largely as a consequence of pressure from gay males. Finally, the fag hags in this community played a much more active, aggressive role and were of greater functional importance than the women interviewed by Warren. The functional importance of the fag hag is well illustrated by the fact that one of the four major cliques at the bar coalesced around a wealthy female. From the gay male perspective, the fag hag fills a functionally important role as counselor, companion, and consultant on dress and clothing.

A major distinction between the community studied by Warren (1974; 1976) and the present research is use of drugs. Aside from alcohol, Warren's sample reported very little drug use. The community under study in our research, however, like its college-aged heterosexual counterpart, is heavily involved in drug use, especially "downers." This resulted in the fag hag playing a crucial role as a major source of such drugs as amyl nitrite, Quaaludes, librium, valium, marijuana (a staple), and even, on occasion, cocaine. Supplying drugs, liquor, and loaning money led many fag hags to believe that there was an element of exploitation involved in their relationships with some gays.

Warren (1976:161) reports that the women in her sample often served as a kind of surrogate through which the gay male could act out tendencies toward adopting the female role, for example, a gay male removing jewelry from a female and wearing it around the room. In our study, the fag hags adopted a more active and aggressive role than that portrayed by Warren. Here, for example, fag hags were indispensable to drag queens by providing a feminine role model for the queens to emulate, helping drag queens buy or sew a dress, assisting them in putting on their makeup, fixing fingernails and hair, and so on. Some fags hags even went beyond a mere surrogate role by actively encouraging certain gays to become drag queens.

While some fag hags believe that their relationship with gays is characterized by exploitation, gay males emphasize the reciprocal nature of their relationship with these women. In return for money and drugs, gay males maintain an environment (a "party" atmosphere) that ensure that all participants will have a good time.

These heterosexual women prefer interacting with gay males because, for one reason, gay bars are "less boring" and "more open." Another reason for interacting with gay males is that fag hags feel they are the beneficiaries of sociability without being the objects of seduction.

Warren (1976:164) notes that an additional reason for females associating with gay males is that these women prefer to avoid competition with other females in society. This competition does not exist in the world of the gay male. Finally, there is the added appeal of being seen in public with a member of the opposite sex.

Each clique at the bar has at least two fag hag members. These women can be extremely hostile or jealous if another fag hag attempts to join the group at the table. In a situation such as invasion of territory, in-group fag hags exhibited *calculated solidarity* in order to prevent collectively an outsider from gaining the attention of the male group members.

Male gays sometimes cast the fag hag into a type of maternal role that she may or may not accept. Fag hags were asked whether they considered their relationship with gay males to be sexual or more along the lines of a brother–sister, mother–sibling relationship.

Even though most female respondents indicated that they felt strictly sisterly or motherly toward the gay males, the majority had had sexual experiences and some had "been in love" with gay men. This is in sharp contrast to Warren (1974:113) who reports that fag hags, at least theoretically, are uninterested in sexual contacts with gay males. Fag hags do not necessarily regard sexual contacts with gays as challenging but instead interact sexually for gratification and to exhibit friendship. One informant had sexual relationships with gay males "to show them that they could succeed with women." Occasionally, a gay male and a fag hag will get married to lower societal reaction to homosexuality by passing as a straight couple, but these relationships usually end in divorce.

Fag hags, through interaction with members of the gay community, come to internalize many of the values of this group. For example, gay males heavily emphasize appearance and attire. Gay male informants indicated that fag hags, when they first begin interacting with gays, may exhibit a rather plain appearance. After a period of interacting with gay males, who stress fashion, neatness, and pride in the way they look, however, the fag hag may begin to internalize this gay orientation concerning appearance. The result is increased attractiveness on the part of these women.

Interaction with gay males also leads many fag hags to question their own sexual preference. Most of the fag hags have had occasional homosexual experiences. These females indicated that being around the gay community definitely affects one's sexual orientation.

One female respondent hypothesized that a reason that most fag hags have homosexual encounters is that they were inclined toward homosexuality *before* they met any male gays and used their association with gays to mask this sexual preference. This hypothesis is also offered in Warren's (1976:263) study in that it was believed that many fag hags were latent homosexuals. Other fag hags in our study reported that they knew of lesbians who became fag hags. However, most interviewees claimed that their experimentation with homosexuality was situationally induced. This behavior evolved because of the environment where there were no sanctions against homosexuality, and active socialization into gay norms and values were experienced.

Conclusion

This research has focused on aspects of two specialized social identities in a college-aged community. Other social identities, numerically more common, have not been considered. The contributions of drag queens and fag hags to the homosexual group have been highlighted. Cliques formed around "reigning" individuals at the bar, foremost being a particular social identity: the drag queen. Drag queens give cliques a sense of exclusiveness and identity by becoming focal points of interaction at the bar. A major reason why drag queens were centrally involved in this community is because these individuals symbolized a value orientation—overtness, "gay pride," and attitudes—that dominates most members sharing this subculture. . . .

A second social identity, which has never been examined in the context of the young gay community, is the fag hag. Warren (1976) found that most women in her study of a middle-class community were not centrally involved in gay social interaction and were functional only in a passive sense. In our community, however, whose basic values revolve around overtness and hedonism, fag hags fill a functionally critical role in that they are providers of services that are related to the central values of the subculture: free drugs and money. Finally, fag hags assist drag queens in preparing for their performances and even assist certain males in adopting the drag queen role.

This research differs from earlier analyses of gay communities (Warren, 1974; Hooker, 1967) because these previous efforts focus on older, middle-class gay groups. While this study deals with a young, college-aged gay community, it is important to note that many values of this group, values that are drastically different from those of the older, middle-class gay community, are not so much peculiar to younger gays as they are characteristic of many young people today. This study has illustrated that young gays have internalized certain values that are prevalent among the younger generation (hedonism, drug use, and sexual experimentation), and it has examined the unique ways in which gays live up to these particular values.

References

Giallombardo, Rose (1966). *Society of Women: A Study of a Women's Prison.* New York: Wiley.

Hooker, Evelyn (1967). "The Homosexual Community." Pp. 176–84 in John H. Gagnon and William Simon (eds.), *Sexual Deviance.* New York: Harper and Row.

Newton, Esther (1972). *Mother Camp: Female Impersonators in America.* Englewood Cliffs, N.J.: Prentice-Hall.

Walinder, Jan (1967). *Transsexualism.* Goteborg, Sweden: Akademiforlaget.

Warren, Carol A. B. (1974). *Identity and Community in the Gay World.* New York: Wiley-Interscience.

—— (1976). "Women Among Men: Females in the Male Homosexual Community," *Archives of Sexual Behavior,* 5:157–69.

21 Pronoia

FRED H. GOLDNER

As you know from your experiences, to maintain a balanced self-concept requires an intricate balancing of information—good, bad, and indifferent—that we receive from others. Sometimes we are "brought down" and feel badly about the negative information others give us about ourselves and our performances. At other times we are "floating on clouds" because of people's positive feedback. Most of us, most of the time, manage to accomplish this juggling act adequately.

Some people, however, never achieve a balanced self-concept. They are simply unable to accomplish a realistic internalization of positive and negative information. Some concentrate on negative information, characteristically blowing it out of all proportion. Others, no matter what people may say, continuously see themselves in a positive light. Out of a whole sequence of information, for example, most of which can be critical, they will pounce on anything that is even remotely positive.

On several occasions Goldner was impressed by this phenomenon of being blind to the negative, but he could find no term to describe it. He then set out to develop a descriptive concept based on his observations, thereby labeling another class of behavior as deviant. Whether pronoia will become a standard descriptive term of mental illness, we cannot say at this point. But I think you will enjoy discussing pronoia—as well as looking for examples of such negative-blindness among your acquaintances.

IN AN ATTEMPT TO UNDERSTAND SOME OF THE CONNECTIONS between organizational and personality processes I have encountered a phenomenon that is rarely discussed and little appreciated for its existence and its effect. It occurred to me a number of years ago that paranoia ought logically to have an opposite. If some people suffered from a disorder characterized by delusions of persecution, then others ought to suffer from delusions of support and exaggerated attractiveness. In 1969 I observed an acquaintance who actually did suffer from this delusion. The subsequent observation of others in many organizations (including academic organizations with which I was familiar and a large corporation in which I was an executive) led me to the conclusion that this phenomenon, which I call *pronoia*, is a real one that both creates problems for individuals and reflects a number of social problems.

Pronoia is the delusion that others think well of one. Actions and the products of one's efforts are thought to be well-received and praised by others who, when they talk behind one's back, must be saying good things, not bad. Mere acquaintances are seen as close friends. Politeness and the exchange of pleasantries are interpreted as expressions of deep attachment and the promise of future support. Because there was no word in our vocabulary to describe these kinds of delusions, I coined the word *pronoia*. The dictionary definition of paranoia does include positive as well as negative delusions (Morris, 1969). However, the negative delusions refer to the negative actions and attitudes of others while the positive delusions refer to feelings of grandeur about oneself. I am concerned not with delusions of grandeur but with delusions about what others think; and such positive delusions are not included in the definition of paranoia. It is not necessary to really think well of oneself to suffer from pronoia, but only to believe that others do.

Organizational Basis for Pronoia

Pronoia seems to be rooted in the social complexity and cultural ambiguity of our lives: We have become increasingly dependent on the opinions of others that are, in turn, based on uncertain criteria (Fromm, 1947:69; Riesman *et al.*, 1950). We do not submit our products to the impersonal forces of a market place. Instead, we increasingly find ourselves either in organizations operating outside of a market place or in market organizations in which our occupational tasks do not produce quantifiable or easily measured outputs. The more uncertain the criteria, then, the less the consensus and objectivity—and the more we are dependent on guesses about where we stand in the eyes of others. As the opinions of others become more important in deciding our fate, the greater the likelihood that neuroses about these relationships will develop. These conditions have increased in our society as we have developed larger, more complex organizations with intricate career paths, and defined success in terms of promotions. Our fates are in the hands of a few specific others.

Looking for Cues

Our lives are shaped by a kind of status ethic fraught with uncertainty: We look for signs that we have been chosen. Instead of looking to our material well-being for indications that we have already been chosen, we search for signs in the actions, behavior, and demeanor of those individuals who do the choosing.

When being chosen is important, when the criteria are vague, and when the decision is long-awaited, it is easy to presume that our every action is being evaluated and that the evaluators are as conscious as we are of the nuances of the interaction. Smiles, frowns, and apparent slights or expressions of interest all become cues about what the evaluators really think of us. Those subject to long-term evaluations assume that the process never stops. The assumption that everything done by someone in a position of authority is related to evaluation, is deliberate, and is significant, encourages the person being evaluated to search for cues to predict future actions of the evaluator.

Case Examples of Pronoid Behavior

The following descriptions of specific individuals are offered as examples of pronoid behavior. I observed each individual during the course of my experiences in academic and non-academic organizations. All the pseudonyms I have chosen are John because all of the individuals I observed were men. I do not know whether this was a coincidence, or whether pronoia is especially prevalent among men—though I suspect it is the latter.

1. John Smith and two partners had been working as consultants for a committee representing a large organization. Smith maintained most of the contact with the committee and kept reporting back to his partners that the committee and others in the organization were pleased with their work. The partners took these reports at face value, until they were each in turn present at meetings that Smith reported positively to the third partner. After comparing notes, the partners discovered that their judgments were considerably more negative than Smith's. Paying closer attention to Smith's reports, they discovered that he always distorted the reactions of others in a positive light. Smith continued to say he was loved and well thought of throughout the three-year contract with the committee, and claimed he was the key to the relationship. Near the end of the contract, the committee asked one of the partners to continue alone for another six months on the project—without Smith. The committee said they had waited until they were alone with this partner to make the offer because they had not wanted to confront Smith. They reported that Smith's assumptions about their positive reactions kept him from listening to their requests. Out of loyalty to Smith the partner talked the committee into a deal that included Smith for three months. Smith criticized the partner for not having obtained a longer contract and claimed he would have done

so if he had been present at the meeting. Significantly, the partner never told Smith what had happened.

2. John White, a high corporate official, referred to any influential person he had met once as a close personal friend. He met many such persons through his job and claimed he had a wide circle of influence. White also assumed that these people supported anything he had to say. He would return from meetings with a highly placed public official to describe how well he had been received, while other executives had direct information to the contrary. Similarly, he claimed that a union leader he had met with had agreed with him about an act he proposed that was against the interests of the union. My own checking revealed that the union leader, after hearing White's arguments, had acknowledged his position but not agreed with it. White, like other pronoids, seldom listened to others and assumed that others always agreed with him.

3. John Brown, a university professor, was applying for tenure. He submitted a long letter from someone in the field as evidence of how well his own work was received. In fact, the only positive aspects of the letter were the opening expression of interest and a closing sentence saying that Brown was involved in an interesting area of research and should keep the letter writer informed. The rest of the letter was a devastating critique of Brown's work. Brown harmed his own cause because he could only see the expressions of interest as positive reactions which then blinded him from seeing the negative content. As confirmed by a phone call, the opening and closing remarks were but the kind attempts of a colleague to soften the blow of criticism.

4. John Black was engaged in a bitter dispute with a department chairman that threatened Black's chances of obtaining tenure. He was convinced, and told outsiders so, that his accusations against the chairman were supported by the rest of the department and the administration, and that the chairman was "on his way out." Not only did Black lose that fight, and his job, but it was clear from talking with other department members that he never did enjoy their support.

Organizational and Interpersonal Encouragement of Pronoia

THE EVALUATIVE PROCESS AND CONDITIONS FOR PRONOIA

Bosses generally avoid criticizing subordinates to their face, thus leaving subordinates ignorant of negative evaluations. This is most likely to happen when the criteria are subjective or, if objective, when there are large numbers of criteria to choose among. If subordinates simply accepted negative evaluations without question, bosses would probably be less likely to avoid the encounter. But a subordinate who demands explicit reasons—where there are no objective, and hence obvious, measures—makes face-to-face evaluation a thankless task for the boss. The best evidence of this avoidance is the failure of most organizations to successfully implement periodic evaluation schemes within their management hierarchy (Sofer and Tuchman, 1970). Such schemes frequently fall into disuse because evaluators frequently give all employees high ratings in an attempt to avoid explaining or defending whatever distinctions among employees they would otherwise have to make (Blau, 1963:214). . . .

Most employees claim they want to know where they stand, but criticizing their work may destroy their self-esteem and render them even less use to the organization. This potential for the subordinate to make even less effort is another reason supervisors avoid evaluations, a factor further compounded when the parties have to continue working together. It is even more difficult to be frank in an evaluation meeting that is simply part of an ongoing process or is to be followed by a long delay before actions follow. Face-to-face negative confrontations are hard enough when the parties subsequently separate, but when their relationship continues it becomes considerably more difficult, and may serve no organizational purpose.

LETTERS OF RECOMMENDATION AS A MAJOR CAUSE OF PRONOIA

Letters of recommendation are notorious for their inflated language, their avoidance of negative factors, and their frequent equivocation (Lewis, 1969). An indication of the suspicion with which positive ones are received is that recipients try to develop schemes by which to obtain more accurate letters. For example, some assure people who write letters of reference that negative statements will not be taken into account unless at least two separate letters are negative, thus freeing the writer from the burden of hurting someone's chances. As mentioned in Brown's case, they also make follow-up phone calls.

This issue of inflated letters and of the expected need for subsequent calls is illustrated by a case reported in the *New York Times* (Butterfield, 1981) of a physician who obtained a hospital position on the basis of positive letters of recommendation from physicians who knew he had been convicted of raping a nurse. The article quotes an official from one of Harvard's teaching hospitals as saying that "all doctors were now aware that letters of recommendation have become cheapened and, in any case, the Buffalo hospital had not followed through with phone calls to check what the letters really meant."

Since letters of recommendation are almost always written for a position or reward in an institution other than the writer's own, it is easy for the writer to avoid the unpleasantness of putting his or her real thoughts on paper. For example, an acquaintance of mine, whom I shall call John Doe, was considered for a position at an institution where one of his friends was employed. The friend, who did not think highly of Doe's ability, was put in the difficult position of having to express his opinion about Doe in a formal letter. At the same time he also knew of Doe's pronoia and did not want to hurt him. However, he was sure Doe would turn down the position even if it were offered to him, thus freeing the friend to write a favorable letter.

The fact that persons see or hear about letters written on their behalf obviously encourages them to think that the writers hold them in higher esteem than they actually do. Similarly, subjects are impressed by the status of people who agree to write letters for them, despite the fact that high-status people frequently write letters simply to avoid the embarrassment of turning someone down. John Black told everyone that a prominent member of his discipline had written on his behalf. What Black did not realize was that some of their mutual acquaintances knew the letter was not an honest expression of the writer's feelings. People writing letters of recommendation may vary what they say depending on their view of the reputation of the institution involved; in this case the letter was positive because the institution involved was not held in high esteem by the writer. . . .

PRONOIA OF THOSE IN SUPERIOR POSITIONS

Superordinates may be as susceptible to pronoia as subordinates. This is especially true in societies where the consent of the governed is required, or where authority has to be legitimated by deed and not just by position. Those at the top are frequently shielded from bad news about themselves. The "yes man" who hides or distorts negative information from below is common to such societies.

Organizations have a number of mechanisms to create awe of the upper levels of the hierarchy among subordinates, in order to legitimate the authority structure (Thompson, 1961). Distance, pomp, ceremony, privileges, and ornate surroundings are all used to create awe. As a result, these top members frequently believe that the awe displayed toward them is intrinsic to their persons, and not to the office or resulting from specific mechanisms set up for that purpose.

We are even likely to encounter the conscious recognition of pronoia, along with subsequent attempts to avoid it, within certain segments of society. The very wealthy or the very powerful are often afraid that everyone who likes them does so for what they have to offer. Hence, they become suspicious of those who flatter them and cautious of all but the equally rich and famous. Pronoia, thus, is explicitly rejected.

Positive Reactions Induced by Pronoids

The previous section discussed some of the organizational mechanisms and interpersonal behavior of *others* that helped create conditions for pronoia. However, some of these conditions are also induced by the pronoids themselves. The aggressive and argumentative character of some people inhibits disagreement; others think such people don't want to listen. And usually there is no need to disagree unless too high a commitment is made by not doing so. . . . It is unpleasant enough to criticize someone; thus, if someone aggressively boasts about themselves or preaches a particular viewpoint it is even easier to avoid criticizing them.

One reacts to aggressive and assertive people the same way one usually reacts to a boor—with silence. One hesitates to respond for fear of encouraging the speaker to continue. Silence is the result, and silence is taken as agreement. John White didn't listen to the union leader's objections to his position, so the union leader simply acknowledged an understanding of White's position, ceased her rebuttal, and lapsed into silence. It was neither a formal nor an informal bargaining session, so the union leader had little to lose by appearing polite. White, however, interpreted the silence as agreement and told everyone that the union leader agreed with his position.

Another example of how silence encourages pronoia is provided by the behavior of John Jones, who had been discharged from a well-paying corporate position. He wrote a memo to the president suggesting how the president should respond to inquiries about him from search firms or prospective employers. In addition to asking the president to tell others that Jones had resigned and not been fired, he then listed in the memo his major strengths that could be praised to a prospective employer. Among them was his: "ability to manage large projects and provide directions"; his "excellent interpersonal skills, particularly in bringing together disparate people to achieve common goals, particularly since people trust me"; and his being "a self starter with little/no need for direction once goals have been set. I don't need to run to my boss on everything." He could not have put together a more accurate list of the weaknesses that led to his discharge. The president did not respond to the memo, nor had he disagreed with Jones in their last meeting when Jones praised himself. There was really no need to do so, because Jones was leaving and it would have been unpleasant to try to correct Jones's misimpressions. This silence encouraged Jones to believe that his former bosses thought highly of his capabilities—even though they fired him.

Displays of confidence reinforce pronoia because they too seldom meet with resistance or disagreement on the part of others. Even if not believed, others hesitate to correct these displays when the risk is small because the effort is not worth the consequences. . . . Displays of confidence, taken at face value without evidence to the contrary, become self-fulfilling. We assume that someone who appears confident must be thought well of by others—that the confidence is based on reality. . . .

"Name dropping" is a major characteristic of a number of pronoids. The briefest encounter with someone of recognized importance is described as an intimate relationship. John White is a perfect example of a name dropper. When he first entered the corporation, everyone was impressed by the important people with whom he appeared to be on intimate terms. He would frequently mention that he had dinner the previous night with this or that important politician; or, whenever the support of a high official was needed he would claim to be a close friend of the official. One day White's colleagues found out that his description of having had dinner with someone the previous night was his interpretation of his attendance, together with scores of other people, at a testimonial dinner for the named personage. White believed that attending a dinner function with other people, no matter how large the group, was the same as having dinner personally with every important guest. Similarly, he described as close friends people he had met the day before for the first time. White's pronoia apparently led him to assume that the merest acquaintance with someone of importance meant that the person was immediately impressed by him and could be counted on as a supporter. Name dropping, thus, is a kind of catalogue of pronoid situations.

Pronoids assume that every aspect of their relationship with someone is satisfactory if the other person describes any one aspect favorably. This leads to a great deal of difficulty for evaluators because every utterance reeks with significance for the person being evaluated. Offhand comments assume crucial importance and lead to complicated interpersonal relations whenever one person attributes greater significance to a statement than the other person does. Mere politeness is taken as proof of a positive, total relationship. Politeness fuels pronoia whenever an evaluator assumes that the person cannot make that distinction and believes everything said is significant.

This inability to distinguish between the trivial and the important is particularly apparent whenever friendship is a factor. Pronoids cannot separate the personal from the impersonal. Signs of friendship are taken as signs of formal business approval. Perhaps this is why subordinates try to personalize their relationships with those above them, and those in authority try to maintain some distance from subordinates.

John Green, another high corporate official, provides an example of such a case. When a new management team was brought into the corporation, Green was told he would soon be replaced and that he should look around for another job. He reacted to the news by reciting what he considered to be his strengths; as with Jones, these were the exact areas that others judged to be his weaknesses and the reasons why he was being fired. During the several months it took to find a successor for Green he was called upon to help the president in a personal situation involving a member of the president's family. Subsequently, Green continued to express friendly remarks to the president who, out of simple courtesy, did not act brusquely or unfriendly. Although nothing positive had been said to Green about his work during that period, when he was told that a successor had finally been found and that he would have to leave he expressed great shock and dismay. He had assumed that the previous negative notice was null and void because the president had not subsequently acted hostile to him. The fact that nothing positive about his work had been said or that the notice had not been rescinded was never considered. He grabbed at any positive signs and assumed they extended to the whole relationship. . . .

[Finally,] pronoia is encouraged during periods of organizational slack (Cyert and March, 1963:36) when there are surplus funds and organizational growth. In times of growth, promotions occur more rapidly, standards of promotions are lowered so that people are promoted who might not otherwise be moved up, and employees are retained who might otherwise be fired. Pronoia occurs if growth periods are preceded by tough times, because those promoted during growth periods assume they are being judged by the same tough standards that were applied during the preceding, more competitive period of scarce resources. . . .

Conclusions

Contemporary society seems to encourage introspection, yet we know little about the effects of this phenomenon. Most of our theories either assume or deny its existence. They do not treat introspection as a variable, and yet it seems clear to me that introspection must vary from culture to culture, from individual to individual, and from situation to situation. Estimating what others think of us is one form of introspection. Pronoia and paranoia are forms of self delusion about these estimates. They resolve, for many, the uncertainty about the opinions of significant people—people who are thrust upon us by the structure of our work rather than those whom we choose to be significant. . . .

References

Blau, Peter M. (1963). *The Dynamics of Bureaucracy*. Chicago: University of Chicago Press.

214 / *Fred H. Goldner*

Butterfield, Fox (1981). "Doctor, ousted in rape, got praise and new job." *New York Times*, October 24, sec. A. p. 16.

Cyert, Richard M., and James G. March (1963). *A Behavioral Theory of the Firm.* Englewood Cliffs, N.J.: Prentice-Hall.

Fromm, Erich (1947). *Man for Himself.* New York: Holt, Rinehart & Winston.

Lewis, Lionel S. (1969). "The puritan ethic in universities and some worldly concerns of sociologists." *American Sociologist*, 4:235–41.

Morris, William (ed.) (1969). *The American Heritage Dictionary of the English Language.* New York: Houghton Mifflin.

Riesman, David, with Ruel Denney and Nathan Glazer (1950). *The Lonely Crowd.* New Haven: Yale University Press.

Sofer, C., and M. Tuchman (1970). "Appraisal interviews and the structure of colleague relations." *Sociological Review*, 18:365–91.

Thompson, Victor A. (1961). *Modern Organization.* New York: Alfred A. Knopf.

22 Techniques of Neutralization

GRESHAM M. SYKES
DAVID MATZA

From our interaction with others, we learn people's expectations of us. As we accept and follow the rules laid down as appropriate for us, we submit to social control. Yet to some extent we all escape social control; that is, we all violate some rules to some degree, knowing that we may face negative reactions if we are caught. Few of us are criminals, but we are all involved in deviances every day. For example, we all fail to meet expectations concerning honesty and openness in intimate relationships, we violate traffic laws, or we shade the truth here and there in order to make things look better for ourselves.

How do we justify what we do? If we know we should do one thing and yet we do another, how do we cope with this? How do we "make it OK" to ourselves so that we do not have to feel guilty—or stop doing what we want to do? While few of us become prostitutes or muggers, we all develop ways of rationalizing, of justifying our deviating actions to ourselves. In this article, Sykes and Matza ask such questions of boys involved in delinquency. In their analysis of what they call *techniques of neutralization* (neutralizing the rules of society), they uncover some basic techniques that we all use. What techniques can you think of that did not show up in their study?

IN ATTEMPTING TO UNCOVER THE ROOTS of juvenile delinquency, the social scientist has long since ceased to search for devils in the mind or stigma of the body. It is now largely agreed that delinquent behavior, like most social behavior, is learned and that it is learned in the process of social interaction.

The classic statement of this position is found in Sutherland's theory of differential association, which asserts that criminal or delinquent behavior involves the learning of (a) techniques of committing crimes and (b) motives, drives, rationalizations, and attitudes favorable to the violation of law.[1] Unfortunately, the specific content of what is learned—as opposed to the process by which it is learned—has received relatively little attention in either theory or research. Perhaps the single strongest school of thought on the nature of this content has centered on the idea of a delinquent subculture. The basic characteristic of the delinquent subculture, it is argued, is a system of values that represents an inversion of the values held by respectable, law-abiding society. The world of the delinquent is the world of the law-abiding society turned upside down and its norms constitute a countervailing force directed against the conforming social order. Cohen[2] sees the process of developing a delinquent subculture as a matter of building, maintaining, and reinforcing a code for behavior which exists by opposition, which stands in point-by-point contradiction to dominant values, particularly those of the middle class. Cohen's portrayal of delinquency is executed with a good deal of sophistication, and he carefully avoids overly simple explanations such as those based on the principle of "follow the leader" or easy generalizations about "emotional disturbances." Furthermore, he does not accept the delinquent subculture as something given, but instead systematically examines the function of delinquent values as a viable solution to the lower-class, male child's problems in the area of social status. Yet in spite of its virtures, this image of juvenile delinquency as a form of behavior based on competing or countervailing values and norms appears to suffer from a number of serious defects. It is the nature of these defects and a possible alternative or modified explanation for a large portion of juvenile delinquency with which this paper is concerned.

The difficulties in viewing delinquent behavior as springing from a set of deviant values and norms—as arising, that is to say, from a situation in which the delinquent defines his delinquency as "right"—are both empirical and theoretical. In the first place, if there existed in fact a delinquent subculture such that the delinquent viewed his illegal behavior as morally correct, we could reasonably suppose that he would exhibit no feelings of guilt or shame at detection or confinement. Instead, the major reaction would tend in the direction of indignation or a sense of martyrdom.[3] It is true that some delinquents do react in the latter fashion, although the sense of martyrdom often seems to be based on the fact that others "get away with it" and indignation appears to be directed against the chance events or lack of skill that led to apprehension. More important, however, is the fact that there is a good deal of evidence suggesting that many delinquents *do* experience a sense of guilt or shame, and its outward expression is not to be dismissed as a purely manipulative gesture to appease those in authority. Much of this evidence is, to be sure, of a clinical nature or in the form of impressionistic judgments of those who must deal first hand with the youthful offender. Assigning a weight to such evidence calls for caution, but it cannot be ignored if we are to avoid the gross stereotype of the juvenile delinquent as a hardened gangster in miniature.

In the second place, observers have noted that the juvenile delinquent frequently accords admiration and respect to law-abiding persons. The "really honest" person is often revered, and if the delinquent is sometimes overly keen to detect hypocrisy in those who conform, unquestioned probity is likely to win his approval. A fierce attachment to a humble, pious mother or a forgiving, upright priest (the former, according to many observers, is often encountered in both juvenile delinquents and adult criminals) might be dismissed as rank sentimentality, but at least it is clear that the delinquent does not necessarily regard those who abide by the legal rules as immoral. In a similar vein, it can be noted that the juvenile delinquent may exhibit great resentment if illegal behavior is imputed to "significant others" in his immediate social environment or to heroes in the world of sport and entertainment. In other words, if the delinquent does hold to a set of values and norms that stand in complete opposition to those of respectable society, his norm-holding is of a peculiar sort. While supposedly thoroughly committed to the deviant system of the delinquent subculture, he would appear to recognize the moral validity of the dominant normative system in many instances.[4]

In the third place, there is much evidence that juvenile delinquents often draw a sharp line between those who can be victimized and those who cannot. Certain social groups are not to be viewed as "fair game" in the performance of supposedly approved delinquent acts while others warrant a variety of attacks. In general, the potentiality for victimization would seem to be a function of the social distance between the juvenile delinquent and others and thus we find implicit maxims in the world of the delinquent such as "don't steal from friends" or "don't commit vandalism against a church of your own faith."[5] This is all rather obvious, but the implications have not received sufficient attention. The fact that supposedly valued behavior tends to be directed against disvalued social groups hints that the "wrongfulness" of such delinquent behavior is more widely recognized by delinquents than the literature has indicated. When the pool of victims is limited by considerations of kinship, friendship, ethnic group, social class, age, sex, etc., we have reason to suspect that the virtue of delinquency is far from unquestioned.

In the fourth place, it is doubtful if many juvenile delinquents are totally immune from the demands for conformity made by the dominant social order. There is a strong likelihood that the family of the delinquent will agree with respectable society that delinquency is wrong, even though the family may be engaged in a variety of illegal activities. That is, the parental posture conducive to delinquency is not apt to be a positive prodding. Whatever may be the influence of parental example, what might be called the "Fagin" pattern of socialization into delinquency is probably rare. Furthermore, as Redl has indicated, the idea that certain neighborhoods are completely delinquent, offering the child a model for delinquent behavior without reservations, is simply not supported by the data.[6]

The fact that a child is punished by parents, school officials, and agencies of the legal system for his delinquency may, as a number of observers have cynically noted, suggest to the child that he should be more careful not to get caught. There is an equal or greater probability, however, that the child will internalize the demands for conformity. This is not to say that demands for conformity cannot be counteracted. In fact, as we shall see shortly, an understanding of how internal and external demands for conformity are neutralized may be crucial for understanding delinquent behavior. But it is to say that a complete denial of the validity of demands for conformity and the substitution of a new normative system is improbable, in light of the child's or adolescent's dependency on adults and encirclement by adults inherent in his status in the social structure. No matter how deeply enmeshed in patterns of delinquency he may be and no matter how much this involvement may outweigh his associations with the law-abiding, he cannot escape the condemnation of his deviance. Somehow the demands for conformity must be met and answered; they cannot be ignored as part of an alien system of values and norms.

In short, the theoretical viewpoint that sees juvenile delinquency as a form of behavior based on the values and norms of a deviant subculture in precisely the same way as law-abiding behavior is based on the values and norms of the larger society is open to serious doubt. The fact that the world of the delinquent is embedded in the larger world of those who conform cannot be overlooked nor can the delinquent be equated with an adult thoroughly socialized into an alternative way of life. Instead, the juvenile delinquent would appear to be at least partially committed to the dominant social order in that he frequently exhibits guilt or shame when he violates its proscriptions, accords approval to certain conforming figures, and distinguishes between appropriate and inappropriate targets for his deviance. It is to an explanation for the apparently paradoxical fact of his delinquency that we now turn.

As Morris Cohen once said, one of the most fascinating problems about human behavior is why men violate the laws in which they believe. This is the problem that confronts us when we attempt to explain why delinquency occurs despite a greater or lesser commitment to the usages of conformity. A basic clue is offered by the fact that social rules or norms calling for valued behavior seldom if ever take the form of categorical imperatives. Rather, values or norms appear as qualified guides for action, limited in their applicability in terms of time, place, persons, and social circumstances. The moral injunction against killing, for example, does not apply to the enemy during combat in time of war, although a captured enemy comes once again under the prohibition. Similarly, the taking and distributing of scarce goods in a time of acute social need is felt by many to be right, although under other circumstances private property is held inviolable. The normative system of a society, then, is marked by what Williams has termed *flexibility;* it does not consist of a body of rules held to be binding under all conditions.[7]

This flexibility is, in fact, an integral part of the criminal law in that measures for "defenses to crimes" are provided in pleas such as non-age, necessity, insanity, drunkenness, compulsion, self-defense, and so on. The individual can avoid moral culpability for his criminal action—and thus avoid the negative sanctions of society—if he can prove that criminal intent was lacking. *It is our argument that much delinquency is based on what is essentially an unrecognized extension of defenses to crimes, in the form of justifications for deviance that are seen as valid by the delinquent but not by the legal system or society at large.*

These justifications are commonly described as rationalizations. They are viewed as following deviant behavior and as protecting the individual from self-blame and the blame of others after the act. But there is also reason to believe that they precede deviant behavior and make deviant behavior possible. It is this possibility that Sutherland mentioned only in passing and that other writers have failed to exploit from the viewpoint of sociological theory. Disapproval flowing from internalized norms and conforming others in the social environment is neutralized, turned back, or deflected in advance. Social controls that serve to check or inhibit deviant motivational patterns are rendered inoperative, and the individual is freed to engage in delinquency without serious damage to his self-image. In this sense, the delinquent both has his cake and eats it too, for he remains committed to the dominant normative system and yet so qualifies its imperatives that violations are "acceptable" if not "right." Thus the delinquent represents not a radical opposition to law-abiding society but something more like an apologetic failure, often more sinned against than sinning in his own eyes. We call these justifications of deviant behavior techniques of neutralization; and we believe these techniques make up a crucial component of Sutherland's "definitions favorable to the violation of law." It is by learning these techniques that the juvenile becomes delinquent, rather than by learning moral imperatives, values or attitudes standing in direct contradiction to those of the dominant society. In analyzing these techniques, we have found it convenient to divide them into five major types.

The Denial of Responsibility. Insofar as the delinquent can define himself as lacking responsibility for his deviant actions, the disapproval of self or others is sharply reduced in effectiveness as a restraining influence. As Justice Holmes has said, even a dog distinguishes between being stumbled over and being kicked, and modern society is no less careful to draw a line between injuries that are unintentional, i.e., where responsibility is lacking, and those that are intentional. As a technique of neutralization, however, the denial of responsibility extends much further than the claim that deviant acts are an "accident" or some similar negation of personal accountability. It may also be asserted that delinquent acts are due to forces outside of the individual and beyond his control such as unloving parents, bad companions, or a slum neighborhood. In effect, the delinquent approaches a "billiard ball" conception of himself in which he sees himself as helplessly propelled into new situations. From a psychodynamic viewpoint, this orientation toward one's own actions may represent a profound alienation from self, but it is important to stress the fact that interpretations of responsibility are cultural constructs and not merely idiosyncratic beliefs. The similarity between this mode of justifying illegal behavior assumed by the delinquent and the implications of a "sociological" frame of reference or a "humane" jurisprudence is readily apparent.[8] It is not the validity of this orientation that concerns us here, but its function of deflecting blame attached to violations of social norms and its relative independence of a particular personality structure.[9] By learning to view himself as more acted upon than acting, the delinquent prepares the way for deviance from the dominant normative system without the necessity of a frontal assault on the norms themselves.

The Denial of Injury. A second major technique of neutralization centers on the injury or harm involved in the delinquent act. The criminal law has long made a distinction between crimes which are *mala in se* and *mala prohibita*—that is between acts that are wrong in themselves and acts that are illegal but not immoral—and the delinquent can make the same kind of distinction in evaluating the wrongfulness of his behavior. For the delinquent, however, wrongfulness may turn on the question of whether or not anyone has clearly been hurt by his deviance, and this matter is open to a variety of interpretations. Vandalism, for example, may be defined by the delinquent simply as "mischief"—after all, it may be claimed, the persons whose property has been destroyed can well afford it. Similarly, auto theft may be viewed as "borrowing," and gang fighting may be seen as a private quarrel, an agreed upon duel between two willing parties, and thus of no concern to the community at large. We are not suggesting that this technique of neutralization, labeled the denial of injury, involves an explicit dialectic. Rather, we are arguing that the delinquent frequently, and in a hazy fashion, feels that his behavior does not really cause any great harm despite the fact that it runs counter to law. Just as the link between the individual and his acts may be broken by the denial of responsibility, so may the link between acts and their consequences be broken by the denial of injury. Since society sometimes agrees with the delinquent, e.g., in matterns such as truancy, "pranks," and so on, it merely reaffirms the idea that the delinquent's neutralization of social controls by means of qualifying the norms is an extension of common practice rather than a gesture of complete opposition.

The Denial of the Victim. Even if the delinquent accepts the responsibility for his deviant actions and is willing to admit that his deviant actions involve an injury or hurt, the moral indignation of self and others may be neutralized by an insistence that the injury is not wrong in light of the circumstances. The injury, it may be claimed, is not really an injury; rather, it is a form of rightful retaliation or punishment. By a subtle alchemy the delinquent moves himself into the position of an avenger and the victim is transformed into a wrongdoer. Assaults on homosexuals or suspected homosexuals, attacks on members of minority groups who are said to have gotten "out of place," vandalism as revenge on an unfair teacher or school official, thefts from a "crooked" store owner—all may be hurts inflicted on a transgressor, in the eyes of the delinquent. As Orwell has pointed out, the type of criminal admired by the general public has probably changed over the course of years and Raffles no longer serves as a hero;[10] but Robin Hood, and his latter day derivatives such as the tough detective seeking justice outside the law, still capture the popular imagination, and the delinquent may view his acts as part of a similar role.

To deny the existence of the victim, then, by transforming him into a person deserving injury is an extreme form of a phenomenon we have mentioned before, namely, the delinquent's recognition of appropriate and inappropriate targets for his delinquent acts. In addition, however, the existence of the victim may be denied for the delinquent, in a somewhat different sense, by the circumstances of the delinquent act itself. Insofar as the victim is physically absent, unknown, or a vague abstraction (as is often the case in delinquent acts committed against property), the awareness of the victim's existence is weakened. Internalized norms and anticipations of the reactions of others must somehow be activated, if they are to serve as guides for behavior; and it is possible that a diminished awareness of the victim plays an important part in determining whether or not this process is set in motion.

The Condemnation of the Condemners. A fourth technique of neutralization would appear to involve a condemnation of the condemners or, as McCorkle and Korn have phrased it, a rejection of the rejectors.[11] The delinquent shifts the focus of attention from his own deviant acts to the motives and behavior of those who disapprove of his violations. His condemners, he may claim, are hypocrites, deviants in disguise, or impelled by personal spite. This orientation toward the conforming world may be of particular importance when it hardens into a bitter cynicism directed against those assigned the task of enforcing or expressing the norms of the dominant society. Police, it may be said, are corrupt, stupid, and brutal. Teachers always show favoritism and parents always "take it out" on their children. By a slight extension, the rewards of conformity—such as material success—become a matter of pull or luck, thus decreasing still further the stature of those who stand on the side of the law-abiding. The validity of this jaundiced viewpoint is not so important as its function in turning back or deflecting the negative sanctions attached to violations of the norms. The delinquent, in effect, has changed the subject of the conversation in the dialogue between his own deviant impulses and the reactions of others; and by attacking others, the wrongfulness of his own behavior is more easily repressed or lost to view.

The Appeal to Higher Loyalties. Fifth, and last, internal and external social controls may be neutralized by sacrificing the demands of the larger society for the demands of the smaller social groups to which the delinquent belongs such as the sibling pair, the gang, or the friendship clique. It is important to note that the delinquent does not necessarily repudiate the imperatives of the dominant normative system, despite his failure to follow them. Rather, the delinquent may see himself as caught up in a dilemma that must be resolved, unfortunately, at the cost of violating the law. One aspect of this situation has been studied by Stouffer and Toby in their research on the conflict between particularistic and universalistic demands, between the claims of friendship and general social obligations, and their results suggest that "it is possible to classify people according to a predisposition to select one or the other horn of a dilemma in a role conflict."[12] For our purposes, however, the most important point is that deviation from certain norms may occur not because the norms are rejected but because other norms, held to be more pressing or involving a higher loyalty, are accorded precedence. Indeed, it is the fact that both sets of norms are believed in that gives meaning to our concepts of dilemma and role conflict.

The conflict between the claims of friendship and the claims of law, or a similar dilemma, has of course long been recognized by the social scientist (and the novelist) as a common human problem. If the juvenile delinquent frequently resolves his dilemma by insisting that he must "always help a buddy" or "never squeal on a friend," even when it throws him into serious difficulties with the dominant social order, his choice remains familiar to the supposedly law-abiding. The delinquent is unusual, perhaps, in the extent to which he is able to see the fact that he acts in behalf of the smaller social groups to which he belongs as a justification for violations of society's norms, but it is a matter of degree rather than of kind.

"I didn't mean it." "I didn't really hurt anybody." "They had it coming to them." "Everybody's picking on me." "I didn't do it for myself." These slogans or their variants, we hypothesize, prepare the juvenile for delinquent acts. These "definitions of the situation" represent tangential or glancing blows at the dominant normative system rather than the creation of an opposing ideology; and they are extensions of patterns of thought prevalent in society rather than something created *de novo*.

Techniques of neutralization may not be powerful enough to fully shield the individual from the force of his own internalized values and the reactions of conforming others, for as we have pointed out, juvenile delinquents often appear to suffer from feelings of guilt and shame when called into account for their deviant behavior. And some delinquents may be so isolated from the world of conformity that techniques of neutralization need not be called into play. Nonetheless, we would argue that techniques of neutralization are critical in lessening the effectiveness of social controls and that they lie behind a large share of delinquent behavior. Empirical research in this area is scattered and fragmentary at the present time, but the work of Redl,[13] Cressey,[14] and others has supplied a body of significant data that has done much to clarify the theoretical issues and enlarge the fund of supporting evidence. Two lines of investigation seem to be critical at this stage. First, there is need for more knowledge concerning the differential distribution of techniques of neutralization, as operative patterns of thought, by age, sex, social class, ethnic group, etc. On *a priori* grounds it might be assumed that these justifications for deviance will be more readily seized by segments of society for whom a discrepancy between common social ideals and social practice is most apparent. It is also possible, however, that the habit of "bending" the dominant normative system—if not "breaking" it—cuts across our cruder social categories and is to be traced primarily to patterns of social interaction within the familial circle. Second, there is need for a greater understanding of the internal structure of techniques of neutralization, as a system of beliefs and attitudes, and its relationship to various types of delinquent behavior. Certain techniques of neutralization would appear to be better adapted to particular deviant acts than to others, as we have suggested, for example, in the case of offenses against property and the denial of the victim. But the issue remains far from clear and stands in need of more information.

In any case, techniques of neutralization appear to offer a promising line of research in enlarging and systematizing the theoretical grasp of juvenile delinquency. As more information is uncovered concerning techniques of neutralization, their origins, and their consequences, both juvenile delinquency in particular, and deviation from normative systems in general may be illuminated.

Notes

1. E. H. Sutherland, *Principles of Criminology*, revised by D. R. Cressey, Chicago: Lippincott, 1955, pp. 77–80.

2. Albert K. Cohen, *Delinquent Boys*, Glencoe, Ill.: The Free Press, 1955.

3. This form of reaction among the adherents of a deviant subculture who fully believe in the "rightfulness" of their behavior and who are captured and punished by the agencies of the dominant social order can be illustrated, perhaps, by groups such as Jehovah's Witnesses, early Christian sects, nationalist movements in colonial areas, and conscientious objectors during World Wars I and II.

4. As Weber has pointed out, a thief may recognize the legitimacy of legal rules without accepting their moral validity. Cf. Max Weber, *The Theory of Social and Economic Organization* (translated by A. M. Henderson and Talcott Parsons), New York: Oxford University Press, 1947, p. 125. We are arguing here, however, that the juvenile delinquent frequently recognizes *both* the legitimacy of the dominant social order and its moral "rightness."

5. Thrasher's account of the "Itschkies"—a juvenile gang composed of Jewish boys—and the immunity from "rolling" enjoyed by Jewish drunkards is a good illustration. Cf. F. Thrasher, *The Gang*, Chicago: The University of Chicago Press, 1947, p. 315.

6. Cf. Solomon Kobrin, "The Conflict of Values in Delinquency Areas," *American Sociological Review*, 16 (October 1951): 653–61.

7. Cf. Robin Williams, Jr., *American Society*, New York: Knopf, 1951, p. 28.

8. A number of observers have wryly noted that many delinquents seem to show a surprising awareness of sociological and psychological explanations for their behavior and are quick to point out the causal role of their poor environment.

9. It is possible, of course, that certain personality structures can accept some techniques of neutralization more readily than others, but this question remains largely unexplored.

10. George Orwell, *Dickens, Dali, and Others*, New York: Reynal, 1946.

11. Lloyd W. McCorkle and Richard Korn, "Resocialization Within Walls," *The Annals of the American Academy of Political and Social Science*, 293 (May 1954): 88–98.

12. See Samuel A. Stouffer and Jackson Toby, "Role Conflict and Personality," in *Toward a General Theory of Action*, edited by Talcott Parsons and Edward A. Shils, Cambridge: Harvard University Press, 1951, p. 494.

13. See Fritz Redl and David Wineman, *Children Who Hate*, Glencoe: The Free Press, 1956.

14. See D. R. Cressey, *Other People's Money*. Glencoe: The Free Press, 1953.

23 The Management of a Mugging

ROBERT LEJEUNE

Hated and feared, that's what muggers are. Hated because of their violations of the individual's person and feared because of the threat they pose to personal safety, they are among the most disrespected of any social group in American society. But, as Berger said in the opening essay to this book, nothing is too sacred or too profane to escape the scrutiny of inquiring sociologists. Motivated by curiosity, the desire to understand the why and how of mugging, Lejeune began interviewing muggers. The result is this remarkable article which takes us behind the scenes of this subterranean activity.

As you read this selection, note that Lejeune manages to avoid expressing judgments about muggers. He simply reports *their* points of view. This does not mean that Lejeune has no negative feelings about muggers, that he advocates mugging, that he is secretly a mugger himself, or any such thing. It is simply that he *suspended* his personal feelings, attitudes, and orientations in order to do this research. Because of this, we are treated to an "insider's" account of this part of our social world.

If you had done this study, do you think that you could have suspended your judgments? When sociologists study deviants, they constantly wrestle with this problem, for the most part successfully.

THE TERM "MUGGING," as it is used in everyday speech, refers to acts of robbery committed in public and semipublic places, usually by young and unskilled predators. In two of its essential aspects, its execution and effect on the members of urban society, the dominant characteristic of the mugging derives from the fact that force or the threat of force is used to obtain compliance from the victim. Robberies of this kind evoke the most fearful image of crime: the possibility of physical violence at the hands of strangers, as well as property theft (Conklin, 1972:5).[1] . . .

This analysis of mugging encounters is based on 28 individual inten-

Author's Note: I thank Nicholas Alex, for his useful comments on an earlier draft of this paper, and Thomas Bratter, Jacqueline Lejeune, and Leona Thompson for valuable leads in obtaining respondents.

sive interviews and four group interviews with 17 other individuals, all of whom had committed at least one mugging in the past six years.[2] The interviews were conducted in New York City during 1973–1974. . . .

Interviews were unstructured, conducted with a guide which focused primarily on ascertaining each respondent's perspective and behavior immediately before, during, and after mugging encounters in which he or she had taken an active part. I tried to obtain, in as great detail as possible, information on the first two muggings, the last mugging, and representative muggings in between. . . .

Preconfrontation Phase

The preconfrontation phase of a "take off" [mugging] is the period of time in which the mugger mobilizes himself for the confrontation with his victim(s). There are two central aspects of this preparatory phase which shall be analyzed here: the mugger's management of his own fears and his selection of victims. . . .

THE MANAGEMENT OF FEAR

The initial and most basic element in the preconfrontation phase is the decision to commit the act. This, the transformation of thought into action, makes manifest the would-be mugger's most critical management problem. He must overcome, or sufficiently suspend, personal fears likely to deter him from initiating a violent confrontation with a stranger.[3] For almost all respondents, even if they have been socialized for violence through numerous prior violent encounters such as street fights and gang fights, coping with fear is a central concern. All but two report fear as the most salient feeling experienced before and during their first take off. Some typical responses to an open-ended question concerning the respondents' first mugging illustrate the variations within this common expression of fear:

> Q: How did you feel about doing this?
> R6: Fear. Cold blooded fear. It's really amazing about people who rip off other people. You know, here you are the victim and saying: "Wow, I'm scared to death. They're gonna cut me and do all these things to me." And meanwhile you don't realize that the dude that's doing the ripping off, man, is just as scared, if not more afraid of you.
> R9: I was scared, but it was exciting. You see, the whole thing, I was scared and excited. And I knew, you know, I had a fifty-fifty chance of either getting away or getting caught. But I figured that was the chance I was going to take. I wanted to get the money. . . .

CHANGING THE DEFINITION OF THE SITUATION: NORMALIZATION

A comparison of accounts of early muggings with the accounts of subsequent muggings by the same respondents indicates that muggers in varying degrees, become more adept over time, and through experience, in the management of their fears. The most important way in which the assessment of the risks involved in doing a mugging is reduced is through a process of *normalization*. The very success experienced in the first few muggings enables the mugger to lower his estimate of the likely risks entailed in future confrontations. . . .

> R17: You scared the first time. But the second time you feel better. The third time you even feel better. You feel like taking off four or five people— even though you've gotten over already. You say to yourself: "Eh, man, I didn't know it was that easy, man. Just go up to a dude: 'give me your money!' "
>
> R9: It just became so easy. It was like a regular payday. Like Friday is the day we gonna have some money. Sometimes we'd do two a night, you know. . . .

The process of normalization is facilitated by experiencing both positive effects and a lack of negative consequences. As in the case of other types of deviance successful execution of the activity becomes a reinforcer for repetition (Becker, 1963: 41–78). Each time that a mugging does not lead to negative consequences it becomes easier to view it as free of major risks. Moreover, some respondents come to experience the activity as intrinsically enjoyable, apart from the monetary rewards. There are several variations in this sense of well-being. Two that stand out are the feeling of power that results from having controlled and dominated the victim, and the experience of retribution for what the mugger views as past injustices inflicted upon him:[4]

> R10: After the first few times I wasn't scared any more. And I felt sort of strongly about it—like I was some kind of god. Because here I am, and there's this person that's scared of *me*. And you know it was so easy to get the money from him that sometimes, you know, it can get habit forming.
>
> R35: I was scared. The first couple of times you felt you would get caught. But then you got used to it. You get a good feeling, like you're getting back at people. . . .

From the mugger's perspective the police, the victim, and witnesses are the three possible sources of danger and causes of fear during the execution of a take off. Each of these represents the threat of personal injury or arrest. Of the three, uniformly, it is the victim that is perceived as potentially the least predictable and least controllable threat.[5] Consequently, "on the stroll"—during that period of time when the mugger walks casually in search of prey—much of his attention and concern is directed toward the selection of the "right" victim.

When asked how they choose their victims almost all respondents indicate two common-sense principles which govern their selection. The victim of choice is one perceived by the mugger as unlikely to resist and likely to yield an acceptable payoff:

> Q: What kind of victim did you look for? . . .
>
> R12: We take our time, you know, but not looking too conspicuous. And just take our time until we see somebody that we think that wouldn't give us no trouble, and have some money.
>
> R15: I was always looking for somebody looked scared to me when I looked at them. You know, people give off vibes. You feel this guy looks scared. He'll give it to you in a minute. . . .

Most respondents also take some pride in their ability to spot such victims; those who are weak (the lames) and those who foolishly flash their money in public (the chumps). There is, however, limited consensus on the specific characteristics of such targets; respondents do not share any clearly formulated set of rules or indicators for implementing the selection of the "right" victim. For example, some will see women or old people as ideal "lames"; others will disagree and prefer middle aged or young men. In each case it is claimed that the preferred type of victim is less likely to resist. Consequently, while almost all respondents justify their choice of victims in terms of the anticipated vulnerability and/or lucrativeness of the target, such statements may only represent rationalizations for actions determined mostly by impulse and circumstances. . . .

Among opportunity factors, the mugger's geographical location at the time he experiences the impulse to mug is most likely to limit his choice of victims. Unlike the professional robber he is usually either too young or down-and-out to own a car. He may use public transportation to seek out victims, both in transit and in distant neighborhoods. But, typically, the mugging takes place within walking distance of the "hangout," where alleyways, rooftops, parks, and other escape routes and hiding places are well known. . . .

DENORMALIZATION OF APPEARANCES

Prior to the confrontation the mugger attempts to cope with his own fears by defining the situation as routine or normal. He selects his victims and generally acts so as to reduce the occasions for "alarms" (Goffman, 1971: 238–47). As he initiates the confrontation he attempts not only to continue to hold his own fears under control, but also to control the situation by inducing fear in his victim. He must, in short, denormalize the situation for the victim as he attempts to define it as relatively normal for himself. . . .

The trouble-free execution of a take off requires that the mugger either surprise, and quickly and unambiguously define the situation to the victim, or rapidly transform a nonthreatening, or less threatening, encounter (e.g., a panhandling or a request for directions) into a robbery. In either case the victim is likely to experience the shock and disbelief which often accompanies rapid deterioration of scenes from benign to malevolent. Such an experience, uniformly reported by victims of muggings (Lejeune and Alex, 1973: 265-76), is also perceived as a management problem by the mugger. Most apprehend this momentary disorientation on the part of the victim as "resistance," and treat it as such—a response which I shall examine in greater detail below. Some muggers are also aware that the victim may not initially comprehend what is going on.

Ironically, the very elements which enable the mugger to limit his risks during the preconfrontation phase, and to facilitate the achievement of maximum surprise, are also likely to accentuate the condition of disbelief for the victim, and consequently the management problem for the mugger during the confrontation phase. Muggers who do not carry weapons, who dress "conventionally," or in other ways do not appear to the victim as credible adversaries to be feared must rectify the impression created by their "respectable" appearance during the initial moments of the confrontation. In such cases unwitting challenge by the victims of what the muggers claim to be, almost inevitably results in the latter's intensification of their threatening manner, or in the use of force:

> R32: I seen like the looks on the victims. They were looking at each other and there was a faint thing of like a smile; like is this some kind of joke boys? Or something like that. And then when they seen me put my hand inside my coat and just start walking toward them, that's when they realized, you know, that it was on.
>
> R31: Like we walked in and my friend had the gun. And he said: "Don't move." And the lady start smiling. I don't know what to do at that moment. I started thinking—looking at her—why is she smiling? It's a robbery, you know. It was funny, man. My friend said: "I'm serious, I'm serious." And she's smiling. I had a knife and I grabbed her son. I yelled to her. "Don't move or your son will get hurt! . . ."

Once the victim has been approached the mugger's success depends on his ability to control his victim. He does this by the way he presents himself—his posture of toughness—and by the use of direct physical force.

THE POSTURE OF TOUGHNESS

In the execution of a mugging the posture of toughness is a dramaturgic device used to intimidate the victim and also, frequently, to impress associates. While more developed as an interactional style and attitude in the lower-class male subculture (Miller, 1958), role models for this kind of behavior can be found in all strata of society as well as the mass media. Those most successful at enacting this role are characterized as having "balls" or "heart"; those who cannot or will not are "punks" or "faggots." . . .

To "show your heart" in a mugging means most emphatically, often quite self-consciously, to play a role that masks any emotion other than toughness. It calls for the use of voice tone and demeanor, as well as physical force, in order to attain rapid and unequivocal dominance over the victim. Those most capable of doing this may earn the label of "take off artist" or "stickup king":

> R28: When you're a take off artist you have to be cold. You gotta show your heart. You gotta show you're not scared to shoot—kill this person if he gives you any hassle. And, you know, if you show you're weak in your emotions then he'll say: "Please don't take it. I need it for such and such. My wife's in the hospital. She's gonna die." You have to say: "Give it up!—you know, period—or I'll shoot you." Not even shake, you know. You have to look cool, like shooting you ain't no big thing. I'm not scared to be caught. You'll be dead. . . .

The intimidation of victims during a mugging depends on the robber's threats and his willingness to use force. The posture of toughness is a dramaturgic adjunct to, or substitute for, the actual use of force. In mugger's accounts, when effectively enacted, it tends to reduce the likelihood of physical injury to the victim. When it fails as a primary method of control the mugger is likely to turn to violent means.

VIOLENCE AND CONTROL

The use of some physical force by young and frequently inept robbers—particularly among those who execute robberies without weapons—occurs more frequently than not (Conklin, 1972: 102–22; Mulvihill et al., 1969: 234–38). Thus, a mugging is essentially a violent encounter in which the possibility that the victim(s) will be seriously hurt is always present. Apart from those cases where the attacker is intent on hurting the victim as a source of gratification, his use of physical violence represents either a means of gaining control, or a loss of control, over the victim. In the first instance force is used as an initial tactic in anticipation of, but prior to, any "resistance" on the part of the victim. In the second instance force is used in response to perceived "resistance" on the part of the victim. The perceived rational use of force among respondents may therefore be classified as either *preemptive* or *reactive*.

The mugger will tend to use preemptive force to quickly define the situation to the victim as a robbery when he is, or feels, unable to control the situation by other means. The younger muggers, particularly the less experienced ones, or in general those for whom mugging has not become normalized, are more likely to rely on preemptive force as an inherent part of the initial moments of the mugging encounter. Thus, for example, one respondent after barely avoiding apprehension by the police during his first take off, describes how he attempted to minimize his risks during the second take off.

> R15: The second time I said, "I'm not gonna fumble up the job. And I'm not gonna let him scream either." You know, I began getting scared of getting caught and I said: "In order for me not to get caught I'm gonna have to make sure that this cat doesn't, you know, scream. . . ." And you know the guy came up the steps and I made believe I was coming down. But this time I didn't even tell him he was getting held up, you know, "Give up your money." I just hit him, you know, to make sure he knew I meant business. I hit him with the pistol. . . .

An initial use of force without warning may also be seen as desirable or not depending on the perceived characteristics of the victim. A strong or tough looking man is either not likely to be attacked, or if he is attacked, is likely to be hit hard or injured prior to any demand for money.

> R7: I thought ahead of what was gonna happen and said: "Well, this cat might fight back." Then my first blow would be a strong blow, or my first grip would be a strong grip—depending on the person.
> R3: It's 5:30 A.M. A man's coming home from work. I walk up to him, throw a kick. He falls on the floor. I take out my chukas, wrap them around his neck. My friend John walks up kicks him in the side. (He was a big black man about thirty-five.)
> Q: Why did you decide to beat him before asking him for his money?
> R3: Because he was too big.

The term reactive force is used here to indicate the second and most frequent type of violent mugging situation, in which the robber fails to obtain, or loses, control over the victim. Respondents, in their accounts of these emergent developments, typically characterize their violence as precipitated by victim "resistance"; as occurring in situations where the victim screamed, fought back or refused to "give it up." Such failures to comply—real or imagined—are interpreted by the attackers as justifications for violent responses. From their perspective reactive force is the inevitable outcome of the victim's failure to accede to the seemingly self-evident social calculus of the situation.

In this perspective the mugger defines the situation as one in which he has attempted, in the first few seconds of the encounter, not only to instill fear but also to communicate to the victim that in return for "cooperation" the use of force will be limited. Having in his own mind established a "coercive exchange" (Goffman, 1971: 329), albeit one that the victim may not understand or may not be able to fulfill, the mugger is likely to define any failure to comply to his expectations as a justified cause for a violent response.

> R30: I went to take off his money. But I didn't go with the intention of hurting him—because I figured he was smart enough to give up the money. But what he did when I had him in the hallway: he screamed. And I got uptight, you know. And me being uptight, I used the knife. And other times people that I went to rob, they gave me a hard time. To get the money that I wanted to get I had to stab them.
>
> R10: Like I tell the man: "Give it up!" And like if he gave it to me, beautiful. I wouldn't climb on him or nothing. You dig it. But if the dude—this is the way I felt, man—if the guy said to me—like I tell him: "Give it up!" He says: "No." He's giving me, you know, trouble. I'm gonna feel like he has a whole lot of nerve. Dig it. I'm gonna get violent. I would get extremely violent. I felt like it was my right; it was my due.

In these and similar accounts the tendency to blame the victim for his injury is evident. Most respondents are well aware of the moral implications of an unprovoked violent attack upon another human being. By shifting the burden of responsibility to the victim they attempt—at least in retrospect—to justify their violence. Whether or not the victim incurs physical injury is no longer seen as a function of the actions of the aggressor but becomes defined as a consequence of the victim's compliance or lack of it. . . .

Conclusion

The mugging is a primitive form of criminal activity. It is practiced by those too young, or otherwise too inept, to execute crimes requiring greater skill and knowledge. Force and the threat of force are substituted for cunning, deception, and expertise. The main advantages of the mugger in his encounter with his victim are surprise and his ability to evoke fear. In addition, the mugger relies for the success of his crime on easily transferred common knowledge and skills learned in play, sport, and everyday street interactions with peers. He relies on the knowledge acquired in childhood; the unconventional use of space—roofs, alleyways, and parks are places for lurking and escaping. Apart from easily obtained weapons his major material resource is his body—used for running and for applying physical force. His interactional skills, relevant to the management of the mugging, are those acquired on the street, in an environment where being cool and being tough are requisites for survival. From the flexibility of his action, the quickness and unpredictability of his strike, and his willingness to use force he gains great advantage over his victim.

Despite these obvious tactical advantages the mugger remains uneasy in his activities. The central theme which emerges from my interviews with persons who have mugged is their concern with loss of control over their victims. The respondents' initial experiences as muggers—most frequently in early adolescence—bear the characteristics of experimentation in dangerous games. The "action" and the sense of power that they experience are often a source of thrills. They are also occasions for fear.

Impelled to continue to mug for a variety of reasons—a persistent desire to prove themselves or the need to maintain an expensive drug habit—individuals seldom mug, in intermittent episodes, for more than two or three years. Interspersed with other acts of delinquency, mugging is usually a sideline activity engaged in when other rip offs and hustles, perceived as more lucrative or less risky, are not available. With experience mugging tends to become "routine." But ultimately it is dropped from the criminal repertoire. Despite the relative normalization that occurs for many participants most retain, underneath the bravado, a sense of their own vulnerability.

Notes

1. Thus, while the mugging is usually a transitory encounter, the consequences for the victims, sometimes physical, but more frequently emotional, are long lasting; victims and their circles of associates are likely to undergo major intensification of their personal sense of vulnerability (Furstenberg, 1971; Lejeune and Alex, 1973).

2. It is difficult to accurately estimate the frequency distribution of the number of muggings committed by the respondents since after the first few take offs they had lost count. However, on the basis of their own gross estimates and their recall of the typical weekly frequency and duration of their mugging episodes(s), the range varies, conservatively, from one to several hundred. Among the 28 respondents interviewed individually, from whom I obtained frequency estimates, 10 are estimated to have mugged from one to 15 times, nine from 16 to 60 times, and the other nine over 60 times.

3. Other feelings, such as moral repugnance and guilt, are mentioned spontaneously only a few times in the interviews. These are "neutralized" through the techniques described by Sykes and Matza (1957).

4. Most respondents articulate some expression of having been victimized by society and its agents. In addition more than half of the respondents report that they have themselves been victims of muggings. Not infrequently such prior victimization—either of the respondent or of a close relative—is seen as justification for the first mugging of another person.

5. The mugger can easily shield his actions from the view of police or bystanders under the cover of darkness, or by attacking in isolated areas and enclosed spaces (Newman, 1972). If his attack remains visible to some witnesses he may (and does) rely on their apathy and fear to deter them from interventions (Freeman, 1966). But the victim, under direct attack, is anticipated to react, from fear

or anger, in ways which may jeopardize the mugger's safety; by screaming or in other ways resisting he may make the attack more visible to the police, or perhaps strike back and physically injure the attacker.

References

Becker, H. S. (1963). *Outsiders* Glencoe, Ill.: Free Press.

Conklin, J. E. (1972). *Robbery and the Criminal Justice System.* Philadelphia: Lippincott.

Freeman, L. (1966). "No response to the cry for help." pp. 170–82 in J. Ratcliffe (ed.), *The Good Samaritan and the Law.* Garden City, N.Y.: Anchor Books.

Furstenberg, F., Jr. (1971). "Public reaction to crime in the streets." *Amer. Scholar*, 40: 601–10.

Goffman, E. (1971). *Relations in Public.* New York: Harper & Row.

Lejeune, R., and N. Alex (1973). "On being mugged: The event and its aftermath." *Urban Life and Culture*, 2: 259–87.

Miller, W. B. (1958). "Lower class culture as a generating milieu of gang delinquency." *J. of Social Issues*, 14: 5–19.

Mulvihill, J., M. M. Tumin; and L. A. Curtis (1969). *Crimes of Violence.* Washington, D.C.: Government Printing Office.

Newman, O. (1972). *Crime Prevention Through Urban Design: Defensible Space.* New York: Macmillan.

Sykes, M., and D. Matza (1957). "Techniques of neutralization: A theory of delinquency." *Amer. Soc. Rev.*, 22: 264–70.

24 The Pathology of Imprisonment

PHILIP G. ZIMBARDO

Why are prisons such powder kegs? Zimbardo provides remarkable insight into some of the reasons. It is not simply due to the kind of people who are locked up, that they are criminals, that they are disposed to violence, that they are antisocial, or that they hate the guards, the food, or the restrictions of prison life. While people often cite such reasons to explain prison violence, it turns out that much more fundamental social issues are involved. As this remarkable experiment uncovered, the basic structures of the prison are a foundation for prison brutality and violence.

While reading this fascinating account, you may begin to think about how prisons could be changed in order to minimize violence, especially changes that might be required in the social structure of prisons.

I was recently released from solitary confinement after being held therein for 37 months [months!]. A silent system was imposed upon me and to even whisper to the man in the next cell resulted in being beaten by guards, sprayed with chemical mace, blackjacked, stomped and thrown into a strip-cell naked to sleep on a concrete floor without bedding, covering, wash basin or even a toilet. The floor served as toilet and bed, and even there the silent system was enforced. To let a moan escape your lips because of the pain and discomfort . . . resulted in another beating. I spent not days, but months there during my 37 months in solitary. . . . I have filed every writ possible against the administrative acts of brutality. The state courts have all denied the petitions. Because of my refusal to let the things die down and forget all that happened during my 37 months in solitary . . . I am the most hated prisoner in [this] penitentiary, and called a "hardcore incorrigible."

Maybe I am an incorrigible, but if true, it's because I would rather die than to accept being treated as less than a human being. I have never complained of my prison sentence as being unjustified except through legal means of appeals. I have never put a knife on a guard's throat and demanded my release. I know that thieves must be punished and I don't justify stealing, even though I am a thief myself. But now I don't think I will be a thief when I am released. No, I'm not rehabilitated. It's just that I no longer think of becoming wealthy by stealing. I now only think of killing—killing those who have beaten me and treated me as if I were a dog. I hope and pray for the sake of my own soul and future life of freedom that I am able to overcome the bitterness and hatred which eats daily at my soul, but I know to overcome it will not be easy.

THIS ELOQUENT PLEA FOR PRISON REFORM— for humane treatment of human beings, for the basic dignity that is the right of every American—came to me secretly in a letter from a prisoner who cannot be identified because he is still in a state correctional institution. He sent it to me because he read of an experiment I recently conducted at Stanford University. In an attempt to understand just what it means psychologically to be a prisoner or a prison guard, Craig Haney, Curt Banks, Dave Jaffe and I created our own prison. We carefully screened over 70 volunteers who answered an ad in a Palo Alto city newspaper and ended up with about two dozen young men who were selected to be part of this study. They were mature, emotionally stable, normal, intelligent college students from middle-class homes throughout the United States and Canada. They appeared to represent the cream of the crop of this generation. None had any criminal record and all were relatively homogeneous on many dimensions initially.

Half were arbitrarily designated as prisoners by a flip of a coin, the others as guards. These were the roles they were to play in our simulated prison. The guards were made aware of the potential seriousness and danger of the situation and their own vulnerability. They made up their own formal rules for maintaining law, order and respect, and were generally free to improvise new ones during their eight-hour, three-man shifts. The prisoners were unexpectedly picked up at their homes by a city policeman in a squad car, searched, handcuffed, fingerprinted, booked at the Palo Alto station house and taken blindfolded to our jail. There they were stripped, deloused, put into a uniform, given a number and put into a cell with two other prisoners where they expected to live for the next two weeks. The pay was good ($15 a day) and their motivation was to make money.

We observed and recorded on videotape the events that occurred in the prison, and we interviewed and tested the prisoners and guards at various points throughout the study. Some of the videotapes of the actual encounters between the prisoners and guards were seen on the NBC News feature "Chronolog" on November 26, 1971.

At the end of only six days we had to close down our mock prison because what we saw was frightening. It was no longer apparent to most of the subjects (or to us) where reality ended and their roles began. The majority had indeed become prisoners or guards, no longer able to clearly differentiate between role playing and self. There were dramatic changes in virtually every aspect of their behavior, thinking and feeling. In less than a week the experience of imprisonment undid (temporarily) a lifetime of learning; human values were suspended, self-concepts were challenged and the ugliest, most base, pathological side of human nature surfaced. We were horrified because we saw some boys (guards) treat others as if they were despicable animals, taking pleasure in cruelty, while other boys (prisoners) became servile, dehumanized robots who thought only of escape, of their own individual survival and of their mounting hatred for the guards.

We had to release three prisoners in the first four days because they had such acute situational traumatic reactions as hysterical crying, confusion in thinking and severe depression. Others begged to be paroled, and all but three were willing to forfeit all the money they had earned if they could be paroled. By then (the fifth day) they had been so programmed to think of themselves as prisoners that when their request for parole was denied, they returned docilely to their cells. Now, had they been thinking as college students acting in an oppressive experiment, they would have quit once they no longer wanted the $15 a day we used as our only incentive. However, the reality was not quitting an experiment but "being paroled by the parole board from the Stanford County Jail." By the last days, the earlier solidarity among the prisoners (systematically broken by the guards) dissolved into "each man for himself." Finally, when one of their fellows was put in solitary confinement (a small closet) for refusing to eat, the prisoners were given a choice by one of the guards: give up their blankets and the incorrigible prisoner would be let out, or keep their blankets and he would be kept in all night. They voted to keep their blankets and to abandon their brother.

About a third of the guards became tyrannical in their arbitrary use of power, in enjoying their control over other people. They were corrupted by the power of their roles and became quite inventive in their techniques of breaking the spirit of the prisoners and making them feel they were worthless. Some of the guards merely did their jobs as tough but fair correctional officers, and several were good guards from the prisoners' point of view since they did them small favors and were friendly. However, no good guard ever interfered with a command by any of the bad guards; they never intervened on the side of the prisoners, they never told the others to ease off because it was only an experiment, and they never even came to me as prison superintendent or experimenter in charge to complain. In part, they were good because the others were bad; they needed the others to help establish their own egos in a positive light. In a sense, the good guards perpetuated the prison more than the other guards because their own needs to be liked prevented them from disobeying or violating the implicit guards' code. At the same time, the act of befriending the prisoners created a social reality which made the prisoners less likely to rebel.

By the end of the week the experiment had become a reality, as if it were a Pirandello play directed by Kafka that just keeps going after the audience has left. The consultant for our prison, Carlo Prescott, an ex-convict with 16 years of imprisonment in California's jails, would get so depressed and furious each time he visited our prison, because of its psychological similarity to his experiences, that he would have to leave. A Catholic priest who was a former prison chaplain in Washington, D.C. talked to our prisoners after four days and said they were just like the other first-timers he had seen.

But in the end, I called off the experiment not because of the horror I saw out there in the prison yard, but because of the horror of realizing that *I* could have easily traded places with the most brutal guard or become the weakest prisoner full of hatred at being so powerless that I could not eat, sleep or go to the toilet without permission of the authorities. *I* could have become Calley at My Lai, George Jackson at San Quentin, one of the men at Attica or the prisoner quoted at the beginning of this article.

Individual behavior is largely under the control of social forces and environmental contingencies rather than personality traits, character, will power or other empirically unvalidated constructs. Thus we create an illusion of freedom by attributing more internal control to ourselves, to the individual, than actually exists. We thus underestimate the power and pervasiveness of situational controls over behavior because: (a) they are often non-obvious and subtle, (b) we can often avoid entering situations where we might be so controlled, (c) we label as "weak" or "deviant" people in those situations who do behave differently from how we believe we would.

Each of us carries around in our heads a favorable self-image in which we are essentially just, fair, humane and understanding. For example, we could not imagine inflicting pain on others without much provocation or hurting people who had done nothing to us, who in fact were even liked by us. However, there is a growing body of social psychological research which underscores the conclusion derived from this prison study. Many people, perhaps the majority, can be made to do almost anything when put into psychologically compelling situations—regardless of their morals, ethics, values, attitudes, beliefs or personal convictions. My colleague, Stanley Milgram, has shown that more than 60 percent of the population will deliver what they think is a series of painful electric shocks to another person even after the victim cries for mercy, begs them to stop and then apparently passes out. The subjects complained that they did not want to inflict more pain but blindly obeyed the command of the authority figure (the experimenter) who said that they must go on. In my own research on violence, I have seen mild-mannered co-eds repeatedly give shocks (which they thought were causing pain) to another girl, a stranger whom they had rated very favorably, simply by being made to feel anonymous and put in a situation where they were expected to engage in this activity.

Observers of these and similar experimental situations never predict their outcomes and estimate that it is unlikely that they themselves would behave similarly. They can be so confident only when they were outside the situation. However, since the majority of people in these studies do act in non-rational, non-obvious ways, it follows that the majority of observers would also succumb to the social psychological forces in the situation.

With regard to prisons, we can state that the mere act of assigning labels to people and putting them into a situation where those labels acquire validity and meaning is sufficient to elicit pathological behavior. This pathology is not predictable from any available diagnostic indicators we have in the social sciences, and is extreme enough to modify in very significant ways fundamental attitudes and behavior. The prison situation, as presently arranged, is guaranteed to generate severe enough pathological reactions in both guards and prisoners as to debase their humanity, lower their feelings of self-worth and make it difficult for them to be part of a society outside of their prison.

For years our national leaders have been pointing to the enemies of freedom, to the fascist or communist threat to the American way of life. In so doing they have overlooked the threat of social anarchy that is building within our own country without any outside agitation. As soon as a person comes to the realization that he is being imprisoned by his society or individuals in it, then, in the best American tradition, he demands liberty and rebels, accepting death as an alternative. The third alternative, however, is to allow oneself to become a good prisoner—docile, cooperative, uncomplaining, conforming in thought and complying in deed.

Our prison authorities now point to the militant agitators who are still vaguely referred to as part of some communist plot, as the irresponsible, incorrigible troublemakers. They imply that there would be no trouble, riots, hostages or deaths if it weren't for this small band of bad prisoners. In other words, then, everything would return to "normal" again in the life of our nation's prisons if they could break these men.

The riots in prison are coming from within—from within every man and woman who refuses to let the system turn them into an object, a number, a thing or a no-thing. It is not communist inspired, but inspired by the spirit of American freedom. No man wants to be enslaved. To be powerless, to be subject to the arbitrary exercise of power, to not be recognized as a human being is to be a slave.

To be a militant prisoner is to become aware that the physical jails are but more blatant extensions of the forms of social and psychological oppression experienced daily in the nation's ghettos. They are trying to awaken the conscience of the nation to the ways in which the American ideals are being perverted, apparently in the name of justice but actually under the banner of apathy, fear and hatred. If we do not listen to the pleas of the prisoners at Attica to be treated like human beings, then we have all become brutalized by our priorities for property rights over human rights. The consequence will not only be more prison riots but a loss of all those ideals on which this country was founded.

The public should be aware that they own the prisons and that their business is failing. The 70 percent recidivism rate and the escalation in severity of crimes committed by graduates of our prisons are evidence that current prisons fail to rehabilitate the inmates in any positive way. Rather, they are breeding grounds for hatred of the establishment, a hatred that makes every citizen a target of violent assault. Prisons are a bad investment for us taxpayers. Until now we have not cared, we have turned over to wardens and prison authorities the unpleasant job of keeping people who threaten us out of our sight. Now we are shocked to learn that their management practices have failed to improve the product and instead turn petty thieves into murderers. We must insist upon new management or improved operating procedures.

The cloak of secrecy should be removed from the prisons. Prisoners claim they are brutalized by the guards, guards say it is a lie. Where is the impartial test of the truth in such a situation? Prison officials have forgotten that they work for us, that they are only public servants whose salaries are paid by our taxes. They act as if it is their prison, like a child with a toy he won't share. Neither lawyers, judges, the legislature nor the public is allowed into prisons to ascertain the truth unless the visit is sanctioned by authorities and until all is prepared for their visit. I was shocked to learn that my request to join a congressional investigating committee's tour of San Quentin and Soledad was refused, as was that of the news media.

There should be an ombudsman in every prison, not under the pay or control of the prison authority, and responsible only to the courts, state legislature and the public. Such a person could report on violations of constitutional and human rights.

Guards must be given better training than they now receive for the difficult job society imposes upon them. To be a prison guard as now constituted is to be put in a situation of constant threat from within the prison, with no social recognition from the society at large. As was shown graphically at Attica, prison guards are also prisoners of the system who can be sacrificed to the demands of the public to be punitive and the needs of politicians to preserve an image. Social scientists and business administrators should be called upon to design and help carry out this training.

The relationship between the individual (who is sentenced by the courts to a prison term) and his community must be maintained. How can a prisoner return to a dynamically changing society that most of us cannot cope with after being out of it for a number of years? There should be more community involvement in these rehabilitation centers, more ties encouraged and promoted between the trainees and family and friends, more educational opportunities to prepare them for returning to their communities as more valuable members of it than they were before they left.

Finally, the main ingredient necessary to effect any change at all in prison reform, in the rehabilitation of a single prisoner or even in the optimal development of a child is caring. Reform must start with people—especially people with power—caring about the well-being of others. Underneath the toughest, society-hating convict, rebel or anarchist is a human being who wants his existence to be recognized by his fellows and who wants someone else to care about whether he lives or dies and to grieve if he lives imprisoned rather than lives free.

PART VI Social Inequality

IN ALL KNOWN PAST SOCIETIES AND EVERY CONTEMPORARY SOCIETY OF THE WORLD the members are characterized by inequalities of some sort. Some people are stronger, learn more quickly, are swifter, shoot weapons more accurately, or have more of whatever is considered important in that particular society. Natural or biological inequalities are a normal part of living in human society. Other inequalities, whatever form they take in a particular society, may appear more contrived, such as distinctions of social rank based on wealth. But no system, whether based on biological characteristics, social skills, or money, is an inevitable way of dividing people into different groups. Rather, each is arbitrary. But all societies rank their members in some way, and all use arbitrary criteria that appear quite reasonable to them.

This fact of social life, called *social inequality* or social stratification, means that people are divided into groups, called *social classes*, that possess more or less of what is valued in a particular society. In our society, three broad bases for ranking people are income, education, and occupation. The more income and education one has and the higher the prestige accorded one's work, the higher one's social class. Conversely, the lower one's income and education and the prestige of one's occupation, the lower one's social class.

On the basis of these three criteria, one can divide Americans into three principal social classes: upper, middle, and lower. The upper are the *very* rich (a million dollars wouldn't buy your way in); the middle, primarily professionals, managers, executives, and other business people, is heavily rewarded with the material goods our society has to offer; the lower class, to understate the matter, receives the least.

Some sociologists add an upper and a lower to each of these divisions and say there are six social classes in the United States: an upper-upper and lower-upper, an upper-middle and a lower-middle, and an upper-lower and a lower-lower. Membership in the upper-upper class is the most exclusive of all, accorded not only on the basis of huge wealth but also on the basis of how long that money has been in the family. The longer the better. Somehow or other, it is difficult to make millions of dollars while remaining scrupulously honest in business dealings. It appears that most people who have entered the monied classes have found it necessary to cut moral corners, at least here and there. This "taint" to the money disappears with time, however, and the later generations of Vanderbilts, Rockefellers, Mellons, DuPonts, Chryslers, Kennedys, Morgans, and so on are considered to have "clean" money simply by virtue of the passage of time. They can be philanthropic as well as rich. They have attended the best private schools and universities, the male heirs have probably entered law, and they protect their vast fortunes and economic empires with far-flung political connections and contributions.

And the lower-upper class? These people have money, but it is new and therefore suspect. They have not gone to the right schools and cannot be depended on for adequate in-group loyalty. Unable themselves to make the leap into the upper-upper class, their hope for social supremacy lies in their children: If their children go to the right schools *and* marry into the upper-upper class, what has been denied the parents will be granted the children.

The upper-middle class consists primarily of people who have entered the professions or higher levels of management. They are doctors, professors, lawyers, dentists, pharmacists, and clergy. They are bank presidents and successful contractors and other business people. Their education is high and their income adequate for most of their needs. The lower-middle class consists largely of lower-level managers, white-collar workers in the service industries, and the more highly paid and skilled blue-collar workers. Their education, income, and the prestige of their work are correspondingly lower than those of their upper-middle class counterparts.

The upper-lower is also known as the working class. (Americans find this term much more agreeable than the term *lower*, as lower brings negative connotations to the American mind, while working elicits more positive images.) This class consists primarily of blue-collar workers who work regularly, not seasonally, at their jobs. Their education is limited, and little prestige is attached to what they do. With more powerful unionization in recent years, however, many have increased their income, and the changes they have made in their life style make it more difficult to distinguish them from the lower-middle class.

At the bottom of the ladder of social inequality is the lower-lower class. This is the social class that gets the worst of everything society has to offer. Its members have the least education and the least income, and often their work is negatively valued, as they do share-cropping and other menial labor. The main difference between the lower-lower and the upper-lower classes is that the upper-lower class works the year round while the lower-lower class does not. Members of the lower-lower class are likely to be drawing welfare and are generally considered the ne'er-do-wells of society.

We can use the example of the automotive industry to illustrate social class membership in American society. The Fords, for example, own and control a manufacturing and financial empire whose net worth is truly staggering. This vast sum of money (and, not incidentally, their ensuing power) is now several generations old. Their children definitely go to the right schools, know how to spend money in the "right" way, and can be trusted to make their family and class interests paramount in life. They are members of the upper-upper class.

Next in line are top Ford executives. While they may have an income of one hundred to several hundred thousand dollars a year (and some, with stock options and bonuses, earn well over a million annually), they are new to wealth and power. Consequently they remain on the rung below and are considered members of the lower-upper class.

A husband and wife who own a successful Ford agency are members of the upper-middle class. They have an income that clearly sets them apart from the majority of Americans and an enviable reputation in the community. More than likely they also exert higher than average influence in their community, but find their capacity to wield power highly limited.

A salesperson, as well as those who work in the office, would be considered members of the lower-middle class. Their income is less, their education likely to be less, and people commonly assign less prestige to the work they do than to the owners of the agency.

A mechanic who repairs customers' cars would ordinarily be considered a member of the upper-lower class. High union wages, however, have blurred this distinction, and he or she might more properly be classified as a member of the lower-middle class. People who service Fords and are paid less, however, such as "detail men" (those who make used cars appear newer by washing and polishing the car, painting the tires and floor mats, and so on) would be members of the upper-lower class.

Window washers and janitors who are hired to clean the agency only during the busy season and then laid off would be members of the lower-lower class. (If they are year round employees of the agency, they would be members of the upper-lower class.) Their income would be the least, as would their education, while the prestige that people give to their work is minimal.

It is significant to note that children are automatically assigned the social class of their parents. It is for this reason that sociologists say that we are *born into* a social class. Sociologists call this *ascribed* membership, as compared with membership one earns on one's own, or *achieved* membership. If a child of the "detail man" goes on to college, works as a salesperson in the agency part time and during vacations, and then eventually buys the agency, he or she has upgraded his/her social class. Because of this *upward social mobility*, the new class membership is said to be achieved membership. (Conversely, if the son of the agency owner becomes an alcoholic, fails to get through college, and takes a lower-status job, he experiences *downward social mobility*. The resulting change in his social class membership is also achieved membership. ("Achieved" does not have to equal "achievement.")

You should note that this division into six social classes is not the only way that sociologists look at the social class system of American society. In fact, sociologists have no single standard, agreed-upon way of overviewing the American class system. Like others, the outline I have presented is both arbitrary and useful but does not do justice to the reality of the nuances and complexities of our class system.

One view in sociology (generally called Marxist) says that to understand social inequality one need focus only on income. What is the source of a person's income and how much of it does he or she have? Know that, and you know his or her social class. There are those with money and those without money. The monied own the means of production—the factories and machinery and buildings—and they live off their investments, while those with little money exchange their labor to produce more money for the wealthy owners. In short, the monied (the capitalist investors) are in the controlling sector of society, while those with little money (the workers) find themselves controlled by the wealthy. With society divided into the haves and the have-nots, it is misleading to pay attention to the fine distinctions among those with or without money.

Be that as it may, and this debate continues among sociologists, society certainly is stratified. And the significance of social inequality is that it determines people's *life chances*, the probabilities as to the fate one may expect in life. It is obvious that not everyone has the same chances in life, and the single most significant factor in deciding a person's life chances in our society certainly is money. Simply put, if you have it, you can do a lot of things you can't do if you haven't got it. And the more you have, the more you can do.

Beyond this obvious point, however, lies a connection between social inequality and life chances that is not so easily seen. It involves such things as one's chances of dying during infancy; dying from accidents, fire, and homicide; being a drug addict; getting arrested; ending up in prison; dropping out of school; getting divorced; or trying to live only on Social Security payments after you reach retirement age. In general, all these things vary indirectly with one's social class. The lower a person's social class, the higher the chances that these things will happen to him or her; conversely, the higher a person's social class the smaller the risk these things pose.

In this Part, as we present an overview of social inequality, we examine some of its major dimensions and emphasize its severe and lifelong effects. G. William Domhoff sets the stage by focusing on the powerful wealthy in the United States, delineating some of the interconnections and associations that serve to maintain their class interests. We are fortunate to have this selection, because so little is known about the wealthy—one use they make of their wealth is to protect themselves from the prying eyes of sociologists.

Have you ever wondered why the poor continue in such vast numbers when we have the material capacity to eliminate poverty? While one could attempt to explain this puzzle in a number of ways, Herbert J. Gans claims that it is because the poor are functional to society, that is, society benefits by keeping some segment in poverty. Richard Sennett and Jonathan Cobb then turn the sociological focus onto parents who are struggling to provide opportunities for their children that they themselves were denied. They stress the pain that results as their children, inevitably learning a new way of looking at life, become estranged from their sacrificing parents. This analysis adds the education/social mobility dimension to our examination of social inequality. Leonard I. Stein then looks at social inequality in the work setting. His focus on physician–nurse interaction adds the sexual/ occupational dimension to our presentation. Elliot Liebow focuses on lower-lower-class men being hired for temporary employment one day at a time. His analysis adds the dimension of race to social inequality, a dimension that runs throughout the American class system. Finally, Everett C. Hughes discusses "the final solution" used by one society to rid itself of those viewed as its undesirables. His article, indeed, is an appropriate closing to this Part on social inequality.

25 The Bohemian Grove and Other Retreats

G. WILLIAM DOMHOFF

In no society on earth are all members equal. In varying ways and to various degrees, the members of all societies are marked by divisions. Some receive more of a society's goods and services, and some far less. This is the way it has been in every known society of the past, is now, and probably—people's hopes to the contrary notwithstanding—always will be.

Our society, as much as many of us would wish it different, is no exception. On the one hand, in some ways we have much equality. This is especially true when we focus on our extensive middle class. Our society, indeed, holds open so many opportunities that thousands and even millions of people are trying to enter our country each year, regardless of the obstacles they face and regardless of the legality of their entry.

On the other hand, we are marked by great divisions. Of those, wealth and power are among the greatest—in extent and in effect on people's lives. Because the poor are the most accessible, in their studies of social inequality sociologists have concentrated on the poor. Domhoff, however, one of the exceptions, presents in this selection an analysis that ought to greatly expand your awareness of power and wealth in American society.

You might ask yourself in what ways life would be different for you if you had been born into one of the families on which this article focuses. Beyond the external differences of material surroundings, how do you suppose your thinking would be different?

The Bohemian Grove

PICTURE YOURSELF comfortably seated in a beautiful open-air dining hall in the midst of twenty-seven hundred acres of giant California redwoods. It is early evening and the clear July air is still pleasantly warm. Dusk has descended, you have finished a sumptuous dinner, and you are sitting quietly with your drink and your cigar, listening to nostalgic welcoming speeches and enjoying the gentle light and the eerie shadows that are cast by the two-stemmed gaslights flickering softly at each of the several hundred outdoor banquet tables.

You are part of an assemblage that has been meeting in this redwood grove sixty-five miles north of San Francisco for [over] a hundred years. It is not just any assemblage, for you are a captain of industry, a well-known television star, a banker, a famous artist, or maybe a member of the President's Cabinet. You are one of fifteen hundred men gathered together from all over the country for the annual encampment of the rich and the famous at the Bohemian Grove.

. . .

["Bohemians" of the 1970s and 1980s include such personages as President Ronald Reagan; Vice President George Bush; Attorney General William French Smith; Secretary of State George P. Shultz; former President Richard Nixon; former President Gerald Ford; Supreme Court Justice Potter Stewart; Herbert Hoover, Jr.; Herbert Hoover III; newspaperman William R. Hearst, Jr.; five members of the Dean Witter family of investment bankers; entertainers Art Linkletter and Edgar Bergen; presidents and chairmen of several oil companies such as Marathon Oil and Standard Oil; the president of Rockefeller University; officers of Anheuser-Busch breweries; the president of Kaiser Industries; bank presidents from California to New York; the president and chairman of Hewlett-Packard Co.; and many other representatives of American industry, finance, government, and entertainment. When these participants arrive for the annual "campout," an elaborate ritual called the Cremation of Care welcomes them and instructs them to leave all cares behind while they join together for two weeks of lavish entertainment, fellowship, and "communion with nature."]

The Cremation of Care is the most spectacular event of the midsummer retreat that members and guests of San Francisco's Bohemian Club have taken every year since 1878. However, there are several other entertainments in store. Before the Bohemians return to the everyday world, they will be treated to plays, variety shows, song fests, shooting contests, art exhibits, swimming, boating, and nature rides.

. . .

A cast for a typical Grove play easily runs to seventy-five or one-hundred people. Add in the orchestra, the stagehands, the carpenters who make the sets, and other supporting personnel, and over three hundred people are involved in creating the High Jinks each year. Preparations begin a year in advance, with rehearsals occurring two or three times a week in the month before the encampment, and nightly in the week before the play.

Costs are on the order of $20,000 to $30,000 per High Jinks, a large amount of money for a one-night production which does not have to pay a penny for salaries (the highest cost in any commercial production). "And the costs are talked about, too," reports my . . . informant. "Hey, did you hear the High Jinks will cost $25,000 this year?' one of them will say to another. The expense of the play is one way they can relate to its worth."

. . .

Entertainment is not the only activity at the Bohemian Grove. For a little change of pace, there is intellectual stimulation and political enlightenment every day at 12:30 P.M. Since 1932 the meadow from which people view the Cremation of Care also has been the setting for informal talks and briefings by people as varied as Dwight David Eisenhower (before he was President), Herman Wouk (author of *The Caine Mutiny*), Bobby Kennedy (while he was Attorney General), and Neil Armstrong (after he returned from the moon).

Cabinet officers, politicians, generals, and governmental advisers are the rule rather than the exception for Lakeside Talks, especially on weekends. Equally prominent figures from the worlds of art, literature and science are more likely to make their appearance during the weekdays of the encampment, when Grove attendance may drop to four or five hundred (many of the members only come up for one week or for the weekends because they cannot stay away from their corporations and law firms for the full two weeks).

. . .

[T]he Grove is an ideal off-the-record atmosphere for sizing up politicians. "Well, of course when a politician comes here, we all get to see him, and his stock in trade is his personality and his ideas," a prominent Bohemian told a *New York Times* reporter who was trying to cover Nelson Rockefeller's 1963 visit to the Grove for a Lakeside Talk. The journalist went on to note that the midsummer encampments "have long been a major showcase where leaders of business, industry, education, the arts, and politics can come to examine each other."[1]

. . .

For 1971, [then] President Nixon was to be the featured Lakeside speaker. However, when newspaper reporters learned that the President planned to disappear into a redwood grove for an off-the-record speech to some of the most powerful men in America, they objected loudly and vowed to make every effort to cover the event. The flap caused the club considerable embarrassment, and after much hemming and hawing back and forth, the club leaders asked the President to cancel his scheduled appearance. A White House press secretary then announced that the President had decided not to appear at the Grove rather than risk the tradition that speeches there are strictly off the public record.[2]

However, the President was not left without a final word to his fellow Bohemians. In a telegram to the president of the club, which now hangs at the entrance to the reading room in the San Francisco clubhouse, he expressed his regrets at not being able to attend. He asked the club president to continue to lead people into the woods, adding that he in turn would redouble his efforts to lead people out of the woods. He also noted that, while anyone could aspire to be President of the United States, only a few could aspire to be president of the Bohemian Club.

. . .

Not all the entertainment at the Bohemian Grove takes place under the auspices of the committee in charge of special events. The Bohemians and their guests are divided into camps which evolved slowly over the years as the number of people on the retreat grew into the hundreds and then the thousands. These camps have become a significant center of enjoyment during the encampment.

At first the camps were merely a place in the woods where a half-dozen to a dozen friends would pitch their tents. Soon they added little amenities like their own special stove or a small permanent structure. Then there developed little camp "traditions" and endearing camp names like Cliff Dwellers, Moonshiners, Silverado Squatters, Woof, Zaca, Toyland, Sundodgers, and Land of Happiness. The next steps were special emblems, a handsome little lodge or specially constructed tepees, a permanent bar, and maybe a grand piano.[3] Today there are 129 camps of varying sizes, structures, and statuses. Most have between 10 and 30 members, but there are one or two with about 125 members and several with less than 10. A majority of the camps are strewn along what is called the River Road, but some are huddled in other areas within five or ten minutes of the center of the Grove.

The entertainment at the camps is mostly informal and impromptu. Someone will decide to bring together all the jazz musicians in the Grove for a special session. Or maybe all the artists or writers will be invited to a luncheon or a dinner at a camp. Many camps have their own amateur piano players and informal musical and singing groups which perform for the rest of the members.

But the joys of the camps are not primarily in watching or listening to performances. Other pleasures are created within them. Some camps become known for their gastronomical specialties, such as a particular drink or a particular meal. The Jungle Camp features mint juleps, Halcyon has a three-foot-high martini maker constructed out of chemical glassware. At the Owl's Nest [President Reagan's club] it's the gin-fizz breakfast—about a hundred people are invited over one morning during the encampment for eggs Benedict, gin fizzes, and all the trimmings.

. . .

The men of Bohemia are drawn in large measure from the corporate leadership of the United States. They include in their numbers directors from major corporations in every sector of the American economy. An indication of this fact is that one in every five resident members and one in every three nonresident members is found in Poor's *Register of Corporations, Executives, and Directors*, a huge volume which lists the leadership of tens of thousands of companies from every major business field except investment banking, real estate, and advertising.

Even better evidence for the economic prominence of the men under consideration is that at least one officer or director from 40 of the 50 largest industrial corporations in America was present, as a member or a guest, on the lists at our disposal. Only Ford Motor Company and Western Electric were missing among the top 25! Similarly, we found that officers and directors from 20 of the top 25 commercial banks (including all of the 15 largest) were on our lists. Men from 12 of the first 25 life-insurance companies were in attendance (8 of these 12 were from the top 10). Other business sectors were represented somewhat less: 10 of 25 in transportation, 8 of 25 in utilities, 7 of 25 in conglomerates, and only 5 of 25 in retailing. More generally, of the top-level businesses ranked by *Fortune* for 1969 (the top 500 industrials, the top 50 commercial banks, the top 50 life-insurance companies, the top 50 transportation companies, the top 50 utilities, the top 50 retailers, and the top 47 conglomerates), *29 percent of these 797 corporations were "represented" by at least 1 officer or director.*

. . .

Other Watering Holes

[Other camps and retreats were founded by wealthy and powerful men, based on the model provided by the Bohemian Grove. One example is the Rancheros Visitadores (Visiting Ranchers) who meet each May for horseback rides through the California ranch land. These are accompanied by feasts, entertainment, and general merrymaking with a Spanish-ranch motif.]

[Among the Rancheros a] common interest in horses and horseplay provides a social setting in which men with different forms of wealth get to know each other better. *Sociologically speaking, the Rancheros Visitadores is an organization which serves the function (whether the originators planned it that way or not) of helping to integrate ranchers and businessmen from different parts of the country into a cohesive social class.*

. . .

[T]he Rancheros had to divide into camps because of a postwar increase in membership. There are seventeen camps, sporting such Spanish names as Los Amigos, Los Vigilantes, Los Tontos (bums), Los Bandidos, and Los Flojos (lazy ones). They range in size from fifteen to ninety-three, with the majority of them listing between twenty and sixty members. Most camps have members from a variety of geographical locations, although some are slightly specialized in that regard. Los Gringos, the largest camp, has the greatest number of members from out of state. Los Borrachos, Los Picadores, and Los Chingadores, the next largest camps, have a predominance of people from the Los Angeles area. Los Vigilantes, with twenty members, began as a San Francisco group, but now includes riders from Oregon, Washington, New York and southern California.

In 1928 the Bohemian Grove provided John J. Mitchell with the inspiration for his retreat on horseback, the Rancheros Visitadores. Since 1930 the RVs have grown to the point where they are an impressive second best to the Grove in size, entertainment, and stature. Their combination of businessmen and ranchers is as unique as the Bohemian's amalgamation of businessmen and artists. It is hardly surprising that wealthy men from Los Angeles, San Francisco, Honolulu, Spokane, and Chicago would join Mitchell in wanting to be members of both.

. . .

[Another club, the Colorado-based Roundup Riders of the Rockies, imitates the RVs in its emphasis on "roughing it" and socializing.]

The riders do not carry their fine camp with them. Instead, twenty camp-hands are employed to move the camp in trucks to the next camp-site. Thus, when the Roundup Riders arrive at their destination each evening they find fourteen large sleeping tents complete with cots, air mattresses, portable toilets, and showers. Also up and ready for service are a large green dining tent and an entertainment stage. A diesel-powered generator provides the camp with electricity.

Food service is provided by Martin Jetton of Fort Worth, Texas, a caterer advertised in the southwest as "King of the Barbecue." Breakfasts and dinners are said to be veritable banquets. Lunch is not as elaborate, but it does arrive to the riders on the trail in a rather unusual fashion that only those of the higher circles could afford: "lunches in rugged country are often delivered by light plane or helicopter."[4] One year the men almost missed a meal because a wind came up and scattered the lunches which were being parachuted from two Cessna 170s.

In addition to the twenty hired hands who take care of the camp, there are twenty wranglers to look after the horses. The horses on the ride—predominantly such fine breeds as Arabian, Quarter Horse, and Morgan—are estimated to be worth more than $200,000. Horses and riders compete in various contests of skill and horsemanship on a layover day in the middle of the week. Skeet shooting, trap shooting, and horseshoes also are a part of this event.

. . .

The Roundup Riders, who hold their trek at the same time the Bohemians hold their encampment, must be reckoned as a more regional organization. Although there are numerous millionaires and executives among them, the members are not of the national stature of most Bohemians and many Rancheros. They can afford to invest thousands of dollars in their horses and tack, to pay a $300 yearly ride fee, and to have their lunch brought to them by helicopter, but they cannot compete in business connections and prestige with those who assemble at the Bohemian Grove. Building from the Denver branch of the upper class, the Roundup Riders reach out primarily to Nebraska (six), Texas (five), Illinois (five), Nevada (three), California (three), and Arizona (three). There are no members from New York, Boston, Philadelphia, or other large Eastern cities.

Several other regional rides have been inspired by the Rancheros, rides such as the Desert Caballeros in Wickenburg, Arizona, and the Verde Vaqueros in Scottsdale, Arizona. These groups are similar in size and membership to the Roundup Riders of the Rockies. Like the Roundup Riders, they have a few overlapping members with the Rancheros. But none are of the status of the Rancheros Visitadores. They are minor legacies of the Bohemian Grove, unlikely even to be aware of their kinship ties to the retreat in the redwoods.

Do Bohemians, Rancheros, and Roundup Riders Rule America?

The foregoing material on upper-class retreats, which I have presented in as breezy a manner as possible, is relevant to highly emotional questions concerning the distribution of power in modern America. In this final [section] I will switch styles somewhat and discuss these charged questions in a sober, simple, and straightforward way. . . .

It is my hypothesis that there is a ruling social class in the United States. This class is made up of the owners and managers of large corporations, which means the members have many economic and political interests in common, and many conflicts with ordinary working people. Comprising at most 1 percent of the total population, members of this class own 25 to 30 percent of all privately held wealth in America, own 60 to 70 percent of the privately held corporate wealth, receive 20 to 25 percent of the yearly income, direct the large corporations and foundations, and dominate the federal government in Washington.

Most social scientists disagree with this view. Some dismiss it out of hand, others become quite vehement in disputing it. The overwhelming majority of them believe that the United States has a "pluralistic" power structure, in which a wide variety of "veto groups" (e.g., businessmen, farmers, unions, consumers) and "voluntary associations" (e.g., National Association of Manufacturers, Americans for Democratic Action, Common Cause) form shifting coalitions to influence decisions on different issues. These groups and associations are said to have differing amounts of interest and influence on various questions. Contrary to my view, pluralists assert that no one group, not even the owners and managers of large corporations, has the cohesiveness and ability to determine the outcome of a large variety of social, economic, and political issues.

. . .

As noted, I believe there is a national upper class in the United States. [T]his means that wealthy families from all over the country, and particularly from major cities like New York, San Francisco, Chicago, and Houston, are part of interlocking social circles which perceive each other as equals, belong to the same clubs, interact frequently, and freely intermarry.

Whether we call it a "social class" or a "status group," many pluralistic social scientists would deny that such a social group exists. They assert that there is no social "cohesiveness" among the various rich in different parts of the country. For them, social registers, blue books, and club membership lists are merely collections of names which imply nothing about group interaction.

There is a wealth of journalistic evidence which suggests the existence of a national upper class. It ranges from Cleveland Amory's *The Proper Bostonians* and *Who Killed Society?* to Lucy Kavaler's *The Private World of High Society* and Stephen Birmingham's *The Right People*. But what is the systematic evidence which I can present for my thesis? There is first of all the evidence that has been developed from the study of attendance at private schools. It has been shown that a few dozen prep schools bring together children of the upper class from all over the country. From this evidence it can be argued that young members of the upper class develop lifetime friendship ties with like-status age-mates in every section of the country.[5]

There is second the systematic evidence which comes from studying high-status summer resorts. Two such studies show that these resorts bring together upper-class families from several different large cities.[6] Third, there is the evidence of business interconnections. Several . . . studies have demonstrated that interlocking directorships bring wealthy men from all over the country into face-to-face relationships at the board meetings of banks, insurance companies, and other corporations.[7]

And finally, there is the evidence developed from studying exclusive social clubs. Such studies have been made in the past, but the present investigation of the Bohemian Club, the Rancheros Visitadores, and the Roundup Riders of the Rockies is a more comprehensive effort. *In short, I believe the present [study] to be significant evidence for the existence of a cohesive American upper class.*

The Bohemian Grove, as well as other watering holes and social clubs, is relevant to the problem of class cohesiveness in two ways. First, the very fact that rich men from all over the country gather in such close circumstances as the Bohemian Grove is evidence for the existence of a socially cohesive upper class. It demonstrates that many of these men do know each other, that they have face-to-face communications, and that they are a social network. In this sense, we are looking at the Bohemian Grove and other social retreats as a *result* of social processes that lead to class cohesion. But such institutions also can be viewed as *facilitators* of social ties. Once formed, these groups become another avenue by which the cohesiveness of the upper class is maintained.

In claiming that clubs and retreats like the Bohemians and the Rancheros are evidence for my thesis of a national upper class, I am assuming that cohesion develops within the settings they provide. Perhaps some readers will find that assumption questionable. So let us pause to ask: Are there reasons to believe that the Bohemian Grove and its imitators lead to greater cohesion within the upper class?

For one thing, we have the testimony of members themselves. There are several accounts by leading members of these groups, past and present, which attest to the intimacy that develops among members. John J. Mitchell, El Presidente of Los Rancheros Visitadores from 1930 to 1955, wrote as follows on the twenty-fifth anniversary of the group:

> All the pledges and secret oaths in the universe cannot tie men, our kind of men, together like the mutual appreciation of a beautiful horse, the moon behind a cloud, a song around the campfire or a ride down the Santa Ynez Valley. These are experiences common on our ride, but unknown to most of our daily lives. Our organization, to all appearances, is the most informal imaginable. Yet there are men here who see one another once a year, yet feel a bond closer than between those they have known all their lives.[8]

F. Burr Betts, chairman of the board of Security Life of Denver, says the following about the Roundup Riders:

> I think you find out about the Roundup Riders when you go to a Rider's funeral. Because there you'll find, no matter how many organizations the man belonged to, almost every pallbearer is a Roundup Rider. I always think of the Roundup Riders as the first affiliation. We have the closest knit fraternity in the world.[9]

. . .

A second reason for stressing the importance of retreats and clubs like the Bohemian Grove is a body of research within social psychology which deals with group cohesion. "Group dynamics" suggests the following about cohesiveness. (1) *Physical proximity is likely to lead to group solidarity.* Thus, the mere fact that these men gather together in such intimate physical settings implies that cohesiveness develops. (The same point can be made, of course, about exclusive neighborhoods, private schools, and expensive summer resorts.) (2) *The more people interact, the more they will like each other*. This is hardly a profound discovery, but we can note that the Bohemian Grove and other watering holes maximize pesonal interactions. (3) *Groups seen as high in status are more cohesive*. The Bohemian Club fits the category of a high-status group. Further, its stringent membership requirements, long waiting lists, and high dues also serve to heighten its valuation in the eyes of its members. Members are likely to think of themselves as "special" people, which would heighten their attractiveness to each other, and increase the likelihood of interaction and cohesiveness. (4) *The best atmosphere for increasing group cohesiveness is one that is relaxed and cooperative*. Again the Bohemian Grove, the Rancheros, and the Roundup Riders are ideal examples of this kind of climate. From a group-dynamics point of view, then, we could argue that one of the reasons for upper-class cohesiveness is the fact that the class is organized into a wide variety of small groups which encourage face-to-face interaction and ensure status and security for members.[10]

In summary, if we take these several common settings together—schools, resorts, corporation directorships, and social clubs—and assume on the basis of members' testimony and the evidence of small-group research that interaction in such settings leads to group cohesiveness, then I think we are justified in saying that wealthy families from all over the United States are linked together in a variety of ways into a national upper class.

Even if the evidence and arguments for the existence of a socially cohesive national upper class are accepted, there is still the question of whether or not this class has the means by which its members can reach policy consensus on issues of importance to them.

A five-year study based upon information obtained from confidential informants, interviews, and questionnaires has shown that social clubs such as the Bohemian Club are an important consensus-forming aspect of the upper class and big-business environment. According to sociologist Reed Powell, "the clubs are a repository of the values held by the upper-level prestige groups in the community and are a means by which these values are transferred to the business environment." Moreover, the clubs are places where problems are discussed:

> On the other hand, the clubs are places in which the beliefs, problems, and values of the industrial organization are discussed and related to other elements in the larger community. Clubs, therefore, are not only effective vehicles of informal communication, but also valuable centers where views are presented, ideas are modified, and new ideas emerge. Those in the interview sample were appreciative of this asset; in addition, they considered the club as a valuable place to combine social and business contacts.[11]

The revealing interview work of Floyd Hunter, an outstanding pioneer researcher on the American power structure, also provides evidence for the importance of social clubs as informal centers of policy making. Particularly striking for our purposes is a conversation he had with one of the several hundred top leaders that he identified in the 1950s. The person in question was a conservative industrialist who was ranked as a top-level leader by his peers:

> Hall [pseudonym] spoke very favorably of the Bohemian Grove group that met in California every year. He said that although over the entrance to the Bohemian Club there was a quotation, "Weaving spiders come not here," there was a good deal of informal policy made in this association. He said that he got to know Herbert Hoover in this connection and that he started work with Hoover in the food administration of World War I.[12]

Despite the evidence presented by Powell and Hunter that clubs are a setting for the development of policy consensus, I do not believe that such settings are the only, or even the primary, locus for developing policy on class-related issues. For policy questions, other organizations are far more important, organizations like the Council on Foreign Relations, the Committee for Economic Development, the Business Council, and the National Municipal League. These organizations, along with many others, are the "consensus-seeking" and "policy-planning" organizations of the upper class. Directed by the same men who manage the major corporations, and financed by corporation and foundation monies, these groups sponsor meetings and discussions wherein wealthy men from all over the country gather to iron out differences and formulate policies on pressing problems.

No one discussion group is *the* leadership council within the upper class. While some of the groups tend to specialize in certain issue areas, they overlap and interact to a great extent. Consensus slowly emerges from the interplay of people and ideas within and among the groups.[13] This diversity of groups is made very clear in the following comments by Frazar B. Wilde, chairman emeritus of Connecticut General Life Insurance Company and a member of the Council on Foreign Relations and the Committee for Economic Development. Mr. Wilde was responding to a question about the Bilderbergers, a big-business meeting group which includes Western European leaders as well as American corporation and foundation directors:

> Business has had over the years many different seminars and discussion meetings. They run all the way from large public gatherings like NAM [National Association of Manufacturers] to special sessions such as those held frequently at Arden House. Bilderberg is in many respects one of the most important, if not the most important, but this is not to deny that other strictly off-the-record meetings and discussion groups such as those held by the Council on Foreign Relations are not in the front rank.[14]

Generally speaking, then, it is in these organizations that leaders within the upper class discuss the means by which to deal with problems of major concern. Here, in off-the-record settings, these leaders try to reach consensus on general issues that have been talked about more casually in corporate boardrooms and social clubs. These organizations, aided by funds from corporations and foundations, also serve several other functions:

1. They are a training ground for new leadership within the class. It is in these organizations, and through the publications of these organizations, that younger lawyers, bankers, and businessmen become acquainted with general issues in the areas of foreign, domestic, and municipal policy.

2. They are the place where leaders within the upper class hear the ideas and findings of their hired experts.

3. They are the setting wherein upper-class leaders "look over" young experts for possible service as corporation or governmental advisers.

4. They provide the framework for expert studies on important issues. Thus, the Council on Foreign Relations undertook a $1 million study of the "China question" in the first half of the 1960s. The Committee for Economic Development created a major study of money and credit about the same time. Most of the money for these studies was provided by the Ford, Rockefeller, and Carnegie foundations.[15]

5. Through such avenues as books, journals, policy statements, discussion groups, press releases, and speakers, the policy-planning organizations greatly influence the "climate of opinion" within which major issues are considered. For example, *Foreign Affairs*, the journal of the Council on Foreign Relations, is considered the most influential journal in its field, and the periodic policy statements of the Committee for Economic Development are carefully attended to by major newspapers and local opinion leaders.

It is my belief, then, that the policy-planning groups are essential in developing policy positions which are satisfactory to the upper class as a whole. As such, I think they are a good part of the answer to any social scientist who denies that members of the upper class have institutions by which they deal with economic and political challenges.

However, the policy-planning groups could not function if there were not some common interests within the upper class in the first place. The most obvious, and most important, of these common interests have to do with the shared desire of the members to maintain the present monopolized and subsidized business system which so generously overrewards them and makes their jet setting, fox hunting, art collecting, and other extravagances possible. But it is not only shared economic and political concerns which make consensus possible. The Bohemian Grove and other upper-class social institutions also contribute to this process: *Group-dynamics research suggests that members of socially cohesive groups are more open to the opinions of other members, and more likely to change their views to those of fellow members.*[16] Social cohesion is a factor in policy consensus because it creates a desire on the part of group members to reconcile differences with other members of the group. It is not enough to say that members of the upper class are bankers, businessmen, and lawyers with a common interest in profit maximization and tax avoidance who meet together at the Council on Foreign Relations, the Committee for Economic Development, and other policy-planning organizations. We must add that they are Bohemians, Rancheros, and Roundup Riders.

Notes

1. Wallace Turner, "Rockefeller Faces Scrutiny of Top Californians: Governor to Spend Weekend at Bohemian Grove among State's Establishment," *New York Times*, July 26, 1963, p. 30. In 1964 Senator Barry Goldwater appeared at the Grove as a guest of retired General Albert C. Wedemeyer and Herbert Hoover, Jr. For that story see Wallace Turner, "Goldwater Spending Weekend in Camp at Bohemian Grove," *New York Times*, July 31, 1964, p. 10.
2. James M. Naughton, "Nixon Drops Plan for Coast Speech," *New York Times*, July 31, 1971, p. 11.
3. There is a special moisture-proof building at the Grove to hold the dozens of expensive Steinway pianos belonging to the club and various camps.
4. Robert Pattridge, "Closer to Heaven on Horseback," *Empire Magazine*, *Denver Post*, July 9, 1972, p. 12. I am grateful to sociologist Ford Cleere for bringing this article to my attention.
5. E. Digby Baltzell, *Philadelphia Gentlemen* (New York: Free Press, 1958), chapter 12. G. William Domhoff, *The Higher Circles* (New York: Random House, 1970), p. 78.
6. Baltzell, *Philadelphia Gentlemen*, pp. 248–51. Domhoff, *The Higher Circles*, pp. 79–82. For recent anecdotal evidence on this point, see Stephen Birmingham, *The Right People* (Boston: Little, Brown, 1968), Part 3.
7. *Interlocks in Corporate Management* (Washington: U.S. Government Printing Office, 1965) summarizes much of this information and presents new evidence as well. See also Peter Dooley, "The Interlocking Directorate," *American Economic Review*, December 1969.
8. Neill C. Wilson, *Los Rancheros Visitadores: Twenty-Fifth Anniversary* (Rancheros Visitadores, 1955), p. 2.
9. Pattridge, "Closer to Heaven on Horseback," p. 11.
10. Dorwin Cartwright and Alvin Zander, *Group Dynamics* (New York: Harper & Row, 1960), pp. 74–82; Albert J. Lott and Bernice E. Lott, "Group Cohesiveness as Interpersonal Attraction," *Psychological Bulletin*, 64 (1965): 259–309; Michael Argyle, *Social Interaction* (Chicago: Aldine Publishing Company, 1969), pp. 220–23. I am grateful to sociologist John Sonquist of the University of California, Santa Barbara, for making me aware of how important the small-groups literature might be for studies of the upper class. Findings on influence processes, communication patterns, and the development of informal leadership also might be applicable to problems in the area of upper-class research.

11. Reed M. Powell, *Race, Religion, and the Promotion of the American Executive*, College of Administrative Science Monograph No. AA-3, Ohio State University, 1969, p. 50.

12. Floyd Hunter, *Top Leadership, U.S.A.* (Chapel Hill: University of North Carolina Press, 1959), p. 109. Hunter also reported (p. 199) that the most favored clubs of his top leaders were the Metropolitan, Links, Century, University (New York), Bohemian, and Pacific Union. He notes (p. 223 n.) that he found clubs to be less important in policy formation on the national level than they are in communities.

13. For a detailed case study of how the process works, see David Eakins, "Business Planners and America's Postwar Expansion," in David Horowitz (ed.), *Corporations and the Cold War* (New York: Monthly Review Press, 1969). For other examples and references, see Domhoff, *The Higher Circles*, chapters 5 and 6.

14. Carl Gilbert, personal communication, June 30, 1972. Mr. Gilbert has done extensive research on the Bilderberg group, and I am grateful to him for sharing his detailed information with me. For an excellent discussion of this group, whose role has been greatly distorted and exaggerated by ultra-conservatives, see Eugene Pasymowski and Carl Gilbert, "Bilderberg, Rockefeller, and the CIA," *Temple Free Press*, No. 6, September 16, 1968. The article is most conveniently located in a slightly revised form in the *Congressional Record*, September 15, 1971, E9615, under the title "Bilderberg: The Cold War Internationale."

15. The recent work of arch-pluralist Nelson Polsby is bringing him dangerously close to this formulation. Through studies of the initiation of a number of new policies, Polsby and his students have tentatively concluded that "innovators are typically professors or interest group experts." Where Polsby goes wrong is in failing to note that the professors are working on Ford Foundation grants and/or Council on Foreign Relations fellowships. If he would put his work in a sociological framework, people would not gain the false impression that professors are independent experts sitting in their ivory towers thinking up innovations for the greater good of humanity. See Nelson Polsby, "Policy Initiation in the American Political System," in Irving Louis Horowitz (ed.), *The Use and Abuse of Social Science* (New Brunswick, N.J.: TransAction Books, 1971), p. 303.

16. Cartwright and Zander, *Group Dynamics*, p. 89; Lott and Lott, "Group Cohesiveness as Interpersonal Attraction," pp. 291–96.

26 The Uses of Poverty: The Poor Pay All

HERBERT J. GANS

Standing in sharp contrast to the preceding selection is this analysis of poverty. We all know that the poor have little money, and sociologists have amply documented how little power the poor are able to exert over their lives. They are subject to debilitating social conditions that make them sicker than most, make it more likely that their marriages will break up, their children drop out of school and get in trouble with the law, make them more likely to be victimized by crime, and even shorten their life span. It is difficult to romanticize the conditions of poverty when one knows what they really are.

Gans presents a different kind of analysis, however. His is not a documentation of the degradation of the poor (although this is intrinsically present), nor of their failing health or trouble with authorities. Nor is his article a plea for social improvement. Rather, from the observation that the poor are always present in society he concludes that this must be because they perform vital services (functions) for society. (An essential assumption of *functionalism*, one of the theoretical schools in sociology, is that conditions persist in society only because they benefit—perform functions for—the society in some way.) In this selection, then, Gans tries to identify those functions.

Do you think the author wrote this article "tongue-in-cheek"? Do you think he has overlooked any "functions" of the poor? If his analysis, which many find startling, is not correct, what alternative explanation could you propose?

SOME 20 YEARS AGO ROBERT K. MERTON APPLIED the notion of functional analysis to explain the continuing though maligned existence of the urban political machine: If it continued to exist, perhaps it fulfilled latent—unintended or unrecognized—positive functions. Clearly it did. Merton pointed out how the political machine provided central authority to get things done when a decentralized local government could not act, humanized the services of the impersonal bureaucracy for fearful citizens, offered concrete help (rather than abstract law or justice) to the poor, and otherwise performed services needed or demanded by many people but considered unconventional or even illegal by formal public agencies.

Today, poverty is more maligned than the political machine ever was; yet it, too, is a persistent social phenomenon. Consequently, there may be some merit in applying functional analysis to poverty, in asking whether it also has positive functions that explain its persistence.

Merton defined functions as "those observed consequences [of a phenomenon] which make for the adaptation or adjustment of a given [social] system." I shall use a slightly different definition; instead of identifying functions for an entire social system, I shall identify them for the interest groups, socioeconomic classes, and other population aggregates with shared values that "inhabit" a social system. I suspect that in a modern heterogeneous society, few phenomena are functional or dysfunctional for the society as a whole, and that most result in benefits to some groups and costs to others. Nor are any phenomena indispensable; in most instances, one can suggest what Merton calls "functional alternatives" or equivalents for them, i.e., other social patterns or policies that achieve the same positive functions but avoid the dysfunction.[1]

Associating poverty with positive functions seems at first glance to be unimaginable. Of course, the slumlord and the loan shark are commonly known to profit from the existence of poverty, but they are viewed as evil men, so their activities are classified among the dysfunctions of poverty. However, what is less often recognized, at least by the conventional wisdom, is that poverty also makes possible the existence or expansion of respectable professions and occupations, for example, penology, criminology, social work, and public health. More recently, the poor have provided jobs for professional and para-professional "poverty warriors," and for journalists and social scientists, this author included, who have supplied the information demanded by the revival of public interest in poverty.

Clearly, then, poverty and the poor may well satisfy a number of positive functions for many nonpoor groups in American society. I shall describe 13 such functions—economic, social, and political—that seem to me most significant.

The Functions of Poverty

First, the existence of poverty ensures that society's "dirty work" will be done. Every society has such work: physically dirty or dangerous, temporary, dead-end and underpaid, undignified, and menial jobs. Society can fill these jobs by paying higher wages than for "clean" work, or it can force people who have no other choice to do the dirty work—and at low wages. In America, poverty functions to provide a low-wage labor pool that is willing—or, rather, unable to be *un*willing—to perform dirty work at low cost. Indeed, this function of the poor is so important that in some Southern states, welfare payments have been cut off during the summer months when the poor are needed to work in the fields. Moreover, much of the debate about the Negative Income Tax and the Family Assistance Plan has concerned their impact on the work incentive, by which is actually meant the incentive of the poor to do the needed dirty work if the wages therefrom are no larger than the income grant. Many economic activities that involve dirty work depend on the poor for their existence: restaurants, hospitals, parts of the garment industry, and "truck farming," among others, could not persist in their present form without the poor.

Second, because the poor are required to work at low wages, they subsidize a variety of economic activities that benefit the affluent. For example, domestics subsidize the upper-middle and upper classes, making life easier for their employers and freeing affluent women for a variety of professional, cultural, civic, and partying activities. Similarly, because the poor pay a higher proportion of their income in property and sales taxes, among others, they subsidize many state and local governmental services that benefit more affluent groups. In addition, the poor support innovation in medical practice as patients in teaching and research hospitals and as guinea pigs in medical experiments.

Third, poverty creates jobs for a number of occupations and professions that serve or "service" the poor, or protect the rest of society from them. As already noted, penology would be minuscule without the poor, as would the police. Other activities and groups that flourish because of the existence of poverty are the numbers game, the sale of heroin and cheap wines and liquors, pentecostal ministers, faith healers, prostitutes, pawn shops, and the peacetime army, which recruits its enlisted men mainly from among the poor.

Fourth, the poor buy goods others do not want and thus prolong the economic usefulness of such goods—day-old bread, fruit and vegetables that would otherwise have to be thrown out, secondhand clothes, and deteriorating automobiles and buildings. They also provide incomes for doctors, lawyers, teachers, and others who are too old, poorly trained, or incompetent to attract more affluent clients.

In addition to economic functions, the poor perform a number of social functions.

Fifth, the poor can be identified and punished as alleged or real deviants in order to uphold the legitimacy of conventional norms. To justify the desirability of hard work, thrift, honesty, and monogamy, for example, the defenders of these norms must be able to find people who can be accused of being lazy, spendthrift, dishonest, and promiscuous. Although there is some evidence that the poor are about as moral and law-abiding as anyone else, they are more likely than middle-class transgressors to be caught and punished when they participate in deviant acts. Moreover, they lack the political and cultural power to correct the stereotypes that other people hold of them and thus continue to be thought of as lazy, spendthrift, etc., by those who need living proof that moral deviance does not pay.

Sixth, and conversely, the poor offer vicarious participation to the rest of the population in the uninhibited sexual, alcoholic, and narcotic behavior in which they are alleged to participate and which, being freed from the constraints of affluence, they are often thought to enjoy more than the middle classes. Thus many people, some social scientists included, believe that the poor not only are more given to uninhibited behavior (which may be true, although it is often motivated by despair more than by lack of inhibition) but derive more pleasure from it than affluent people (which research by Lee Rainwater, Walter Miller, and others shows to be patently untrue). However, whether the poor actually have more sex and enjoy it more is irrelevant; so long as middle-class people believe this to be true, they can participate in it vicariously when instances are reported in factual or fictional form.

Seventh, the poor also serve a direct cultural function when culture created by or for them is adopted by the more affluent. The rich often collect artifacts from extinct folk cultures of poor people; and almost all Americans listen to the blues, Negro spirituals, and country music, which originated among the Southern poor. Recently they have enjoyed the rock styles that were born, like the Beatles, in the slums; and in the last year, poetry written by ghetto children has become popular in literary circles. The poor also serve as culture heroes, particularly, of course, to the left; but the hobo, the cowboy, the hipster, and the mythical prostitute with a heart of gold have performed this function for a variety of groups.

Eighth, poverty helps to guarantee the status of those who are not poor. In every hierarchical society someone has to be at the bottom; but in American society, in which social mobility is an important goal for many and people need to know where they stand, the poor function as a reliable and relatively permanent measuring rod for status comparisons. This is particularly true for the working class, whose politics is influenced by the need to maintain status distinctions between themselves and the poor, much as the aristocracy must find ways of distinguishing itself from the *nouveaux riches*.

Ninth, the poor also aid the upward mobility of groups just above them in the class hierarchy. Thus a goodly number of Americans have entered the middle class through the profits earned from the provision of goods and services in the slums, including illegal or nonrespectable ones that upper-class and upper-middle-class businessmen shun because of their low prestige. As a result, members of almost every immigrant group have financed their upward mobility by providing slum housing, entertainment, gambling, narcotics, etc., to later arrivals—most recently to blacks and Puerto Ricans.

Tenth, the poor help to keep the aristocracy busy, thus justifying its continued existence. "Society" uses the poor as clients of settlement houses and beneficiaries of charity affairs; indeed, the aristocracy must have the poor to demonstrate its superiority over other elites who devote themselves to earning money.

Eleventh, the poor, being powerless, can be made to absorb the costs of change and growth in American society. During the nineteenth century, they did the backbreaking work that built the cities; today, they are pushed out of their neighborhoods to make room for "progress." Urban renewal projects to hold middle-class taxpayers in the city and expressways to enable suburbanites to commute downtown have typically been located in poor neighborhoods, since no other group will allow itself to be displaced. For the same reason, universities, hospitals, and civic centers also expand into land occupied by the poor. The major costs of the industrialization of agriculture have been borne by the poor, who are pushed off the land without recompense; and they have paid a large share of the human cost of the growth of American power overseas, for they have provided many of the foot soldiers for Vietnam and other wars.

Twelfth, the poor facilitate and stabilize the American political process. Because they vote and participate in politics less than other groups, the political system is often free to ignore them. Moreover, since they can rarely support Republicans, they often provide the Democrats with a captive constituency that has no other place to go. As a result, the Democrats can count on their votes, and be more responsive to voters—for example, the white working class—who might otherwise switch to the Republicans.

Thirteenth, the role of the poor in upholding conventional norms (see the *fifth* point, above) also has a significant political function. An economy based on the ideology of laissez-faire requires a deprived population that is allegedly unwilling to work or that can be considered inferior because it must accept charity or welfare in order to survive. Not only does the alleged moral deviancy of the poor reduce the moral pressure on the present political economy to eliminate poverty, but socialist alternatives can be made to look quite unattractive if those who will benefit most from them can be described as lazy, spendthrift, dishonest, and promiscuous.

The Alternatives

I have described 13 of the more important functions poverty and the poor satisfy in American society, enough to support the functionalist thesis that poverty, like any other social phenomenon, survives in part because it is useful to society or some of its parts. This analysis is not intended to suggest that because it is often functional, poverty *should* exist, or that it *must* exist. For one thing, poverty has many more dysfunctions than functions; for another, it is possible to suggest functional alternatives.

For example, society's dirty work could be done without poverty, either by automation or by paying "dirty workers" decent wages. Nor is it necessary for the poor to subsidize the many activities they support through their low-wage jobs. This would, however, drive up the costs of these activities, which would result in higher prices to their customers and clients. Similarly, many of the professionals who flourish because of the poor could be given other roles. Social workers could provide counseling to the affluent, as they prefer to do anyway; and the police could devote themselves to traffic and organized crime. Other roles would have to be found for badly trained or incompetent professionals now relegated to serving the poor, and someone else would have to pay their salaries. Fewer penologists would be employable, however. And pentecostal religion could probably not survive without the poor—nor would parts of the second- and thirdhand-goods market. And in many cities, "used" housing that no one else wants would then have to be torn down at public expense.

Alternatives for the cultural functions of the poor could be found more easily and cheaply. Indeed, entertainers, hippies, and adolescents are already serving as the deviants needed to uphold traditional morality and as devotees of orgies to "staff" the fantasies of vicarious participation.

The status functions of the poor are another matter. In a hierarchical society, some people must be defined as inferior to everyone else with respect to a variety of attributes, but they need not be poor in the absolute sense. One could conceive of a society in which the "lower class," though last in the pecking order, received 75 percent of the median income, rather than 15–40 percent, as is now the case. Needless to say, this would require considerable income redistribution.

The contribution the poor make to the upward mobility of the groups that provide them with goods and services could also be maintained without the poor's having such low incomes. However, it is true that if the poor were more affluent, they would have access to enough capital to take over the provider role, thus competing with, and perhaps rejecting, the "outsiders." (Indeed, owing in part to antipoverty programs, this is already happening in a number of ghettos, where white storeowners are being replaced by blacks.) Similarly, if the poor were more affluent, they would make less willing clients for upper-class philanthropy, although some would still use settlement houses to achieve upward mobility, as they do now. Thus "Society" could continue to run its philanthropic activities.

The political functions of the poor would be more difficult to replace. With increased affluence the poor would probably obtain more political power and be more active politically. With higher incomes and more political power, the poor would be likely to resist paying the costs of growth and change. Of course, it is possible to imagine urban renewal and highway projects that properly reimbursed the displaced people, but such projects would then become considerably more expensive, and many might never be built. This, in turn, would reduce the comfort and convenience of those who now benefit from urban renewal and expressways. Finally, hippies could serve also as more deviants to justify the existing political economy—as they already do. Presumably, however, if poverty were eliminated, there would be fewer attacks on that economy.

In sum, then, many of the functions served by the poor could be replaced if poverty were eliminated, but almost always at higher costs to others, particularly more affluent others. Consequently, a functional analysis must conclude that poverty persists not only because it fulfills a number of positive functions but also because many of the functional alternatives to poverty would be quite dysfunctional for the affluent members of society. A functional analysis thus ultimately arrives at much the same conclusion as radical sociology, except that radical thinkers treat as manifest what I describe as latent: that social phenomena that are functional for affluent or powerful groups and dysfunctional for poor or powerless ones persist; that when the elimination of such phenomena through functional alternatives would generate dysfunctions for the affluent or powerful, they will continue to persist; and that phenomena like poverty can be eliminated only when they become dysfunctional for the affluent or powerful, or when the powerless can obtain enough power to change society.

Note

1. I shall henceforth abbreviate positive functions as functions and negative functions as dysfunctions. I shall also describe functions and dysfunctions, in the planner's terminology, as benefits and costs.

27 Some Hidden Injuries of Class

RICHARD SENNETT
JONATHAN COBB

Parents often want their children to have what they themselves were denied. In order to realize such dreams, some parents make extreme sacrifices for their children. They work at two jobs and go without luxuries. In some instances, they even do without necessities, such as medical and dental care, so that they can give their children more.

While some people can understand such self-sacrifice on the part of parents, many cannot understand the children's response. It is not infrequently the case that the children are ungrateful and even filled with resentment toward their parents. Instead of bonding their children to them, such sacrificing tends to alienate. Why? This at first appears contrary to reason, and certainly is contrary to the parent's expectations. It is precisely this dilemma that Sennett and Cobb consider in this article, documenting the ingratitude and resentment and analyzing why these unexpected attitudes exist. The hurt experienced by both parents and children, the alienation that crops up between children and the parents who encourage them to be upwardly mobile—the deep gulf and pain that permeate their basic relationship—are but two of the many hidden injuries of social class.

Do you know anyone who has experienced this problem? Do you think it is possible for parents to encourage their children's upward social mobility and avoid the problems these parents face? If so, how?

IN THE LATE 1950S THE YALE POLITICAL SCIENTIST ROBERT LANE sat down with a group of fifteen men in New Haven to find out "why the American common man believes what he does." The first book to result from these interviews, *Political Ideology*, is a moving document; in part, it touches on the same conflict that has so far appeared in this book [*The Hidden Injuries of Class*]. "Most of my subjects," Lane writes, "accepted the view that America opens up opportunity to all people, if not in equal proportions then at least enough so that a person must assume responsibility for his own status." Yet subordination in social position also appears to them as the result of circumstances of birth and class, over which the people in New Haven felt they had no control.

We want to analyze what has changed in America's social structure during the last decade, so that this conflict has now assumed major proportions in the lives of workingmen. However, Lane poses a more immediate question for us to consider. He asks what kind of resolution the people caught up in this conflict try to make:

> When something is painful to examine, people look away, or, if they look at it, they see only the parts they want to see. They deny that it is an important something. So is it often with a person's class status when the reference is upward, when people must account not for the strength of their position, but for its weakness.

Lane sees this feeling dealt with in three ways. A man he interviewed who said, "It's pretty hard for me to think there is anyone in the upper class and I'm not in the upper class," resolves first to insulate himself: "I have my own little unit to take care of." For an urban worker ten years ago, that was still possible culturally; there were still strong ethnic enclaves to reinforce his desire to insulate himself.

Secondly, the workers he interviewed denied the importance of the conflict itself, dismissing at various points the power of social class in their lives—even though at other times they did speak of how much class had placed them in circumstances beyond their control. Something has changed in the America known to the Boston workers we interviewed, so that we never heard the sheer power of social class dismissed.

Finally, Lane found resignation as a response to this conflict, "a reluctant acceptance of one's fate." In some cases, he noted, he was not really convinced that the pose of resignation was genuine: he could still sense a restless drive beneath the resignation; in other cases, people really did seem to deal with this conflict in the end by deciding they could do nothing.

The workingmen of Boston almost never voiced resignation in face of the injuries of class. The people we encountered had a powerful though complicated, sense of mission in their lives: they were determined that, if circumstances of class had limited their freedom in comparison to that of educated people, they would *create* freedom for themselves. By that we mean that they were resolved to shape the actions open to them so that, in their own minds, they felt as though they acted from choice rather than necessity. It is not a question of lying about how free you are, existential philosophers have said of such resolves in general, it is a matter of thinking about your circumstances in terms of an end you choose, you want. No matter how much the world has enslaved you, in this way you keep alive your dignity as a man. The dignity the people in Boston hoped to wrest from their circumstances was expressed, however, in a paradoxical morality of personal sacrifice.

The grandson of an immigrant tailor, John Bertin works six days and two nights a week. He grosses $12,000,* an amount that seems enormous to him in comparison to his parents' income, yet quite meager considering inflation, taxes, and the daily needs of his wife and five children. Mr. and Mrs. Bertin both grew up in an all-white, working-class neighborhood. In school, John Bertin barely made it through the ninth grade. "I was like runna-the-mill," he says, "the kid that didn't care. I never really enjoyed school—I hate being cooped up, I hafta be outside."

The outlines of Bertin's life form a microcosm of a development we have traced in larger terms. He felt "stupid" in school, and so came to think that his power to understand was undercut by *his* defects of character, *his* lack of perseverance, of willpower to perform well. During his earliest years, therefore, a definite connection was formed between a failure to perform for authority and a failure to develop resources of character and understanding in himself. As Bertin moved into adult life, this connection of failure in competence with loss of personal worth grew stronger; he paints delivery equipment for a large factory, people treat him like nothing. Bertin feels that his experience—his hopes, his failures, even his present struggle—has in itself no power to gain his children's respect.

He has, however, one claim on them: the fact that he is sacrificing himself, his time, his effort, for them. He has still his power to act as an agent for others, to give his wife and children the material means to move away from him. That stewardship he can indeed control. He is acting as a free man when he thinks of himself as *choosing* to sacrifice. Having been so repeatedly denied by the social order outside himself, now he will usurp the initiative, he will do the denying, the sacrifice of himself will become a voluntary act. Ricca Kartides's words return: "I am their father . . . and they *have* to respect me—because of that, and . . . because I want to do things for them." The outer face of this process is a great harshness on the part of the father; the inner face is one of self-contempt, the plea that the children not become the same as he.

Bertin's son came home from school during a talk.

"What did you do today in school, boy?" Bertin asked.

"Nothin'."

"But you were there six hours, now you must have learned something."

"Oh yeah, some calculus, some chem lab on photosynthesis, you know . . ."

"Well, that's real fine."

After his son left the room, Bertin turned to the interviewer and said

---

*This sum represents about $25,000 in today's purchasing power.—Ed.

proudly, "Now, did you understand any of that? Well, I suppose you did—not me. I haven't got it up here," tapping his head, "but my kids are smart—*I make 'em be that way.*"

Such fathers are determined that their children shall be very different from themselves; they do not allow the young to be indifferent about school, for it was their own failure to develop in school that has made them "run of the mill."

Again and again the fathers interviewed in Boston mixed an ideology of self-denial with assertions of their right therefore to tell children how to behave; yet these are not unambiguously authoritarian parents. "Look," said one man, "six days is a lot of work, right? Now somebody got to enjoy that, someone's got to get something from it, right?" If he is always working, his children deserve the freedom to "slack off," to be occasionally free of his discipline. He is "permissive" as long as his children follow a course that takes them from "the hard world I knew as a boy in the Depression to something decent where they can do what they want." A railroad man told us, "See, I think about that, 'specially on long trips when I'm away from home taking freight up to Maine . . . I'm thinking that's what it all adds up to now, why I spend this time away from them, because then they can take advantage of a good home."

There is a terrible paradox here, however. The "good home" can only be supported by longer hours of labor, only by the father's physical absence. But the "terrible homes" of the children of the Great Depression were curiously the same: "See, my father never played with me," says yet another man. "My father was always out, outta town, like three, four, five weeks at a time. So my mother actually brought me up, and there was only discipline with my mother; like a lot of mothers, she never hesitated to backhand me, punch me, or whatever it was. But I think it was on accounta my old man that I want to be different in *my* life."

To devote oneself and one's life to the children has an obvious set of class limits: you must have something to give them. A destitute worker, perennially out of a job, can't feel that his sacrifices give meaning to his family life. Desperately as he may want the children to lead different lives from his own, he must struggle just to eat; everything he does concerns present survival.

Crossing that line, however, we come back to a familiar problem: isn't it characteristic of most American families, not just manual-laboring ones, to see the struggles of adult life redeemed by sacrifice for the children? A study of affluent Jewish community life, *Children of the Gilded Ghetto*, shows men who have made a go of it in business, who have not suffered the worldly constraints John Bertin knows, feeling that the strains of their jobs are also justified by the privileges work creates for their children. Indeed, the whole line of thinking about performance and respect laid out in this book leads logically to the same class-less idea: if you feel inadequate and unfulfilled in demonstrating your worth, thinking you are doing it for the good of someone else makes the performance legitimate for you. If wearing a badge of ability is alienating, wear it so that the rewards will give a person whom you love a better life.

However, class gets entangled in sacrifice in two ways. The first is a matter of economics. A wage-worker is attempting to perform the most difficult of balancing acts: on the one hand, he wishes to be with his wife and children, to play with and show concern for them; on the other hand, he knows that the only way he can provide decently for his wife and children, and give his life some greater meaning, is by working longer hours, and thus spending much free time away from his family.

But that material calculation is not enough. Sacrifice, as an attempt to redeem the traumas in a person's life, becomes divided into unequal classes of experience. By this we mean that a working-class person has less chance than a middle-class person of sacrificing successfully; class definitions intrude to derail him from a sense that he has made an effective gift of his own struggles to someone else. To understand the inability of a working-class person to sacrifice "successfully," we should start by looking at an unspoken social contract demanded by sacrificial acts.

Sacrifice as a Contract

Sacrificial rites in "savage" tribes manipulate time. An animal or man is sacrificed to the gods for some past misdeed of the tribe; a sacrifice is made to bring good fortune in the future; a sacrifice serves as a rite of passage for individuals in the tribe, easing them over the time of their childhood to the time of their adulthood.

Self-sacrifice in a modern family also manipulates time. To sacrifice for the children is to future-orient oneself, to delay gratification. The gratification will come when they, as adults, have moved up to a social position where anyone could respect them. Their future position will redeem the unsatisfying effort a parent makes now. Yet sacrifice in a family like John Bertin's or William O'Malley's means that the sacrificer is also making demands in the present on those for whom he is struggling.

When William O'Malley was growing up during the Depression, . . . his parents were very poor, and his mother as well as his father spent all day at work, leaving the children alone to fend for themselves. For O'Malley, work is an act he performs alone so that his wife can have more free time at home than his mother had. Mrs. O'Malley, however, does not feel that her life at home is freedom. It bores her, it seems an imposition of her husband's authority. The effort O'Malley puts in at work is the answer for him to the historical conditions of his childhood; that his wife today has needs not consonant with the reparation of a wound in his past, this he does not, perhaps cannot, permit himself to see. Where he feels that by working alone he is making a sacrifice of himself *for* her, he is rather sacrificing her freedom to that wound of his past.

Men acquire status, said Max Weber, by usurpation. William O'Malley has usurped the roles of provider and intermediary to the "real" world outside the home for his family. But for a man like O'Malley this usurpation is not made without expectations. His sacrifice for his family, he believes, gives him the right to expect his family to act as he wishes; in other words, taking away their freedom is legitimate because he has denied himself out of love for them.

Sacrifice to the husband and father may thus seem here a kind of reciprocal "contract" with his family. But it is in fact only a pseudo-mutual relationship: the sacrificer does not ask his family whether *they* want him to sacrifice; the very power of this "one-way" contract lies in the fact that one person has wholly usurped the act of giving, and so prevented the others from asserting countervailing personal rights. Any accusation against the usurper is undercut *a priori* by the fact of the usurper's self-denial.

Shame, Helen Lynd has written in *On Shame and the Search for Identity*, is harder to "pass off" than guilt. When we have broken a law and feel guilty about it, being punished by others helps us make a symbolic closure to the period of wrongdoing; we are not endlessly guilty. But shame, she argues—which concerns inability, which concerns doing poorly rather than doing wrong—shame is harder to get rid of.

In some cultures, where tests of an individual come at specific points in life (tests of a man passing from childhood to puberty, for instance) a failure to perform the ritual tests well can be closed off simply as the individual grows older. Sacrifice is an attempt to deal with shaming in this most unritualistic of cultures, but the contract of rights-for-self-denial does not pass off; in Lynd's terms, there is no ritualized point the person involved reaches where he feels the shaming expunged and therefore the moral necessity for his self-denial ended.

A number of studies of the differences between middle- and working-class family attitudes point to the greater importance placed on the father's authority and discipline in working-class homes. (The best series of studies has been conducted by Melvin L. Kohn. See his *Class and Conformity: A Study in Values* [Homewood, Ill.: Dorsey Press; 1969]). Furthermore, these "authoritarian" parental attitudes stretch over family time so that they are as pronounced in the babyhood of a child as they are in his adolescence. The conclusion usually drawn is that the parent is trying to make up for his lack of status in the outer world by imposing it unendingly at home.

That conclusion is in a way true, but also in a way misleading. A middle-class father may pass off the tensions of his work by thinking he is doing it for the kids, but in the process he needn't desire that they rise to a higher class—i.e., that they become unlike him. Working-class fathers like O'Malley and Bertin see the whole point of sacrificing for their children to be that the children *will* become unlike themselves; through education and the right kind of peer associations, the kids will learn the arts of rational control and acquire the power to make wide choices which in sum should make the kids better armed, less vulnerable in coping with the world than the fathers are. If the child succeeds in becoming better armed, the father does so only by proxy: his sacrifice does not end in his own life the social conditions that have made him feel open to shame, prey to feelings of inadequacy. To call the pressure working-class fathers put on their kids "authoritarian" is misleading in that the father doesn't ask the child to take the parents' lives as a model, but as a warning.

Working-class sacrifice is not a ritual, then. It creates no closure to shame because, indeed, the ascription of weakness the society forces on men has no limits in time; the weakness is built into who they are. The contract in sacrificing is not therefore a simple transaction of, I will give myself to you, you will therefore do what I want, that will make me feel better, and I can stop feeling I have no life except through you.

If sacrifice is not a ritual, it is at least a routine. The women with whom we spoke expect their husbands to sacrifice and provide for them, and this expectation, too, they often justify in terms of their own sacrifices as women, as wives, and as mothers. There is created in many families a kind of exchange relationship, a series of unspoken, individual expectations of obligation towards each other based on the respective sacrifices of each.

The expectations husbands had of their wives were often felt by the women to be hopelessly contradictory. The wives have to shoulder most of the work of child-raising, most of the heavy as well as light maintenance of the home, most of the shopping, bill-paying, and other clerical labor of the house. "I *can* do all these things," said one women. "After all, that is what a man expects from a good wife. Where I feel caught is, that Eddie also wants me to be a glamour girl—I spend twelve or fourteen hours a day making the house work, and then he expects me to be sexy in bed. He says, 'If I can work hard all day and be a man at night, why can't you be a woman?' It's a whole thing about the way he wants me to act. I mean, he wants me to spend a lot of time fixing myself up and being seductive, and at the same time if I'm a good wife, I'm supposed to spend from morning to night being *the* parent and *the* bill-payer—you know, coping with life."

This divide is the mirror of the conflicting codes of love and social competence that affect young men and boys. On the one hand there is the sexual being, the "woman," and on the other hand there is the competent manager, achieving some control over the problems of running a family and a household. A woman does not appear more attractive, more sensual, more desirable in the eyes of her husband, and in her own eyes, because she can raise the children or deal with the neighbors; this ability in coping appears divorced from and in conflict with the sexual dimension.

If the women feel it impossible to satisfy adequately the demands their husbands make of them, they nevertheless often retain a profound sympathy for their husbands' burdens. This was expressed as a wish to protect the men; because their husbands were working so hard to bring home an adequate income, many wives felt they ought to cope with all the daily household cares. This was the sacrifice they felt was owed the husband, even if, as with Mrs. O'Malley, it made them deeply unhappy.

The contract implicit in sacrifice has, in sum, these lines: the sacrificer resolves to look at his own actions as essentially serving the welfare of another. Applied to children, the service is for the future; applied to either a spouse or children, the self-denial in the present legitimates limiting the present freedom of the other. Sacrifice in the home, like legitimized power in the school or factory, thus creates a conflict between freedom and self-respect.

Unlike middle-class fathers, the men we interviewed can only make sacrifices of free time. The cost of sacrifice is special also in that fathers like O'Malley and Bertin are trying, not to create a web of stability in the home, but to spur the children to develop themselves, so that they will enter a social life higher than their own.

That image of transformation across the generations gives a clue to a hidden class anger implicit in this personal resolve, beyond considerations of money and time, an image of injustice spreading beyond the home. What this transformation invites the child to do is to desert his past, to leave it and the parents who have sacrificed for him all behind. And if he does that, if he becomes a man of rank where he can command the respect of anyone, isn't he in a way betraying them, by having risen above them? Isn't betrayal the inevitable result when you try to endow your life with a moral purpose greater than your own survival?

Sacrifice and Images of Betrayal

For very few does redemption come so completely as it apparently has for Tom DeWolfe and his wife. They have four sons, all of whom respect their parents, have done well in sports, and have been well-liked school leaders. All four have either graduated from or are about to enter college. The DeWolfes are laboring people of little formal education who have struggled hard to provide thier children with an education and resources in the home commensurate with what they considered the boys' abilities. "That's been my whole life," says DeWolfe, "trying to get enough money ahead so my boys'd get what I didn't have. . . . Now my next ambition's to retire when I'm sixty-two, so I can enjoy a few years." They have been strict parents, requiring the children to apply themselves and study, and have laid down strict rules to keep the boys as much as possible shielded from the influence of the street.

They take pride in the accomplishments of their sons, and feel a reflected glory. They also feel that the successes of their sons give them an edge on their neighbors, a basis for feeling individual, i.e., superior to the other families on the street. "There is something wonderful when you think of how many people here alone *can't* get their boys to, you know, any type of college, let alone a major college. So this is the satisfaction we're getting out of it."

Such a vicarious life through one's children, however, carries with it enormous dangers. For children are not merely extensions of oneself, embodiments of one's dreams, but themselves independent beings. What is happening in the DeWolfe family is the most direct kind of betrayal these independent beings can practice.

The DeWolfe boys, caught up in the contemporary shift in values among young people, are becoming increasingly unwilling to carry out the fantasies of retribution and justification cherished by their parents and their parents' era. They are beginning to question why they should work so hard, why they should be "Mommy and Daddy's little jewels," as one of them put it: "I look at my father and I want to cry . . . but he's getting almost to hate me because I don't want to be a lawyer or doctor or someone respectable."

As the children consider dropping out of school, or becoming artistic craftsmen, their parents worry below the surface of self-congratulation that their children may not after all redeem them in quite the same way they expected. But the young who do not let their parents down also betray them.

"I always let them fear me," says Frank Rissarro, speaking of his boys in college: " 'Because you got an education under you, you gonna push me around,' I says, 'I'll throw you out of this house bodily. I don't need you.' I make them understand who is the boss and they respect me. 'Cause if I let them get away with it, they'd start, you know . . . working on me."

This is an extraordinary statement—first in its honesty, but more in the fear it expresses. Unlike DeWolfe, Rissarro is seeing his boys move up, fulfilling their part of the contract he has imposed on them, by staying in school. But this means they will now have power over him, will be able to "pull rank" on him and, he fears, start "pushing him around" if he "lets them get away with it."

Indeed, if the father's sacrifices do succeed in transforming his children's lives, he then becomes a burden to them, an embarrassment. A great moment of pathos occurred in our interviews when a laborer described one of the "great events of my life." This was when we went to visit his son on parents' day at the fraternity house of the community college the boy attended. His wife baked a ham, so "we have an 'in,' you know," and this was his reaction when they walked through the front door:

"I never thought I'd have my boys in a fraternity house at a university. We met some of the nicest people you'd ever want to meet. In their class and out of our class, let's put it that way. If they ever saw where I came from, the back slums of East Boston, they'd say it's impossible to even put him in our circle. I mean, let's face it, we have to be a little respectful of where we came from. That's the category he's in right now. Now he's in with a group of fellows who are educated. Now, if he goes around the corner where he came from, they're a bunch of hoodlums, hoods, period."

The destruction of respect that sacrifice most strongly creates within a home, however, does not turn on the success or failure of the young; the more direct problem is whether love can survive under contract.

The tragedy of loving as sacrifice is that those who are pushed to feel grateful cannot. Sacrifice appears to the children as a way parents have of manipulating them, rather than really loving them. The eldest son of a hard-working laborer, for instance, resents his father, and gets angry when he feels his father is "doing things" for him. He sees that it is not a sacrifice called into being because of something he, the son, has asked for; he sees it, therefore, as a hidden and rather cowardly power play by his father, a man who won't stand up for himself.

The son thus feels betrayed because his father has taken him on a "guilt trip." The father, however, also feels betrayed, by his boy's refusal to say or show that he is grateful for what the father has done. The ungratefulness of a child who has had advantages the father lacked, where the advantages were earned by the father's own sacrifices—this seems to him like ultimate injustice.

It is not so much that the father has "internalized" the values of a repressive society in his treatment of his children as that he has, rather, tried to replace the society in a certain sense, so that *he* is the one who decides to sink back to a subordinate or passive role. It is not in order to feel more debased that he makes this sacrifice. The need for dignity is a hunger pushing a person to get from day to day with the feeling that he is building some meaning, that he is adding something to the world in which he was born. That this parental sacrifice appears to the son as insidious manipulation, an imposition of a demand for blind love, is a necessary consequence neither the father nor the son can avoid.

The theme of giving oneself, and receiving ingratitude in return, stretches beyond the home to the more general awareness working men have of their class position in America. There is a feeling that the anxieties they have taken upon themselves, the tensions they have to bear, ought to give them the right to demand that society give something in return, that government and large institutions should not make class tensions any worse. But ingratitude is the return they feel from society, too, a refusal to acknowledge that their sacrifices finally create a claim on the respect of others.

28 The Doctor–Nurse Game

LEONARD I. STEIN

The socialization into sex roles that we studied in Part III is an essential part of the basic social inequality in American society. This socialization has far-reaching and only inadequately understood effects on perhaps all our interactions as adults. Because men are socialized for dominance, they tend to play a dominant role in most of what they do; if women are socialized into supportive roles, that is what they tend to perform in most aspects of their lives.

Male–female positions in American occupations are certainly no exception. You yourself are directly familiar with sex roles functioning in occupations to maintain inequality. To select an example that is close to your own situation at present, in colleges and universities almost without exception the higher-paid positions belong to men (the presidencies, deanships, departmental headships, and, disproportionately, also the full professorships), while the lower-paid supportive positions are usually occupied by women (secretaries, clerks, and, disproportionately, the lower teaching ranks).

In addition to the positions that men and women tend to hold is the related matter of how males and females interact with one another when they are at work. It is how socialization into dominant or supportive roles actually works out in the occupational setting that Stein analyzes in this article on doctors and nurses at work.

Can you supplement Stein's observations through your own work experiences? In what ways have you seen men and women play out their basic sex roles at work, even though those roles were irrelevant to the tasks to be performed? Do you think things are changing? In what ways?

THE RELATIONSHIP BETWEEN THE DOCTOR AND THE NURSE is a very special one. There are few professions where the degree of mutual respect and cooperation between co-workers is as intense as that between the doctor and nurse. Superficially, the stereotype of this relationship has been dramatized in many novels and television serials. When, however, it is observed carefully in an interactional framework, the relationship takes on a new dimension and has a special quality which fits a game model. The underlying attitudes which demand that this game be played are unfortunate. These attitudes create serious obstacles in the path of meaningful communications between physicians and nonmedical professional groups.

The physician traditionally and appropriately has total responsibility for making the decisions regarding the management of his patients' treatment. To guide his decisions he considers data gleaned from several sources. He acquires a complete medical history, performs a thorough physical examination, interprets laboratory findings, and at times obtains recommendations from physician-consultants. Another important factor in his decision making is the recommendations he receives from the nurse. The interaction between doctor and nurse through which these recommendations are communicated and received is unique and interesting.

The Game

One rarely hears a nurse say, "Doctor, I would recommend that you order a retention enema for Mrs. Brown." A physician, upon hearing a recommendation of that nature, would gape in amazement at the effrontery of the nurse. The nurse, upon hearing the statement, would look over her shoulder to see who said it, hardly believing the words actually came from her own mouth. Nevertheless, if one observes closely, nurses make recommendations of more import every hour and physicians willingly and respectfully consider them. If the nurse is to make a suggestion without appearing insolent and the doctor is to seriously consider that suggestion, their interaction must not violate the rules of the game.

OBJECT OF THE GAME

The object of the game is as follows: the nurse is to be bold, have initiative, and be responsible for making significant recommendations, while at the same time she must appear passive. This must be done in such a manner so as to make her recommendations appear to be initiated by the physician.

Both participants must be acutely sensitive to each other's nonverbal and cryptic verbal communications. A slight lowering of the head, a minor shifting of position in the chair, or a seemingly nonrelevant comment concerning an event which occurred eight months ago must be interpreted as a powerful message. The game requires the nimbleness of a high wire acrobat, and if either participant slips, the game can be shattered; the penalties for frequent failure are apt to be severe.

RULES OF THE GAME

The cardinal rule of the game is that open disagreement between the players must be avoided at all costs. Thus, the nurse must communicate her recommendations without appearing to be making a recommendation statement. The physician, in requesting a recommendation from a nurse, must do so without appearing to be asking for it. Utilization of this technique keeps anyone from committing themselves to a position before a sub-rosa agreement on that position has already been established. In that way open disagreement is avoided. The greater the significance of the recommendation, the more subtly the game must be played.

To convey a subtle example of the game with all its nuances would require the talents of a literary artist. Lacking these talents, let me give you the following example, which is unsubtle but happens frequently. The medical resident on hospital call is awakened by telephone at 1:00 A.M., because a patient on a ward, not his own, has not been able to fall asleep. Dr. Jones answers the telephone and the dialogue goes like this:

> This is Dr. Jones.
> (An open and direct communication.)
> Dr. Jones, This is Miss Smith on 2W—Mrs. Brown, who learned today of her father's death, is unable to fall asleep.
> (This message has two levels. Openly, it describes a set of circumstances: a woman who is unable to sleep and who that morning received word of her father's death. Less openly, but just as directly, it is a diagnostic and recommendation statement; i.e., Mrs. Brown is unable to sleep because of her grief, and she should be given a sedative. Dr. Jones, accepting the diagnostic statement and replying to the recommendation statement, answers.)
> What sleeping medication has been helpful to Mrs. Brown in the past?
> (Dr. Jones, not knowing the patient, is asking for a recommendation from the nurse, who does know the patient, about what sleeping medication should be prescribed. Note, however, his question does not appear to be asking her for a recommendation. Miss Smith replies.)
> Pentobarbital mg 100 was quite effective night before last.
> (A disguised recommendation statement. Dr. Jones replies with a note of authority in his voice.)
> Pentobarbital mg 100 before bedtime as needed for sleep; got it?
> (Miss Smith ends the conversation with the tone of a grateful supplicant.)
> Yes, I have, and thank you very much doctor.

The above is an example of a successfully played doctor–nurse game. The nurse made appropriate recommendations which were accepted by the physician and were helpful to the patient. The game was successful because the cardinal rule was not violated. The nurse was able to make her recommendation without appearing to, and the physician was able to ask for recommendations without conspicuously asking for them.

THE SCORING SYSTEM

Inherent in any game are penalties and rewards for the players. In game theory, the doctor–nurse game fits the non-zero-sum-game model. It is not like chess, where the players compete with each other and whatever one player loses the other wins. Rather, it is the kind of game in which the rewards and punishments are shared by both players. If they play the game successfully they both win rewards, and if they are unskilled and the game is played badly, they both suffer the penalty.

The most obvious reward from the well-played game is a doctor–nurse team that operates efficiently. The physician is able to utilize the nurse as a valuable consultant, and the nurse gains self-esteem and professional satisfaction from her job. The less obvious rewards are no less important. A successful game creates a doctor–nurse alliance; through this alliance the physician gains the respect and admiration of the nursing service. He can be confident that his nursing staff will smooth the path for getting his work done. His charts will be organized and waiting for him when he arrives, the ruffled feathers of patients and relatives will have been smoothed down, his pet routines will be happily followed, and he will be helped in a thousand and one other ways.

The doctor–nurse alliance sheds its light on the nurse as well. She gains a reputation for being a "damn good nurse." She is respected by everyone and appropriately enjoys her position. When physicians discuss the nursing staff it would not be unusual for her name to be mentioned with respect and admiration. Their esteem for a good nurse is no less than their esteem for a good doctor.

The penalties for a game failure, on the other hand, can be severe. The physician who is an unskilled gamesman and fails to recognize the nurses' subtle recommendation messages is tolerated as a "clod." If, however, he interprets these messages as insolence and strongly indicates he does not wish to tolerate suggestions from nurses, he creates a rocky path for his travels. The old truism "If the nurse is your ally you've got it made, and if she has it in for you, be prepared for misery" takes on life-size proportions. He receives three times as many phone calls after midnight as his colleagues. Nurses will not accept his telephone orders, because "telephone orders are against the rules." Somehow, this rule gets suspended for the skilled players. Soon he becomes like Joe Bfstplk in the "Li'l Abner" comic strip. No matter where he goes, a black cloud constantly hovers over his head.

The unskilled gamesman-nurse also pays heavily. The nurse who does not view her role as that of consultant, and therefore does not attempt to communicate recommendations, is perceived as a dullard and is mercifully allowed to fade into the woodwork.

The nurse who does see herself as a consultant but refuses to follow the rules of the game in making her recommendations has hell to pay. The outspoken nurse is labeled a "bitch" by the surgeon. The psychiatrist describes her as unconsciously suffering from penis envy, and her behavior is the acting out of her hostility towards men. Loosely translated, the psychiatrist is saying she is a bitch. The employment of the unbright, outspoken nurse is soon terminated. The outspoken, bright nurse whose recommendations are worthwhile remains employed. She is, however, constantly reminded in a hundred ways that she is not loved.

Genesis of the Game

To understand how the game evolved, we must comprehend the nature of the doctors' and nurses' training which shaped the attitudes necessary for the game.

MEDICAL STUDENT TRAINING

The medical student in his freshman year studies as if possessed. In the anatomy class he learns every groove and prominence on the bones of the skeleton as if life depended on it. As a matter of fact, he literally believes just that. He not infrequently says, "I've got to learn it exactly; a life may depend on me knowing that." A consequence of this attitude, which is carefully nurtured throughout medical school, is the development of a phobia: the overdetermined fear of making a mistake. The development of this fear is quite understandable. The burden the physician must carry is at times almost unbearable. He feels responsible in a very personal way for the lives of his patients. When a man dies leaving young children and a widow, the doctor carries some of her grief and despair inside himself; and when a child dies, some of him dies too. He sees himself as a warrior against death and disease. When he loses a battle, through no fault of his own, he nevertheless feels pangs of guilt, and he relentlessly searches himself to see if there might have been a way to alter the outcome. For the physician a mistake leading to a serious consequence is intolerable, and any mistake reminds him of his vulnerability. There is little wonder that he becomes phobic. The classical way in which phobias are managed is to avoid the source of the fear. Since it is impossible to avoid making some mistakes in an active practice of medicine, a substitute defensive maneuver is employed. The physician develops the belief that he is omnipotent and omniscient and therefore incapable of making mistakes. This belief allows the phobic physician to actively engage in his practice rather than avoid it. The fear of committing an error in a critical field like medicine is unavoidable and appropriately realistic. The physician, however, must learn to live with the fear rather than handle it defensively through a posture of omnipotence. This defense markedly interferes with his interpersonal professional relationships.

Physicians, of course, deny feelings of omnipotence. The evidence, however, renders their denials whispers in the wind. The slightest mistake inflicts a large narcissistic wound. Depending on his underlying personality structure, the physician may be obsessed for days about it, quickly rationalize it away, or deny it. The guilt produced is unusually exaggerated, and the incident is handled defensively. The ways in which physicians enhance and support each other's defenses when an error is made could be the topic of another paper. The feeling of omnipotence becomes generalized to other areas of his life. A report of the Federal Aviation Agency (FAA), as quoted in *Time* (August 5, 1966), states that in 1964 and 1965, physicians had a fatal-accident rate four times as high as the average for all other private pilots. Major causes of the high death rate were risk-taking attitudes and judgments. Almost all of the accidents occurred on pleasure trips and were therefore not necessary risks to get to a patient needing emergency care. The trouble, suggested an FAA official, is that too many doctors fly with "the feeling that they are omnipotent." Thus, the extremes to which the physician may go in preserving his self-concept of omnipotence may threaten his own life. This overdetermined preservation of omnipotence is indicative of its brittleness and its underlying foundation of fear of failure.

The physician finds himself trapped in a paradox. He fervently wants to give his patient the best possible medical care, and being open to the nurses' recommendations helps him accomplish this. On the other hand, accepting advice from nonphysicians is highly threatening to his omnipotence. The solution for the paradox is to receive sub-rosa recommendations and make them appear to be initiated by himself. In short, he must learn to play the doctor–nurse game.

Some physicians never learn to play the game. Most learn in their internship, and a perceptive few learn during their clerkships in medical school. Medical students frequently complain that the nursing staff treats them as if they had just completed a junior Red Cross first-aid class instead of two years of intensive medical training. Interviewing nurses in a training hospital sheds considerable light on this phenomenon. In their words they said:

> A few students just seem to be with it, they are able to understand what you are trying to tell them and they are a pleasure to work with; most, however, pretend to know everything and refuse to listen to anything we have to say and I guess we do give them a rough time.

In essence, they are saying that those students who quickly learn the game are rewarded, and those that do not are punished.

Most physicians learn to play the game after they have weathered a few experiences like the one described below. On the first day of his internship, the physician and nurse were making rounds. They stopped at the bed of a fifty-two-year-old woman who, after complimenting the young doctor on his appearance, complained to him of her problem with constipation. After several minutes of listening to her detailed description of peculiar diets, family home remedies, and special exercises that have helped her constipation in the past, the nurse politely interrupted the patient. She told her the doctor would take care of the problem and that he had to move on because there were other patients waiting to see him. The young doctor gave the nurse a stern look, turned toward the patient, and kindly told her he would order an enema for her that very afternoon. As they left the bedside, the nurse told him the patient has had a normal bowel movement every day for the past week and that in the twenty-three days the patient has been in the hospital she has never once passed up an opportunity to complain of her constipation. She quickly added that *if* the doctor wanted to order an enema, the patient would certainly receive one. After hearing this report the intern's mouth fell open, and the wheels began turning in his head. He remembered the nurse's comment to the patient that "the doctor had to move on," and it occurred to him that perhaps she was really giving him a message. This experience and a few more like it, and the young doctor learns to listen for the subtle recommendations the nurses make.

NURSING STUDENT TRAINING

Unlike the medical student who usually learns to play the game after he finishes medical school, the nursing student begins to learn it early in her training. Throughout her education she is trained to play the doctor–nurse game.

Student nurses are taught how to relate to physicians. They are told he has infinitely more knowledge than they, and thus he should be shown the utmost respect. In addition, it was not many years ago when nurses were instructed to stand whenever a physician entered a room. When he would come in for a conference, the nurse was expected to offer him her chair, and when both entered a room the nurse would open the door for him and allow him to enter first. Although these practices are no longer rigidly adhered to, the premise upon which they were based is still promulgated. One nurse described that premise as, "He's God almighty and your job is to wait on him."

To inculcate subservience and inhibit deviancy, nursing schools, for the most part, are tightly run, disciplined institutions. Certainly, there is great variation among nursing schools, and there is little question that the trend is toward giving students more autonomy. However, in too many schools this trend has not gone far enough, and the climate remains restrictive. The student's schedule is firmly controlled, and there is very little free time. Classroom hours, study hours, mealtime, and bedtime with lights out are rigidly enforced. In some schools meaningless chores are assigned, such as cleaning bedsprings with cotton applicators. The relationship between student and instructor continues this military flavor. Often their relationship is more like that between recruit and drill sergeant than between student and teacher. Open dialogue is inhibited by attitudes of strict black and white with few, if any, shades of gray. Straying from the rigidly outlined path is sure to result in disciplinary action.

The inevitable result of these practices is to instill in the student nurse a fear of independent action. This inhibition of independent action is most marked when relating to physicians. One of the students' greatest fears is making a blunder while assisting a physician and being publicly ridiculed by him. This is really more a reflection of the nature of their training than the prevalence of abusive physicians. The fear of being humiliated for a blunder while assisting in a procedure is generalized to the fear of humiliation for making any independent act in relating to a physician, especially the act of making a direct recommendation. Every nurse interviewed felt that making a suggestion to a physician was equivalent to insulting and belittling him. It was tantamount to questioning his medical knowledge and insinuating he did not know his business. In light of her image of the physician as an omniscient and punitive figure, the questioning of his knowledge would be unthinkable.

The student, however, is also given messages quite contrary to the ones described above. She is continually told that she is an invaluable aid to the physician in the treatment of the patient. She is told that she must help him in every way possible and that she is imbued with a strong sense of responsibility for the care of her patient. Thus she, like the physician, is caught in a paradox. The first set of messages implies that the physician is omniscient and that any recommendation she might make would be insulting to him and leave her open to ridicule. The second set of messages implies that she is an important aspect to him, has much to contribute, and is duty-bound to make those contributions. Thus, when her good sense tells her a recommendation would be helpful to him, she is not allowed to communicate it directly, nor is she allowed not to communicate it. The way out of the bind is to use the doctor–nurse game and communicate the recommendation without appearing to do so.

29 Tally's Corner

ELLIOT LIEBOW

Liebow studied black streetcorner men, lower-lower-class males whose chief activities and satisfactions take place "on the street." The men are materially poor because of the convergence of income, race, education, and residence. Focusing on the adaptations these streetcorner men have made to their life circumstances. Liebow analyzes their survival strategies.

In his analysis, Liebow applies the concept of the *self-fulfilling prophecy,* a prediction that, by the mere fact of being made, makes the predicted event come true. This happens when people's beliefs about coming events become part of the way they look at the world and they then change their behavior to match what they feel is on its way. When this occurs, their changed behavior sometimes makes the prediction a reality—hence the term self-fulfilling prophecy.

An example might help clarify the term. Let us suppose that reporters begin to discuss the possibility of a coming recession. They quote economists who see indicators that a recession might occur. The economists don't predict a recession, however, but carefully cover themselves with a lot of "ifs, ands, and buts." Some people who read the stories skip the disclaimers of the economists, however, and focus on the recession part of their statements. More and more, as they talk about the matter, people come to believe that a recession might be on its way. Consequently, they cut down on their purchases "just in case." When enough people cut back, inventories of unsold goods build up, factory orders diminish, economic indexes begin to decline, and worried business people cut back on expansion plans—making ripples felt throughout the economy. The recession arrives, because it was predicted and people changed their behavior accordingly.

Although this oversimplifies economic matters, the above scenario illustrates a significant concept in social life. As Liebow applies the concept, it becomes apparent that a self-fulfilling prophecy can create a vicious cycle that drastically affects people's lives. The perceptions of the men he studied both predict failure at work and help cause the predicted failure.

Can you think of other self-fulfilling prophecies? Which have you personally experienced? What effect did they have on your life? How do you think the streetcorner men's cycle of self-fulfilling prophecies could be broken?

IN SUMMARY OF OBJECTIVE JOB CONSIDERATIONS [of street-corner men], the most important fact is that a man who is able and willing to work cannot earn enough money to support himself, his wife, and one or more children. A man's chances for working regularly are good only if he is willing to work for less than he can live on, and sometimes not even then. On some jobs, the wage rate is deceptively higher than on others, but the higher the wage rate, the more difficult it is to get the job, and the less the job security. Higher-paying construction work tends to be seasonal and, during the season, the amount of work available is highly sensitive to business and weather conditions and to the changing requirements of individual projects.[1] Moreover, high-paying construction jobs are frequently beyond the physical capacity of some of the men, and some of the low-paying jobs are scaled down even lower in accordance with the self-fulfilling assumption that the man will steal part of his wages on the job.[2]

Bernard assesses the objective job situation dispassionately over a cup of coffee, sometimes poking at the coffee with his spoon, sometimes staring at it as if, like a crystal ball, it holds tomorrow's secrets. He is twenty-seven years old. He and the woman with whom he lives have a baby son, and she has another child by another man. Bernard does odd jobs—mostly painting—but here it is the end of January, and his last job was with the Post Office during the Christmas mail rush. He would like postal work as a steady job, he says. It pays well (about $2.00 an hour) but he has twice failed the Post Office examination (he graduated from a Washington high school) and has given up the idea as an impractical one. He is supposed to see a man tonight about a job as a parking attendant for a large apartment house. The man told him to bring his birth certificate and driver's license, but his license was suspended because of a backlog of unpaid traffic fines. A friend promised to lend him some money this evening. If he gets it, he will pay the fines tomorrow morning and have his license reinstated. He hopes the man with the job will wait till tomorrow night.

A "security job" is what he really wants, he said. He would like to save up money for a taxi cab. (But having twice failed the postal examination and having a bad driving record as well, it is highly doubtful that he could meet the qualifications or pass the written test.) That would be "a good life." He can always get a job in a restaurant or as a clerk in a drugstore but they don't pay enough, he said. He needs to take home at least $50 to $55 a week. He thinks he can get that much driving a truck somewhere. . . . Sometimes he wishes he had stayed in the army. . . . A security job, that's what he wants most of all, a real security job. . . .

When we look at what the men bring to the job rather than at what the job offers the men, it is essential to keep in mind that we are not looking at men who come to the job fresh, just out of school perhaps, and newly prepared to undertake the task of making a living, or from another job where they earned a living and are prepared to do the same on this job. Each man comes to the job with a long job history characterized by his not being able to support himself and his family. Each man carries this knowledge, born of his experience, with him. He comes to the job flat and stale, wearied by the sameness of it all, convinced of his own incompetence, terrified of responsibility—of being tested still again and found wanting. Possible exceptions are the younger men not yet, or just, married. They suspect all this but have yet to have it confirmed by repeated personal experience over time. But those who are or have been married know it well. It is the experience of the individual and the group; of their fathers and probably their sons. Convinced of their inadequacies, not only do they not seek out those few better-paying jobs which test their resources, but they actively avoid them, gravitating in a mass to the menial, routine jobs which offer no challenge—and therefore pose no threat—to the already diminished images they have of themselves.

Thus Richard does not follow through on the real estate agent's offer. He is afraid to do on his own—minor plastering, replacing broken windows, other minor repairs and painting—exactly what he had been doing for months on a piece-work basis under someone else (and which provided him with a solid base from which to derive a cost estimate).

Richard once offered an important clue to what may have gone on in his mind when the job offer was made. We were in the Carry-out, at a time when he was looking for work. He was talking about the kind of jobs available to him.

> I graduated from high school [Baltimore] but I don't know anything. I'm dumb. Most of the time I don't even say I graduated, 'cause then somebody asks me a question and I can't answer it, and they think I was lying about graduating. . . . They graduated me but I didn't know anything. I had lousy grades but I guess they wanted to get rid of me.
>
> I was at Margaret's house the other night and her little sister asked me to help her with her homework. She showed be some fractions and I knew right away I couldn't do them. I was ashamed so I told her I had to go to the bathroom.

And so it must have been, surely, with the real estate agent's offer. Convinced that "I'm dumb . . . I don't know anything," he "knew right away" he couldn't do it, despite the fact that he had been doing just that sort of work all along.

Thus, the man's low self-esteem generates a fear of being tested and prevents him from accepting a job with responsibilities or, once on a job, from staying with it if responsibilities are thrust on him, even if the wages are commensurately higher. Richard refuses such a job, Leroy leaves one, and another man, given more responsibility and more pay, knows he will fail and proceeds to do so, proving he was right about himself all along. The self-fulfilling prophecy is everywhere at work. In a hallway, Stanton,

Tonk and Boley are passing a bottle around. Stanton recalls the time he was in the service. Everything was fine until he attained the rank of corporal. He worried about everything he did then. Was he doing the right thing? Was he doing it well? When would they discover their mistake and take his stripes (and extra pay) away? When he finally lost his stripes, everything was all right again.

Lethargy, disinterest and general apathy on the job, so often reported by employers, has its streetcorner counterpart. The men do not ordinarily talk about their jobs or ask one another about them.[3] Although most of the men know who is or is not working at any given time, they may or may not know what particular job an individual man has. There is no overt interest in job specifics as they relate to this or that person, in large part perhaps because the specifics are not especially relevant. To know that a man is working is to know approximately how much he makes and to know as much as one needs or wants to know about how he makes it. After all, how much difference does it make to know whether a man is pushing a mop and pulling trash in an apartment house, a restaurant, or an office building, or delivering groceries, drugs, or liquor, or, if he's a laborer, whether he's pushing a wheelbarrow, mixing mortar, or digging a hole? So much does one job look like every other that there is little to choose between them. In large part, the job market consists of a narrow range of nondescript chores calling for nondistinctive, undifferentiated, unskilled labor. "A job is a job."

A crucial factor in the streetcorner man's lack of job commitment is the overall value he places on the job. *For his part, the streetcorner man puts no lower value on the job than does the larger society around him.* He knows the social value of the job by the amount of money the employer is willing to pay him for doing it. In a real sense, every pay day, he counts in dollars and cents the value placed on the job by society at large. He is no more (and frequently less) ready to quit and look for another job than his employer is ready to fire him and look for another man. Neither the streetcorner man who performs these jobs nor the society which requires him to perform them assesses the job as one "worth doing and worth doing well." Both employee and employer are contemptuous of the job. The employee shows his contempt by his reluctance to accept it or keep it, the employer by paying less than is required to support a family.[4] Nor does the low-wage job offer prestige, respect, interesting work, opportunity for learning or advancement, or any other compensation. With few exceptions, jobs filled by the streetcorner man are at the bottom of the employment ladder in every respect, from wage level to prestige. Typically, they are hard, dirty, uninteresting and underpaid. The rest of society (whatever its ideal values regarding the dignity of labor) holds the job of the dishwasher or janitor or unskilled laborer in low esteem if not outright contempt.[5] So does the streetcorner man. He cannot do otherwise. He cannot draw from a job those social values which other people do not put into it.[6]

Only occasionally does spontaneous conversation touch on these matters directly. Talk about jobs is usually limited to isolated statements of intention, such as "I think I'll get me another gig [job]," "I'm going to look for a construction job when the weather breaks," or "I'm going to quit. I can't take no more of this shit." Job assessments typically consist of nothing more than a noncommittal shrug and "It's O.K." or "It's a job."

One reason for the relative absence of talk about one's job is, as suggested earlier, that the sameness of job experiences does not bear reiteration. Another and more important reason is the emptiness of the job experience itself. The man sees middle-class occupations as a primary source of prestige, pride and self-respect; his own job affords him none of these. To think about his job is to see himself as others see him, to remind him of just where he stands in this society.[7] And because society's criteria for placement are generally the same as his own, to talk about his job can trigger a flush of shame and a deep, almost physical ache to change places with someone, almost anyone, else.[8] The desire to be a person in his own right, to be noticed by the world he lives in, is shared by each of the men on the streetcorner. Whether they articulate this desire (as Tally does below) or not, one can see them position themselves to catch the attention of their fellows in much the same way as plants bend or stretch to catch the sunlight.[9]

Tally and I were in the Carry-out. It was summer, Tally's peak earning season as a cement finisher, a semiskilled job a cut or so above that of the unskilled laborer. His take-home pay during these weeks was well over a hundred dollars—"a lot of bread." But for Tally, who no longer had a family to support, bread was not enough.

"You know that boy came in last night? That Black Moozlem? That's what I ought to be doing. I ought to be in his place."

"What do you mean?"

"Dressed nice, going to [night] school, got a good job."

"He's no better off than you, Tally. You make more than he does."

"It's not the money. [Pause] It's position, I guess. He's got position. When he finish school he gonna be a supervisor. People respect him. . . . Thinking about people with position and education gives me a feeling right here [pressing his fingers into the pit of his stomach]."

"You're educated, too. You have a skill, a trade. You're a cement finisher. You can make a building, pour a sidewalk."

"That's different. Look, can anybody do what you're doing? Can anybody just come up and do your job? Well, in one week I can teach you cement finishing. You won't be as good as me 'cause you won't have the experience but you'll be a cement finisher. That's what I mean. Anybody can do what I'm doing and that's what gives me this feeling. [Long pause]

Suppose I like this girl. I go over to her house and I meet her father. He starts talking about what he done today. He talks about operating on somebody and sewing them up and about surgery. I know he's a doctor 'cause of the way he talks. Then she starts talking about what she did. Maybe she's a boss or a supervisor. Maybe she's a lawyer and her father says to me, 'And what do you do, Mr. Jackson?' [Pause] Your remember at the courthouse, Lonny's trial? You and the lawyer was talking in the hall? You remember? I just stood there listening. I didn't say a word. You know why? 'Cause I didn't even know what you was talking about. That's happened to me a lot."

"Hell, you're nothing special. That happens to everybody. Nobody knows everything. One man is a doctor, so he talks about surgery. Another man is a teacher, so he talks about books. But doctors and teachers don't know anything about concrete. You're a cement finisher and that's your specialty."

"Maybe so, but when was the last time you saw anybody standing about talking about concrete?"

The streetcorner man wants to be a person in his own right, to be noticed, to be taken account of, but in this respect, as well as in meeting his money needs, his job fails him. The job and the man are even. The job fails the man and the man fails the job.

Furthermore, the man does not have any reasonable expectation that, however bad it is, his job will lead to better things. Menial jobs are not, by and large, the starting point of a track system which leads to even better jobs for those who are able and willing to do them. The busboy or dishwasher in a restaurant is not on a job track which, if negotiated skillfully, leads to chef or manager of the restaurant. The busboy or dishwasher who works hard becomes, simply, a hard-working busboy or dishwasher. Neither hard work nor perseverance can conceivably carry the janitor to a sitdown job in the office building he cleans up. And it is the apprentice who becomes the journeyman electrician, plumber, steam fitter or bricklayer, not the common unskilled Negro laborer.

Thus, the job is not a stepping stone to something better. It is a dead end. It promises to deliver no more tomorrow, next month or next year than it does today.

Delivering little, and promising no more, the job is "no big thing." The man appears to treat the job in a cavalier fashion, working and not working as the spirit moves him, as if all that matters is the immediate satisfaction of his present appetites, the surrender to present moods, and the indulgence of whims with no thought for the cost, consequences, the future. To the middle-class observer, this behavior reflects a "present-time orientation"—an "inability to defer gratification." It is this "present-time" orientation—as against the "future orientation" of the middle-class person—that "explains" to the outsider why Leroy chooses to spend the day at the Carry-out rather than report to work; why Richard who was paid Friday, was drunk Saturday and Sunday and penniless Monday; why

Sweets quits his job today because the boss looked at him "funny" yesterday.

But from the inside looking out, what appears as a "present-time" orientation to the outside observer is, to the man experiencing it, as much a future orientation as that of his middle-class counterpart.[10] The difference between the two men lies not so much in their different orientations to time as in their different orientations to future time or, more specifically, to their different futures.[11]

The future orientation of the middle-class person presumes, among other things, a surplus of resources to be invested in the future and a belief that the future will be sufficiently stable both to justify his investment (money in a bank, time and effort in a job, investment of himself in marriage and family, etc.) and to permit the consumption of his investment at a time, place and manner of his own choosing and to his greater satisfaction. But the streetcorner man lives in a sea of want. He does not, as a rule, have a surplus of resources, either economic or psychological. Gratification of hunger and the desire for simple creature comforts cannot be long deferred. Neither can support for one's flagging self-esteem. Living on the edge of both economic and psychological subsistence, the streetcorner man is obliged to expend all his resources on maintaining himself from moment to moment.[12]

As for the future, the young streetcorner man has a fairly good picture of it. In Richard or Sea Cat or Arthur he can see himself in his middle twenties; he can look at Tally to see himself at thirty, at Wee Tom to see himself in his middle thirties, and at Budder and Stanton to see himself in his forties. It is a future in which everything is uncertain except the ultimate destruction of his hopes and the eventual realization of his fears. The most he can reasonably look forward to is that these things do not come too soon. Thus, when Richard squanders a week's pay in two days it is not because, like an animal or a child, he is "present-time oriented," unaware of or unconcerned with his future. He does so precisely because he is aware of the future and the hopelessness of it all.

Sometimes this kind of response appears as a conscious, explicit choice. Richard had had a violent argument with his wife. He said he was going to leave her and the children, that he had had enough of everything and could not take any more, and he chased her out of the house. His chest still heaving, he leaned back against the wall in the hallway of his basement apartment.

> "I've been scuffling for five years," he said. "I've been scuffling for five years from morning till night. And my kids still don't have anything, my wife don't have anything, and I don't have anything."
>
> "There," he said, gesturing down the hall to a bed, a sofa, a couple of chairs and a television set, all shabby, some broken. "There's everything I have and I'm having trouble holding onto that."

Leroy came in, presumably to petition Richard on behalf of Richard's wife, who was sitting outside on the steps, afraid to come in. Leroy started to say something but Richard cut him short.

"Look, Leroy, don't give me any of that action. You and me are entirely different people. Maybe I look like a boy and maybe I act like a boy sometimes but I got a man's mind. You and me don't want the same things out of life. Maybe some of the same, but you don't care how long you have to wait for yours and I—*want—mine—right—now*."[13]

Thus apparent present-time concerns with consumption and indulgences—material and emotional—reflect a future-time orientation. "I want mine right now" is ultimately a cry of despair, a direct response to the future as he sees it.[14]

In many instances, it is precisely the streetcorner man's orientation to the future—but to a future loaded with "trouble"—which not only leads to a greater emphasis on present concerns ("I want mine right now") but also contributes importantly to the instability of employment, family and friend relationships, and to the general transient quality of daily life.

Let me give some concrete examples. One day, after Tally had gotten paid, he gave me four twenty-dollar bills and asked me to keep them for him. Three days later he asked me for the money. I returned it and asked why he did not put his money in a bank. He said that the banks close at two o'clock. I argued that there were four or more banks within a two-block radius of where he was working at the time and that he could easily get to any one of them on his lunch hour. "No, man, " he said, "you don't understand. They close at two o'clock and they closed Saturday and Sunday. Suppose I get into trouble and I got to make it [leave]. Me get out of town, and everything I got in the world layin' up in that bank? No good! No good!"

In another instance, Leroy and his girl friend were discussing "trouble." Leroy was trying to decide how best to go about getting his hands on some "long green" (a lot of money), and his girl friend cautioned him about "trouble." Leroy sneered at this, saying he had had "trouble" all his life and wasn't afraid of a little more. "Anyway," he said, "I'm famous for leaving town."[15]

Thus, the constant awareness of a future loaded with "trouble" results in a constant readiness to leave, to "make it," to "get out of town," and discourages the man from sinking roots into the world he lives in.[16] Just as it discourages him from putting money in the bank, so it discourages him from committing himself to a job, especially one whose payoff lies in the promise of future rewards rather than in the present. In the same way, it discourages him from deep and lasting commitments to family and friends or to any other persons, places or things, since such commitments could hold him hostage, limiting his freedom of movement and thereby compromising his security which lies in that freedom.

What lies behind the response to the driver to the pickup truck [Liebow is referring to an example from earlier in his book], then, is a complex combination of attitudes and assessments. The streetcorner man is under continuous assault by his job experiences and job fears. His experiences and fears feed on one another. The kind of job he can get—and frequently only after fighting for it, if then—steadily confirms his fears, depresses his self-confidence and self-esteem until finally, terrified of an opportunity even if one presents itself, he stands defeated by his experiences, his belief in his own self-worth destroyed and his fears a confirmed reality.

Notes

1. The overall result is that, in the long run, a Negro laborer's earnings are not substantially greater—and may be less—than those of the busboy, janitor, or stock clerk. Herman P. Miller, for example, reports that in 1960, 40 percent of all jobs held by Negro men were as laborers or in the service trades. The average annual wage for nonwhite nonfarm laborers was $2,400. The average earning of non-white service workers was $2,500. *Rich Man, Poor Man*, (New York: Crowell-Collier Press, 1964), p. 90. Francis Greenfield estimates that in the Washington vicinity, the 1965 earnings of the union laborer who works whenever work is available will be about $3,200. Even this figure is high for the man on the streetcorner. Union men in heavy construction are the aristocrats of the laborers. Casual day labor and jobs with small firms in the building and construction trades, or with firms in other industries, pay considerably less.

2. For an excellent discussion of the self-fulfilling assumption (or prophecy) as a social force, see "The Self-Fulfilling Prophecy," Ch. XI in Robert K. Merton's *Social Theory and Social Structure*, Rev. ed. (Glencoe, Ill.: The Free Press, 1957).

3. This stands in dramatic contrast to the leisure-time conversation of stable, working-class men. For the coal miners (of Ashton, England), for example, "the topic [of conversation] which surpasses all others in frequency is work—the difficulties which have been encountered in the day's shift, the way in which a particular task was accomplished, and so on." Josephine Klein, *Samples from English Cultures* (London: Routledge and Kegan Paul, 1965), I: 88.

4. It is important to remember that the employer is not entirely a free agent. Subject to the constraints of the larger society, he acts for the larger society as well as for himself. Child labor laws, safety and sanitation regulations, minimum wage scales in some employment areas, and other constraints are already on the books; other control mechanisms, such as a guaranteed annual wage, are to be had for the voting.

5. See, for example, the U.S. Bureau of the Census, *Methodology and Scores of Socioeconomic Status*. The assignment of the lowest SES ratings to men who hold such jobs is not peculiar to our own society. A low SES rating for "the shoe-shine boy or garbage man. . . seems to be true for all [industrial] countries." Alex Inkeles, "Industrial Man," *The American Journal of Sociology*, 66 (1960):8.

6. That the streetcorner man downgrades manual labor should occasion no surprise. Merton points out that "the American stigmatization of manual labor

. . . *has been found to hold rather uniformly in all social classes"* (emphasis in original). *Social Theory and Social Structure*, p. 145. That he finds no satisfaction in such work should also occasion no surprise: "[There is] a clear positive correlation between the over-all status of occupations and the experience of satisfaction in them." Inkeles, "Industrial Man," p. 12.

7. "[In our society] a man's work is one of the things by which he is judged, and certainly one of the more significant things by which he judges himself. . . . A man's work is one of the more important parts of his social identity, of his self; indeed, of his fate in the one life he has to live." Everett C. Hughes, *Men and Their Work* (Glencoe, Ill.: The Free Press, 1958), pp. 42–43.

8. Noting that lower-class persons "are constantly exposed to evidence of their own irrelevance," Lee Rainwater spells out still another way in which the poor are poor: "The identity problems of lower class persons make the soul-searching of middle class adolescents and adults seem rather like a kind of conspicuous consumption of psychic riches." "Work and Identity in the Lower Class," paper prepared for Washington University Conference on Planning for the Quality of Urban Life, April 1965 (mimeographed), p. 3.

9. Sea Cat cuts his pants legs off at the calf and puts a fringe on the raggedy edges. Tony breaks his "shades" and continues to wear the horn-rimmed frames minus the lenses. Richard cultivates a distinctive manner of speech. Lonny gives himself a birthday party. And so on.

10. Taking a somewhat different point of view, S. M. Miller and Frank Riessman suggest that "the entire concept of deferred gratification may be inappropriate to understanding the essence of workers' lives." "The Working Class Subculture: A New View," *Social Problems*, 9(1961):87.

11. This sentence is a paraphrase of a statement made by Marvin Cline at a 1965 colloquium at the Mental Health Study Center, National Institute of Mental Health.

12. And if, for the moment, he does sometimes have more money than he chooses to spend or more food than he wants to eat, he is pressed to spend the money and eat the food anyway since his friends, neighbors, kinsmen, or acquaintances will beg or borrow whatever surplus he has or, failing this, they may steal it. In one extreme case, one of the men admitted taking the last of a woman's surplus food allotment after she had explained that, with four children, she could not spare any food. The prospect that consumer soft goods not consumed by oneself will be consumed by someone else may be related to the way in which portable consumer durable goods, such as watches, radios, television sets or phonographs, are sometimes looked at as a form of savings. When Shirley was on welfare, she regularly took her television set out of pawn when she got her monthly check. Not so much to watch it, she explained, as to have something to fall back on when her money runs out toward the end of the month. For her and others, the television set or the phonograph is her savings, and the pawn ticket is her bankbook.

13. This was no simple rationalization for irresponsibility. Richard had indeed "been scuffling for five years" trying to keep his family going. Until shortly after this episode, Richard was known and respected as one of the hardest-working men on the street. Richard had said, only a couple of months earlier, "I figure you got to get out there and try. You got to try before you can get anything." His wife Shirley confirmed that he had always tried. "If things get tough with me I'll

get all worried. But Richard get worried, he don't want me to see him worried. . . . He *will* get out there. He's shoveled snow, picked beans, and he's done some of everything. . . . He's not ashamed to get out there and get us something to eat." At the time of the episode reported above, Leroy was just starting marriage and raising a family. He and Richard were not, as Richard thought, "entirely different people." Leroy had just not learned, by personal experience over time, what Richard had learned. But within two years Leroy's marriage had broken up and he was talking and acting like Richard. "He just let go completely," said one of the men on the street.

14. There is no mystically intrinsic connection between "present-time" orientation and lower-class persons. Whenever people of whatever class have been uncertain, skeptical or downright pessimistic about the future, "I want mine right now" has been one of the characteristic responses, although it is usually couched in more delicate terms: e.g., Omar Khayyam's "Take the cash and let the credit go," or Horace's "*Carpe diem.*" In wartime, especially, all classes tend to slough off conventional restraints on sexual and other behavior (i.e., become less able or less willing to defer gratification). And when inflation threatens, darkening the fiscal future, persons who formerly husbanded their resources with commendable restraint almost stampede one another rushing to spend their money. Similarly, it seems that future-time orientation tends to collapse toward the present when persons are in pain or under stress. The point here is that, the label notwithstanding, (what passes for) present-time orientation appears to be a situation-specific phenomenon rather than a part of the standard psychic equipment of Cognitive Lower Class Man.

15. And proceeded to do just that the following year when "trouble"—in this case, a grand jury indictment, a pile of debts, and a violent separation from his wife and children—appeared again.

16. For a discussion of "trouble" as a focal concern of lower-class culture, see Walter Miller, "Lower Class Culture as a Generating Milieu of Gang Delinquency," *Journal of Social Issues*, 14 (1958): 7,8.

30 Good People and Dirty Work

EVERETT C. HUGHES

Assume that there is much hatred of some group; then assume that the people who are filled with that hatred take control of society; assume further that moving against the hated group seems to many to be in the best interest of the country. You then have the makings of "the final solution," the use of state power to commit genocide, destroying an entire group of people on the basis of their presumed race or ethnicity. I use the word "presumed" because people around the world have intermarried and intermated to such a degree that there is serious doubt whether there is, on a genetic basis, any such thing as a race. For this reason, some researchers are now substituting for race the term "genetic pool." Because most sociological sources and people in our society use the term "race," however, we shall also use it.

Could it happen here? Even the thought is abhorrent, and most people are inclined to answer immediately, "No! In no way could that happen here. The Holocaust was simply an aberration of history. We would not allow it." While such statements might be comforting, they beg the question: Could it happen here? To answer it, we need to deal with the issues raised above. Is there hatred of groups on the basis of presumed racial characteristics? If so, is it possible for those with that hatred to gain control of society? If that happened, would it then be possible for them to use the machinery of the state to attempt to destroy the group they hate?

As you grapple with these issues, think about the fact that Germany had perhaps the most educated citizens in the world—with perhaps more Ph.D.s per square mile than any place on the face of the earth. Remember also that Germany was a world leader in the arts, the sciences, technology, and theology. Think also about the fact that about fifty years ago the Nazis were a small group of powerless fanatics who were not taken seriously.

That is enough to make me shiver. And where were the "regular" people, the ones who could have prevented it all? What were they doing while humans were being turned into soap and the stink of the crematoriums rose over towns and villages? That is what Hughes discusses.

300

THE NATIONAL SOCIALIST GOVERNMENT OF GERMANY, with the arm of its fanatical inner sect, the S.S., commonly known as the Brown Shirts or Elite Guard, perpetrated and boasted of the most colossal and dramatic piece of social dirty work the world has ever known. Perhaps there are other claimants to the title, but they could not match this one's combination of mass, speed and perverse pride in the deed. Nearly all peoples have plenty of cruelty and death to account for. How many Negro Americans have died by the hands of lynching mobs? How many more from unnecessary disease and lack of food or of knowledge of nutrition? How many Russians died to bring about collectivization of land? And who is to blame if there be starving millions in some parts of the world while wheat molds in the fields of other parts?

I do not revive the case of the Nazi *Endloesung* (final solution) of the Jewish problem in order to condemn the Germans, or make them look worse than other peoples, but to recall to our attention dangers which lurk in our midst always. Most of what follows was written after my first post-war visit to Germany in 1948. The impressions were vivid. The facts have not diminished and disappeared with time, as did the stories of alleged German atrocities in Belgium in the first World War. The fuller the record, the worse it gets.

Several millions of people were delivered to the concentration camps, operated under the leadership of Heinrich Himmler with the help of Adolf Eichmann. A few hundred thousand survived in some fashion. Still fewer came out sound of mind and body. A pair of examples, well attested, will show the extreme of perverse cruelty reached by the S. S. guards in charge of the camps. Prisoners were ordered to climb trees; guards whipped them to make them climb faster. Once they were out of reach, other prisoners, also urged by the whip, were put to shaking the trees. When the victims fell, they were kicked to see whether they could rise to their feet. Those too badly injured to get up were shot to death, as useless for work. A not inconsiderable number of prisoners were drowned in pits full of human excrement. These examples are so horrible that your minds will run away from them. You will not, as when you read a slightly salacious novel, imagine the rest. I therefore thrust these examples upon you and insist that the people who thought them up could, and did, improvise others like them, and even worse, from day to day over several years. Many of the victims of the Camps gave up the ghost (this Biblical phrase is the most apt) from a combination of humiliation, starvation, fatigue and physical abuse. In due time, a policy of mass liquidation in the gas chamber was added to individual virtuosity in cruelty.

This program—for it was a program—of cruelty and murder was carried out in the name of racial superiority and racial purity. It was directed mainly, although by no means exclusively, against Jews, Slavs and

Gypsies. It was thorough. There are few Jews in the territories which were under the control of the Third German Reich—the two Germanys, Holland, Czechoslovakia, Poland, Austria, Hungary. Many Jewish Frenchmen were destroyed. There were concentration camps even in Tunisia and Algiers under the German occupation.

When, during my 1948 visit to Germany, I became more aware of the reactions of ordinary Germans to the horrors of the concentration camps, I found myself asking not the usual question, "How did racial hatred rise to such a high level?", but this one, "How could such dirty work be done among and, in a sense, *by* the millions of ordinary, civilized German people?" Along with this came related questions. How could these millions of ordinary people live in the midst of such cruelty and murder without a general uprising against it and against the people who did it? How, once freed from the regime that did it, could they be apparently so little concerned about it, so toughly silent about it, not only in talking with outsiders—which is easy to understand—but among themselves? How and where could there be found in a modern civilized country the several hundred thousand men and women capable of such work? How were these people so far released from the inhibitions of civilized life as to be able to imagine, let alone perform, the ferocious, obscene and perverse actions which they did imagine and perform? How could they be kept at such a height of fury through years of having to see daily at close range the human wrecks they made and being often literally spattered with the filth produced and accumulated by their own actions?

You will see that there are here two orders of questions. One set concerns the good people who did not themselves do this work. The other concerns those who did do it. But the two sets are not really separate; for the crucial question concerning the good people is their relation to the people who did the dirty work, with a related one which asks under what circumstances good people let the others get away with such actions.

An easy answer concerning the Germans is that they were not so good after all. We can attribute to them some special inborn or ingrained race consciousness, combined with a penchant for sadistic cruelty and unquestioning acceptance of whatever is done by those who happen to be in authority. Pushed to its extreme, this answer simply makes us, rather than the Germans, the superior race. It is the Nazi tune, put to words of our own.

Now there are deep and stubborn differences between peoples. Their history and culture may make the Germans especially susceptible to the doctrine of their own racial superiority and especially acquiescent to the actions of whoever is in power over them. These are matters deserving of the best study that can be given them. But to say that these things could happen in Germany simply because Germans are different—from us—

buttresses their own excuses and lets us off too easily from blame for what happened there and from the question whether it could happen here.

Certainly in their daily practice and expression before the Hitler regime, the Germans showed no more, if as much, hatred of other racial or cultural groups than we did and do. Residential segregation was not marked. Intermarriage was common, and the families of such marriages had an easier social existence than they generally have in America. The racially exclusive club, school and hotel were much less in evidence than here. And I well remember an evening in 1933 when a Montreal business man—a very nice man, too—said in our living room, "Why don't we admit that Hitler is doing to the Jews just what we ought to be doing?" That was not an uncommon sentiment, although it may be said in defense of the people who expressed it that they probably did not know and would not have believed the full truth about the Nazi program of destroying Jews. The essential underlying sentiments on racial matters in Germany were not different in kind from those prevailing throughout the western and especially the Anglo-Saxon, countries. But I do not wish to over-emphasize this point. I only want to close one easy way out of serious consideration of the problem of good people and dirty work, by demonstrating that the Germans were and are about as good and about as bad as the rest of us on this matter of racial sentiments and, let us add, their notions of decent human behaviour.

But what was the reaction of ordinary Germans to the persecution of the Jews and to the concentration camp mass torture and murder? A conversation between a German school-teacher, a German architect and myself gives the essentials in a vivid form. It was in the studio of the architect, and the occasion was a rather casual visit, in Frankfurt am Main in 1948.

> The artchitect: "I am ashamed for my people whenever I think of it. But we didn't know about it. We only learned about all that later. You must remember the pressure we were under; we had to join the party. We had to keep our mouths shut and do as we were told. It was a terrible pressure. Still, I am ashamed. But you see, we had lost our colonies, and our national honour was hurt. And these Nazis exploited that feeling. And the Jews, they *were* a problem. They came from the east. You should see them in Poland; the lowest class of people, full of lice, dirty and poor, running about in their Ghettos in filthy caftans. They came here, and got rich by unbelievable methods after the first war. They occupied all the good places. Why, they were in the proportion of ten to one in medicine and law and government posts!"
>
> At this point the architect hesitated and looked confused. He continued: "Where was I? It is the poor food. You see what misery we are in here, Herr Professor. If often happens that I forget what I was talking about. Where was I now? I have completely forgotten."

(His confusion was, I believe, not at all feigned. Many Germans said they suffered losses of memory such as this, and laid it to their lack of food.)

I said firmly: "You were talking about loss of national honour and how the Jews had got hold of everything."

The architect: "Oh, yes! That was it! Well, of course that was no way to settle the Jewish problem. But there *was* a problem and it had to be settled some way."

The school-teacher: "Of course, they have Palestine now."

I protested that Palestine would hardly hold them.

The architect: "The professor is right. Palestine can't hold all the Jews. And it was a terrible thing to murder people. But we didn't know it at the time. But I am glad I am alive now. It is an interesting time in men's history. You know, when the Americans came it was like a great release. I really want to see a new ideal in Germany. I like the freedom that lets me talk to you like this. But, unfortunately this is not the general opinion. Most of my friends really hang on to the old ideas. They can't see any hope, so they hang on to the old ideas."

This scrap of talk gives, I believe the essential elements as well as the flavor of the German reaction. It checks well with formal studies which have been made, and it varies only in detail from other conversations which I myself recorded in 1948.

One of the most obvious points in it is unwillingness to think about the dirty work done. In this case—perhaps by chance, perhaps not—the good man suffered an actual lapse of memory in the middle of this statement. This seems a simple point. But the psychiatrists have shown that it is less simple than it looks. They have done a good deal of work on the complicated mechanisms by which the individual mind keeps unpleasant or intolerable knowledge from consciousness, and have shown how great may, in some cases, be the consequent loss of effectiveness of the personality. But we have taken collective unwillingness to know unpleasant facts more or less for granted. That people can and do keep a silence about things whose open discussion would threaten the group's conception of itself, and hence its solidarity, is common knowledge. It is a mechanism that operates in every family and in every group which has a sense of group reputation. To break such a silence is considered an attack against the group; a sort of treason, if it be a member of the group who breaks the silence. This common silence allows group fictions to grow up; such as, that grandpa was less a scoundrel and more romantic than he really was. And I think it demonstrable that it operates especially against any expression, except in ritual, of collective guilt. The remarkable thing in present-day Germany is not that there is so little reference to something about which people do feel deeply guilty, but that it is talked about at all.

In order to understand this phenomenon we would have to find out who talks about the concentration camp atrocities, in what situations, in what mood, and with what stimulus. On these points I know only my own limited experiences. One of the most moving of these was my first post-war meeting with an elderly professor whom I had known before the Nazi time; he is an heroic soul who did not bow his head during the Nazi time and who keeps it erect now. His first words, spoken with tears in his eyes, were:

"How hard it is to believe that men will be as bad as they say they will. Hitler and his people said: 'Heads will roll,' but how many of us—even his bitterest opponents—could really believe that they would do it."

This man could and did speak, in 1948, not only to the likes of me, but to his students, his colleagues and to the public which read his articles, in the most natural way about the Nazi atrocities whenever there was occasion to do it in the course of his tireless effort to reorganize and to bring new life into the German universities. He had neither the compulsion to speak, so that he might excuse and defend himself, nor a conscious or unconscious need to keep silent. Such people were rare; how many there were in Germany I do not know.

Occasions of another kind in which the silence was broken were those where, in class, public lecture or in informal meetings with students, I myself had talked frankly of race relations in other parts of the world, including the lynchings which sometimes occur in my own country and the terrible cruelty visited upon natives in South Africa. This took off the lid of defensiveness, so that a few people would talk quite easily of what happened under the Nazi regime. More common were situations like that with the architect, where I threw in some remark about the atrocities in response to Germans' complaint that the world is abusing them. In such cases, there was usually an expression of shame, accompanied by a variety of excuses (including that of having been kept in ignorance), and followed by a quick turning away from the subject.

Somewhere in consideration of this problem of discussion versus silence we must ask what the good (that is, ordinary) people in Germany did know about these things. It is clear that the S.S. kept the more gory details of the concentration camps a close secret. Even high officials of the government, the army and the Nazi party itself were in some measure held in ignorance, although of course they kept the camps supplied with victims. The common people of Germany knew that the camps existed; most knew people who had disappeared into them; some saw the victims, walking skeletons in rags, being transported in trucks or trains, or being herded on the road from station to camp or to work in fields or factories near the camps. Many knew people who had been released from concentration camps; such released persons kept their counsel on pain of death. But secrecy was cultivated and supported by fear and terror. In the absence of a determined and heroic will to know and publish the truth, and in the absence of all the instruments of opposition, the degree of knowledge was undoubtedly low, in spite of the fact that all knew that something both stupendous and horrible was going on; and in spite of the fact that Hitler's *Mein Kampf* and the utterances of his aides said that no fate was too horrible for the Jews and other wrong-headed or inferior people. This must make us ask under what conditions the will to know and to discuss is strong, determined and effective; this, like most of the important questions I have raised, I leave unanswered except as answers may be contained in the statement of the case.

But to return to our moderately good man, the architect. He insisted over and over again that he did not know, and we may suppose that he knew as much and as little as most Germans. But he also made it quite clear that he wanted something done to the Jews. I have similar statements from people of whom I knew that they had had close Jewish friends before the Nazi time. This raises the whole problem of the extent to which those pariahs who do the dirty work of society are really acting as agents for the rest of us. To talk of this question one must note that, in building up his case, the architect pushed the Jews firmly into an out-group: they were dirty, lousy and unscrupulous (an odd statement from a resident of Frankfurt, the home of old Jewish merchants and intellectual families long identified with those aspects of culture of which Germans are most proud). Having dissociated himself clearly from these people, and having declared them a problem, he apparently was willing to let someone else do to them the dirty work which he himself would not do, and for which he expressed shame. The case is perhaps analogous to our attitude toward those convicted of crime. From time to time, we get wind of cruelty practiced upon the prisoners in penitentiaries or jails; or, it may be, merely a report that they are ill-fed or that hygienic conditions are not good. Perhaps we do not wish that the prisoners should be cruelly treated or badly fed, but our reaction is probably tempered by a notion that they deserve something, because of some dissociation of them from the in-group of good people. If what they get is worse than what we like to think about, it is a little bit too bad. It is a point on which we are ambivalent. Campaigns for reform of prisons are often followed by counter-campaigns against a too high standard of living for prisoners and against having prisons run by softies. Now the people who run prisons are our agents. Just how far they do or could carry out our wishes is hard to say. The minor prison guard, in boastful justification of some of his more questionable practices, says, in effect: "If those reformers and those big shots upstairs had to live with these birds as I do, they would soon change their fool notions about running a prison." He is suggesting that the good people are either naive or hypocritical. Furthermore, he knows quite well that the wishes of his employers, the public, are by no means unmixed. They are quite as likely to put upon him for being too nice as for being too harsh. And if, as sometimes happens, he is a man disposed to cruelty, there may be some justice in his feeling that he is only doing what others would like to do, if they but dared; and what they would do, if they were in his place.

There are plenty of examples in our own world which I might have picked for comparison with the German attitude toward the concentration camps. For instance, a newspaper in Denver made a great scandal out of the allegation that our Japanese compatriots were too well fed in the camps where they were concentrated during the war. I might have mentioned some feature of the sorry history of the people of Japanese background in Canada. Or it might have been lynching, or some aspect of racial discrimination. But I purposely chose prisoners convicted of crime. For convicts are formally set aside for special handling. They constitute an out-group in all countries. This brings the issue clearly before us, since few people cherish the illusion that the problem of treating criminals can be settled by propaganda designed to prove that there aren't any criminals. Almost everyone agrees that something has to be done about them. The question concerns what is done, who does it, and the nature of the mandate given by the rest of us to those who do it. Perhaps we give them an unconscious mandate to go beyond anything we ourselves would care to do or even to acknowledge. I venture to suggest that the higher and more expert functionaries who act in our behalf represent something of a distillation of what we may consider our public wishes, while some of the others show a sort of concentrate of those impulses of which we are or wish to be less aware.

Now the choice of convicted prisoners brings up another crucial point in inter-group relations. All societies of any great size have in-groups and out-groups; in fact, one of the best ways of describing a society is to consider it a network of smaller and larger in-groups and out-groups. And an in-group is one only because there are out-groups. When I refer to *my* children I obviously imply that they are closer to me than other people's children and that I will make greater efforts to buy oranges and cod-liver oil for them than for others' children. In fact, it may mean that I will give them cod-liver oil if I have to choke them to get it down. We do our own dirty work on those closest to us. The very injunction that I love my neighbor as myself starts with me; if I don't love myself and my nearest, the phrase has a very sour meaning.

Each of us is a center of a network of in and out-groups. Now the distinctions between *in* and *out* may be drawn in various ways, and nothing is more important for both the student of society and the educator than to discover how these lines are made and how they may be redrawn in more just and sensible ways. But to believe that we can do away with the distinction between *in* and *out*, *us* and *them* in social life is complete nonsense. On the positive side, we generally feel a greater obligation to in-groups; hence less obligation to out-groups; and in the case of such groups as convicted criminals, the out-group is definitely given over to the hands of our agents for punishment. That is the extreme case. But there are other out-groups toward which we may have aggressive feelings and dislike, although we give no formal mandate to anyone to deal with them in our behalf, and although we profess to believe that they should not suffer restrictions or disadvantages. The greater their social distance from us, the more we leave in the hands of others a sort of mandate by default to deal with them on our behalf. Whatever effort we put on reconstructing the lines which divide in and out-groups, there remains the eternal problem of our treatment, direct or delegated, of whatever groups are considered somewhat outside. And here it is that the whole matter of our professed and possible deeper unprofessed wishes comes up for consideration; and the related problem of what we know, can know and want to know about it. In Germany, the agents got out of hand and created such terror that it was best not to know. It is also clear that it was and is easier to the conscience of many Germans not to know. It is, finally, not unjust to say that the agents were at least working in the direction of the wishes of many people, although they may have gone beyond the wishes of most. The same questions can be asked about our own society, and with reference not only to prisoners but also to many other groups upon whom there is no legal or moral stigma. Again I have not the answers. I leave you to search for them.

In considering the question of dirty work we have eventually to think about the people who do it. In Germany, these were the members of the S.S. and of that inner group of the S.S. who operated the concentration camps. Many reports have been made on the social backgrounds and the personalities of these cruel fanatics. Those who have studied them say that a large proportion were "gescheiterte Existenzen," men or women with a history of failure, of poor adaptation to the demands of work and of the classes of society in which they had been bred. Germany between wars had large numbers of such people. Their adherence to a movement which proclaimed a doctrine of hatred was natural enough. The movement offered something more. It created an inner group which was to be superior to all others, even Germans, in their emancipation from the usual bourgeois morality; people above and beyond the ordinary morality. I dwell on this, not as a doctrine, but as an organizational device. For, as Eugen Kogon, author of the most penetrating analysis of the S.S. and their camps, has said, the Nazis came to power by creating a state within a state; a body with its own counter-morality, and its own counter-law, its courts and its own execution of sentence upon those who did not live up to its orders and standards. Even as a movement, it had inner circles within inner circles; each sworn to secrecy as against the next outer one. The struggle between these inner circles continued after Hitler came to power; Himmler eventually won the day. His S.S. became a state within the Nazi state, just as the Nazi movement had become a state within the Weimar state. One is reminded of the oft quoted but neglected statement of Sighele: "At the center of a crowd look for the sect." He referred, of course, to the political sect; the fanatical inner group of a movement seeking power by revolutionary methods. Once the Nazis were in power, this inner sect, while becoming now the recognized agent of the state and, hence, of the masses of the people, could at the same time dissociate itself more completely from them in action, because of the very fact of having a mandate. It was now beyond all danger of interference and investigation. For it had the instruments of interference and investigation its own hands. These are also the instruments of secrecy. So the S.S. could and did build up a powerful system in which they had the resources of the state and of the economy of Germany and the conquered countries from which to steal all that was needed to carry out their orgy of cruelty luxuriously as well as with impunity.

Now let us ask, concerning the dirty workers, questions similar to those concerning the good people. Is there a supply of candidates for such work in other societies? It would be easy to say that only Germany could produce such a crop. The question is answered by being put. The problem of people who have run aground (gescheiterte Existenzen) is one of the most serious in our modern societies. Any psychiatrist will, I believe, testify that we have a sufficient pool or fund of personalities warped toward perverse punishment and cruelty to do any amount of dirty work that the good people may be inclined to countenance. It would not take a very great turn of events to increase the number of such people, and to bring their discontents to the surface. This is not to suggest that every movement based on discontent with the present state of things will be led by such people. That is obviously untrue; and I emphasize the point lest my remarks give comfort to those who would damn all who express militant discontent. But I think study of militant social movements does show that these warped people seek a place in them. Specifically, they are likely to become the plotting, secret police of the group. It is one of the problems of militant social movements to keep such people out. It is of course easier to do this if the spirit of the movement is positive, its conception of humanity high and inclusive, and its aims sound. This was not the case of the Nazi movement. As Kogon puts it: "The SS were but the arch-type of the Nazis in general." But such people are sometimes attracted, for want of something better, to movements whose aims are contrary to the spirit of cruelty and punishment. I would suggest that all of us look well at the leadership and entourage of movements to which we attach ourselves for signs of a negativistic, punishing attitude. For once such a spirit develops in a movement, punishment of the nearest and easiest victim is likely to become more attractive than striving for the essential goals. And, if the Nazi movement teaches us anything at all, it is that if any shadow of a mandate be given to such people, they will—having compromised us—

make it larger and larger. The processes by which they do so are the development of the power and inward discipline of their own group, a progressive dissociation of themselves from the rules of human decency prevalent in their culture, and an ever-growing contempt for the welfare of the masses of people.

The power and inward discipline of the S.S. became such that those who once became members could get out only by death; by suicide, murder or mental breakdown. Orders from the central offices of the S.S. were couched in equivocal terms as a hedge against a possible day of judgment. When it became clear that such a day of judgment would come, the hedging and intrigue became greater; the urge to murder also became greater, because every prisoner became a potential witness.

Again we are dealing with a phenomenon common in all societies. Almost every group which has a specialized social function to perform is in some measure a secret society, with a body of rules developed and enforced by the members and with some power to save its members from outside punishment. And here is one of the paradoxes of social order. A society without smaller, rule-making and disciplining powers would be no society at all. There would be nothing but law and police; and this is what the Nazis strove for, at the expense of family, church, professional groups, parties and other such nuclei of spontaneous control. But apparently the only way to do this, for good as well as for evil ends, is to give power into the hands of some fanatical small group which will have a far greater power of self-discipline and a far greater immunity from outside control than the traditional groups. The problem is, then, not of trying to get rid of all the self-disciplining, protecting groups within society, but one of keeping them integrated with one another and as sensitive as can be to a public opinion which transcends them all. It is a matter of checks and balances, of what we might call the social and moral constitution of society. . . .

PART VII Social Institutions

"SOCIAL INSTITUTIONS" IS A TERM THAT APPEARS at first glance far removed from life. But in fact it refers to concrete and highly relevant realities. Parents and their children, the basic family unit, constitute a social institution. So does the church, with its sacred books, clergy, and worship, and the law with its police, lawyers, judges, courts, and prisons. Social institutions also means politics, the gamut of the American political process, including broken campaign promises, Congress, and the president and his Cabinet. Social institutions means the economic order, with new plants opening and old ones closing, working for a living or drawing unemployment or welfare or retirement. Schools, colleges and universities—places where people are socialized, as sociologists put it, or where they go to learn, as most other people put it—are also examples of social institutions. Social institutions means science, with its test tubes and experiments and its interviewers and questionnaires. It refers to doctors and nurses and hospitals, as well as to the patients they treat, and the Medicare and Blue Cross and Blue Shield that people struggle to pay for in order to keep the American medical enterprise from destroying one's present and future finances. And social institutions means the military, with its generals and privates and tanks and planes, and the whole war game that at times threatens to become too real.

Social institutions means all these things. It is far from antiseptically removed from life as one might think. On the contrary, this term refers to social life and to how our lives are affected by social structure.

One might say that to understand social life it is absolutely necessary to understand the institutions of a society. It is not enough to understand what people do when they are in one another's presence. That certainly is important, but it is only part of the picture. Social institutions provide the structure within which interaction takes place. The characteristics of a society's institutions, in fact, dictate much of that interaction. For example, because of the way our economic order is arranged, we normally work eight hours a day, are off sixteen, and repeat this pattern five days a week. There is nothing natural about the pattern. Its regularity is but an arbitrary temporal arrangement for work and leisure and personal concerns. Yet, this one aspect of a single social institution has far-reaching affects on how we structure our own time and activities, how we deal with our family and friends, meet our personal needs and nonwork obligations, and, indeed, on how we view time and life.

Each social institution has similarly far-reaching effects on our lives and outlooks. By shaping our society as a whole and establishing the context in which we live, these institutions shape almost everything that is of concern to us. We can, in fact, say that if the social institutions of our society were different we would be different people. We certainly could not be the same, for our ideas and attitudes and other orientations to the social world, and even to life itself, would be different.

To demonstrate the relevance of social institutions for our lives, Annabelle B. Motz leads off with an examination of the American family. Tying directly into Erving Goffman's analysis in Part II, she focuses on how family activities commonly center on projecting socially acceptable images. By focusing on a military academy in the second selection, Sanford M. Dornbusch deals with a broad aspect of education—the use of schools and the educational process to assimilate students into conformity. Then to turn the focus onto the religious institution, Lawrence K. Hong and Marion V. Dearman analyze streetcorner preachers, looking at their approaches, motives, views, and relationships. As a representation of the social institution of organized sports, Charles W. Smith analyzes the role and point of view of the referee. Barney G. Glaser and Anselm L. Strauss present an analysis of the medical institution, focusing on death as it occurs in the hospital. William A. Westley examines the legal institution, looking at the how and why of police violence. Finally, C. Wright Mills concludes this Part with a penetrating and disturbing analysis of interrelationships among our military, economic, and political institutions, a partially subterranean intertwining that vitally affects the daily lives of all of us.

31 The Family as a Company of Players

ANNABELLE B. MOTZ

In a direct application of ideas that Erving Goffman presented in the seventh selection of this book, Motz suggests that *performances* are a focal concern of the American family—presenting a socially acceptable image of who and what the family members are. The leading lady in these family performances is the wife-mother, the leading man the husband-father, while the younger children are understudies who are still learning their lines. The main concern of the family drama is saying and doing the "right" thing, making certain that the presentation of self to others is done in a "socially acceptable" manner.

Beyond its humor, this analysis contains serious implications. For example, can the American family really be "working so hard on its lines that it is forgetting what the play is all about," as Motz suggests? If so, it is similar to people who hate their jobs, feel they are ruining almost every aspect of their lives, but stoically stick with it for decades in the hope of building up a pension in order "one day to begin to enjoy life." By the time retirement comes, such people have almost inevitably lost the capacity to enjoy life. They see the dark side only, are morose, regretful, perhaps bitter, and no longer have the hope of "one day" to mitigate their sorrowful and sorry existence.

If people in families have the capacity to enjoy one another in the here and now, how do you think they can move beyond performances put forward for the consumption of others and begin to relate more genuinely to one another, to help one another's development, and to appreciate the others fully? In other words, how can family members decide what their potential as a family is, and then take steps to go beyond performances and reach that potential?

ALL THE WORLD'S A STAGE, AND WE ARE ALL PLAYERS. Erving Goffman in his *The Presentation of Self in Everyday Life* views our everyday world as having both front stage and back. Like professionals, we try to give a careful and superior performance out front. Back stage we unzip, take off our masks, complain of the strain, think back over the last act, and prepare anxiously for the next.

Sometimes the "on stage" performances are solos; sometimes we act in teams or groups. The roles may be carefully planned, rehearsed, and executed; or they may be spontaneous or improvised. The presentation can be a hit; or it can flop badly.

Picture a theater starring the family. The "stars" are the husband, wife and children. But the cast includes a wide range of persons in the community—fellow workers, friends, neighbors, delivery men, shopkeepers, doctors, and everyone who passes by. Usually husband and wife are the leads; and the appeal, impact, and significance of their performances vary with the amount of time on stage, the times of day and week, the circumstances of each presentation, and the moods of the audience.

Backstage for the family members is generally to be found in their homes, as suggested by the expression, "a man's home is his castle." The front stage is where they act out their dramatic parts in schools, stores, places of employment, on the street, in the homes of other persons; or, as when entertaining guests, back in their own homes.

My aim is to analyze the performances of family members before the community audience—their *front stage* appearances. The behavior conforms to the rules and regulations that society places upon its members; perhaps the analysis of the family life drama will provide insights into the bases of the problems for which an increasing number of middle-class persons are seeking professional help.

Many years ago, Thorstein Veblen noted that although industrialization made it possible for the American worker to live better than at any previous time in history, it made him feel so insignificant that he sought ways to call attention to himself. In *The Theory of the Leisure Class*, Veblen showed that all strata of society practiced "conspicuous consumption"—the ability to use one's income for non-essential goods and services in ways readily visible to others. A man's abilities were equated with his monetary worth and the obvious command he had in the marketplace to purchase commodities beyond bare necessities. Thus, a family that lives more comfortably than most must be a "success."

While conspicuous consumption was becoming an essential element of front stage performance, the ideal of the American as a completely rational person—governed and governing by reason rather than emotion—was being projected around the world. The writings of the first four decades of this century stress over and over again the importance of the individual and individual opinion. (The growth of unionism, the Social Security program, public opinion polling, and federal aid to education are a few examples of the trend toward positive valuation of each human being—not to mention the impact of Freud and Dewey and their stress on individual worth.) The desirability of rule by majority and democratic debate and voting as the best means of reaching group decisions—all these glorified rationality.

As population, cities, and industry grew, so also did anonymity and complexity; and rationality in organizations (more properly known as bureaucritization) had to keep pace. The individual was exposed to more and more people he knew less and less. The face to face relationships of small towns and workshops declined. Job requirements, duties and loyalties, hiring and firing, had to "go by the book." Max Weber has described the bureaucratic organization: each job is explicitly defined, the rights of entry and exit from the organization can be found in the industry's manual, and the rights and duties of the worker and of the organization toward the worker are rationally defined; above all, the worker acts as a rational being on the job—he is never subject to emotional urges.

With the beams and bricks of "fronts" and rationality the middle-class theater is built; with matching props the stage is set.

There are two basic scenes. One revolves about family and close personal relationships. It takes place in a well-furnished house—very comfortable, very stylish, but not "vulgar." The actors are calm, controlled, reasonable.

The other scene typically takes place in a bureaucratic anteroom cluttered with physical props and with people treated like physical props. The actors do not want the audience to believe that they *are* props—so they attract attention to themselves and dramatize their individuality and worth by spending and buying far more than they need.

What does this mean in the daily life of the family stars?

Take first the leading lady, wife, and mother. She follows Veblen and dramatizes her husband's success by impressing any chance onlookers with her efficient house management. How does one run a house efficiently? All must be reasoned order. The wife-housekeeper plans what has to be done and does it simply and quickly. Kitchen, closets, and laundry display department store wares as attractively as the stores themselves. The house is always presentable, and so is she. Despite her obviously great labors, she does not seem to get flustered, over-fatigued, or too emotional. (What would her neighbors or even a passing door-to-door salesman think if they heard her screaming at the children?) With minimal household help she must appear the gracious hostess, fresh and serene—behind her a dirty kitchen magically cleaned, a meal effortlessly prepared, and husband and children well behaved and helpful.

Outside the home, too, she is composed and rational. She does not show resentment toward Johnny's teacher, who may irritate her or give

Johnny poor marks. She does not yawn during interminable and dull PTA programs (what would they think of her and her family?). At citizen meetings she is the embodiment of civic-minded, responsible property-ownership (even if the mortgage company actually owns the property). Her supermarket cart reflects her taste, affluence, efficiency, and concern. At church she exhibits no unchurchly feelings. She prays that her actions and facial expression will not give away the fact that her mind has wandered from the sermon; she hopes that as she greets people, whether interested in them or not, she will be able to say the "right" thing. Her clothes and car are extremely important props—the right make, style, finish; and they project her front stage character, giving the kind of impression she thinks she and the other members of the family want her to give.

Enter Father Center Stage

The male lead is husband, father, and man-of-affairs. He acts in ways that, he hopes, will help his status, and that of his family. At all times he must seem to be in relaxed control of difficult situations. This often takes some doing. For instance, he must be both unequal and equal to associates; that is, he is of course a good fellow and very democratic, but the way he greets and handles his superiors at work is distinctly, if subtly, different from the way he speaks to and handles inferiors. A superior who arrives unexpectedly must find him dynamically at work, worth every cent and more of his income; an inferior must also find him busy, demonstrating how worthy he is of superior status and respect. He must always be in control. Even when supposedly relaxing, swapping dirty jokes with his colleagues, he must be careful to avoid any that offend their biases. He has to get along; bigots, too, may be able to do him good or harm.

The scene shifts back to the home. The other stars greet him—enter loving wife and children. He may not yet be ready or able to re-establish complete emotional control—after all, a man's home is his backstage—and the interplay of the sub-plots begins. If his wife goes on with her role, she will be the dutiful spouse, listening sympathetically, keeping the children and her temper quiet. If she should want to cut loose at the same time, collision will probably still be avoided because both have been trained to restrain themselves and present the right front as parents to their children—if not to each other.

Leisure is not rest. At home father acts out his community role of responsible family head. The back yard is kept up as a "private" garden; the garage as a showroom for tools on display. He must exhibit interest—but not too much enthusiasm—in a number of activities, some ostensibly recreational, retaining a nice balance between appearing a dutiful husband and a henpecked one. Reason must rule emotion.

The children of old vaudevillians literally were born and reared in the theater—were nursed between acts by mothers in spangles, trained as toddlers to respond to footlights as other children might to sunlight. The young in the middle-class family drama also learn to recognize cues and to perform.

Since "front" determines the direction and content of the drama, they are supposed to be little ladies and gentlemen. Proper performances from such tyros require much backstage rehearsal. Unfortunately, the middle-class backstage is progressively disappearing, and so the children too must be prepared to respond appropriately to the unexpected—whether an unwanted salesman at the door who must be discreetly lied to about mother's whereabouts or a wanted friend who must not be offended. They are taught rationality and democracy in family councils—where they are also taught what behavior is expected of them. Reason is rife; even when they get out of hand the parents "reason" with them. As Dorothy Barclay says when discussing household chores and the child, "Appealing to a sense of family loyalty and pride in maturity is the tack most parents take first in trying to overcome youngsters' objections (to household chores). Offering rewards come second, arguing and insisting third."

"Grown-up" and "good" children do family chores. They want the house to look "nice"; they don't tell family secrets when visitors are present, and even rush to close closet and bedroom doors when the doorbell rings unexpectedly.

The child, of course, carries the family play into school, describing it in "show and tell" performances and in his deportment and dress. Part of the role of responsible parenthood includes participation in PTA and teacher conferences, with the child an important player, even if offstage.

To the child, in fact, much of the main dynamic of the play takes place in the dim realm of offstage (not always the same as backstage)—his parents' sex activities, their real income and financial problems, and many other things, some of them strange and frightening, that "children are not old enough to understand."

They learn early the fundamental lesson of front stage: be prepared; know your lines. Who knows whether the neighbors' windows are open? The parent who answers a crying child with, "Calm down now, let's sit down and talk this over," is rehearsing him in stage presence, and in his character as middle-class child and eventually middle-class adult.

Often the family acts as a team. The act may be rehearsed, but it must appear spontaneous. Watch them file in and out of church on Sunday mornings. Even after more than an hour of sitting, the children seem fresh and starched. They do not laugh or shout as on the playground. The parents seem calm, in complete control. Conversations and postures are confined to those appropriate for a place of worship.

Audience reaction is essential to a play. At church others may say, "What nice children you have!" or, "We look forward to seeing you next Sunday." Taken at face value, these are sounds of audience approval and applause; the performers may bask in them. Silence or equivocal remarks may imply disapproval and cause anxiety. What did they really mean? What did we do wrong? Sometimes reaction is delayed, and the family will be uncertain of their impression. In any case, future performances will be affected.

Acting a role, keeping up a front, letting the impressions and expectations of other people influence our behavior, does result in a great deal of good. Organized society is possible only when there is some conformity to roles and rules. Also a person concerned with the impressions others have of him feels that he is significant to them and they to him. When he polishes his car because a dirty one would embarrass him, when his wife straightens her make-up before answering the door, both exhibit a sense of their importance and personal dignity in human affairs. Those who must, or want to, serve as models or exemplars must be especially careful of speech and performance—they are always on stage. When people keep up appearances they are identifying themselves with a group and its standards. They need it; presumably it needs them.

Moreover, acting what seems a narrow role may actually broaden experience and open doors. To tend a lawn, or join a PTA, social club, or art group—"to keep up appearances"—may result in real knowledge and understanding about horticulture, education, or civic responsibility.

For the community, front produces the positive assets of social cohesion. Well-kept lawns, homes, cars, clean children and adults have definite aesthetic, financial, and sanitary value. People relate to one another, develop common experiences. People who faithfully play their parts exhibit personal and civic responsibility. The rules make life predictable and safe, confine ad-libs within acceptable limits, control violence and emotional tangents, and allow the show to go on and the day's work to be done. Thus, the challenging game of maintaining front relates unique personalities to one another and unites them in activity and into a nation.

So much for the good which preoccupation with front and staging accomplishes; what of the bad?

First, the inhibition of the free play of emotion must lead to frustration. Human energies need outlets. If onstage acting does not allow for release of tension, then the escape should take place backstage. But what if there is virtually no backstage? Perhaps then the releases will be found in the case histories of psychiatrists and other counselors. Communication between husband and wife may break down because of the contrast between the onstage image each has of the other as a perfect mate and the unmasked actuality backstage. Perhaps when masks crumble and crack, when people can no longer stand the strain of the front, then what we call nervous breakdown occurs.

Growing Up with Bad Reviews

And how does the preoccupation with front affect the growth and development of the child? How can a child absorb and pattern himself after models which are essentially unreal? A mother may "control" her emotions when a child spills milk on her freshly scrubbed floor, and "reason" with him about it; she may still retain control when he leaves the refrigerator open after repeated warnings; but then some minor thing such as loud laughter over the funnies may suddenly blow off the lid, and she will "let him have it, but good!" What can he learn from such treatment? To respect his mother's hard work at keeping the house clean? To close the refrigerator door? Not to laugh loudly when reading the comics? That mother is a crab? Or, she's always got it in for him? Whatever he has learned, it is doubtful it was what his mother wanted! Whatever it was it will probably not clarify his understanding of such family values as pride in work, reward for effort, consideration of other people, or how to meet problems. Too, since the family's status is vitally linked with the maintenance of fronts, any deviance by the child, unless promptly rectified, threatens family standing in the community. This places a tremendous burden on a child actor.

Moreover, a concentration on front rather than content must result in a leveling and deadening of values and feelings. If a man buys a particular hat primarily because of what others may think, then its intrinsic value as a hat—in fact, even his own judgment and feelings about it—become secondary. Whether the judgment of those whose approval he covets is good or bad is unimportant—just so they approve. Applause has taken the place of value.

A PTA lecture on "The Future of America" will call for the same attentive front from him as a scientist's speech on the "Effects of Nuclear Warfare on Human Survival." Reading a newspaper on a crowded bus, his expression undergoes little change whether he is reading about nuclear tests, advice to the lovelorn, or Elizabeth Taylor's marital problems. To his employer he presents essentially the same bland, non-argumentative, courteous front whether he has just been refused a much deserved pay raise or told to estimate the cost of light bulbs. He seems impartial, objective, rational—and by so doing he also seems to deny that there is any difference to him between the pay raise and the light bulbs, as well as to deny his feelings.

The Price of Admission

What price does the community pay for its role as audience?

The individual human talents and energies are alienated from assuming responsibility for the well-being and survival of the group. The exaggerated self-consciousness of individuals results in diluted and superficial concern with the community at a time when deep involvement, new visions, and real leadership are needed. Can the world afford to have overzealous actors who work so hard on their lines that they forget what the play is all about?

It is probable that this picture will become more general in the near future and involve more and more people—assuming that the aging of the population continues, that the Cold War doesn't become hot and continues to need constant checks on loyalty and patriotism, that automation increases man's leisure at the same time as it keeps up or increases the production of consumer goods, and that improved advertising techniques make every home a miniature department store. The resulting conformity, loyalty, and patriotism may foster social solidarity. It may also cause alienation, immaturity, confusion, and much insecurity when new situations, for which old fronts are no longer appropriate, suddenly occur. Unless people start today to separate the important from the tinsel and to assume responsibility for community matters that are vital, individual actors will feel even more isolated; and the society may drift ever further from the philosophy that values every person.

Tomorrow's communities will need to provide new backstages, as the home, work place, and recreation center become more and more visible. Psychiatrists, counselors, confessors, and other professional listeners must provide outlets for actors who are exhausted and want to share their backstage thoughts. With increased leisure, businessmen will probably find it profitable to provide backstage settings in the form of resorts, rest homes, or retreats.

The state of the world is such today that unless the family and the community work together to evaluate and value the significant and direct their energies accordingly, the theater with its actors, front stage, backstage, and audience may end in farce and tragedy.

32 The Military Academy as an Assimilating Institution

SANFORD M. DORNBUSCH

As we saw in Parts IV and V, each society has a general interest in making people conform to expectations. A major social institution for which conformity is one of its major goals is education. Educators want to graduate people who are acceptable to the community, not only in terms of marketable skills but also in terms of their ideas, attitudes, and behaviors. Whether it be grade school, high school, or college, educational administrators want instructors to teach standard ideas and facts, to steer clear of radical politics, and not to stir up trouble in the school or community. *Then* the social institution can go about its business—and that business, when you delve beyond official utterances and get at the "hidden curriculum," is producing conformists who fit well in society.

Although Dornbusch's focus is the military academy, this article was chosen to represent the educational institution because it focuses on this essential nature of education, training in conformity. If this is what education is really about, where is stimulation, the excitement of discovery, and creativity? The answer is that they may occur as long as they are noncontroversial (that is, they are expected to reflect the conformist nature of this social institution).

Based on your own extensive experiences with education, how do you react to the idea that the essence of the educational institution is training into conformity? What good and bad points do you see in your own educational experiences? What would you change about American education if you had the opportunity? How would you go about making those changes?

The function of a military academy is to make officers out of civilians or enlisted men. The objective is accomplished by a twofold process of transmitting technical knowledge and of instilling in the candidates an outlook considered appropriate for members of the profession. This paper is concerned with the latter of these processes, the assimilating function of the military academy.[1] Assimilation is viewed as "a process of interpenetration and fusion in which persons and groups acquire the memories, sentiments, and attitudes of other persons and groups, and, by sharing their experience and history, are incorporated with them in a common cultural life. . . . The unity thus achieved is not necessarily or even normally like-mindedness; it is rather a unity of experience and of orientation, out of which may develop a community of purpose and action."[2]

Data for this study consists almost entirely of retrospective material, based on ten months spent as a cadet at the United States Coast Guard Academy. The selective nature of memory obviously may introduce serious deficiencies in the present formulation. Unfortunately, it is unlikely that more objective evidence on life within the Academy will be forthcoming. Cadets cannot keep diaries, are formally forbidden to utter a word of criticism of the Academy to an outsider, and are informally limited in the matters which are to be discussed in letters or conversations. The lack of objective data is regrettable, but the process of assimilation is present here in an extreme form. Insight into this process can better be developed by the study of such an explicit, overt case of assimilation.

The Coast Guard Academy, like West Point and Annapolis, provides four years of training for a career as a regular officer. Unlike the other service academies, however, its cadet corps is small, seldom exceeding 350 cadets. This disparity in size probably produces comparable differences in the methods of informal social control. Therefore, all the findings reported here may not be applicable to the other academies. It is believed, however, that many of the mechanisms through which this military academy fulfills its assimilating function will be found in a wide variety of social institutions.

The Suppression of Pre-existing Statuses

The new cadet, or "swab" is the lowest of the low. The assignment of low status is useful in producing a correspondingly high evaluation of successfully completing the steps in an Academy career and requires that there be a loss of identity in terms of pre-existing statuses. This clean break with the past must be achieved in a relatively short period. For two months, therefore, the swab is not allowed to leave the base or to engage in social intercourse with non-cadets. This complete isolation helps to produce a unified group of swabs, rather than a heterogeneous collection of persons of high and low status. Uniforms are issued on the first day, and discussions of wealth and family background are taboo. Although the pay of the cadet is very low, he is not permitted to receive money from home. The role of the cadet must supersede other roles the individual has been accustomed to play. There are few clues left which will reveal social status in the outside world.[3]

It is clear that the existence of minority-group status on the part of some cadets would tend to break down this desired equality. The sole minority group present was the Jews, who, with a few exceptions, had been informally excluded before 1944. At that time 18 Jews were admitted in a class of 162. Their status as Jews made them objects of scrutiny by the upper classmen, so that their violations of rules were more often noted. Except for this "spotlight," however, the Jews reported no discrimination against them—they too, were treated as swabs.

Learning New Rules and Adjustment to Conflicts Between Rules

There are two organized structures of rules which regulate the cadet's behavior. The first of these is the body of regulations of the Academy, considered by the public to be the primary source of control. These regulations are similar to the code of ethics of any profession. They serve in part as propaganda to influence outsiders. An additional function is to provide negative sanctions which are applied to violations of the second set of expectations, the informal rules. Offenses against the informal rules are merely labeled as breaches of the formal code, and the appropriate punishment according to the regulations is then imposed. This punitive system conceals the existence of the informal set of controls.

The informal traditions of the Academy are more functionally related to the existing set of circumstances than are the regulations, for although these traditions are fairly rigid, they are more easily forgotten or changed than are the formal regulations. Unlike other informal codes, the Academy code of traditions is in part written, appearing in a manual for entering cadets.

In case of conflict between the regulations and tradition, the regulations are superseded. For example, it is against the regulations to have candy in one's room. A first classman orders a swab to bring him candy. Caught en route by an officer, the swab offers no excuse and is given 15 demerits. First classmen are then informally told by the classmate involved that they are to withhold demerits for this swab until he has been excused for offenses totaling 15 demerits. Experience at any Academy teaches future officers that regulations are not considered of paramount importance when they conflict with informal codes—a principle noted by other observers.[4]

Sometimes situations arise in which the application of either form of control is circumvented by the commanding officer. The following case is an example. Cadets cannot drink, cannot smoke in public, can never go above the first floor in a hotel. It would seem quite clear, therefore, that the possessor of a venereal disease would be summarily dismissed. Cadets at the Academy believed that two upper-class cadets had contracted a venereal disease, were cured, and given no punishment. One of the cadets was an outstanding athlete, brilliant student, and popular classmate. Cadets were told that a direct appeal by the commanding officer to the Commandant of the Coast Guard resulted in the decision to hush up the entire affair, with the second cadet getting the same treatment as his more popular colleague. The event indicated the possibility of individualization of treatment when rules are violated by officers.

The Development of Solidarity

The control system operated through the class hierarchy. The first class, consisting of cadets in their third or fourth year at the Academy, are only nominally under the control of the officers of the Academy. Only one or two officers attempt to check on the activities of the first classmen, who are able to break most of the minor regulations with impunity. The first class is given almost complete control over the rest of the cadet corps. Informally, certain leading cadets are even called in to advise the officers on important disciplinary matters. There are one or two classes between the first classmen and the swabs, depending on the existence of a three or four-year course. These middle classes haze the swabs. Hazing is forbidden by the regulations, but the practice is a hallowed tradition of the Academy. The first class demands that this hazing take place, and, since they have the power to give demerits, all members of the middle classes are compelled to haze the new cadets.

As a consequence of undergoing this very unpleasant experience together, the swab class develops remarkable unity. For example, if a cadet cannot answer an oral question addressed to him by his teacher, no other member of his class will answer. All reply, "I can't say, sir," leaving the teacher without a clue to the state of knowledge of this student compared to the rest of the class. This group cohesion persists throughout the academy period, with first classmen refusing to give demerits to their classmates unless an officer directly orders them to do so.

The Honor system, demanding that offenses by classmates be reported, is not part of the Coast Guard Academy tradition. It seems probable that the honor system, if enforced, would tend to break down the social solidarity which the hazing develops within each class.

The basis for interclass solidarity, the development of group feeling on the part of the entire cadet corps, is not so obvious. It occurs through informal contacts between the upper classmen and swabs, a type of fraternization which occurs despite the fact it traditionally is discouraged. The men who haze the swab and order him hazed live in the same wing of the dormitory that he does. Coming from an outside world which disapproves of authoritarian punishment and aggressiveness, they are ashamed of their behavior. They are eager to convince the swab that they are good fellows. They visit his room to explain why they are being so harsh this week or to tell of a mistake he is making. Close friendships sometimes arise through such behavior. These friendships must be concealed. One first classman often ordered his room cleaned by the writer as a "punishment," then settled down for an uninterrupted chat. Such informal contacts serve to unite the classes and spread a "we-feeling" through the Academy.

In addition, the knowledge of common interests and a common destiny serves as a unifying force that binds together all Academy graduates. This is expressed in the identification of the interest of the individual with the interest of the Coast Guard. A large appropriation or an increase in the size of the Coast Guard will speed the rate of promotion for all, whether ensign or captain. A winning football team at the Academy may familiarize more civilians with the name of their common alma mater. Good publicity for the Coast Guard raises the status of the Coast Guard officer.

The Coast Guard regulars are united in their disdain for the reserves. There are few reserve officers during peacetime, but in wartime the reserve officers soon outnumber the regulars. The reserves do not achieve the higher ranks, but they are a threat to the cadets and recent graduates of the Academy. The reserves receive in a few months the rank that the regulars reach only after four grueling years. The Academy men therefore protectively stigmatize the reserves as incompetents. If a cadet falters on the parade ground, he is told, "You're marching like a reserve." Swabs are told to square their shoulders while on liberty, "or else how will people know you are not a reserve?" Myths spring up—stories of reserve commanders who must call on regular ensigns for advice. The net effect is reassurance that although the interlopers may have the same rank, they do not have equal status.

Another out-group is constituted by the enlisted men, who are considered to be of inferior ability and eager for leadership. Segregation of cadets and enlisted men enables this view to be propagated. Moreover, such segregation helps to keep associations within higher status social groups. There is only one leak in this insulating dike. The pharmacist mates at sick bay have direct contact with the cadets, and are the only enlisted personnel whom cadets meet on an equal basis. The pharmacist mates take pleasure in reviling the Academy, labeling it "the p—k factory." Some of the cadets without military experience are puzzled by such an attitude, which is inconsistent with their acquired respect for the Academy.

The Development of a Bureaucratic Spirit

The military services provide an excellent example of a bureaucratic structure. The emphasis is upon the office with its set of rights and duties, rather than on the man. It is a system of rules with little regard for the individual case. The method of promotion within the Coast Guard perfectly illustrates this bureaucratic character. Unlike the Army or Navy, promotions in the Coast Guard up to the rank of lieutenant-commander do not even depend on the evaluation of superior officers. Promotion comes solely according to seniority, which is based on class standing at the Academy. The 50th man in the 1947 class will be lieutenant-commander before the 51st man, and the latter will be promoted before the 1st man in the 1948 class.

The hazing system contributes directly to acceptance of the bureaucratic structure of the Coast Guard, for the system is always viewed by its participants as not involving the personal character of the swab or upper classman. One is not being hazed because the upper classman is a sadist, but because one is at the time in a junior status. Those who haze do not pretend to be superior to those who are being hazed. Since some of those who haze you will also try to teach you how to stay out of trouble, it becomes impossible to attribute evil characteristics to those who injure you. The swab knows he will have his turn at hazing others. At most, individual idiosyncrasies will just affect the type of hazing done.[5]

This emphasis on the relativity of status is explicitly made on the traditional Gizmo Day, on which the swabs and their hazers reverse roles. The swabs-for-a-day take their licking without flinching and do not seek revenge later, for they are aware that they are under the surveillance of the first classmen. After the saturnalia, the swabs are increasingly conscious of their inability to blame particular persons for their troubles.

Upper classmen show the same resentment against the stringent restrictions upon their lives, and the manner in which they express themselves indicates a feeling of being ruled by impersonal forces. They say, "You can't buck the System." As one writer puts it, "The best attitude the new cadet can have is one of unquestioning acceptance of tradition and custom."

There is a complete absence of charismatic veneration of the Coast Guard heroes of the past and present. Stirring events are recalled, not as examples of the genius of a particular leader but as part of the history of the great organization which they will serve. A captain is a cadet thirty years older and wiser. Such views prepare these men for their roles in the bureaucracy.

New Satisfactions in Interaction

A bureaucratic structure requires a stable set of mutual expectations among the occupants of offices. The Academy develops this ability to view the behavior of others in terms of a pre-ordained set of standards. In addition to preparing the cadet for later service as an officer, the predictability of the behavior of his fellows enables the cadet to achieve a high degree of internal stability. Although he engages in a continual bustle of activity, he always knows his place in the system and the degree to which he is fulfilling the expectations of his role.

Sharing common symbols and objects, the cadets interact with an ease of communication seldom found in everyday life. The cadet is told what is right and wrong, and, if he disagrees, there are few opportunities to translate mental reservations into action. The "generalized other" speaks with a unitary voice which is uncommon in modern societies. To illustrate, an upper classman ordered a swab to pick up some pieces of paper on the floor of a washroom. The latter refused and walked away. There were no repercussions. The swab knew that, if he refused, the upper classman would be startled by the choice of such an unconventional way of getting expelled from the Academy. Wondering what was happening, the upper classman would redefine his own behavior, seeing it as an attack on the high status of the cadet. Picking up litter in a washroon is "dirty work," fit only for enlisted men. The swab was sure that the upper classman shared this common universe of discourse and never considered the possibility that he would not agree on the definition of the situation.

Interaction with classmates can proceed on a level of confidence that only intimate friends achieve in the outside world. These men are in a union of sympathy, sharing the same troubles, never confiding secrets to upper classmen, never criticizing one another to outsiders. Each is close to only a few but is friendly with most of the men in his class.

When interacting with an upper classman in private, a different orientation is useful. The swab does not guess the reason why he is being addressed, but instead assumes a formal air of deference. If the upper classman says, "Aw cut it out," the swab relaxes. In this manner the role of the upper classman is explicitly denoted in each situation.

In addition to providing predictability of the behavior of others, the Academy provides a second set of satisfactions in the self-process. An increase in the cadet's self-esteem develops in conjunction with identification in his new role. Told that they are members of an elite group respected by the community, most cadets begin to feel at ease in a superordinate role. One may be a low-ranking cadet, but cadets as a group have high status. When cadets visit home for the first time, there is a conflict between the lofty role that they wish to play and the role to which their parents are accustomed. Upon return to the Academy, much conversation is concerned with the way things at home have changed.

This feeling of superiority helps to develop self-confidence in those cadets who previously had a low evaluation of themselves. It directly enters into relationships with girls, with whom many boys lack self-confidence. It soon becomes apparent that any cadet can get a date whenever he wishes, and he even begins to feel that he is a good "catch." The cadet's conception of himself is directly influenced by this new way of viewing the behavior of himself and others. As one cadet put it, "I used to be shy. Now I'm reserved."

Social Mobility

A desire for vertical social mobility on the part of many cadets serves as one means of legitimizing the traditional practices of the Academy. The cadets are told that they will be members of the social elite during the later stages of their career. The obstacles they meet at the Academy are then viewed as the usual barriers to social mobility in the United States, a challenge to be surmounted.

Various practices at the Academy reinforce the cadets' feeling that they are learning how to enter the upper classes. There is a strong emphasis on etiquette, from calling cards to table manners. The Tactics Officer has been known to give long lectures on such topics as the manner of drinking soup from an almost empty bowl. The cadet must submit for approval the name of the girl he intends to take to the monthly formal dance. Girls attending the upper-class college in the vicinity are automatically acceptable, but some cadets claim that their dates have been rejected because they are in a low status occupation such as waitress.

Another Academy tradition actively, though informally, encourages contact with higher status girls. After the swabs have been completely isolated for two months, they are invited to a dance at which all the girls at the nearby college have a dance for the swabs. The next weekend finds the swab compelled to invite an acceptable girl to a formal reception. He must necessarily choose from the only girls in the area whom he knows, those that he met during the recent hours of social intercourse.

Justification of Institutional Practices

In addition to the social mobility theme which views the rigors of Academy life as obstacles to upward mobility, there is a more open method of justifying traditionally legitimated ways of doing things. The phrase "separating the men from the boys" is used to meet objections to practices which seem inefficient or foolish. Traditional standards are thus redefined as further tests of ability to take punishment. Harsh practices are defined as methods by which the insincere, incompetent, or undisciplined cadets are weeded out. Cadets who rebel and resign are merely showing lack of character.[6]

Almost all cadets accept to some extent this traditional view of resignations as admissions of defeat. Of the 162 entering cadets in 1944, only 52 graduated in 1948. Most of the 110 resignations were entirely voluntary without pressure from the Academy authorities. Most of these resignations came at a time when the hazing was comparatively moderate. Cadets who wish to resign do not leave at a time when the hazing might be considered the cause of their departure. One cadet's history illustrates this desire to have the resignation appear completely voluntary. Asked to resign because of his lack of physical coordination, he spent an entire year building up his physique, returned to the Academy, finished his swab year, and then joyously quit. "It took me three years, but I showed them."

Every cadet who voluntarily resigns is a threat to the morale of the cadet corps, since he has rejected the values of the Academy. Although cadets have enlisted for seven years and could theoretically be forced to remain at the Academy, the usual procedure is to isolate them from the swabs and rush acceptance of their resignation. During the period before the acceptance is final, the cadets who have resigned are freed from the usual duties of their classmates, which action effectively isolates them from cadets who might be affected by their contagious disenchantment.

Reality Shock

Everett C. Hughes has developed the concept of "reality shock," the sudden realization of the disparity between the way a job is envisaged before beginning work and the actual work situation.[7] In the course of its 75-year history the Coast Guard Academy has wittingly or unwittingly developed certain measures to lessen reality shock in the new ensign. The first classmen, soon to be officers, are aided in lessening the conflict between the internalized rules of the Academy world and the standards for officer conduct.

On a formal level the first classmen are often reminded that they are about to experience a relative decline in status. On their first ship they will be given the most disagreeable duties. The first classmen accept this and joke about how their attitudes will change under a harsh captain. On a more concrete level, first classmen are given weekend leaves during the last six months of their stay at the Academy. These leaves allow them to escape from the restrictive atmosphere of the nearby area. It is believed wise to let them engage in orgiastic behavior while still cadets, rather than suddenly release all controls upon graduation.

Rumors at the Academy also help to prepare the cadets for their jobs as officers. Several of the instructors at the Academy were supposed to have been transferred from sea duty because of their incompetence. Such tales protect the cadets from developing a romantic conception of the qualities of Coast Guard officers, as well as providing a graphic illustration of how securely the bureaucratic structure protects officers from their own derelictions. In addition, many stories were told about a junior officer whose career at the Academy had been singularly brilliant. He had completely failed in his handling of enlisted men because he had carried over the high standards of the Academy. The cadets were thus oriented to a different conception of discipline when dealing with enlisted personnel.

Conclusion

The United States Coast Guard Academy performs an assimilating function. It isolates cadets from the outside world, helps them to identify themselves with a new role, and thus changes their self-conception. The manner in which the institution inculcates a bureaucratic spirit and prevents reality shock is also considered in this analysis.

The present investigation is admittedly fragmentary. Much of the most relevant material is simply not available. It is also clear that one cannot assume that this analysis applies completely to any other military academy. However, as an extreme example of an assimilating institution, there is considerable material which can be related to other institutions in a comparative framework.

Notes

1. The writer is indebted to Harold McDowell, Frank Miyamoto, Charles Bowerman, and Howard S. Becker for their constructive criticism of this paper.
2. Robert E. Park and Ernest W. Burgess, *Introduction to the Science of Sociology* (Chicago: University of Chicago Press, 1921), pp. 735, 737.
3. Cf. Arnold Van Gennep, *Les Rites de Passage* (Paris: Emile Nourry, 1909). Translated by Everett C. Hughes in *Anthropology-Sociology 240, Special Readings* (Chicago: University of Chicago Bookstore, 1948), Pt. II, p. 9.
4. Ralph H. Turner, "The Navy Disbursing Officer as a Bureaucrat, *American Sociological Review*, 12 (June 1946): 344 and 348; Arnold Rose, "The Social Structure of the Army," *American Journal of Sociology*, 51 (March 1946): 361.
5. Compare this viewpoint with that expressed in Hugh Mullan, "The Regular Service Myth," *American Journal of Sociology*, 53 (January 1948): 280, where

hazing is viewed as the expression of "pent-up sadism." Such individualistic interpretations do not take into account the existence of an institutional structure, or else they give psychological interpretations to social processes.

6. "At each step of the ceremonies he feels that he is brought a little closer, until at last he can feel himself a man among men." A. R. Radcliffe-Brown, *The Andaman Islanders* (Glencoe, Ill.: The Free Press, 1948), p. 279.

7. Miriam Wagenschein, "Reality Shock," unpublished M.A. thesis, Department of Sociology, University of Chicago, 1950.

33 The Streetcorner Preacher

LAWRENCE K. HONG
MARION V. DEARMAN

Religion is vital to American society, and if someone misses this point they fail to understand Americans. Although in previous years some professionals prophesied that with the rise of science and the general secularization of American culture religion would quietly fade into the background, this has not happened. Americans repeatedly go through periods of decreased religious involvement— and to some it then looks as though religion is on the way out— only to enter an inevitable period of increased religious participation. Although church and synagogue membership and attendance ebb and flow, in American society there always remains a strong current of genuine religiosity based on sincere convictions.

It is no exaggeration, then, to say that religion is one of the principal social institutions in American society. In it Americans find solace and courage, as well as the answers to many of the perplexing questions that contemporary social life poses. Those who have religious convictions grasp the meaning of what I am writing, while those with few or none must remain "outsiders," somewhat perplexed by all the activity of which they are not a part.

While most of us are at least "somewhat" religious, most of us also think that religion should remain primarily a private matter. "We believe what we believe, and it is no one else's business" is likely to be the attitude most of us take. Consequently, few of us are likely to preach on streetcorners or accost people on the sidewalk with a religious message—or to approve those who do. Streetcorner preaching strikes most of us somewhat humorous, somehow unseemly, and undesirably "pushy," an invasion of our privacy.

In spite of such common reactions, however, some people persist in preaching on streetcorners. Focusing on just this one aspect of the fascinatingly multifaceted social institution we call religion, Hong and Dearman's analysis helps the unfamiliar take on just a little more familiarity. From the lens of these sociologists, then, we gain greater understanding of another aspect of our social world.

Alleluia, alleluia, Lord, I glorify your name. Thank you,
Jesus, Heaven come to your heart, heaven come to your
heart. Amen, amen. Devil is here, but Jesus is right here.
Alleluia, alleluia. Praise the Lord. Thank you, Jesus.

ON A BUSY DOWNTOWN STREET CORNER a black man in his
late fifties, clapping his hands, striking his arms, striding back and forth,
preaches at the top of his voice to the ceaseless streams of pedestrians.
Adults avert their eyes in apparent embarrassment for the preacher; children stare at him while being jerked forward by their mothers who admonish them to pay no attention. Police walk or drive by, glance at him
indifferently, and go their way. These sights and sounds are part of the
permanent landscape of most major cities from New York to Los Angeles.
The experienced city dweller apparently takes the streetcorner preachers
for granted, along with slow traffic, stale air, sleazy movies, and monotonous neon signs. But to the novice or newcomer, they add excitement
and color to the kaleidoscopic, carnival atmosphere which inner city life
presents to him.

Who are these streetcorner preachers? Where do they come from?
What do they try to accomplish? These and other questions have brought
the authors of this paper to the streets of downtown Los Angeles. Over a
period of three months, we observed and interviewed the preachers, a
spokesman of the church of which many were members, different types
of pedestrians, and the police in an attempt to search for the answers. . . .

One Situation, Multiple Definitions

With few exceptions, all the passers-by whom we interviewed regard the
streetcorner preachers as "crazy," "insane," or "mentally disturbed." The
following comment from a regular downtown shopper is typical:

> I think he is crazy. Mentally unbalanced, you know. There are many of
> them. They always stand over in that corner, making a lot of noise. Nobody
> ever listens to them. I think they are nuts.

Policemen agreed with this opinion, although a desk sergeant con-
fided to us that "some of them [the preachers] are righteous but most of
them are squirrels, nuts, kooks." Another policeman told us that "they are
definitely a nuisance but, you know, free speech and all that jazz" makes
it impossible to eliminate them.

The preachers, in turn, define the passers-by as sinners—heathens,
drunkards, thieves, and worse; the policemen are seen as would-be per-
secutors of God's spokesmen, the preachers. By thus defining themselves
as the representatives of God, the creator and master of the universe, the
preachers perceive themselves as the "winners" while the others become

poor, pitiful "losers" who are going to Hell if they fail to heed their warnings.

Very much contrary to the definitions of the police and pedestrians,
we soon discovered that these preachers are quite rational, intelligent people and sincere, dedicated Christians. Our basis for this definition will
emerge in the remaining pages of this paper.

Organization of "Frenetic" Behavior

It did not take us long to discover that just beneath the surface of their
seemingly erratic behavior was a close group of people who share many
of the system characteristics—mutual obligations, common goals, status
hierarchy, and territoriality—of the streetcorner society that Whyte (1943)
has described. The permanent cadre, or nucleus, of the street preachers
are members of a major Pentecostal denomination—the Church of God
in Christ (CGC)—that claims national membership of around three million.[1] Although these preachers are neither licensed to preach, nor ordained by their church, they are well organized and follow a schedule
almost as regular as that of suburban churches in conducting their religious services. They begin their preaching around noon every day and
finish around five. During this five-hour interval, three or four preachers
will take turns preaching, each having a time slot of about half an hour.
Other preachers may also stand by, but only a few will have a chance to
preach on the same day.

The street preachers feel very close to one another, and frequently
have lunch or coffee breaks together in a cafeteria in the immediate area.
In the cafeteria, they will also meet with other "brothers" and "sisters"
who perform other religious services in the vicinity such as passing out
religious tracts and mini-bibles. Their interactions are characterized by
warmth and rapport. This observation is also confirmed by an ordained
minister of their church (who does not preach in the street but has a regular pastoral appointment):

> They have a way to be aware of each other's needs. They preach by turns
> and help one another out. They get to know each other very well. Some-
> times, they even live together. Some of them share the same apartment. They
> are very close.

When a preacher is preaching, his voice may appear to be emotional
and his utterances disjunct, but the whole presentation is delivered with
a deliberate effort and what appears to be a carefully considered style. He
fully understands that very few individuals will stop and listen to his
preaching and, therefore, it is not necessary to deliver a coherent, logical
discourse on Christianity and salvation. . . . Hence, in contrast to other
downtown religious groups such as the Skid Row Missions (Bibby and

Mauss, 1974), the goal of the street preacher is not concerned with immediate conversion; his goal, rather, is to "sow the seeds" by scattering discrete words and phrases of virtue and holiness to the downtown crowds, hoping that someone will pick up a word or two here and there.[2] As one of the preachers explains their technique:

> What we try to accomplish here is to sow the seeds. What we do out here is like spreading the germs. They get into the air and someone may pick them up. They may not know it now, but one of these days when he is in trouble, he may remember what he has heard here today. It may turn him to the Lord. All it takes is one word, and he may be saved.

. . . The organization of the streetcorner preachers is also manifested in their informal status hierarchy. This status differentiation is determined by the style of delivery and paraphernalia. On the top of the hierarchy is "Brother James," who is a black man in his late forties. Brother James is a recognized virtuoso of streetcorner preachers. His voice is firm and forceful. He does not rattle like many of the other preachers in the lower hierarchy. He always preaches with a high degree of confidence and considerable skill. He also has a charismatic quality which holds the attention of his listeners. Furthermore, he dresses differently than the other streetcorner preachers. His suit is well tailored and his shirt well pressed, while many of the other preachers wear old clothes which desperately need a thorough cleaning. . . .

The preaching styles and dress of the other preachers are visibly inferior. Accordingly, their status in the eyes of their peers is also lower. This is evident in the magnitude of support and the size of the gathering accorded to them by their colleagues while they are preaching. Brother James has the largest gathering. When he preaches, all the other preachers gather along the opposite edge of the sidewalk and respond to his utterances enthusiastically. They repeat after him, clap their hands rhythmically, and fix their attention on him intensively:

> BROTHER JAMES: Alleluia, alleluia
> OTHER PREACHERS: Alleluia
> BROTHER JAMES: Lord, I glorify your name
> OTHER PREACHERS: I glorify your name
> BROTHER JAMES: Thank you Jesus
> OTHER PREACHERS: Thank you Jesus
> BROTHER JAMES: Lord, give us strength through this journey
> OTHER PREACHERS: Through this journey

But, when a lower status preacher preaches, at most one or two of his colleagues give him support. The type of support is also less enthusiastic. Instead of repeating in full or partially what he actually says, they tend to use standard responses such as "Praise the Lord" and "Alleluia." Furthermore, they rarely clap their hands. Sometimes, they even suspend their support by engaging in social talks. Brother James also occupies an interstitial role between the regular Church of God in Christ and the street-corner preachers. He is an evangelist who travels from city to city preaching the gospel to down-and-outers and street people. He represents the church and his role allows church members to feel comfortable that their group is both ministering to the lost ones on the downtown streets as well as assisting the streetcorner preachers in their humble and, at first glance, unrewarding task. . . .

Another manifestation of the organization of the street preachers is their concern over territoriality. The corners where they preach are located on certain of the busiest intersections of downtown Los Angeles. The street preachers have more or less occupied these intersections as their own; other downtown religious groups such as the Salvation Army, Jesus People, and Hare Krishna respect, perhaps reluctantly, their "right" to be there and seldom conduct their activities on those corners. . . .

We have observed only one territorial violation during the period of study. The violator was a Hare Krishna who was giving out his sect's newspapers to the passers-by in the exact location where the preachers usually conduct their activities. He took over the area while the preachers were taking their coffee break inside a cafeteria. Upon discovering their spot had been occupied by an intruder (after their coffee break), the immediate response of the preachers was motionless silence. They stood across from the Hare Krishna, stared at him in silence and remained almost motionless. But the Hare Krishna ignored their "silent treatment." After waiting for a couple of minutes in futility, the preachers tried a different technique; they flooded the area with their own people and tried to crowd the Hare Krishna out.

One of the preachers walked over to the Hare Krishna, positioned next to him, and started to preach in the highest decibel. His audio output was matched by the ferocity of his bodily movement. The Hare Krishna adjusted his distance, moving a few feet away from the preacher. The preacher readjusted his position to keep close to the Hare Krishna. Standing across from the couple, the "brothers" and "sisters" of the preacher clapped their hands and responded "alleluia" and "thank you Jesus" to the beat of the preacher's delivery. Finally, the Hare Krishna left the location and moved to a new area about a block away. Although we have observed only one episode, the spontaneity of the preachers' actions and the effortlessness of their coordination in defending their territory strongly suggest that they have employed these techniques before.

Rebirth of the Evangelist

Who are these street preachers? What are their backgrounds? These are some of the most difficult questions that we encountered in our research. As a group, the street preachers are below average in education—most of them have not finished high school. We have met only one preacher who has some college experience, a geography major who dropped out from college after the second year. In spite of their lack of education, the preachers are intelligent, knowledgeable persons who have a good grasp of themselves and happenings in society. In great contrast to the style they preach in the street, they speak conventionally and coherently when they engage in social talks.

They are gregarious and interesting to talk to. Not unlike people in other walks of life, during a typical coffee break they comment on a wide variety of subjects, ranging from politics to personal events. However, there is one topic that is almost a taboo—their past life, that is, their life before their religious conversion. In a way, the street preachers are very much like the streetcorner men in Tally's corner (Liebow, 1967): They do not like to talk about their past, and not even their best friends know about the details of their past. When asked, they speak in generality. One of the preachers speaks of his past in this way:

> Before I became a Christian, I was in sin. Drink, women, and all kinds of troubles. But, I don't do that anymore. One day, I talked to myself. I didn't want to do that anymore. Jesus came into my heart. Now, I am as happy as I can be.

Another preacher relates a similar story:

> I was born in Texas, and then I moved to Tennessee. I came out here 10 years ago. I have been to many places, seen all kinds of people. I did almost everything. I have worked all kinds of jobs. I always had troubles with the laws, nothing serious, you know. Traffic tickets and things like that. Nothing big. And then the Lord spoke to me in my heart. He asked me to come out here. This is where He wants me to be. I follow Him. Jesus cannot be wrong.

To the best of our reconstruction of their past, all the street preachers have gone through an experience of "rebirth."[3] Throughout their early adulthood, they worked on low-paying jobs in various cities. They were the drifters, moving from one city to another. Like many other people in similar circumstances, they had a long history of minor infractions with the law. However, unlike many of their peers, they did not get deeper into trouble. At some moments in their middle years, they decided that they could not live like that anymore and resolved to do something that they considered to be meaningful. Perhaps, through the influence of a friend, or the contact with a preacher, or the experience in a revival meeting, they concluded that ministry was their vocation.

Preaching in Church

Why don't they become regular ministers? Why don't they preach in a church? In our conversation with the street preachers, it is evident that they are interested in conducting religious service in a church. When asked, they usually become somewhat defensive; one of the preachers retorted:

> I can preach in a church. Sometimes, I do. I'm a minister of Jesus Christ just like all other ministers. I am doing the same work. Jesus sent me here just like the others. If I want to preach in a church, I can.

However, they are also quick to point out that they see street preaching as their vocation, and they are satisfied with it. As one preacher puts it:

> Yeah, I preach in the church sometime. I like to preach in a church. But, this is my calling, out here in the street. This is where the Lord sent me. There is no difference where you preach, in the street, on TV, or in the church. They are all the same. The Lord has many ways to reach people. This is the way He wants me to do. And I am doing as He says.

But, according to a pastor in their church, the street preachers never preach in the church. However, he did point out that it is common practice for members of his congregation to "testify" during religious service. In view of the fact that these testimonials are quite long—sometimes so long that the leader of the testimony service will discreetly terminate the "testimonial" by singing a hymn, joined by the congregation, lest the testifier intrude too far into the prerogatives of the pastor—it is unclear where they end and preaching per se begins. Furthermore, according to the same pastor, no street preacher has ever been appointed as a regular minister in a church, and therefore street preaching cannot be viewed as a stepping stone for advancing toward a pastoral appointment. He explains:

> The street preachers are lay preachers. They are not ordained ministers. Our church believes that every Christian has the right to witness. It is a personal thing. Many of them feel the call to witness in the street. Witnessing in the street is just as significant as witnessing in the church. They are just different forms of evangelism. There might be more effective ways to preach, but I dont' discourage them because I do not want to lessen their intensity, feeling and freedom. To the best of my knowledge, no street preacher has ever become a pastor in our church.

When pressed as to why their church does not ordain at least some of the preachers, he replies:

> To be ordained, you have to have education. Most of these people have very little education. It also takes time to gather your congregation. You have to have a congregation before you can have a pastoral appointment. As I said before, what they are doing in the street is very significant. It is as significant as witnessing in the church. I do not want to discourage them.

It is obvious that there is a paradox here. The street preachers view themselves as regular ministers and want to preach in a church, but their church encourages them to preach in the street and does not accept them as ordained ministers. While their lack of education may be one of the reasons that has kept them from being ordained, other factors apparently are also involved. Possibly, another factor is their church's lack of confidence in the street preachers' ability to attract and maintain a congregation. As their pastor mentioned earlier: "You have to have a congregation before you can have a pastoral appointment." This appears to be a major factor that keeps the street preachers away from the mainstream of the ministry. . . .

Summary and Conclusion

In this paper, we have attempted to demonstrate that the seemingly frenetic streetcorner preachers are actually rational, intelligent, dedicated Christians. Furthermore, their activities on the street corner display many organizational characteristics such as goals, status hierarchy, and territoriality. Thus, in a way, our findings give support to the highly publicized observation that Whyte (1943) made more than [forty] years ago—i.e., an ostensibly disorganized street corner may have a complex and well-established organization of its own. . . .

Notes

1. This figure, provided by a spokesman of the church, is most likely too high. A yearbook of churches (Jacquet, 1973) gives the Church of God in Christ membership as 501,000 in 1971. This figure, however, is only an estimate; the last census was taken in the late 1960s. At the time of our research, the spokesman informed us that a new census is at the planning stage. Three things are certain regarding the CGC: as with all pentecostals, it is very difficult to determine their membership precisely; they are a very large and fast-growing pentecostal group and one of the largest black pentecostal sects.

2. It should be noted this method is somewhat similar to that used by the sophisticated advertising agencies on their billboard and spot radio and television messages.

3. "Rebirth" for pentecostals usually requires some kind of proof of genuine repentance of their sins, baptism in water as a sign of this repentance, and baptism "in the Spirit," the initial sign of which is "speaking in tongues" (glossolalia).

References

Bibby, R. W., and A. L. Mauss (1974). "Skidders and their servants; variable goals and functions of the skid road rescue mission." *J. for the Scientific Study of Religion*, 13: 421–36.

Jacquet, C. H. (1973). *Yearbook of American and Canadian Churches 1973*. New York: Abingdon.

Liebow, E. (1967). *Tally's Corner*. Boston: Little, Brown.

Whyte, W. F. (1943). *Street Corner Society*. Chicago: University of Chicago Press.

34 The Wrestling Referee

CHARLES W. SMITH

Are you active in sports? If not, you have probably participated in them many times, if only as a school requirement. Some of us play varsity sports. For some sports even become a near obsession, and seemingly living and breathing the latest football or baseball game they have a difficult time understanding why the rest of us don't get as excited as they do. For our parts, we put up with their conversations with as good grace as we can muster.

For most of us sports are something to watch, not something to do. We turn on the television and sometimes get excited by boxing, the Olympics, swim meets, or college and professional games. And always in these sports, whether we play or passively participate at the television screen, there is someone who is almost invisible. It is on this person (or more accurately this social role) that Smith focuses. As he examines the referee, he attempts to gain and impart an "insider's" understanding of that activity. If he is successful, you should acquire an understanding of not only why referees do what they do but also how they feel as they do those things and why they feel that way.

[NORMS] ARE THE PRODUCT of complex social negotiations occurring within and influenced by specific social situations. Certain social situations allow for a good deal of negotiation; others do not. This ethnographic essay seeks to document this process in a specific setting, namely, interscholastic wrestling meets; its primary focus of concern is the role of the referee. The central thesis, which I shall attempt to document, is that the more fragile and tenuous the social structure, the less likely open negotiation and the more likely ritualistic performance.

The Ethnographic Setting

"And refereeing tonight's contest, Charlie Smith." The silence which greets the announcement of my name—even the visiting coach got a brief burst of applause—reminds me that as the referee I have no friends. I am on my own.

I began to realize this sometime during my first year as a referee. I was commenting to a number of more experienced referees about how alone I felt when refereeing as compared to simply watching or even wrestling. (Like most referees, I had participated in the sport myself when in school.) They all gave me "knowing" nods; one then said "Just remember, no one likes a zebra." (The "zebra" label is derived from the black and white striped shirt which referees wear.) It was like having a cold glass of water thrown in my face. He said it so calmly, so matter of factly, but that was the hard "truth" which I had refused to accept. It was not that they disliked me personally—though they often made me feel that way—but rather that they did not like referees and as far as they were concerned that is all I was. To them I was just a uniform. This awareness led me to rethink how I had gotten involved in refereeing in the first place.

I had become a wrestling referee by accident. In high school and college, I had been an ardent wrestler; I had also done some high school and college coaching while in graduate school. One day on the spur of the moment after having had nothing to do with wrestling for close to twelve years, I stopped by the local high school to watch a workout. A few visits later, I was being urged to become a referee. It was not any latent refereeing talent that I had exhibited; there was simply a desperate need for more referees. I agreed to look into the matter and with the beginning of the next season (ten months later)—after some study, a fairly rigorous multiple choice exam, and a number of hours refereeing under the critical stares of half a dozen experienced referees—I became a probationary referee.

Though I had acquired a new vocation, my primary occupation remained that of sociologist; furthermore, I found myself continually looking at this new world through sociological eyes. Initially, I tried to resist this tendency, believing that the last thing I needed as a referee was a sociologist looking over my shoulder. The more I confronted the apparent contradictions of my refereeing role: i.e., refereeing a major dual meet in front of over 500 people, calling the captains to the center of the mat, flipping the coin, starting and stopping each match, making all the calls, awarding all the points, in short running the whole show, and yet being treated in many respects as if I wasn't even there; the more I felt like I needed some sage sociological advice.

Method

In an attempt to "objectify" my observations, I began to carry with me on all refereeing assignments a tape recorder into which I dictated my observations. (Most dictation occurred immediately following a given meet.) On returning home, I replayed what I had dictated and supplemented my observations with more "theoretical" comments. These observations took place over a two-year period, during which I officiated at approximately fifty dual meets and three tournaments. In addition to recording my personal observations, I began a fairly systematic process of interviewing fellow referees; in total I questioned individually approximately ten other referees and eight coaches. These interviews occurred over a period of approximately 18 months. On two other occasions, I initiated a group discussion among my fellow referees at referee meetings. All of this material was transcribed and later coded.

Observations

From my own experiences and discussions with others I began to see quite early the role of the referee in highly ritualistic terms. Put a slightly different way, the referee was perceived and related to outside the normal "rules" of interpersonal empathy. Most people, most of the time, did not hate, or even dislike, referees though this is what I had originally believed; for the most part they just did not care one way or another. The referee, though in the center of the action, was seen and treated as an outsider. . . .

This unwillingness or inability to identify with referees seemed to explain many of my own findings from the tentative, awkward way people tended to treat me when I was in uniform to the heavy abuse I often received while refereeing. I had always been willing to accept that people might get upset with me if I had made a decision which they thought was wrong, especially if it went against their team. I was not, however, ready for the abusive form in which such criticism was expressed. It was not so much what they said or did—there are fairly severe restrictions on what you can and cannot say to a referee without incurring certain automatic penalties—as the complete indifference they showed for me as a person. To put it simply, no one seemed to care how I, the referee, felt. The contrast with other social situations was striking. In most everyday life situations, no matter how angry or upset you are with someone, the mores of sociability require that you show some sort of consideration for the feelings of the persons with whom you are dealing and that you somehow attempt to negotiate your differences. No such rules seemed to apply to relationships with a referee.

The first time I confronted this—it was the third meet I had refereed—I was flabbergasted. What had I done to deserve such abuse? What was going on? What was even more amazing, however, was that a week later when I ran into the coach who had abused me, he greeted me as if nothing at all had happened. In our brief conversation the only reference he made to our previous encounter—in which I had had to charge him with a technical violation and threaten to throw him out of the gym; and he had accused me of a litany of sins covering prejudice, stupidity, etc.— was to say "I hope you didn't take anything I said personally."

He meant it: he had been arguing with a referee; I just happened to have been that referee.

Initially it might seem as if this extreme disregard for the referee reflects a general disdain for the referee. Nothing could be farther from the truth. While the referee is treated at one level as if he or she is a nonentity, at another, he or she is treated almost with awe (the tentative, awkward quality mentioned earlier). In some ways I found this formal deference more off-putting than the abuse. Whatever the contestants and coaches may think of you personally or professionally, as the referee you are in charge and they know it. Moreover, they are not going to let you forget it or allow you to share your responsibility with anyone else.

This situation was made very clear to me early in my refereeing career. I was working my second or third varsity meet. Ideally, first-year referees are limited to junior high and junior varsity competitions. Given my past experience, age, and most importantly the shortage of referees, I was also assigned to a number of varsity meets my first year. . . .

One of the responsibilities of a varsity referee, which is not normally a responsibility of a junior high or a junior varsity referee, is to supervise the weighing in of the wrestlers. In actuality, the coaches usually do the weighing in, but the referee is there to make the decision if the coaches cannot agree. I had never run a weigh-in before though I had been told what to do. Specifically, I had been told to (1) set the scale for the proper weight, (2) hold the indicator up, (3) have the wrestler step on the scale, and (4) let the indicator go. If it dropped off the top, the wrestler "made weight." This is the procedure I followed under the watchful eyes of not only both coaches but also the athletic director of one of the schools who was also a certified referee. In one case, as I let go of the indicator it dropped approximately a quarter of an inch then went back up. Since it had dropped, I said the contestant had "made weight" and the weighing-in proceeded. Approximately, ten minutes later, while the wrestlers were getting into uniform, the athletic director-referee came over to me to inform me that the boy had not "made weight," explaining that, in determining eligibility, the indicator could not go back up. Furthermore, he told me that both coaches and the wrestler himself felt that he had not made weight. I asked him why no one had said anything. His answer: "You're the referee. Your decision."

Such deference was not, however, always forthcoming. I was surprised, however, how often it was. A suggestion, on my part, to the effect that the mats were not taped properly would lead to the retaping of the mats. Hair and nails judged too long by me would be immediately cut. My nod toward fans sitting too close to the mat would bring supervisory personnel running. Moreover, this deferential behavior was just as much, if not more, likely to be exhibited by the same people who the next moment treated me as if I did not exist.

This deference was consistent with a comment I kept hearing during my first year. Often, during my first year, a more experienced referee observed me while I refereed. If I had been assigned to a junior varsity meet, the referee assigned to the varsity meet would often be present to watch me judge the last few matches. Similarly, there would often be two referees assigned to do a junior high school meet because of the number of matches involved. From these referees and also from a few of the more experienced coaches who knew it was my first year, I kept hearing "nice job, but be a little more decisive." To be honest I did not really know what they meant. When I asked, I got a range of answers: "Yell out your calls louder." "Use your hands more." "Hesitate less, when making your calls."

I was struck by another thing which I originally did not connect with any of this. No one seemed to mind, or at least not to mind nearly as much as I would have thought, when I penalized a wrestler for breaking some rule, even when the infraction was minuscule. High school wrestlers are not allowed to lock their hands in certain situations, or grab clothing; similarly, certain holds become illegal if pushed beyond a certain limit. In all situations the idea is to protect the wrestlers from injury and to prevent one wrestler from taking unfair advantage of the other. The problem is that during a match one wrestler may inadvertently break one of these rules in a manner which really does not take unfair advantage of the other wrestler, but for a period of time which cannot be dismissed as not having happened or as due solely to "reaction time." The rules require that such infractions be penalized by awarding points to the other wrestler; points which may very well determine the outcome of a match. I quickly learned that if I saw such an infraction, no matter how trivial, I was better off calling it than letting it go.

What all these things: the formal deference, the request that I be decisive, the desire to go by the book, had in common was the notion that I was expected to maintain order "no matter what." Everyone else—participants, fans, even coaches—could, and in fact, was expected to, get emotionally involved in the contest; it was my responsibility as the referee to insure that the show proceeded in an orderly manner. In short, in order for everyone else to enjoy and to be able to participate in the contest, I as the referee had to remain an outsider.

As a non-person/outsider, my contact with everyone was governed by procedures which were highly ritualistic. I was part of a performance. Nowhere did this become more apparent than in what could be called "sideline confrontations," i.e., situations where a coach loudly questions some action or decision from on or near the team's bench.

The first time I was exposed to such "questioning" I responded to it much as I might have responded to such heated comments in any other situation. I tried to calm the coach down and to explain as clearly as possible why I had done what I had done with extensive and adequate reference to the governing rules. Rather than calming him down, everything I said seemed to make him angrier and more abusive. Finally, in desperation I said: "That's it, sit down and be quiet!" Without a peep, that is exactly what he did. Initially, I did not give the incident much thought. I figured that he really knew that I was right and had decided not to argue anymore. When this chain of events happened for a third time, however, I began to realize that it was more complicated than that. I remember going over to the coach after this third incident when the meet was over and asking him to explain why he had questioned me on a rule when he knew I was right. His answer, especially the matter of fact way he gave it, floored me: "Oh, I did that for my boys; if I ever really want to question you on anything I would not do it that way." His point was clear: I had been part of a ritual performance and had not been aware of it.

Reviewing my own experiences and discussions with other referees, it became clear that coaches follow two very different procedures when they criticize a referee. The performance is just that and is not meant to be taken seriously by the referee. Its purpose is to arouse the team and perhaps the fans. While it is usually based on some incident which could be questioned, the legitimacy of the call is seldom really in question. In fact, the last thing a coach wants from a referee in such a situation is a rational explanation of why he or she did what was done. All such a discussion can accomplish is to show that the coach is wrong and undercut his or her position. What the coach wants is an opportunity to yell and then to be told to sit down or risk being thrown out. The coach wants to be threatened, not reasoned with. . . .

If, in contrast to this situation, a coach really does want to question how a referee has interpreted a rule, the approach is quite different. The coach will approach the scorer's table and indicate that he or she would like to speak to the referee if possible. (This is the procedure stipulated in the rules.) The referee and the coach will then move "off stage" behind the scorer's table. The coach will then ask the referee in a most polite fasion to explain what had happened. If the coach thinks a rule has been misapplied or ignored, he or she will say so. If the coach is correct, it is very possible that the referee will change the call. If the referee still disagrees, the coach is likely to go back to the bench with little more than an unhappy nod. Usually what happens is that such situations prove not to represent differences of opinion regarding the rules, but rather a difference of judgment which makes different rules applicable. For example, the referee stops the match and breaks a hold one wrestler has on another. The coach of the wrestler on whom the hold had been used comes over to question why a penalty point was not given out since "illegal" holds should be penalized. The referee answers that he or she judged it to be a potentially dangerous hold, not an illegal hold, i.e., while the arm was being pushed in a potentially dangerous way it did not reach the point of being illegal.

Such situations, of course, may end up in heated arguments. For the most part, however, they do not. The discussions are relatively calm and well mannered. In a sideline performance nothing could be more different.

Despite the differences in the way a referee is likely to be treated in these two situations, they are similar in that in both situations there is a maintenance of distance. The referee is treated more as a symbol of authority than as a real person. In one case the symbol is ritually attacked whereas in the other case it is formally beseeched. In neither case, however, are the rules of give and take, mutual sensitivity, and reciprocity which govern most social interactions likely to apply. Insofar as they do apply, however, they are likely to apply in the "off stage" interactions. I judged only three out of over 50 such situations as entailing any sort of mutual sensitivity, and all three occurred "off stage."

Little if any creative negotiation occurs during a meet, but a fair amount of such negotiation does occur before a meet. It is not unusual, for example, for both coaches and the referee to negotiate how rigidly certain rules will be interpreted before the meet begins. This is especially the case with the rules which apply to "stalling." (Each wrestler is expected to be aggressive and can be penalized for being too defensive.) Similar negotiations occur over uniforms, hair length, and even acceptable weight limits. All such negotiations, however, must occur before the meet and in private.

While these procedures are followed in general in all contests, the strictness with which they are adhered to varies with the type of meet, i.e., junior high, junior varsity, varsity, and tournaments. As might be expected, it is generally the case that the more important the meet, i.e., the higher the level of competition, the more rigorously the procedures are followed. In the case of junior high and junior varsity meets, coaches and referees generally work on the principle that the meet is as much a learning experience for the contestants as anything else. As such there is greater cooperation and less confrontation between referee and coaches. From my own observations, however, another factor plays a more important role, namely that in such meets there are normally other professionals present. (As noted above in junior high and junior varsity meets, two or more referees are normally present.) The presence of the other referees plus the fact that the junior high and junior varsity coaches are usually less experienced allows for more open discussion of rules, judgments, etc. without threatening the referee's overall control of the situation.

The extent to which such group support allows for more substantive discussion without loss of control accounts for what otherwise would be a paradoxical situation, namely that in what are probably the most important matches—i.e., tournaments—there is more substantive negotiation than in varsity dual meets. While I observed no such discussions in varsity dual meets, I observed a number of such discussions in tournaments. The reason for this is that in a tournament match, the referee on the mat is not alone; he is supported by two other referees who serve as judges observing the match from the sidelines. This allows for much more open discussion of calls without jeopardizing official control since the referees as a group can impose closure whenever they choose.

The overriding need for some mechanism imposing "official" closure is due to the fact that it is impossible to be a "perfect" referee. Every referee is going to make mistakes, usually mistakes of judgment. Furthermore, every referee is going to find himself in a position, sooner or later, where in order to fulfill one rule, he or she will have to ignore another rule. There are a number of reasons for this: the rules never cover all situations; the referee cannot be in all places at once; referees work under considerable pressure, requiring them to make instantaneous judgments, referees are "human." Every referee knows this; more importantly, at one level so does everyone else. However, to admit this publicly can undermine the very legitimacy and meaning of the contest. Consequently there is need to gloss the whole issue.[1]

The fact that every referee is bound to make at least one or two errors in any contest makes it that much more difficult to correct an error once it is made. This is one of the true ironies of refereeing. Everyone knows that the referee is going to make a mistake somewhere, but everyone also has a vested interest in maintaining the illusion that such mistakes do not in fact happen. To admit that such mistakes not only happen, but happen regularly would create a situation where every close call would be disputed as if it was the "one," i.e., the mistake. The result would be constant bickering and the end to the orderly running of the contest. As a consequence, the mistake is normally buried and treated as if it was not a mistake. A coach might object, knowing that "this time, he is right," but also knowing that the way the game is played, the referee is not about to change the call once it has been made. The referee, for his or her part, also knows that even if a second later he or she realizes the call was a mistake, he or she is "stuck" with it. (The exception here is that a referee can often change the ruling if it has not yet been challenged.) . . .

Final Comments

To a large extent the role of the referee is an idiosyncratic one. Nevertheless, it sheds considerable light on the process of normative negotiations.

The role of the referee is clearly a more ritualistic role than most. The reasons for this, as I have shown, are that the referee has responsibility for maintaining social order in an extremely tenuous social situation. In a very real sense he or she functions as the communal "scape goat." Participants, coaches, and audience all know that their vision of the "idealized" sporting contest can never be realized, but they remain committed to their vision. It is the referee's job to personally take on the inconsistencies and ambiguities of reality and to ritualistically transform the actual contest into the ordered contest they all desire. Creative social negotiations of rules and meanings are called for when dealing with "social reality;" when people are engaged in accepted social rituals as means of insulating them from this reality, they demand correct performances.

Note

1. Not everyone, of course, plays as fairly as everyone else. There are always one or two coaches who want a slight edge. If they can get a referee to favor them ever so slightly, all the better. The most obvious way to do this is to try to intimidate the referee; to let the referee know that any close call that goes against their team will be met by argumentation and aggravation. A second approach is to be very friendly. To an experienced referee one approach is as unappealing as the other. Furthermore, though an inexperienced referee might be influenced by a well-orchestrated attack once or twice, he or she will become immune within a year. Most experienced coaches know this and consequently only try to work on the feelings of inexperienced referees. It is nearly always only inexperienced coaches who attempt to work on the feelings of experienced referees.

35 After Death in the Hospital

BARNEY G. GLASER
ANSELM L. STRAUSS

Many aspects of our daily lives have left the private sphere and come under the control of organizations. Such is the case with death in American society. Today more than half of all deaths occur in hospitals. Even in cases where families want very much to keep dying relatives at home, they typically send them to the hospital for the death scene. This is in sharp contrast to such places as Greece, Malaya, and Italy, where families typically insist that hospitalized patients who come near the point of death be moved home so that they can be with family when they die.

Studying the process of dying in hospitals, Glaser and Strauss found that although nursing and medical students are taught skills to treat the bodies of patients, their training neglects the psychosocial aspects of dying. The behavior of medical personnel in the presence of dying patients and their families is primarily influenced by "common sense" assumptions, not by professional training.

At your own death (which, granted, is seldom pleasant to consider), would you prefer to be in a hospital or at home? If you prefer the hospital, in most instances this is easy to arrange. If you prefer being at home, however, how do you think you could arrange it? What obstacles do you think you would have to overcome? Finally, what changes do you think could be made in the training of medical personnel so they could be more comforting at the time of death?

The Death Announcement

IF FAMILY MEMBERS ARE AT THE HOSPITAL but not at the death scene, the death first must be announced to them. Several conditions give this crucial announcement greater or less potential for creating a "wailing scene" that may disturb the ward. Various conditions of the patient's dying trajectory [An individual's particular course or process of dying], as well as the kinsmen's reputation for behavior, which has developed among staff, will have provided some indication of how they will react to this announcement.

If, during a lingering trajectory, the family have been made aware by successive preannouncements that the patient was dying, and have also been told when he was likely to die, then staff usually expect them—or at least the strongest members—to be able to take the news with composure. Little explanation is required. Nor is any special announcement ritual needed. Almost any of the nurses or residents can convey the news; it can be passed on in the hallway, or waiting room, or even at the nursing station. Under this configuration of conditions, the death announcement is, in effect, the confirmation of a long-expected event. Since this is the easiest interactional situation for staff to handle at this trying moment, some doctors and nurses try whenever possible to prepare family members by keeping them continually informed. Once told of the dying trajectory, some family members, too, try to create a reputation for being easily informed, so as to encourage staff unhesitatingly to make successive preannouncements and the death announcement on time.

It is more difficult to announce death when the family of the lingering patient has been "left out" of the dying situation—when they have not been made clearly aware of the approach of death. They may have been denied access to clues or may have perceived them ambiguously; or they may have pretended not to recognize them. In any case, if kinsmen's knowledge of impending death has not been clear or has been denied in the eyes of staff, their reputation is one of less than adequate preparation, indicating that they are likely not to take a simple death announcement well. The news must then come from the doctor, the only legitimate source of such information; some sort of explanation is needed to fill in their vague knowledge and erase their doubts or denial of what had been happening earlier. The explanation usually includes a temporalized resume of the dying trajectory and the hospital career provided for it: "As you know, his chances weren't very good, but we did everything we could." If possible, the announcement is made in an office or an empty room in order both to provide a quiet, somewhat formal setting for the solemn news and to insulate family reactions. These crucial announcements, then, are spatially and temporally managed with care to avoid scenes that may spill over to disrupt the sentimental order of the ward.

Announcing death to family members of a patient whose death ended a quick dying trajectory is usually difficult. There has been little time to prepare them. Preannouncements a few days ahead are few, brief, and usually grave. The death itself must be announced while family members are still trying to accept the fact that the patient is dying. However, explanations of quick death are generally specific, and the death announcement ("He had a coronary") may not require any addition to what the preannouncements provided. Therefore, the announcement can be made by a nurse as well as the doctor. The fact of death is all that needs to be communicated, and the intensity of care at the death might prevent the doctor from appearing as speedily as the nurse. But with the announcement must come consolations about the rapidity of the dying trajectory. The nurse expects to spend some time in helping the family remain composed; if her consoling is not adequate, she may call other nurses, aides, chaplains, nuns, clerks, or other family members, depending on who is available for such backstopping. The doctor may be called upon later to provide explanations as to why medical science cannot as yet prevent this kind of quick death. In all these cases, an effort is made to provide privacy for the announcement.

As we stated elsewhere, the unexpected quick death comes as a surprise to the family. With no preannouncement to help prepare the family, staff have no idea how they may react. They usually expect the worst. Moreover, since the unexpected quick death is also a surprise to staff members, they must, first of all, announce the death to each other and maintain or regain their own composure. Then one of them—preferably the doctor, who can legitimize the death and its suddenness—approaches the family, usually ushers them into the privacy of a closed room, and engages in a "prolonged announcement." That is, he builds up to the news of the death. This build-up describes the patient's condition, tells what he was doing before the surprise, and explains why saving him was impossible. Then follows a more general explanation about how people die this way, why death cannot be forestalled by medicine, or under what conditions it could be prevented. This general kind of announcement may be truncated by a doctor who is too upset to go on. Or the announcement may be stopped also by family members going into shock, wailing loudly, threatening suicide, or making accusations. Further talk is not meaningful.

Without any reputation for potential behavior, kinsmen are fully expected to "go to pieces" until they prove otherwise to staff. Doctors and nurses have several coping strategies in this explosive situation. Personnel in emergency wards are especially adept at these strategies. For example, if an accident case is brought in DOA ("dead on arrival") or dies soon after entry, his family may initially be notified that he had had an accident and that his condition is undetermined but could be grave. Or on a medical ward the nurse phones and says, "The patient has taken a turn for the worse. Would you please come?" Thus the trip to the hospital gives family members time to get somewhat used to the idea of possible death, even if they can hardly be expected to be adequately prepared for it. The nursing staff also likes such strategies because they feel the doctor should be the one to announce the death.

A similar false preannouncement leading to brief preparations may be used for families who are at the hospital waiting for news about someone in the ICU, in surgery, or in the emergency ward, when the timing of the death allows the staff a chance to act as if the dying trajectory were still in progress. The staff can then, since the family cannot invade the sick room or get information elsewhere, have time to wait before giving the death announcement. This situation may be created even if the family is at the patient's bedside when he suddenly starts to die quickly. The alert nurse quickly ushers the family out, saying that the patient requires a quick treatment or procedure done in private. The mildly panicked family then waits until the nurse reports on the patient, preparing themselves for the worst. The nurse must find a doctor both to pronounce death and then to tell the family. If none is immediately available, and if she fears the family may come back into the patient's room to see what is going on, she may then announce the death herself. This alternative of earlier announcing outside the room reduces the dangers of a potential scene.

Another strategy is to choose the best person for giving the surprise announcement, letting the doctor explain later. The person may be someone who is good at giving consolation, such as a social worker, a chaplain, or a nun. Or it may be someone close to the family—a friend who has visited with them, or, after an accident, the family doctor who has been called. The family may be sized up quickly and then the strongest member told, leaving to him the job of telling others in the family. These strategies build into the announcement a variety of specialized people who are ready to help the family through the shock and to prevent scenes. In any case, the staff stands ready to tranquilize or sedate and possibly provide a hospital bed to any family member needing it.

The importance both of preparation and of careful strategy in announcing a death is highlighted by instances in which neither was used. In one unusual case a physician on an emergency ward, shocked at the death of a patient, ran to the waiting room and told the mother, who suspected nothing, that her son had just died. The woman shrieked and wailed. Others in the waiting room became highly agitated. The nurses, horrified at what the doctor had done, attempted to restore calm to the doctor as well as to the visitors. When the doctor recovered, he returned to the grieving woman and with apologies took her into a private office and started to explain what he knew of the sudden death—an effort that also consoled the staff.

Sometimes, regardless of the preannouncement conditions or the kind of death, a doctor who finds this job particularly difficult finds ways to avoid announcing to the family. He may leave the hospital before the death, giving no instructions but knowing that in his absence someone else must announce to the waiting family. Or, upon leaving, he may instruct the nurse to tell the family members (whom he had told the patient was dying) if the patient should die. One nurse caught in this situation realized that the doctor had slipped away precisely to avoid the death announcement. She became furious. Her countertactic was to notify the doctor and "let him tell the family." A doctor might answer with an "order" for the nurse to call the family. Other nurses have suffered through their anger or have turned the task over to the resident who pronounced the death. Doctors tend to use this tactic to avoid being bothered at night.

Successive preannouncements do not necessarily prepare family members adequately. Indeed, their preannouncement reactions may establish for them poor reputations for maintaining composure. They cry too easily and too loudly, faint or become accusing, barrage staff with questions without listening to the answers, or ask unanswerable questions ("Why him of all people?"). Announcements are made to such family members as carefully as to the unprepared kinsmen during a quick, sudden trajectory. Again, the strongest member may be told, and sent home with the family with orders to tell them there. In some cases, staff almost never directly inform certain family members, either for the time being or "forever"—for example, relatives who are severely ill themselves, mothers of premature babies, or aged grandparents who might die from the news. The hospital then may search for a strong family member to tell—usually a distant relative—asking him to sign necessary papers. A husband of a wife who has given birth to a "preemie" who then dies may receive an immediate announcement and be asked to tell his wife when she wakes or is "ready" for the news.

The Last Look

There are several distinct phases of the end of the trajectory when family members may take their last looks at the patient. They may do so during a farewell or during the death watch; at death, if they participate in the death scene; or after death in the hospital, before his body is sent to the funeral home. Some do not take a last look, preferring to remember the patient "as he was."

The hospital staff is usually generous in allowing the last looks before death. Indeed, sometimes they suggest them. "Now you go over and look at him tonight," said one nurse to a mother, implying that she might never see him alive again. After death, however, staff seldom suggest a last look. It is unusual to hear a nurse say after death, as one did, "You can see the patient if you wish." For staff members consider the risks of emotional upset during an after-death last look too great, particularly if the mode of death is not "viewable" to laymen. Moreover, it is an unusual hospital indeed which has personnel both available and prepared for the task of ushering the family into the room for its look and handling the consequences for the sentimental order.

Requests for such post-death last looks mainly occur on the quick-dying wards (ICU, operating room, emergency, and premature babies). On these wards family members are not allowed at the death scene, since their presence would interfere with the intense efforts to save the patient. As we have stated, these families are relatively unprepared for the death. They may not have had any chance to see the patient after the quick trajectory started, and hence are not directly aware of the often drastically changed appearance. Yet, precisely because they have not seen the patient during his dying, they are likely to need a last look after death, to say goodbye and to recognize the reality of the death. They wish to see for themselves; they wish to come to terms with the *mystic gap* between their kinsman alive and their kinsman suddenly and astoundingly dead. Hence, after announcing death the doctor must be ready to manage the family's request for one last look at the patient.

On the lingering dying wards, requests for a last look after death are less frequent, and those who ask are likely to be better able to maintain composure. Family members, unless kept completely unaware, usually have had sufficient time to make farewells and take tentative last looks before death, and to become prepared for the death. As we have pointed out, intimate family members often participate in the death scene and thus have a last look at the time of death.

When relatives request or even demand a last look at the body before it goes to the funeral home, the doctor's or nurse's decision rests on several conditions. First and foremost, the possibility of a scene (especially in cases of quick deaths) is considered. How insistent is the family member? Insistence itself is prime evidence for the probability of a scene. Yet, adequately supervised, the last look can afford the staff an opportunity to help the distressed, insistent family member gain composure. If they appear to be going to pieces, less insistent family members may be talked out of taking a last look.

Another decision that must be made about the family's last look is how long it will last and where it will take place. In the United States, the hospital viewing is usually expected to last only a few moments, to be taken up later in the funeral home. The family member who breaks down, then, can be whisked out of the room to control the scene. The family can take its last look anywhere in the hospital without threatening the sentimental order too much, although the staff may think twice about permitting it on an open or crowded ward where even brief crying is disturbing to many. Also, in only a few moments on an ICU or an emergency ward, a family member can knock over precious equipment. If the risk of a scene is great, the body may be moved to a private or treatment room for the viewing; or it may take place in the hospital morgue or autopsy room.

In Asia the last look may be considerably longer; in Japan, for example, it may be many hours. Since in these hospitals patients often die on open wards, the potential for disturbing scenes is great. In Japan, a post-mortem room (in the basement or on the grounds) is provided for the whole family and the body until the following day; thus the affair is isolated from everyone. In Malaya, a Chinese family just floods the open ward and wails at least ceremoniously, while an Indian family may take its last look on the ward and then repair to the courtyard to cry and moan.

The number of people involved is also an important consideration for averting scenes. In the United States, only a few close family members typically are allowed to see the body at the hospital. The remainder of the family and friends must wait until the undertaker has prepared the body. American hospitals, therefore, can become chaotic when a foreign person dies and his entire family, following their home custom, invades the ward for a last look. We learned of an extreme situation that arose when an Italian Gypsy queen died in a county hospital; not only her family but hundreds of her followers piled into the ward for a last look. The staff had no ready strategy to handle such a disturbance. In some Japanese hospitals, however, the whole family may come for the last look, but there is no problem because they are isolated in the patient's room. In Asia and Europe the ward may simply have to put up with many grief-stricken family members.

Also related to the "scene potential" is the presentability of the patient. This factor has an inverse relationship with the family's "need" for an after-death last look: relatives of quick-dying patients are more likely to request last looks after death, but less likely to be prepared for the fact of death. Patients who have had quick deaths are often more dreadful to view than others are. The causal accident or seizure often disfigures; the consequent heroic treatment often compounds the unpleasantness. Viewing bodies of lingering patients who have withered away or whose bodies have partly degenerated can also be devastating to kinsmen; but, since post-death viewing is less common in these cases, and since kinsmen have been aware of dying's toll, it poses fewer problems.

Mode of death thus compounds the problem of preventing scenes during last looks. When an awesome mode of death makes the patient unviewable by the uninitiated, the doctor or nurse usually tries to talk the relative out of a last look. They almost routinely do so, for example, with parents of premature babies. If the mother never saw it alive, nurses maneuver to prevent a last look, usually by saying firmly that "it's just as well" she not see it. If the mother or father insists, the doctor is called to counsel strongly against it. With surgical deaths, when the body is mutilated, the doctor advises the family to wait until the body is prepared at the funeral home. He suggests that the relative would probably prefer to "remember him as he was," and the relative usually acquiesces, particularly when assured that the patient died peacefully, which gives the relative an imaginary or symbolic last look. In the case of accidents, which have a high scene potential if the body is mutilated, the strategy is to re-move it to the hospital morgue or to the coroner as fast as possible. Prompt removal precludes a last look. As one nurse said when the relatives arrived on a county emergency ward, "They want to see him, so you'd better get him out of here in a hurry." Faced with a fait accompli, the relatives must wait until they can view the body at the funeral home.

In effect, when the mode of death is too unpleasant to allow the rel-ative a last look, the hospital staff provides relatives with a "symbolic" last look. In the case of preemies, mothers are left to their idealized images of babies. In the case of accident, surgical or other intensive-care cases, the relatives are asked to remember their best image of the person until they view him at the funeral home (where experts attempt to recreate this im-age). For these relatives, the mystic gap between life and death is closed symbolically. This may make the gap harder to grasp at the moment, but eases the threat to the ward's sentimental order posed by a potential hys-terical scene.

When the relative does have a last look, the mystic gap may be closed more realistically—but sometimes more harshly. To ease the harsh reality when the mode of death has disfigured the body, the staff makes an effort to make it more presentable. They try to make the patient appear as the relatives might "remember him." They put a smile on his face to replace a grimace of pain. They dress him in fresh pajamas or even street clothes. They hide, bandage, or disguise mutilated or severely damaged parts of the body that would be exposed. A chaplain reported of a surgical death that he "stalled and handled the relatives while the doctors went out and fixed the body just the way the body is sometimes fixed in the funeral parlor, and they put something on the patient's head so he wouldn't look so bloody." The staff may also remove the body from a surgical or emer-gency ward to an empty room in order to help "neutralize" the viewing. Sometimes staff insist that relatives who have requested a last look take it before the autopsy, in case the body is further disfigured beyond repair at the funeral home.

All in all, then, the patient's presentability is a temporally organized phenomenon that occurs quickly within the routines of the hospital. The staff has only a short time to fix up the body and to allow a last look before it is removed to the morgue, autopsy room, or funeral home. Seldom will they keep a body on a ward for hours while a family comes from afar for a last look; the delay would be too disturbing for the staff and too intrusive on needed hospital space.

The patient's appearance is also of concern to family members wish-ing to protect other, more upset members from a last look. A strong rel-ative sometimes forbids a weaker one from seeing the body, particularly when damage or distortion is great. The strong member immediately, in trying to protect the living, makes and enforces the decision. In one such case, a daughter discovered her father's death upon arrival at the hospital; although surprised, she immediately recovered her control. Once the fact of death was established, her immediate reaction was, "I'll go catch mother." She intercepted her approaching mother in the hall, asserted that there was no point in her going into the patient's room, and sent her home with assurances that she would handle details.

The Last Touch and Ushering

The last look also presents a control problem beyond that of maintaining composure. The person who users in or escorts the relative must be able to handle a relative's need for a last touch—a none-too-easy task. Touching the body is part of relatives' effort to help close the mystic gap between life and death. It is typical for the relative at first to stand silently with disbelief and just look at the body. As the realization of death seeps in he touches it. The touch may be highly charged, may trigger highly emotional outbursts. In one instance reported to us, parents grabbed hold of their child and cried, "He's not dead, he's not dead," as they hugged and hugged the small boy. The nurse, a practiced "usher," was able to dislodge them after fifteen minutes. In another case, a daughter buried her face in her dead father's neck; the nurse could not free her and an orderly was called to help tear the girl loose. Thus, the mystic gap between life and death was forcefully closed. In another instance, a boy became hysterical on viewing his dead father, tore the cushions from the chairs, beat his fists on the walls, then grabbed the body and would not let go. He screamed, "You killed my father, he can't be dead." Again the nurse had to call for help. A chaplain, in this case, "talked" the boy away; by talking, the mystic gap closed. The doctor then gave him a sedative.

Happily, many last touches are gentle and moving, bringing to both the relative and the usher a modicum of composure—and perhaps closure. The relative may kiss the body, stroke the cheek, caress the hands, run hands through the hair, touch all the face areas. These touches seem to be a matter of assuring oneself that "everything is in place"; and thus they help close the mystic gap. Such a final, formal farewell is made even more real by touching a body that is still warm. The relative realizes he is saying goodbye at the point of genuine departure. The staff member watches and waits for the right moment, when the disbelief in death disappears, then gently ushers the relative out and takes him back to the family group.

The usher for these delicate situations often is a nurse who has a demonstrated flair for handling herself and family members. But others, too, may serve: a clerk, social worker, doctor, resident, aide, chaplain, nun. By and large however, personnel adept at ushering are relatively rare, and the task itself is sometimes not well understood. On one ward a head nurse was so unnerved by the last-look situation that she would not allow even capable nurses to usher in relatives. Rather than preserving the ward's sentimental order, her prohibition jolted it, for the nurses "felt the family should have an opportunity to see the body just to *realize* that the patient was really dead." Moreover, the relatives' closure of the mystic gap concerns the nurses also, because it helps reinforce their own closure on the death.

36 Violence and the Police

WILLIAM A. WESTLEY

My personal contacts with the police have been infrequent and brief. Nevertheless, I have seen a policeman handcuff a suspect to a tree and slap him in the face in front of a group of citizen-witnesses. I have heard another threaten the life of a suspect he was escorting near a stream, saying he wished the suspect would attempt to flee so he "could shoot her and watch her body float down the river." And in Mexico, after recovering my billfold and apprehending the two men who had picked my pocket, the police offered to hold the culprits while I beat them. They felt this would be justified because the men had caused me (and presumably them) so much trouble.

These random events have convinced me that police violence is no random matter but is a regular part of the occupation. Why should this be so? Is it because the police recruit certain personality types? Westley, as a sociologist, examines interactions, social constraints, community norms, and relationships between groups to uncover the answer to this question.

If you were a social reformer and wanted to decrease police violence, where would you start? Remember to keep in mind the support for police violence that is built into the occupation.

BRUTALITY AND THE THIRD DEGREE have been identified with the municipal police of the United States since their inauguration in 1844.[1] These aspects of police activity have been subject to exaggeration, repeated exposure, and virulent criticism. Since they are a breach of the law by the law-enforcement agents, they constitute a serious social, but intriguing sociological, problem. Yet there is little information about or understanding of the process through which such activity arises or of the purposes which it serves.

This paper is concerned with the genesis and function of the illegal use of violence by the police and presents an explanation based on an interpretative understanding of the experience of the police as an occupational group.[2] It shows that (a) the police accept and morally justify their legal use of violence; (b) such acceptance and justification arise through their occupational experience; and (c) its use is functionally related to the collective occupational, as well as to the legal, ends of the police.

The analysis which follows offers both an occupational perspective on the use of violence by the police and an explanation of policing as an occupation, from the perspective of the illegal use of violence. Thus the meaning of this use of violence is derived by relating it to the general behavior of policemen as policemen, and occupations in general are illuminated through the delineation of the manner in which a particular occupation handles one aspect of its work.

The technical demands of a man's work tend to specify the kinds of social relationships in which he will be involved and to select the groups with whom these relationships are to be maintained. The social definition of the occupation invests its members with a common prestige position. Thus, a man's occupation is a major determining factor of his conduct and social identity. This being so, it involves more than man's work, and one must go beyond the technical in the explanation of work behavior. One must discover the occupationally derived definitions of self and conduct which arise in the involvements of technical demands, social relationships between colleagues and with the public, status, and self-conception. To understand these definitions, one must track them back to the occupational problems in which they have their genesis.[3]

The policeman finds his most pressing problems in his relationships to the public. His is a service occupation but of an incongruous kind, since he must discipline those whom he serves. He is regarded as corrupt and inefficient by, and meets with hostility and criticism from, the public. He regards the public as his enemy, feels his occupation to be in conflict with the community, and regards himself to be a pariah. The experience and the feeling give rise to a collective emphasis on secrecy, an attempt to coerce respect from the public, and a belief that almost any means are legitimate in completing an important arrest. These are for the policeman basic occupational values. They arise from his experience, take precedence over his legal responsibilities, are central to an understanding of his conduct, and form the occupational contexts within which violence gains its meaning. This then is the background for our analysis.[4]

The materials which follow are drawn from a case study of a municipal police department in an industrial city of approximately one hundred and fifty thousand inhabitants. This study included participation in all types of police activities, ranging from walking the beat and cruising with policemen in a squad car to the observation of raids, interrogations, and the police school. It included intensive interviews with over half the men in the department who were representative as to rank, time in service, race, religion, and specific type of police job.

Duty and Violence

In the United States the use of violence by the police is both an occupational prerogative and a necessity. Police powers include the use of violence, for to them, within civil society, has been delegated the monopoly of the legitimate means of violence possessed by the state. Police are obliged by their duties to use violence as the only measure adequate to control and apprehension in the presence of counterviolence.

Violence in the form of the club and the gun is for the police a means of persuasion. Violence from the criminal, the drunk, the quarreling family, and the rioter arises in the course of police duty. The fighting drunk who is damaging property or assailing his fellows and who looks upon the policeman as a malicious intruder justifies for the policeman his use of force in restoring order. The armed criminal who has demonstrated a casual regard for the lives of others and a general hatred of the policeman forces the use of violence by the police in the pursuit of duty. Every policeman has some such experiences, and they proliferate in police lore. They constitute a common-sense and legal justification for the use of violence by the police and for training policemen in the skills of violence. Thus, from experience in the pursuit of their legally prescribed duties, the police develop a justification for the use of violence. They come to see it as good, as useful, and as their own. Furthermore, although legally their use of violence is limited to the requirements of the arrest and the protection of themselves and the community, the contingencies of their occupation lead them to enlarge the area in which violence may be used. Two kinds of experience—that with respect to the conviction of the felon and that with respect to the control of sexual conduct—will illustrate how and why the illegal use of violence arises.

1. *The conviction of the felon.*—The apprehension and conviction of the felon is, for the policeman, the essence of police work. It is the source of prestige both within and outside police circles, it has career implications, and it is a major source of justification for the existence of the police before a critical and often hostile public. Out of these conditions a legitimation for the illegal use of violence is wrought.

The career and prestige implication of the "good pinch"[5] elevate it to a major end in the conduct of the policeman. It is an end which is justified both legally and through public opinion as one which should be of great concern to the police. Therefore it takes precedence over other duties and tends to justify strong means. Both trickery and violence are such means. The "third degree" has been criticized for many years, and extensive administrative controls have been devised in an effort to eliminate it. Police persistence in the face of that attitude suggests that the illegal use of violence is regarded as functional to their work. It also indicates a tendency to regard the third degree as a legitimate means for obtaining the conviction of the felon. However, to understand the strength of this legitimation, one must include other factors: the competition between patrolman and detectives and the publicity value of convictions for the police department.

The patrolman has less access to cases that might result in the "good pinch" than the detective. Such cases are assigned to the detective, and for their solution he will reap the credit. Even where the patrolman first detects the crime, or actually apprehends the possible offender, the case is likely to be turned over to the detective. Therefore patrolmen are eager to obtain evidence and make the arrest before the arrival of the detectives. Intimidation and actual violence frequently come into play under these conditions. This is illustrated in the following case recounted by a young patrolman when he was questioned as to the situations in which he felt the use of force was necessary.

> One time Joe and I found three guys in a car, and we found that they had a gun down between the seats. We wanted to find out who owned that gun before the dicks arrived so that we could make a good pinch. They told us.

Patrolmen feel that little credit is forthcoming from a clean beat (a crimeless beat), while a number of good arrests really stands out on the record. To a great extent this is actually the case, since a good arrest results in good newspaper publicity, and the policeman who has made many "good pinches" has prestige among his colleagues.

A further justification for the illegal use of violence arises from the fact that almost every police department is under continuous criticism from the community, which tends to assign its own moral responsibilities to the police. The police are therefore faced with the task of justifying themselves to the public, both as individuals and as a group. They feel that the solution of major criminal cases serves this function. This is illustrated in the following statement:

> There is a case I remember of four Negroes who held up a filling station. We got a description of them and picked them up. Then we took them down to the station and really worked them over. I guess that everybody that came into the station that night had a hand in it, and they were in pretty bad shape. Do you think that sounds cruel? Well, you know what we got out of it? We broke a big case in—. There was a mob of twenty guys, burglars and stick-up men, and eighteen of them are in the pen now. Sometimes you have to get rough with them, see. The way I figure it is, if you can get a clue that a man is a pro and if he won't cooperate, tell you what you want to know, it is justified to rough him up a little, up to a point. You know how it is. You feel that the end justifies the means.

It is easier for the police to justify themselves to the community through the dramatic solution of big crimes than through orderly and responsible completion of their routine duties. Although they may be criticized for failures in routine areas, the criticism for the failure to solve big crimes is more intense and sets off a criticism of their work in noncriminal areas. The pressure to solve important cases therefore becomes strong. The following statement, made in reference to the use of violence in interrogations, demonstrates the point:

If it's a big case and there is a lot of pressure on you and they tell you you can't go home until the case is finished, then naturally you are going to lose patience.

The policeman's response to this pressure is to extend the use of violence to its illegal utilization in interrogations. The apprehension of the felon or the "good pinch" thus constitutes a basis for justifying the illegal use of violence.

2. *Control of sexual conduct.*—The police are responsible for the enforcement of laws regulating sexual conduct. This includes the suppression of sexual deviation and the protection of the public from advances and attacks of persons of deviant sexual tendencies. Here the police face a difficult task. The victims of such deviants are notoriously unwilling to cooperate, since popular curiosity and gossip about sexual crimes and the sanctions against the open discussion of sexual activities make it embarrassing for the victim to admit or describe a deviant sexual advance or attack and cause him to feel that he gains a kind of guilt by association from such admissions. Thus the police find that frequently the victims will refuse to identify or testify against the deviant.

These difficulties are intensified by the fact that, once the community becomes aware of sexual depredations, the reports of such activity multiply well beyond reasonable expectations. Since the bulk of these reports will be false, they add to the confusion of the police and consequently to the elusiveness of the offender.

The difficulties of the police are further aggravated by extreme public demand for the apprehension of the offender. The hysteria and alarm generated by reports of a peeping Tom, a rapist, or an exhibitionist result in great public pressure on the police; and, should the activities continue, the public becomes violently critical of police efficiency. The police, who feel insecure in their relationship to the public, are extremely sensitive to this criticism and feel that they must act in response to the demands made by the political and moral leaders of the community.

Thus the police find themselves caught in a dilemma. Apprehension is extremely difficult because of the confusion created by public hysteria and the scarcity of witnesses, but the police are compelled to action by extremely public demands. They resolve this dilemma through the illegal utilization of violence.

A statement of this "misuse" of police powers is represented in the remarks of a patrolman:

Now in my own case when I catch a guy like that I just pick him up and take him into the woods and beat him until he can't crawl. I have had seventeen cases like that in the last couple of years. I tell that guy that if I catch him doing that again I will take him out to those woods and I will shoot him. I tell him that I carry a second gun on me just in case I find guys like him and that I will plant it in his hand and say that he tried to kill and that no jury will convict me.

This statement is extreme and is not representative of policemen in general. In many instances the policeman is likely to act in a different fashion. This is illustrated in the following statement of a rookie who described what happened when he and his partner investigated a parked car which had aroused their suspicions:

> He [the partner] went up there and pretty soon he called me, and there were a couple of fellows in the car with their pants open. I couldn't understand it. I kept looking around for where the woman would be. They were both pretty plastered. One was a young kid about eighteen years old, and the other was an older man. We decided, with the kid so drunk, that bringing him in would only really ruin his reputation, and we told him to go home. Otherwise we would have pinched them. During the time we were talking to them they offered us twenty-eight dollars, and I was going to pinch them when they showed the money, but my partner said, "Never mind, let them go."

Nevertheless, most policemen would apply no sanctions against a colleague who took the more extreme view of the right to use violence and would openly support some milder form of illegal coercion. This is illustrated in the statement of another rookie:

> They feel that it's okay to rough a man up in the case of sex crimes. One of the older men advised me that if the courts didn't punish a man we should. He told me about a sex crime, the story of it, and then said that the law says the policeman has the right to use the amount of force necessary to make an arrest and that in that kind of a crime you can use just a little more force. They feel definitely, for example, in extreme cases like rape, that if a man was guilty he ought to be punished even if you could not get any evidence on him. My feeling is that all the men on the force feel that way, at least from what they have told me.

Furthermore, the police believe, and with some justification it seems, that the community supports their definition of the situation and that they are operating in terms of an implicit directive.

The point of this discussion is that the control of sexual conduct is so difficult and the demand for it so incessant that the police come to sanction the illegal use of violence in obtaining that control. This does not imply that all policemen treat all sex deviants brutally, for, as the above quotations indicate, such is not the case. Rather, it indicates that this use of violence is permitted and condoned by the police and that they come to think of it as a resource more extensive than is included in the legal definition.

Legitimation of Violence

The preceding discussion has indicated two ways in which the experience of the police encourages them to use violence as a general resource in the achievement of their occupational ends and thus to sanction its illegal use. The experience, thus, makes violence acceptable to the policeman as a generalized means. We now wish to indicate the particular basis on which this general resource is legitimated. In particular we wish to point out the extent to which the policeman tends to transfer violence from a legal resource to a personal resource, one which he uses to further his own ends.

Seventy-three policemen, drawn from all ranks and constituting approximately 50 per cent of the policemen, were asked, "When do you think a policeman is justified in roughing a man up?" The intent of the question was to get them to legitimate the use of violence. Their replies are summarized in the following table.

An inspection of the types and distribution of the responses indicates (1) that violence is legitimated by illegal ends (A, C, E, F, G) in 69 per cent of the cases; (2) that violence is legitimated in terms of purely personal or group ends (A) in 37 per cent of the cases (this is important, since it is the largest single reason for the use of violence given); and (3) that legal ends are the bases for legitimation in 31 per cent of the cases (B and D). However, this probably represents a distortion of the true feelings of some of these men, since both the police chief and the community had been severely critical of the use of violence by the men, and the respondents had a tendency to be very cautious with the interviewer, whom some of

Bases for the Use of Force Named by 73 Policemen

TYPE OF RESPONSE*		FREQUENCY	PERCENTAGE
(A)	Disrespect for police	27	37
(B)	When impossible to avoid	17	23
(C)	To obtain information	14	19
(D)	To make an arrest	6	8
(E)	For the hardened criminal	5	7
(F)	When you know man is guilty	2	3
(G)	For sex criminals	2	3
	Total	73	100

*Many respondents described more than one type of situation which they felt called for the use of violence. The "reason" which was either (a) given most heatedly and at greatest length and/or (b) given first was used to characterize the respondent's answer to the question. However, this table is exhaustive of the types of replies which were given.

them never fully trusted. Furthermore, since all the men were conscious
of the chief's policy and of public criticism, it seems likely that those who
did justify the use of violence for illegal and personal ends no longer recognized the illegality involved. They probably believed that such ends fully
represented a moral legitimation for their use of violence.

The most significant finding is that at least 37 per cent of the men
believed that it was legitimate to use violence to coerce respect. This suggests that policemen use the resource of violence to persuade their audience
(the public) to respect occupational status. In terms of the policeman's
definition of the situation, the individual who lacks respect for the police,
the "wise guy" who talks back, or any individual who acts or talks in a
disrespectful way, deserves brutality. This idea is epitomized in admoni-
tions given to the rookies such as, "You gotta make them respect you" and
"You gotta act tough." Examples of some of the responses to the preceding
question that fall into the "disrespect for the police" category follow:

> Well, there are cases. For example, when you stop a fellow for a routine
> questioning, say a wise guy, and he starts talking back to you and telling
> you you are no good and that sort of thing. You know you can take a man
> in on a disorderly conduct charge, but you can practically never make it
> stick. So what you do in a case like that is to egg the guy on until he makes
> a remark where you can justifiably slap him and, then, if he fights back,
> you can call it resisting arrest.

> Well, it varies in different cases. Most of the police use punishment if the
> fellow gives them any trouble. Usually you can judge a man who will give
> you trouble though. *If there is any slight resistance*, you can go all out on
> him. You shouldn't do it in the street though. Wait until you are in the squad
> car, because, even if you are in the right and a guy takes a poke at you, just
> when you are hitting back somebody's just likely to come around the corner,
> and what he will say is that you are beating the guy with your club.

> Well, a prisoner deserves to be hit when he goes to the point where he tries
> to put you below him.

> You gotta get rough when a man's language becomes very bad, when he is
> trying to make a fool of you in front of everybody else. I think most police-
> men try to treat people in a nice way, but usually you have to talk pretty
> rough. That's the only way to set a man down, to make him show a little
> respect.

> If a fellow calls a policeman a filthy name, a slap in the mouth would be a
> good thing, especially if it was out in the public where calling a policeman
> a bad name would look bad for the police.

> There was the incident of a fellow I picked up. I was on the beat, and I was
> taking him down to the station. There were people following us. He kept

saying that I wasn't in the army. Well, he kept going on like that, and I finally had to bust him one. I had to do it. The people would have thought I was afraid otherwise.

These results suggest (1) that the police believe that these private or group ends constitute a moral legitimation for violence which is equal or *superior* to the legitimation derived from the law and (2) that the monopoly of violence delegated to the police, by the state, to enforce the ends of the state has been appropriated by the police as a personal resource to be used for personal and group ends.

The Use of Violence

The sanctions for the use of violence from occupational experience and the fact that policemen morally justify even its illegal use may suggest that violence is employed with great frequency and little provocation. Such an impression would be erroneous, for the actual use of violence is limited by other considerations, such as individual inclinations, the threat of detection, and a sensitivity to public reactions.

Individual policemen vary of course in psychological disposition and past experience. All have been drawn from the larger community which tends to condemn the use of violence and therefore have internalized with varying degrees of intensity this other definition of violence. Their experience as policemen creates a new dimension to their self-conceptions and gives them a new perspective on the use of violence. But individual men vary in the degree to which they assimilate this new conception of self. Therefore, the amount of violence which is used and the frequency with which it is employed will vary among policemen according to their individual propensities. However, policemen cannot and do not employ sanctions against their colleagues for using violence,[6] and individual men who personally condemn the use of violence and avoid it whenever possible[7] refuse openly to condemn acts of violence by other men on the force. Thus, the collective sanctions for the use of violence permits those men who are inclined to its use to employ it without fear.

All policemen, however, are conscious of the dangers of the illegal use of violence. If detected, they may be subject to a lawsuit and possibly dismissal from the force. Therefore, they limit its use to what they think they can get away with. Thus, they recognize that, if a man is guilty of a serious crime, it is easy to "cover up" for their brutality by accusing him of resisting arrest, and the extent to which they believe a man guilty tends to act as a precondition to the use of violence.[8]

The policeman, in common with members of other occupations, is sensitive to the evaluation of his occupation by the public. A man's work is an important aspect of his status, and to the extent that he is identified with his work (by himself and/or the community) he finds that his self-esteem requires the justification and social elevation of his work. Since policemen are low in the occupational prestige scale, subject to continuous criticism, and in constant contact with this criticizing and evaluating public, they are profoundly involved in justifying their work and its tactics to the public and to themselves. The way in which the police emphasize the solution of big crimes and their violent solution to the problem of the control of sexual conduct illustrate this concern. However, different portions of the public have differing definitions of conduct and are of differential importance to the policeman, and the way in which the police define different portions of the public has an effect on whether or not they will use violence.

The police believe that certain groups of persons will respond only to fear and rough treatment. In the city studied they defined both Negroes and slum dwellers in this category. The following statements, each by a different man, typify the manner in which they discriminate the public:

> In the good districts you appeal to people's judgment and explain the law to them. In the South Side the only way is to appear like you are the boss.

> You can't ask them a question and get an answer that is not a lie. In the South Side the only way to walk into a tavern is to walk in swaggering as if you own the place and if somebody is standing in your way give him an elbow and push him aside.

> The colored people understand one thing. The policeman is the law, and he is going to treat you rough and that's the way you have to treat them. Personally, I don't think the colored are trying to help themselves one bit. If you don't treat them rough, they will sit right on top of your head.

Discriminations with respect to the public are largely based on the political power of the group, the degree to which the police believe that the group is potentially criminal, and the type of treatment which the police believe will elicit respect from it.

Variations in the administration and community setting of the police will introduce variations in their use of violence. Thus, a thoroughly corrupt police department will use violence in supporting the ends of this corruption, while a carefully administered nonpolitical department can go a long way toward reducing the illegal use of violence. However, wherever the basic conditions here described are present, it will be very difficult to eradicate the illegal use of violence.

Given these conditions, violence will be used when necessary to the pursuit of duty or when basic occupational values are threatened. Thus a threat to the respect with which the policeman believes his occupation should be regarded or the opportunity to make a "good pinch" will tend to evoke its use.

Conclusions

This paper sets forth an explanation of the illegal use of violence by the police based on an interpretative understanding of their occupational experience. Therefore, it contains a description and analysis of *their* interpretation of *their* experience.

The policeman uses violence because such usage is seen as just, acceptable, and, at times, expected by his colleague group and because it constitutes an effective means for solving problems in obtaining status and self-esteem which policemen as policemen have in common. Since the ends for which violence is illegally used are conceived to be both just and important, they function to justify, to the policeman, the illegal use of violence as a general means. Since "brutality" is strongly criticized by the larger community, the policeman must devise a defense of his brutality to himself and the community, and the defense in turn gives a deeper and more lasting justification to the "misuse of violence." This process then results in a transfer in property from the state to the colleague group. The means of violence which were originally a property of the state, in loan to its law-enforcement agent, the police, are in a psychological sense confiscated by the police, to be conceived of as a personal property to be used at their discretion. This, then, is the explanation of the illegal use of violence by the police which results from viewing it in terms of the police as an occupational group.

The explanation of the illegal use of violence by the police offers an illuminating perspective on the social nature of their occupation. The analysis of their use of brutality in dealing with sexual deviants and felons shows that it is a result of their desire to defend and improve their social status in the absence of effective legal means. This desire in turn is directly related to and makes sense in terms of the low status of the police in the community, which results in a driving need on the part of policemen to assert and improve their status. Their general legitimation of the use of violence *primarily* in terms of coercing respect and making a "good pinch" clearly points out the existence of occupational goals, which are independent of and take precedence over their legal mandate. The existence of such goals and patterns of conduct indicates that the policeman has made of his occupation a preoccupation and invested in it a large aspect of his self.

Notes

1. The writer is indebted to Joseph D. Lohman for his assistance in making contact with the police and for many excellent suggestions as to research procedure and insights into the organization of the police. This paper presents part of a larger study of the policy by the writer. For the complete study see William A. Westley, "The Police: A Sociological Study of Law, Custom, and Morality," unpublished Ph.D dissertation, University of Chicago, Department of Sociology, 1951.

2. Interpretative understanding is here used as defined by Max Weber. See *The Theory of Social and Economic Organization*, trans. Talcott Parsons (New York: Oxford University Press, 1947), p. 88.

3. The ideas are not original. I am indebted for many of them to Everett C. Hughes, although he is in no way responsible for their present formulation. See E. C. Hughes, "Work and the Self," in Rohrer and Sherif, *Social Psychology at the Crossroads* (New York: Harper & Bros., 1951).

4. The background material will be developed in subsequent papers which will analyze the occupational experience of the police and give a full description of police norms.

5. Policemen, in the case studied, use this term to mean an arrest which (a) is politically clear and (b) likely to bring them esteem. Generally it refers to felonies, but in the case of a "real" vice drive it may include the arrest and conviction of an important bookie.

6. The emphasis on secrecy among the police prevents them from using legal sanctions against their colleagues.

7. Many men who held jobs in the police station rather than on beats indicated to the interviewer that their reason for choosing a desk job was to avoid the use of violence.

8. In addition, the policeman is aware that the courts are highly critical of confessions obtained by violence and that, if violence is detected, it will "spoil his case."

37 The Structure of Power in American Society

C. WRIGHT MILLS

". . . we must understand the elite today in connection with . . . the development of a permanent war-establishment, alongside a privately incorporated economy, inside a virtual political vacuum."
—C. Wright Mills

The preceding articles in this Part have focused on six American social institutions. We now turn to what is probably the most critical question concerning American institutions: Who has the power? Just who is it that makes those "big" decisions that drastically affect our lives and influence the course of world events?

Mills says that in order to understand modern society, we must grasp the central fact of the enlargement and centralization of the means of power. Our political, military, and economic institutions have not only grown tremendously in size but have also become centralized and powerfully interconnected. Consequently, they have outstripped our other institutions in importance in decision making. There is no longer a separation of politics, the economy, and the military. Rather, we now have a "triangle of power," built on overlapping leadership with mutuality of interests. The electorate (the "public") is at the bottom of the hierarchy, while the majority of politicians, labor leaders, and business heads reach only to the middle of the hierarchy. They are secondary when it comes to making the crucial policy decisions that critically affect the nation, for it is a *power elite*, those top persons in the political, the economic, and the military sectors, who make the significant decisions that affect our welfare so vitally.

You may wish to review article 25, as it provides a relevant context for understanding Mills's analysis of the operation of power in American society.

I

POWER HAS TO DO WITH whatever decisions men make about the arrangements under which they live, and about the events which make up the history of their times. Events that are beyond human decision do happen;

social arrangements do change without benefit of explicit decision. But in so far as such decisions are made, the problem of who is involved in making them is the basic problem of power. In so far as they could be made but are not, the problem becomes who fails to make them?

We cannot today merely assume that in the last resort men must always be governed by their own consent. For among the means of power which now prevail is the power to manage and to manipulate the consent of men. That we do not know the limits of such power, and that we hope it does have limits, does not remove the fact that much power today is successfully employed without the sanction of the reason or the conscience of the obedient.

Surely nowadays we need not argue that, in the last resort, coercion is the "final" form of power. But then, we are by no means constantly at the last resort. Authority (power that is justified by the beliefs of the voluntary obedient) and manipulation (power that is wielded unbeknown to the powerless) must also be considered, along with coercion. In fact, the three types must be sorted out whenever we think about power.

In the modern world, we must bear in mind, power is often not so authoritative as it seemed to be in the medieval epoch: Ideas which justify rulers no longer seem so necessary to their exercise of power. At least for many of the great decisions of our time—especially those of an international sort—mass "persuasion" has not been "necessary"; the fact is simply accomplished. Furthermore, such ideas as are available to the powerful are often neither taken up nor used by them. Such ideologies usually arise as a response to an effective debunking of power; in the United States such opposition has not been effective enough recently to create the felt need for new ideologies of rule.

There has, in fact, come about a situation in which many who have lost faith in prevailing loyalties have not acquired new ones, and so pay no attention to politics of any kind. They are not radical, not liberal, not conservative, not reactionary. They are inactionary. They are out of it. If we accept the Greek's definition of the idiot as an altogether private man, then we must conclude that many American citizens are now idiots. And I should not be surprised, although I do not know, if there were not some such idiots even in Germany. This—and I use the word with care—this spiritual condition seems to me the key to many modern troubles of political intellectuals, as well as the key to much political bewilderment in modern society. Intellectual "conviction" and moral "belief" are not necessary, in either the rulers or the ruled, for a ruling power to persist and even to flourish. So far as the role of ideologies is concerned, their frequent absences and the prevalence of mass indifference are surely two of the major political facts about the western societies today.

How large a role any explicit decisions do play in the making of history is itself an historical problem. For how large that role may be depends very much upon the means of power that are available at any given time in any given society. In some societies, the innumerable actions of innumerable men modify their milieux, and so gradually modify the structure itself. These modifications—the course of history—go on behind the backs of men. History is drift, although in total "men make it." Thus innumerable entrepreneurs and innumerable consumers by ten-thousand decisions per minute may shape and reshape the free-market economy. Perhaps this was the chief kind of limitation Marx had in mind when he wrote, in *The 18th Brumaire* that: "Men make their own history, but they do not make it just as they please; they do not make it under circumstances chosen by themselves. . . ."

But in other societies—certainly in the United States and in the Soviet Union today—a few men may be so placed within the structure that by their decisions they modify the millieux of many other men, and in fact nowadays the structural conditions under which most men live. Such elites of power also make history under circumstances not chosen altogether by themselves, yet compared with other men, and compared with other periods of world history, these circumstances do indeed seem less limiting.

I should contend that "men are free to make history," but that some men are indeed much freer than others. For such freedom requires access to the means of decision and of power by which history can now be made. It has not always been so made; but in the later phases of the modern epoch it is. It is with reference to this epoch that I am contending that if men do not make history, they tend increasingly to become the utensils of history-makers as well as the mere objects of history.

The history of modern society may readily be understood as the story of the enlargement and the centralization of the means of power—in economic, in political, and in military institutions. The rise of industrial society has involved these developments in the means of economic production. The rise of the nation-state has involved similar developments in the means of violence and in those of political administration.

In the western societies, such transformations have generally occurred gradually, and many cultural traditions have restrained and shaped them. In most of the Soviet societies, they are happening very rapidly indeed and without the great discourse of western civilization, without the Renaissance and without the Reformation, which so greatly strengthened and gave political focus to the idea of freedom. In those societies, the enlargement and the coordination of all the means of power has occurred more brutally, and from the beginning under tightly centralized authority. But in both types, the means of power have now become international in scope and similar in form. To be sure, each of them has its own ups and downs; neither is as yet absolute; how they are run differs quite sharply.

Yet so great is the reach of the means of violence, and so great the economy required to produce and support them, that we have in the immediate past witnessed the consolidation of these two world centers, either of which dwarfs the power of Ancient Rome. As we pay attention to the awesome means of power now available to quite small groups of men we come to realize that Caesar could do less with Rome than Napoleon with France; Napoleon less with France than Lenin with Russia. But what was Caesar's power at its height compared with the power of the changing inner circles of Soviet Russia and the temporary administrations of the United States? We come to realize—indeed they continually remind us— how a few men have access to the means by which in a few days continents can be turned into thermonuclear wastelands. That the facilities of power are so enormously enlarged and so decisively centralized surely means that the powers of quite small groups of men, which we may call elites, are now of literally inhuman consequence.

My concern here is not with the international scene but with the United States in the middle of the twentieth century. I must emphasize "in the middle of the twentieth century" because in our attempt to understand any society we come upon images which have been drawn from its past and which often confuse our attempt to confront its present reality. That is one minor reason why history is the shank of any social science: we must study it if only to rid ourselves of it. In the United States, there are indeed many such images and usually they have to do with the first half of the nineteenth century. At that time the economic facilities of the United States were very widely dispersed and subject to little or to no central authority. The state watched in the night but was without decisive voice in the day. One man meant one rifle and the militia were without centralized orders.

Any American, as old-fashioned as I, can only agree with R. H. Tawney that "Whatever the future may contain, the past has shown no more excellent social order than that in which the mass of the people were the masters of the holdings which they ploughed and the tools with which they worked, and could boast . . . 'It is a quietness to a man's mind to live upon his own and to know his heir certain.' "

But then we must immediately add: all that is of the past and of little relevance to our understanding of the United States today. Within this society three broad levels of power may now be distinguished. I shall begin at the top and move downward.

II

The power to make decisions of national and international consequence is now so clearly seated in political, military, and economic institutions that other areas of society seem off to the side and, on occasion, readily subordinated to these. The scattered institutions of religion, education and family are increasingly shaped by the big three, in which history-making decisions now regularly occur. Behind this fact there is all the push and drive of a fabulous technology; for these three institutional orders have incorporated this technology and now guide it, even as it shapes and paces their development.

As each has assumed its modern shape, its effects upon the other two have become greater, and the traffic between the three has increased. There is no longer, on the one hand, an economy, and, on the other, a political order, containing a military establishment unimportant to politics and to money-making. There is a political economy numerously linked with military order and decision. This triangle of power is now a structural fact, and it is the key to any understanding of the higher circles in America today. For as each of these domains has coincided with the others, as decisions in each have become broader, the leading men of each—the high military, the corporation executives, the political directorate—have tended to come together to form the power elite of America.

The political order, once composed of several dozen states with a weak federal center, has become an executive apparatus which has taken up into itself many powers previously scattered, legislative as well as administrative, and which now reaches into all parts of the social structure. The long-time tendency of business and government to become more closely connected has, since World War II, reached a new point of explicitness. Neither can now be seen clearly as a distinct world. The growth of executive government does not mean merely the "enlargement of government" as some kind of autonomous bureaucracy; under American conditions, it has meant the ascendancy of the corporation man into political eminence. Already during the New Deal, such men had joined the political directorate; as of World War II, they came to dominate it. Long involved with government, now they have moved into quite full direction of the economy of the war effort and of the post-war era.

The economy, once a great scatter of small productive units in somewhat automatic balance, has become internally dominated by a few hundred corporations, administratively and politically interrelated, which together hold the keys to economic decision. This economy is at once a permanent-war economy and a private-corporation economy. The most important relations of the corporation to the state now rest on the coincidence between military and corporate interests, as defined by the military and the corporate rich, and accepted by politicians and public. Within the elite as a whole, this coincidence of military domain and corporate realm strengthens both of them and further subordinates the merely political man. Not the party politician but the corporation executive, is now more likely to sit with the military to answer the question: what is to be done?

The military order, once a slim establishment in a context of civilian distrust, has become the largest and most expensive feature of government;

behind smiling public relations, it has all the grim and clumsy efficiency of a great and sprawling bureaucracy. The high military have gained decisive political and economic relevance. The seemingly permanent military threat places a premium upon them and virtually all political and economic actions are now judged in terms of military definitions of reality; the higher military have ascended to a firm position within the power elite of our time.

In part, at least, this is a result of an historical fact, pivotal for the years since 1939: the attention of the elite has shifted from domestic problems—centered in the thirties around slump—to international problems—centered in the forties and fifties around war. By long historical usage, the government of the United States has been shaped by domestic clash and balance; it does not have suitable agencies and traditions for the democratic handling of international affairs. In considerable part, it is in this vacuum that the power elite has grown.

1. To understand the unity of this power elite, we must pay attention to the psychology of its several members in their perspective milieux. In so far as the power elite is composed of men of similar origin and education, of similar career and style of life, their unity may be said to rest upon the fact that they are of similar social type, and to lead to the fact of their easy intermingling. This kind of unity reaches its frothier apex in the sharing of that prestige which is to be had in the world of the celebrity. It achieves a more solid culmination in the fact of the interchangeability of positions between the three dominant institutional orders. It is revealed by considerable traffic of personnel within and between these three, as well as by the rise of specialized go-betweens as in the new style high-level lobbying.

2. Behind such psychological and social unity are the structure and the mechanics of those institutional hierarchies over which the political directorate, the corporate rich, and the high military now preside. How each of these hierarchies is shaped and what relations it has with the others determine in large part the relations of their rulers. Were these hierarchies scattered and disjointed, then their respective elites might tend to be scattered and disjointed; but if they have many interconnections and points of coinciding interest, then their elites tend to form a coherent kind of grouping. The unity of the elite is not a simple reflection of the unity of institutions, but men and institutions are always related; that is why we must understand the elite today in connection with such institutional trends as the development of a permanent war-establishment, alongside a privately incorporated economy, inside a virtual political vacuum. For the men at the top have been selected and formed by such institutional trends.

3. Their unity however, does not rest solely upon psychological similarity and social intermingling, nor entirely upon the structural blending

of commanding positions and common interests. At times it is the unity of a more explicit coordination.

To say that these higher circles are increasingly coordinated, that this is *one* basis of their unity, and that at times—as during open war—such coordination is quite wilful, is not to say that the coordination is total or continuous, or even that it is very surefooted. Much less is it to say that the power elite has emerged as the realization of a plot. Its rise cannot be adequately explained in any psychological terms.

Yet we must remember that institutional trends may be defined as opportunities by those who occupy the command posts. Once such opportunities are recognized, men may avail themselves of them. Certain types of men from each of these three areas, more far-sighted than others, have actively promoted the liaison even before it took its truly modern shape. Now more have come to see that their several interests can more easily be realized if they work together, in informal as well as in formal ways, and accordingly they have done so.

The idea of the power elite is of course an interpretation. It rests upon and it enables us to make sense of major institutional trends, the social similarities and psychological affinities of the men at the top. But the idea is also based upon what has been happening on the middle and lower levels of power, to which I now turn.

III

There are of course other interpretations of the American system of power. The most usual is that it is a moving balance of many competing interests. The image of balance, at least in America, is derived from the idea of the economic market: in the nineteenth century, the balance was thought to occur between a great scatter of individuals and enterprises; in the twentieth century, it is thought to occur between great interest blocs. In both views, the politician is the key man of power because he is the broker of many conflicting powers.

I believe that the balance and the compromise in American society—the "countervailing powers" and the "veto groups," of parties and associations, of strata and unions—must now be seen has having mainly to do with the middle levels of power. It is these middle levels that the political journalist and the scholar of politics are most likely to understand and to write about—if only because, being mainly middle class themselves, they are closer to them. Moreover these levels provide the noisy content of most "political" news and gossip; the images of these levels are more or less in accord with the folklore of how democracy works; and, if the master-image of balance is accepted, many intellectuals, especially in their current patrioteering, are readily able to satisfy such political optimism as they wish. Accordingly, liberal interpretations of what is happening in the United States are now virtually the only interpretations that are widely distributed.

But to believe that the power system reflects a balancing society is, I think, to confuse the present era with earlier times, and to confuse its top and bottom with its middle levels.

By the top levels, as distinguished from the middle, I intend to refer, first of all, to the scope of the decisions that are made. At the top today, these decisions have to do with all the issues of war and peace. They have also to do with slump and poverty which are now so very much problems of international scope. I intend also to refer to whether or not the groups that struggle politically have a chance to gain the positions from which such top decisions are made, and indeed whether their members do usually hope for such top national command. Most of the competing interests which make up the clang and clash of American politics are strictly concerned with their slice of the existing pie. Labor unions, for example, certainly have no policies of an international sort other than those which given unions adopt for the strict economic protection of their members; neither do farm organizations. The actions of such middle-level powers may indeed have consequence for top-level policy; certainly at times they hamper these policies. But they are not truly concerned with them, which means of course that their influence tends to be quite irresponsible.

The facts of the middle levels may in part be understood in terms of the rise of the power elite. The expanded and centralized and interlocked hierarchies over which the power elite preside have encroached upon the old balance and relegated it to the middle level. But there are also independent developments of the middle levels. These, it seems to me, are better understood as an affair of entrenched and provincial demands than as a center of national decision. As such, the middle level often seems much more of a stalemate than a moving balance.

1. The middle level of politics is not a forum in which there are debated the big decisions of national and international life. Such debate is not carried on by nationally responsible parties representing and clarifying alternative policies. There are no such parties in the United States. More and more, fundamental issues never come to any point of decision before the Congress, much less before the electorate in party campaigns. In the case of Formosa, in the spring of 1955 the Congress abdicated all debate concerning events and decisions which surely bordered on war. The same is largely true of the 1957 crisis in the Middle East. Such decisions now regularly bypass the Congress, and are never clearly focused issues for public decision.

The American political campaign distracts attention from national and international issues but that is not to say that there are no issues in these campaigns. In each district and state, issues are set up and watched by organized interests of sovereign local importance. The professional politician is of course a party politician, and the two parties are semifeudal organizations: they trade patronage and other favors for votes and for protection. The differences between them so far as national issues are concerned, are very narrow and very mixed up. Often each seems to be fifty parties, one for each state; and accordingly, the politician as campaigner and as Congressman is not concerned with national party lines, if any are discernible. Often he is not subject to any effective national party discipline. He speaks for the interests of his own constituency, and he is concerned with national issues only in so far as they affect the interests effectively organized there, and hence his chances of re-election. That is why, when he does speak of national matters, the result is so often such an empty rhetoric. Seated in his sovereign locality, the politician is not at the national summit. He is on and of the middle levels of power.

2. Politics is not an arena in which free and independent organizations truly connect the lower and middle levels of society with the top levels of decision. Such organizations are not an effective and major part of American life today. As more people are drawn into the political arena, their associations become mass in scale, and the power of the individual becomes dependent upon them; to the extent that they are effective, they have become larger, and to that extent they have become less accessible to the influence of the individual. This is a central fact about associations in any mass society; it is of most consequence for political parties and for trade unions.

In the thirties, it often seemed that labor would become an insurgent power independent of corporation and state. Organized labor was then emerging for the first time on an American scale, and the only political sense of direction it needed was the slogan, "organize the unorganized." Now without the mandate of the slump, labor remains without political direction. Instead of economic and political struggles it has become deeply entangled in administrative routines with both corporation and state. One of its major functions, as a vested interest of the new society, is the regulation of such irregular tendencies as may occur among the rank and file.

There is nothing, it seems to me, in the make-up of the current labor leadership to allow us to expect that it can or that it will lead, rather than merely react. In so far as it fights at all, it fights over a share of the goods of a single way of life and not over that way of life itself. The typical labor leader in the U.S.A. today is better understood as an adaptive creative creature of the main business drift than as an independent actor in a truly national context.

3. The idea that this society is a balance of powers requires us to assume that the units in balance are of more or less equal power and that they are truly independent of one another. These assumptions have rested,

it seems clear, upon the historical importance of a large and independent middle class. In the latter nineteenth century and during the Progressive Era, such a class of farmers and small businessmen fought politically— and lost—their struggle for a paramount role in national decision. Even then, their aspirations seemed bound to their own imagined past.

This old, independent middle class has of course declined. On the most generous count, it is now 40 percent of the total middle class (at most 20 percent of the total labor force). Moreover, it has become politically as well as economically dependent upon the state, most notably in the case of the subsidized farmer.

The *new* middle class of white-collar employees is certainly not the political pivot of any balancing society. It is in no way politically unified. Its unions, such as they are, often serve merely to incorporate it as hanger-on of the labor interest. For a considerable period, the old middle class *was* an independent base of power; the new middle class cannot be. Political freedom and economic society *were* anchored in small and independent properties; they are not anchored in the worlds of the white-collar job. Scattered property holders were economically united by more or less free markets; the jobs of the new middle class are integrated by corporate authority. Economically, the white-collar classes are in the same condition as wage workers; politically, they are in a worse condition, for they are not organized. They are no vanguard of historic change; they are at best a rear-guard of the welfare state.

The agrarian revolt of the nineties, the small-business revolt that has been more or less continuous since the eighties, the labor revolt of the thirties—each of these has failed as an independent movement which could countervail against the powers that be; they have failed as politically autonomous third parties. But they have succeeded, in varying degrees, as interests vested in the expanded corporation and state; they have succeeded as parochial interests seated in particular districts, in local divisions of the two parties, and in the Congress. What they would become, in short, are well-established features of the *middle* levels of balancing power, on which we may now observe all those strata and interest which in the course of American history have been defeated in their bids for top power or which have never made such bids.

Fifty years ago many observers thought of the American state as a mask behind which an invisible government operated. But nowadays, much of what was called the old lobby visible or invisible, is part of the quite visible government. The "governmentalization of the lobby" has proceeded in both the legislative and the executive domain, as well as between them. The executive bureaucracy becomes not only the center of decision but also the arena within which major conflicts of power are resolved or denied resolution. "Administration" replaces electorial politics; the maneuvering of cliques (which include leading Senators as well as civil servants) replaces the open clash of parties.

The shift of corporation men into the political directorate has accelerated the decline of the politicians in the Congress to the middle levels of power; the formation of the power elite rests in part upon this relegation. It rests also upon the semiorganized stalemate of the interests of sovereign localities, into which the legislative function has so largely fallen; upon the virtually complete absence of a civil service that is a politically neutral but politically relevant, depository of brainpower and executive skill; and it rests upon the increased official secrecy behind which great decisions are made without benefit of public or even of Congressional debate.

IV

There is one last belief upon which liberal observers everywhere base their interpretations and rest their hopes. That is the idea of the public and the associated idea of public opinion. Conservative thinkers, since the French Revolution, have of course Viewed With Alarm the rise of the public, which they have usually called the masses, or something to that effect. "The populace is sovereign," wrote Gustave LeBon, "and the tide of barbarism mounts." But surely those who have supposed the masses to be well on their way to triumph are mistaken. In our time, the influence of publics or of masses within political life is in fact decreasing, and such influence as on occasion they do have tends, to an unknown but increasing degree, to be guided by the means of mass communication.

In a society of publics, discussion is the ascendant means of communication, and the mass media, if they exist, simply enlarge and animate this discussion, linking one face-to-face public with the discussions of another. In a mass society, the dominant type of communication is the formal media, and publics become mere markets for these media: the "public" of a radio program consists of all those exposed to it. When we try to look upon the United States today as a society of publics, we realize that it has moved a considerable distance along the road to the mass society.

In official circles, the very term, "the public," has come to have a phantom meaning, which dramatically reveals its eclipse. The deciding elite can identify some of those who clamor publicly as "Labor," others as "Business," still others as "Farmer." But these are not the public. "The public" consists of the unidentified and the nonpartisan in a world of defined and partisan interests. In this faint echo of the classic notion, the public is composed of these remnants of the old and new middle classes whose interests are not explicitly defined, organized, or clamorous. In a curious adaptation, "the public" often becomes, in administrative fact, "the disengaged expert," who, although never so well informed, has never taken a clear-cut and public stand on controversial issues. He is the "public" member of the board, the commission, the committee. What "the public" stands for, accordingly, is often a vagueness of policy (called "openmindedness"), a lack of involvement in public affairs (known as "reasonableness"), and a professional disinterest (known as "tolerance").

All this is indeed far removed from the eighteenth century idea of the public of public opinion. The idea parallels the economic idea of the magical market. Here is the market composed for freely competing entrepreneurs; there is the public composed of circles of people in discussion. As price is the result of anonymous, equally weighted, bargaining individuals, so public opinion is the result of each man's having thought things out for himself and then contributing his voice to the great chorus. To be sure, some may have more influence on the state of opinion than others, but no one group monopolizes the discussion, or by itself determines the opinions that prevail.

In this classic image, the people are presented with problems. They discuss them. They formulate viewpoints. These viewpoints are organized, and they compete. One viewpoint "wins out." Then the people act on this view, or their representatives are instructed to act it out, and this they promptly do.

Such are the images of democracy which are still used as working justifications of power in America. We must now recognize this description as more a fairy tale than a useful approximation. The issues that now shape man's fate are neither raised nor decided by any public at large. The idea of a society that is at bottom composed of publics is not a matter of fact; it is the proclamation of an ideal, and as well the assertion of a legitimation masquerading as fact.

I cannot here describe the several great forces within American society as well as elsewhere which have been at work in the debilitation of the public. I want only to remind you that publics, like free associations, can be deliberately and suddenly smashed, or they can more slowly wither away. But whether smashed in a week or withered in a generation, the demise of the public must be seen in connection with the rise of centralized organizations, with all their new means of power, including those of the mass media of distraction. These, we now know, often seem to expropriate the rationality and the will of the terrorized or—as the case may be—the voluntarily indifferent society of masses. In the more democratic process of indifference, the remnants of such publics as remain may only occasionally be intimidated by fanatics in search of "disloyalty." But regardless of that, they lose their will for decision because they do not possess the instruments for decision; they lose their sense of political belonging because they do not belong; they lose their political will because they see no way to realize it.

The political structure of a modern democratic state requires that such a public as is projected by democratic theorists not only exist but that it be the very forum within which a politics of real issues is enacted.

It requires a civil service that is firmly linked with the world of knowledge and sensibility, and which is composed of skilled men who, in their careers and in their aspirations, are truly independent of any private, which is to say, corporation, interests.

It requires nationally responsible parties which debate openly and clearly the issues which the nation, and indeed the world, now so rigidly confronts.

It requires an intelligentsia, inside as well as outside the universities, who carry on the big discourse of the Western world, and whose work is relevant to and influential among parties and movements and publics.

And it certainly requires, as a fact of power, that there be free associations standing between families and smaller communities and publics, on the one hand, and the state, the military, the corporation, on the other. For unless these do exist, there are no vehicles for reasoned opinion, no instruments for the rational exertion of public will.

Such democratic formations are not now ascendant in the power structure of the United States, and accordingly the men of decision are not selected and formed by careers within such associations and by their performance before such publics. The top of modern American society is increasingly unified, and often seems wilfully coordinated: at the top there has emerged an elite whose power probably exceeds that of any small group of men in world history. The middle levels are often a drifting set of stalemated forces: the middle does not link the bottom with the top. The bottom of this society is politically fragmented, and even as a passive fact, increasingly powerless: at the bottom there is emerging a mass society.

These developments, I believe, can be correctly understood neither in terms of the liberal nor the Marxian interpretation of politics and history. Both these ways of thought arose as guidelines to reflection about a type of society which does not now exist in the United States. We confront there a new kind of social structure, which embodies elements and tendencies of all modern society, but in which they have assumed a more naked and flamboyant prominence.

That does not mean that we must give up the ideals of these classic political expectations. I believe that both have been concerned with the problem of rationality and of freedom: liberalism, with freedom and rationality as supreme facts about the individual; Marxism, as supreme facts about man's role in the political making of history. What I have said here, I suppose, may be taken as an attempt to make evident why the ideas of freedom and of rationality now so often seem so ambiguous in the new society of the United States of America.

PART VIII — Social Change

SHIFTING EVENTS SWIRL AROUND US, at times seeming to engulf us in a sea of change. Nothing seems to remain the same. Familiar landmarks are torn down and replaced, seemingly overnight, by a supermarket or fast food outlet. Ideas of proper relations between the sexes become outmoded so fast that the guidelines of only a few years ago are outdated. Drugs move into middle-class homes. Males grow their hair to controversial lengths, then abruptly decide to crop it. Divorce rates soar while the marriage rate declines, increases, and again declines. Clothing styles of the 1950s, cars of the 1940s, furniture of the 1930s come back into fashion. Pocket calculators and hand-held computers. Microwave ovens and autos that get 50 mpg. Price scanners in the supermarkets and digital clocks. LED watches and wrist televisions. Video games and video recorders. Talking water meters and talking automobiles.

While change is an essential part of modern society, it is anything but new. Twenty-five hundred years ago Heraclitus said: "Everything flows, nothing stands still." Six hundred years later Marcus Aurelius Antoninus wrote, "The universe *is* change." A more recent observer of the social scene put it this way: "The only thing constant is the certainty of change."

While social change was also a part of ancient civilizations, there is an essential difference between those changes and what we are experiencing. Barring catastrophe in the form of human or natural disaster, change in ancient times was slow and orderly. It sometimes was so slow that even over generations the change was barely perceptible. In all societies of the world, in fact, it was routinely the case that the father passed his occupation down to his son, who in turn passed it on to his son, and so on. It was the same with the women. Mothers passed their occupation to their daughters. For all intents and purposes, the society the son or daughter lived in was identical to that of his or her parents. Although the players had changed, the basic social institutions, with their usual ways of handling things, remained the same over generations.

But this is no longer true. Most children are amazed at how different they and their parents are—with some amazed that they have any similarities at all. Their worlds are so different that it is not uncommon for a grown child visiting his or her parents after an absence of months or years to find that after the first hour or two they have little or nothing left to talk about. Social change has separated them into different worlds, with their differing experiences making them people with contrastive orientations.

"Adapt or die" may be the maxim under which living creatures exist. Only the organisms that adapt to changing circumstances survive, and humans are no exception. Confronted with challenge, humans adapt. They change their social institutions to match changed circumstances. Those changes affect not only their outward behaviors but also their ideas and beliefs, the fundamental concepts that make up their basic orientations to the world.

It is with discussions of this vital aspect of social life that we conclude the book. Setting the tone for this Part is our first selection by Alvin Toffler, who coined the term "future shock." We then look at how one individual experienced profound changes in his personal identity as he underwent life-transforming experiences in the educational institution. Some of you should be able to identify strongly with Richard Rodriguez's personal account of his search for lost roots. Andrew Cherlin and Frank F. Furstenberg, Jr., then turn their sociological imagination loose as they explore what family life will probably be like at the turn of the century. Highlighting the implications of technological developments for the same time period, and still using the family as a focus, Charles J. Leslie examines other aspects of what our future may be like.

It is with this fitting consideration of the future that we close this book.

In conclusion, I would like to add that you, the reader, are the future. Yet you cannot escape being shaped by your experiences in this society, and even by others' anticipations of what the future will be. For all of this to make sense, and for you to make better sense of your social experiences, I highly recommend the sociological imagination—the idea with which we began this book.

38 Future Shock

ALVIN TOFFLER

In *Future Shock*, Alvin Toffler relates this incident:

> Some time ago my wife sent my daughter, then twelve, to a
> supermarket a few blocks from our Manhattan apartment.
> Our little girl had been there only once or twice before. Half
> an hour later she returned perplexed. "It must have been torn
> down," she said. "I couldn't find it." It hadn't been. New to
> the neighborhood, Karen had merely looked on the wrong
> block. But she is a child of the Age of Transience, and her
> immediate assumption—the building had been razed and re-
> placed—was a natural one for a twelve-year-old growing up
> in the United States at this time.

Toffler adds that "Such an idea would probably never have
occurred to a child faced with a similar predicament even half a
century ago" for "the "physical environment was far more durable"
and "our links with it less transient."

The speed, extent, and intensity of the social change of our
civilization is mind-boggling. We barely get used to one changed
idea or object or relationship when another overtakes and over-
powers it—and us. Simultaneously, other replacing changes are on
their way. It is to this steady barrage of social change to which we
have no leisure or opportunity to adjust, making us dizzy with its
speed, that Toffler is referring by the term *future shock*. It is the
vertigo, the confusion, the internal disorientation that people experience when rapidly occurring social change suddenly pulls their
familiar assumptions and expectations of reality out from under
them.

Because future shock is here to stay (one of the constants of
rapid social change), it is fitting to open this Part with Toffler's
explanation of the concept.

IN THE [SHORT TIME REMAINING] between now and the twenty-
first century, millions of ordinary, psychologically normal people will face
an abrupt collision with the future. Citizens of the world's richest and
most technologically advanced nations, many of them will find it increasingly painful to keep up with the incessant demand for change that characterizes our time. For them, the future will have arrived too soon. . . .

Western society for the past 300 years has been caught up in a fire storm of change. This storm, far from abating, now appears to be gathering force. Change sweeps through the highly industrialized countries with waves of ever accelerating speed and unprecedented impact. It spawns in its wake all sorts of curious social flora—from psychedelic churches and "free universities" to science cities in the Arctic and wifeswap clubs in California.

It breeds odd personalities, too: children who at twelve are no longer childlike; adults who at fifty are children of twelve. There are rich men who playact poverty, computer programmers who turn on with LSD. There are anarchists who, beneath their dirty denim shirts, are outrageous conformists, and conformists who, beneath their button-down collars, are outrageous anarchists. There are married priests and atheist ministers and Jewish Zen Buddhists. . . .

Much that now strikes us as incomprehensible would be far less so if we took a fresh look at the racing rate of change that makes reality seem, sometimes, like a kaleidoscope run wild. For the acceleration of change does not merely buffet industries or nations. It is a concrete force that reaches deep into our personal lives, compels us to act out new roles, and confronts us with the danger of a new and powerfully upsetting psychological disease. This new disease can be called "future shock," and a knowledge of its sources and symptoms helps explain many things that otherwise defy rational analysis. . . .

The parallel term "culture shock" has already begun to creep into the popular vocabulary. Culture shock is the effect that immersion in a strange culture has on the unprepared visitor. Peace Corps volunteers suffer from it in Borneo or Brazil. Marco Polo probably suffered from it in Cathay. Culture shock is what happens when a traveler suddenly finds himself in a place where yes may mean no, where a "fixed price" is negotiable, where to be kept waiting in an outer office is no cause for insult, where laughter may signify anger. It is what happens when the familiar psychological cues that help an individual to function in society are suddenly withdrawn and replaced by new ones that are strange or incomprehensible. . . .

Future shock is a time phenomenon, a product of the greatly accelerated rate of change in society. It arises from the superimposition of a new culture on an old one. It is culture shock in one's own society. But its impact is far worse. For most Peace Corps men, in fact most travelers, have the comforting knowledge that the culture they left behind will be there to return to. The victim of future shock does not.

Take an individual out of his own culture and set him down suddenly in an environment sharply different from his own, with a different set of cues to react to—different conceptions of time, space, work, love, religion, sex, and everything else—then cut him off from any hope of retreat to a more familiar social landscape, and the dislocation he suffers is doubly severe. Moreover, if this new culture is itself in constant turmoil, and if—

worse yet—its values are incessantly changing, the sense of disorientation will be still further intensified. Given few clues as to what kind of behavior is rational under the radically new circumstances, the victim may well become a hazard to himself and others.

Now imagine not merely an individual, but an entire society, an entire generation—including its weakest, least intelligent, and most irrational members—suddenly transported into this new world. The result is mass disorientation, future shock on a grand scale.

This is the prospect that man now faces. Change is avalanching upon our heads and most people are grotesquely unprepared to cope with it.

39 Searching for Roots in a Changing World

RICHARD RODRIGUEZ

Americans are certainly among the most geographically mobile of all people. Approximately 17 percent of our population moves each year; that is, in every six-year period, a number equal to our *entire* population changes residence. One of the basic reasons for this American restlessness is the attempt to better oneself, to climb another rung on the social class ladder. As Sennett and Cobb discussed in Part VI, the personal costs of social mobility are high—especially the severing of roots, a breaking with family and its customs and orientations. This tearing away can lead to personal disorientation, to a questioning of who one is. In this selection, Richard Rodriguez relates how he realized that he had cut himself off from his roots, that the costs of this rupture were extremely difficult to bear, and how he felt the need to embark on a search to rediscover himself by examining his past.

If you are strongly rooted (and, in the extreme case, a few of you have probably lived in the same house from childhood and you intend your college education to be a means to maintain your social class membership), you can contrast your experiences with those analyzed by Rodriguez. Some of you, however, like Rodriguez, are likely to be using the educational institution to take huge leaps in social mobility. As you identify with Rodriguez's experiences, you might ask yourself—as he does—how much of your roots are you willing to give up?

TODAY I AM ONLY TECHNICALLY the person I once felt myself to be—a Mexican-American, a Chicano. Partly because I had no way of comprehending my racial identity except in this technical sense, I gave up long ago the cultural consequences of being a Chicano.

The change came gradually but early. When I was beginning grade school, I noted to myself the fact that the classroom environment was so different in its styles and assumptions from my own family environment that survival would essentially entail a choice between both worlds. When I became a student, I was literally "remade"; neither I nor my teachers considered anything I had known before as relevant. I had to forget most of what my culture had provided, because to remember it was a disadvantage. The past and its cultural values became detachable, like a piece of clothing grown heavy on a warm day and finally put away.

Strangely, the discovery that I have been inattentive to my cultural past has arisen because others—student colleagues and faculty members—have started to assume that I am a Chicano. The ease with which the assumption is made forces me to suspect that the label is not meant to suggest cultural, but racial, identity. Nonetheless, as a graduate student and a prospective university faculty member, I am routinely expected to assume intellectual leadership *as a member of a racial minority*. Recently, for example, I heard the moderator of a panel discussion introduce me as "Richard Rodriguez, a Chicano intellectual." I wanted to correct the speaker—because I felt guilty representing a non-academic cultural tradition that I had willingly abandoned. So I can only guess what it would have meant to have retained my culture as I entered the classroom, what it would mean for me to be today a *Chicano intellectual*. (The two words juxtaposed excite me; for years I thought a Chicano had to decide between being one or the other.)

Does the fact that I barely spoke any English until I was nine, or that as a child I felt a surge of *self*-hatred whenever a passing teenager would yell a racial slur, or that I saw my skin darken each summer—do any of these facts shape the ideas which I have or am capable of having? Today, I suspect they do—in ways I doubt the moderator who referred to me as a "Chicano intellectual" intended. The peculiar status of being a "Chicano intellectual" makes me grow restless at the thought that I have lost at least as much as I have gained through education.

I remember when, 20 years ago, two grammar-school nuns visited my childhood home. They had come to suggest—with more tact than was necessary, because my parents accepted without question the church's authority—that we make a greater effort to speak as much English around the house as possible. The nuns realized that my brothers and I led solitary lives largely because we were barely able to comprehend English in a school where we were the only Spanish-speaking students. My mother and father complied as best they could. Heroically, they gave up speaking to us in Spanish—the language that formed so much of the family's sense of intimacy in an alien world—and began to speak a broken English. Instead of Spanish sounds, I began hearing sounds that were new, harder, less friendly. More important, I was encouraged to respond in English.

The change in language was the most dramatic and obvious indication that I would become very much like the "gringo"—a term which was used descriptively rather than pejoratively in my home—and unlike the Spanish-speaking relatives who largely constituted my preschool world. Gradually, Spanish became a sound freighted with only a kind of sentimental significance, like the sound of the bedroom clock I listened to in my aunt's house when I spent the night. Just as gradually, English became the language I came not to *hear* because it was the language I used every day, as I gained access to a new, larger society. But the memory of Spanish persisted as a reminder of the society I had left. I can remember occasions when I entered a room and my parents were speaking to one another in Spanish, seeing me, they shifted into their more formalized English. Hearing them speak to me in English troubled me. The bonds their voices once secured were loosened by the new tongue.

This is not to suggest that I was being *forced* to give up my Chicano past. After the initial awkwardness of transition, I committed myself, fully and freely, to the culture of the classroom. Soon what I was learning in school was so antithetical to what my parents knew and did that I was careful about the way I talked about myself at the evening dinner table. Occasionally, there were moments of childish cruelty: a son's condescending to instruct either one of his parents about a "simple" point of English pronunciation or grammar.

Social scientists often remark, about situations such as mine, that children feel a sense of loss as they move away, from their working-class identifications and models. Certainly, what I experienced, others have also—whatever their race. Like other generations of, say, Polish-American or Irish-American children coming home from college, I was to know the silence that ensues so quickly after the quick exchange of news and the dwindling of common interests.

In addition, however, education seemed to mean not only a gradual dissolving of familial and class ties but also a change of racial identity. The new language I spoke was only the most obvious reason for my associating the classroom with "gringo" society. The society I knew as Chicano was barely literate—in English *or* Spanish—and so impatient with either prolonged reflection or abstraction that I found the academic environment a sharp contrast. Sharpening the contrast was the stereotype of the Mexican as a mental inferior. (The fear of this stereotype has been so deep that only recently have I been willing to listen to those, like D. H. Lawrence, who celebrate the "non-cerebral" Mexican as an alternative to the rational and scientific European man.) Because I did not know how to distinguish the healthy non-rationality of Chicano culture from the mental incompetency of which Chicanos were unjustly accused, I was willing to abandon my non-mental skills in order to disprove the racist's stereotype.

I was wise enough not to feel proud of the person education had helped me to become. I knew that education had led me to repudiate my race. I was frequently labeled a *pocho*, a Mexican with gringo pretentions, not only because I could not speak Spanish but also because I would respond in English with precise and careful sentences. Uncles would laugh good-naturedly, but I detected scorn in their voices. For my grandmother, the least assimilated of my relations, the changes in her grandson since entering school were especially troubling. She remains today a dark and silently critical figure in my memory, a reminder of the Mexican-Indian ancestry that somehow my educational success has violated.

Nonetheless, I became more comfortable reading or writing careful prose than talking to a kitchen filled with listeners, withdrawing from situations to reflect on their significance rather than grasping for meaning at the scene. I remember, one August evening, slipping away from a gathering of aunts and uncles in the backyard, going into a bedroom tenderly lighted by a late sun, and opening a novel about life in nineteenth-century England. There, by an open window, reading, I was barely conscious of the sounds of laughter outside.

With so few fellow Chicanos in the university, I had no chance to develop an alternative consciousness. When I spent occasional weekends tutoring lower-class Chicano teenagers or when I talked with Mexican-American janitors and maids around the campus, there was a kind of sympathy—a sense, however privately held—that we knew something about one another. But I regarded them all primarily as people from my past. The maids reminded me of my aunts (similarly employed); the students I tutored reminded me of my cousins (who also spoke English with barrio accents).

When I was young, I was taught to refer to my ancestry as Mexican-American. *Chicano* was a word used among friends or relatives. It implied a familiarity based on shared experience. Spoken casually, the term easily became an insult. In 1968 the word *Chicano* was about to become a political term. I heard it shouted into microphones as Third World groups agitated for increased student and faculty representation in higher education. It was not long before I *became* a Chicano in the eyes of students and faculty members. My racial identity was assumed for only the simplest reasons: my skin color and last name.

On occasion I was asked to account for my interests in Renaissance English literature. When I explained them, declaring a need for cultural assimilation on the campus, my listener would disagree. I sensed suspicion on the part of a number of my fellow minority students. When I could not imitate Spanish pronunciations of the dialect of the barrio, when I was plainly uninterested in wearing ethnic costumes and could not master a special handshake the minority students often used with one another, they knew I was different. And I was. I was assimilated into the culture of a graduate department of English. As a result, I watched how in less than five years nearly every minority graduate student I knew dropped out of school, largely for cultural reasons. Often they didn't understand the value of analyzing literature in professional jargon, which others around them readily adopted. Nor did they move as readily to lofty heights of abstraction. They became easily depressed by the seeming uselessness of the talk they heard around them. "It's not for real," I still hear a minority student murmur to herself and perhaps to me, shaking her head slowly, as we sat together in a class listening to a discussion on punctuation in a Renaissance epic.

I survived—thanks to the accommodation I had made long before. In fact, I prospered, partly as a result of the political movement designed to increase the enrollment of minority students less assimilated than I in higher education. Suddenly grants, fellowships, and teaching offers became abundant.

In 1972 I went to England on a Fulbright scholarship. I hoped the months of brooding about racial identity were behind me. I wanted to concentrate on my dissertation, which the distractions of an American campus had not permitted. But the freedom I anticipated did not last for long. Barely a month after I had begun working regularly in the reading room of the British Museum, I was surprised, and even frightened, to have to acknowledge that I was not at ease living the rarefied life of the academic. With my pile of research file cards growing taller, the mass of secondary materials and opinions was making it harder for me to say anything original about my subject. Every sentence I wrote, every thought I had, became so loaded with qualifications and footnotes that it said very little. My scholarship became little more than an exercise in caution. I had an accompanying suspicion that whatever I did manage to write and call my dissertation would be of little use. Opening books so dusty that they must not have been used in decades, I began to doubt the value of writing what only a few people would read.

Obviously, I was going through the fairly typical crisis of the American graduate student. But with one difference: After four years of involvement with questions of racial identity, I now saw my problems as a scholar in the context of the cultural issues that had been raised by my racial situation. So much of what my work in the British Museum lacked, my parents' culture possessed. They were people not afraid to generalize or to find insights in their generalities. More important, they had the capacity to make passionate statements, something I was beginning to doubt my dissertation would ever allow me to do. I needed to learn how to trust the use of "I" in my writing the way they trusted its use in their speech. Thus developed a persistent yearning for the very Chicano culture that I had abandoned as useless.

Feelings of depression came occasionally but forcefully. Some days I found my work so oppressive that I had to leave the reading room and stroll through the museum. One afternoon, appropriately enough, I found myself in an upstairs gallery containing Mayan and Aztec sculptures. Even there the sudden yearning for a Chicano past seemed available to me only as nostalgia. One morning, as I was reading a book about Puritan autobiography, I overheard two Spaniards whispering to one another. I did not hear what they said, but I did hear the sound of their Spanish—and it embraced me, filling my mind with swirling images of a past long abandoned.

I returned from England, disheartened, a few months later. My dissertation was coming along well, but I did not know whether I wanted to submit it. Worse, I did not know whether I wanted a career in higher education. I detested the prospect of spending the rest of my life in libraries and classrooms, in touch with my past only through the binoculars nostalgia makes available. I knew that I could not simply re-create a version of what I would have been like had I not become an academic. There was no possibility of going back. But if the culture of my birth was to survive, it would have to animate my academic work. That was the lesson of the British Museum.

I frankly do not know how my academic autobiography will end. Sometimes I think I will have to leave the campus, in order to reconcile my past and present. Other times, more optimistically, I think that a kind of negative reconciliation is already in progress, that I can make creative use of my sense of loss. For instance, with my sense of the cleavage between past and present, I can, as a literary critic, identify issues in Renaissance pastoral—a literature which records the feelings of the courtly when confronted by the alternatives of rural and rustic life. And perhaps I can speak with unusual feeling about the price we must pay, or have paid, as a rational society for confessing seventeenth-century Cartesian faiths. Likewise, because of my sense of cultural loss, I may be able to identify more readily than another the ways in which language has meaning simply as sound and what the printed word can and cannot give us. At the very least, I can point up the academy's tendency to ignore the cultures beyond its own horizons.

February 1974

On my job interview the department chairman has been listening to an oral version of what I have just written. I tell him he should be very clear about the fact that I am not, at the moment, confident enough to call myself a Chicano. Perhaps I never will be. But as I say all this, I look at the interviewer. He smiles softly. Has he heard what I have been trying to say? I wonder. I repeat: I have lost the ability to bring my past into my present; I do not know how to be a Chicano reader of Spenser or Shakespeare. All that remains is a desire for the past. He sighs, preoccupied, looking at my records. Would I be interested in teaching a course on the Mexican novel in translation? Do I understand that part of my duties would require that I become a counselor of minority students? What was the subject of that dissertation I did in England? Have I read the book on the same subject that was published this month?

Behind the questioner, a figure forms in my imagination: my grandmother, her face solemn and still.

40 The American Family in the Year 2000

ANDREW CHERLIN
FRANK F. FURSTENBERG, JR.

The fast-moving currents of social change have not left the American family untouched. We are all familiar with many of the changes that the American family is experiencing. Divorce, illegitimacy, abortion, and cohabitation—all are up. Some of us have come from broken homes; others of us have been divorced. Hardly any of us expect our marriage to be the way our grandparents' was, and many of us even expect our approach to being husband or wife to be markedly different from our parents'.

But few of us can adequately anticipate what life will be like in the future nor the contingencies that will confront us and force further changes in our ideas and our actions. In an attempt to identify what life will be like in the near future, Cherlin and Furstenberg project current trends and apply them to family life. If changes occur as they foresee, how do you think you will like the future? Can you think of other implications of these changes for family life?

• AT CURRENT RATES, half of all American marriages begun in the early 1980s will end in divorce.
• The number of unmarried couples living together has more than tripled since 1970.
• One out of four children is not living with both parents.

The list could go on and on. Teenage pregnancies: up. Adolescent suicides: up. The birthrate: down. Over the past decade, popular and scholarly commentators have cited a seemingly endless wave of grim statistics about the shape of the American family. The trends have caused a number of concerned Americans to wonder if the family, as we know it, will survive the twentieth century.

And yet, other observers ask us to consider more positive developments:

• Seventy-eight percent of all adults in a recent national survey said they get "a great deal" of satisfaction from their family lives; only 3 percent said "a little" or "none."

- Two-thirds of the married adults in the same survey said they were "very happy" with their marriages; only 3 percent said "not too happy."
- In another recent survey of parents of children in their middle years, 88 percent said that if they had to do it over, they would choose to have children again.
- The vast majority of the children (71 percent) characterized their family life as "close and intimate."

Family ties are still important and strong, the optimists argue, and the predictions of the demise of the family are greatly exaggerated.

Neither the dire pessimists who believe that the family is falling apart nor the unbridled optimists who claim that the family has never been in better shape provide an accurate picture of family life in the near future. But these trends indicate that what we have come to view as the "traditional" family will no longer predominate.

Diverse Family Forms

In the future, we should expect to see a growing amount of diversity in family forms, with fewer Americans spending most of their life in a simple "nuclear" family consisting of husband, wife, and children. By the year 2000, three kinds of families will dominate the personal lives of most Americans: families of first marriages, single-parent families, and families of remarriages.

In first-marriage families, both spouses will be in a first marriage, frequently begun after living alone for a time or following a period of cohabitation. Most of these couples will have one, two, or, less frequently, three children.

A sizable minority, however, will remain childless. Demographer Charles F. Westoff predicts that about one-fourth of all women currently in their childbearing years will never bear children, a greater number of childless women than at any time in U.S. history.

One other important shift: in a large majority of these families, both the husband and the wife will be employed outside the home. In 1940 only about one out of seven married women worked outside the home; today the proportion is one out of two. We expect this proportion to continue to rise, although not as fast as it did in the past decade or two.

Single-Parent Families

The second major type of family can be formed in two ways. Most are formed by a marital separation, and the rest by births to unmarried women. About half of all marriages will end in divorce at current rates, and we doubt that the rates will fall substantially in the near future.

When the couple is childless, the formerly married partners are likely to set up independent households and resume life as singles. The high rate of divorce is one of the reasons why more men and women are living in single-person households than ever before.

But three-fifths of all divorces involve couples with children living at home. In at least nine out of ten cases, the wife retains custody of the children after a separation.

Although joint custody has received a lot of attention in the press and in legal circles, national data show that it is still uncommon. Moreover, it is likely to remain the exception rather than the rule because most ex-spouses can't get along well enough to manage raising their children together. In fact, a national survey of children aged 11 to 16 conducted by one of the authors demonstrated that fathers have little contact with their children after a divorce. About half of the children whose parents had divorced hadn't seen their father in the last year; only one out of six had managed to see their father an average of once a week. If the current rate of divorce persists, about half of all children will spend some time in a single-parent family before they reach 18.

Much has been written about the psychological effects on children of living with one parent, but the literature has not yet proved that any lasting negative effects occur. One effect, however, does occur with regularity: women who head single-parent families typically experience a sharp decline in their income relative to before their divorce. Husbands usually do not experience a decline. Many divorced women have difficulty reentering the job market after a long absence; other find that their low-paying clerical or service-worker jobs aren't adequate to support a family. . . .

Families of Remarriages

The experience of living as a single parent is temporary for many divorced women, especially in the middle class. Three out of four divorced people remarry, and about half of these marriages occur within three years of the divorce.

Remarriage does much to solve the economic problems that many single-parent families face because it typically adds a male income. Remarriage also relieves a single parent of the multiple burdens of running and supporting a household by herself.

But remarriage also frequently involves blending together two families into one, a difficult process that is complicated by the absence of clear-cut ground rules for how to accomplish the merger. Families formed by remarriages can become quite complex, with children from either spouse's previous marriage or from the new marriage and with numerous sets of grandparents, stepgrandparents, and other kin and quasi-kin.

The divorce rate for remarriages is modestly higher than for first marriages, but many couples and their children adjust successfully to their remarriage and, when asked, consider their new marriage to be a big improvement over their previous one. . . .

Convergence and Divergence

The family lives of Americans vary according to such factors as class, ethnicity, religion, and region. But recent evidence suggests a convergence among these groups in many features of family life. The clearest example is in childbearing, where the differences between Catholics and non-Catholics or between Southerners and Northerners are much smaller than they were 20 years ago. We expect this process of convergence to continue, although it will fall far short of eliminating all social class and subcultural differences.

The experiences of blacks and whites also have converged in many respects, such as in fertility and in patterns of premarital sexual behavior, over the past few decades. But with respect to marriage, blacks and whites have diverged markedly since about 1960.

Black families in the United States always have had strong ties to a large network of extended kin. But in addition, blacks, like whites, relied on a relatively stable bond between husbands and wives. But over the past several decades—and especially since 1960—the proportion of black families maintained by a woman has increased sharply; currently, the proportion exceeds four in ten. In addition, more young black women are having children out of wedlock; in the late 1970s about two out of three black women who gave birth to a first child were unmarried.

These trends mean that we must qualify our previously stated conclusion that marriage will remain central to family life. This conclusion holds for Americans in general. For many low-income blacks, however, marriage is likely to be less important than the continuing ties to a larger network of kin.

Marriage is simply less attractive to a young black woman from a low-income family because of the poor prospects many young black men have for steady employment and because of the availability of alternative sources of support from public-assistance payments and kin. Even though most black women eventually marry, their marriages have a very high probability of ending in separation or divorce. Moreover, they have a lower likelihood of remarrying.

Black single-parent families sometimes have been criticized as being "disorganized" or even "pathological." What the critics fail to note is that black single mothers usually are embedded in stable, functioning kin networks. These networks tend to center around female kin—mothers, grandmothers, aunts—but brothers, fathers, and other male kin also may be active. The members of these networks share and exchange goods and services, thus helping to share the burdens of poverty. The lower-class black extended family, then, is characterized by strong ties among a network of kin but fragile ties between husband and wife. The negative aspects of this family system have been exaggerated greatly; yet it need not be romanticized, either. It can be difficult and risky for individuals to leave the network in order to try to make it on their own; thus, it may be hard for individuals to raise themselves out of poverty until the whole network is raised.

The Disintegrating Family?

By now, predictions of the demise of the family are familiar to everyone. Yet the family is a resilient institution that still retains more strength than its harshest critics maintain. There is, for example, no evidence of a large-scale rejection of marriage among Americans. To be sure, many young adults are living together outside of marriage, but the evidence we have about cohabitation suggests that it is not a lifelong alternative to marriage; rather, it appears to be either another stage in the process of courtship and marriage or a transition between first and second marriages.

The so-called alternative life-styles that received so much attention in the late 1960s, such as communes and lifelong singlehood, are still very uncommon when we look at the nation as a whole.

Young adults today do marry at a somewhat older age, on average, than their parents did. But the average age at marriage today is very similar to what it was throughout the period from 1890 to 1940.

To be sure, many of these marriages will end in divorce, but three out of four people who divorce eventually remarry. Americans still seem to desire the intimacy and security that a marital relationship provides.

Much of the alarm about the family comes from reactions to the sheer speed at which the institution changed in the last two decades. Between the early 1960s and the mid-1970s, the divorce rate doubled, the marriage rate plunged, the birthrate dropped from a twentieth-century high to an all-time low, premarital sex became accepted, and married women poured into the labor force. But since the mid-1970s the pace of change has slowed. The divorce rate has risen modestly and the birthrate even has increased a bit. We may have entered a period in which American families can adjust to the sharp changes that occurred in the 1960s and early 1970s. We think that, by and large, accommodations will be made as expectations change and institutions are redesigned to take account of changing family practices.

Despite the recent difficulties, family ties remain a central part of American life. Many of the changes in family life in the 1960s and 1970s were simply a continuation of long-term trends that have been with us for generations.

The birthrate has been declining since the 1820s, the divorce rate has been climbing since at least the Civil War, and over the last half century a growing number of married women have taken paying jobs. Employment outside the home has been gradually eroding the patriarchal system of values that was a part of our early history, replacing it with a more egalitarian set of values.

The only exception occurred during the late 1940s and the 1950s. After World War II Americans raised during the austerity of depression and war entered adulthood at a time of sustained prosperity. The sudden turnabout in their fortunes led them to marry earlier and have more children than any generation before or since in this century. Because many of us were either parents or children in the baby-boom years following the war, we tend to think that the 1950s typify the way twentieth-century families used to be. But the patterns of marriage and childbearing in the 1950s were an aberration resulting from special historical circumstances; the patterns of the 1960s and 1970s better fit the long-term trends. Barring unforeseen major disruptions, small families, working wives, and impermanent marital ties are likely to remain with us indefinitely.

A range of possible developments could throw our forecasts off the mark. We do not know, for example, how the economy will behave over the next 20 years, or how the family will be affected by technological innovations still at the conception stage. But, we do not envision any dramatic changes in family life resulting solely from technological innovations in the next two decades. . . .

Were we to be transported suddenly to the year 2000, the families we would see would look very recognizable. There would be few unfamiliar forms—not many communes or group marriages, and probably not a large proportion of lifelong singles. Instead, families by and large would continue to center around the bonds between husbands and wives and between parents and children. One could say the same about today's families relative to the 1960s: the forms are not new. What is quite different, comparing the 1960s with the 1980s, or the 1980s with a hypothetical 2000, is the distribution of these forms.

In the early 1960s there were far fewer single-parent families and families formed by remarriages after divorce than is the case today; and in the year 2000 there are likely to be far more single-parent families and families of remarriage than we see now. Moreover, in the early 1960s both spouses were employed in a much smaller percentage of two-parent families; in the year 2000, the percentage with two earners will be greater still. Cohabitation before marriage existed in the 1960s, but it was a frowned-upon, bohemian style of life. Today, it has become widely accepted; it will likely become more common in the future. Yet we have argued that cohabitation is less an alternative to marriage than a precursor to marriage, though we expect to see a modest rise in the number of people who never marry.

41 Life in the 21st Century

CHARLES J. LESLIE

The author of this selection foresees current trends accelerating, and out of them the development of an almost new society in but a few years. While it is certain that we have or soon could have the technology Leslie discusses, it is not nearly as certain that the future will look like the one he projects. If these technological developments take place, as they probably will, they are more likely to characterize the daily life of the relatively few. The elite of the middle class will perhaps be living in the way depicted, as well, of course, as the rich. But the majority? That is questionable. And the poor? That is unlikely, most unlikely.

But I do not wish to become too much of a futurologist myself, nor a pessimist, and will terminate such suggestions. Rather, as you read this selection, think both of what life would be like for you if the author's projections come true, as well as what life would be like for most people. To what extent do you think the author's envisioning of the future would apply to the poor?

AVA NIRAY FLIPPED ON THE VIDEO MONITOR and the screen glowed softly. She kept the volume low because she did not wish to disturb her husband and son. The monitor was running through some sports scores of the previous evening. There were hockey and basketball scores, but also Ultra Bridge and Compumaze. Across the lower portion of the screen, bright green letters spelled out, "Good morning . . . Today is Monday, Dec. 17, 2001."

Ava dressed quickly. She seldom cooked anything and never prepared breakfast. Like most of the tenants of her apartment complex, she got a quick nutritious morning meal in the dining hall. Except for a few old-fashioned folks and gourmet chefs, nobody cooked at home anymore. The home range had become as obsolete as the home dishwasher and clothes washers and dryers, since they used too much energy.

After breakfast, Ava walked the short distance to the carport and found her LTD parked in its usual spot under the neatly lettered sign with her name on it. The tiny blue light glowing on the dash indicated that its batteries had been fully charged during the night. She and her husband, Dave, had just bought the LTD the month before. It was considered the flagship of Ford's line, capable of squeezing more speed and distance out of an ordinary overnight battery charge than any other car in its class. At $17,974, it was considered a real bargain. Ava was lucky that her drive to work was only 16 kilometers—not bad for a resident of one of the nation's largest cities.

High above the parking lot, Dave Niray had just arisen and happened to glance out the window as the LTD pulled into the street. Dave stretched before the window, then finished his cylinder of Nutri-Juice. He scowled. It was time to get to work. He sat down before the video screen in his study and punched in the code to receive a rapid feed of the morning headlines. He halted the headline scan when "Food Riots Hit Brazil" flowed across the screen. He instructed the machine to present a summary of the story. The Brazilian situation was shaping up as a major story and he decided he had better be prepared.

Dave was an editor and feature writer for Trans Com News Service, one of the world's largest electronic news organizations. Although he routinely worked on stories of national and international events, he seldom left the apartment. His video screen gave him access to all of Trans Com's files. He could interview almost anyone in the world—from prime minister to Eskimo trader—via Vision Phone. In fact, it was almost time for a scheduled interview with the minister of agriculture in Buenos Aires. On the video screen, he scanned the notes he had made the previous day in preparation for the interview, then turned to the keyboard of the Vision Phone for the Argentine call.

It took only a few moments to finish the interview. Using the electronic record of the interview and information on Argentine commodities he summoned from Trans Com's computer, Dave quickly composed his story on the video screen. When the story was done, Dave instructed the computer to transmit it to his boss, an editor he had met only once in person a few years ago. Within minutes, the story would be available on the video screens of Trans Com subscribers all over the country and would be transmitted overseas via satellites.

Feeling pleased about finishing the story, Dave activated the house-monitor computer system, which compiled lists of various household needs as they arose. It reminded Dave that Rent-a-Robot would be coming in to clean the apartment. Dave decided he would go to the gymnasium for a workout before the robot arrived. He hoped some vigorous exercise would help him shake off the tired feeling that had been nagging him lately. Just before leaving, he checked the hourly mail on the video screen. Finding only bills, he keyed them to the appropriate bank accounts and departed.

Dave pulled out of the carport and accelerated past the BioLeen station at the corner. This station was one of the few left in the Midland City area. Here were dispensed the various mixtures of bio-fuel (made with organic material) and gasoline that powered older cars and trucks. Dave was still driving his 1989 Impala. As gasoline prices had gone up, it had been modified several times to use higher and higher proportions of bio-fuel. Even so, the car was eating up too much of their income.

Since they now had the LTD for a family car, it would be possible for Dave to get a smaller car for his own use. He was thinking about a new Malibu. At four meters in length, the Malibu was a good compromise between the big cars and the tiny urban scooters designed strictly for short-range errands. The Malibu cost only $12,000 to $13,000 and you could expect it to last for 15 years, but, for now, the Impala would have to do. He eased the car into a narrow space just inside the gym entrance. He stepped out and pressed a button labeled "Park." While Dave walked to the elevator, the car would automatically be deposited in a free storage space.

Ava Niray pulled into her reserved parking place at World Wide Master Metals, Plant No. 7. Other workers were leaving their cars and hurrying into the plant to begin the morning shift. There was plenty of room in the lot. Although the factory covered more than 10,000 square meters, only 50 production workers were needed for each shift.

Ava hurried to the building and turned a key in a lock beside a thick door. It slid open, then closed behind her. She was now in the control room, where she would work for most of the next eight hours. The control room was heavily insulated, air-conditioned, and carpeted. It was kept as spotless as an operating room for the benefit of its principal occupant, an enormous console of keyboards, video screens, and ranks and files of tiny lights.

Six persons were on duty in the control room at all times and 12 were there as Ava's shift replaced the third shift. Ava strode to station No. 5, her regular work place. The man she would replace, Ralph Swansea, was seated there in a heavily upholstered swivel chair, typing rapidly at a small keyboard as she approached. Ralph looked up and smiled at her. He finished his typing and walked toward the door. He had been using the keyboard to notify the "front office" that he was leaving and turning the equipment over to Ava. The "front office" was the workers' name for the central computer that kept track of the men and women and machines of World Wide Master Metals.

Ava slipped into the chair and typed her own identification code on the keyboard, then leaned forward to begin her first inspection of the day. Although she was good at her work, Ava was dubious about her chances of further promotion with only an associate degree in technology. She was already taking some evening classes and was considering getting a degree in engineering.

Barely four meters away, beyond thick glass, toiled Ava's crew. Persons at each of the other supervisory stations controlled similar groups. On this day, all crews were at work on parts for big industrial compressors that were designed for China—one of America's biggest trading partners.

Ava's crew had been working on the Chinese order since mid-October. Except for a breakdown which had shut the operation down for 15 minutes last week, the crew members had been working steadily without a break 24 hours a day, seven days a week. They were, of course, robots.

ALAS (Articulated Lift and Swing) seized each casting as it entered the room on a conveyor. It passed the part to AMDRAF (Automatic Milling, Drilling, and Finishing). Using high-speed, synthetic-diamond cutters, AMDRAF planed and drilled each cylinder unit to make it ready for assembly. As a final touch, the machine cleaned each part with a blast of compressed air from multiple nozzles.

GAR (Grasp and Remove) took each completed manifold from AMDRAF and passed it through the probing laser beams of LIAC (Light Inspector and Communicator). If LIAC approved a piece, GAR deposited it on a conveyor for transmission to the next work room, where a robotic arm would pick it up and position it at the automatic-assembly station. If LIAC found a mistake, it notified GAR to set the manifold aside in a special receptacle. Although she was called a supervisor, Ava really did no supervision. AMDRAF and the rest of the crew got their instructions from the "front office." All Ava had to do was make sure nothing went wrong.

Ava checked the status of her crew on the video displays and typed the appropriate message on her keyboard to let the "front office" know that she had done so. She usually sent such messages to the "front office" 30 times during her seven-and-one-half-hour tour of duty. If 20 minutes elapsed without a message from Ava, the "front office" would check up on her by flashing a message on a video screen. If she did not respond at once, a hollow voice would ask one of the other supervisors to find her.

Seldom did anything go wrong with the machines, but the "front office" occasionally would flash a light or print an emergency message on a display screen to make the supervisor think a mishap had occurred. When that happened, the supervisor would have to make a quick check to diagnose the problem and get things running again as soon as possible. Ava looked at these exercises as a game and enjoyed solving the problems.

The shift passed quickly for Ava. She had elected to fulfill her 30-hour workweek requirement with four shifts of seven-and-one-half hours. She had plenty of time for her class in contemporary dance and her courses at the university. . . .

At Home

It was late afternoon and neither Ava's husband, Dave, nor their son, Billy, was at home. It was a perfect time for Ava to buy their Christmas gifts.

One of the pluses of living in Midland City was its excellent communications system. Every dwelling in the region was connected to a central computer and communication network. Although people still spoke of the "wired city," it was really a "city of light." Data streamed into and out of every home on beams of light carried in bundles of hairlike glass fibers. The system was extremely efficient and—once the lines were in place—very cheap.

Ava activated the portable video set beside her chair and punched the code for Tele-Mart, the city's largest department store. She knew exactly what she wanted to order for Billy and asked for sporting goods. The Tele-Mart logo appeared on the screen, then a human figure came into focus. "May I help you, Mrs. Niray?" the salesman asked.

Ava looked at a dozen Skycycles, although she knew from the first that the one in brilliant orange and silver would be Billy's favorite. She hardly listened as the salesman described the safety features and accessories. Ava okayed payment for the cycle by punching her bank account number on the keyboard. Her bank would automatically deduct the proper amount from her account. The store would deliver the cycle to their apartment the next day. Now, she faced the task of getting Dave's gift. Perhaps one of those new plastine jump suits? She punched another code and was soon asking a saleman in men's wear to help her browse.

She was interrupted by a soft buzzing at her throat. Most persons carried their personal telephones in their pockets. A few wore them on their wrists. Ava had hers styled into a medallion and wore it as a necklace. She switched on her microphone and spoke. As she expected, Billy answered. He wanted her to know that he would be staying late at school because of an extra rehearsal for the class play. He would get a snack for supper and come home on the bus.

She was still pondering what might look nice on Dave when she heard him unlocking the door. After greeting each other and chatting for a moment, Dave and Ava decided to go to the top-floor restaurant of their apartment building for dinner. The theme there this week was Indonesian, so they could look forward to something special. When they returned, Billy was at home. Billy and Ava sat down for a game of Ricco-Bound, a new form of triple handball played by two persons on a video screen.

Dave headed for the kitchen. He wrinkled his nose slightly as he finished a glass of water. The taste was OK, but he had never quite gotten used to the idea of drinking water recycled directly from sewage. By every scientific test, the water was pure, but still. . . . Almost all Americans drank tap water recovered from sewage. Some families had individual systems in their homes to recover water and provide lawn fertilizer. Large communities like Midland City had citywide systems. Like Dave, many people didn't like the idea, but there was really little choice. The wells had gone dry throughout most of the country years ago and only an idiot would try to purify the stuff that came out of lakes and streams in the year 2001. . . .

In the living room, Billy tired of Ricco-Bound after a couple of games and went to his room. His mother began to leaf through the evening's schedule of television offerings. Among other things, there was a football game and a symphony concert. The X channel was featuring a revival of the classic musical, "Hair." There was nothing here she cared to watch, especially since the cheapest would cost $12.

Ava flipped the page and there saw advertised the show she wanted. She punched the appropriate buttons to activate the Mega-Vision and to bill their account for the $25 the show would cost. She watched fascinated as the whirling figures danced across the opposite end of the room. It was one of her favorites, the Folies Bergere telecast from Paris via satellite and reproduced in full color and three dimensions by a holographic projection device. "Come here, Dave," she called. "You've got to see this."

Some weeks later, Ava sat at home watching a much different type of TV program. It was a videotaped lecture from the university on nu-clear-reactor engineering, a subject she needed to know more about if she intended to get her degree. Ava's mind wandered and she missed some of the professor's remarks. She pressed a button to back up the tape stored in the university library many miles away. She listened intently to the replay and typed notes into the memory of her home computer. She wished that her own memory was as efficient as the computer's. With a sigh, she switched off the video.

Ava was too worried to concentrate on a lecture. She missed her hus-band, Dave, who was off on a short vacation in Rio, but the real cause of her concern was their son, Billy. Ava and Billy had argued a few days ago, when Billy announced that he was dropping out of school to look for a job. Billy had only a year to go to get his high school diploma, but he was determined to make a change.

She heard a slam of the hall door. Billy had apparently just left the apartment. She wondered where he could be going so early in the day and pressed a button on her console to see if he had left a message for her on the household video. Bright letters spelled out his note on the screen: "Mom . . . I'm going to check on a job. I'll be home this evening . . . Love, Billy."

Transportation and Farming

The youth was already walking along the street 14 stories below. Billy did not have his own car, but for his 17th birthday the previous month he had received the next best thing. He reached into his pocket for it now, the magnetic card that gave him access to Midland City's Metro-Trans system.

Billy slipped the card into a slot on the hood of a tiny Metronaire parked at the curb. The car's doors instantly unlocked. Billy slid behind the wheel, switched on the main electric circuit, and pulled smoothly away from the curb. He steered the car with one hand and punched his destination code on a small keyboard with the other. He would steer the Metronaire to the freeway and then let the guideway take over. His car would automatically link up with the others headed the same way and they would run on power picked up from the guideway while the batteries in the individual Metronaires were recharged. Metronaires traveled together on the freeway like baby elephants linked nose to tail. They were hooked together because it was safer for the passengers. The guideway could control them more easily in groups.

Midland City maintained thousands of Metronaires for use of its residents and visitors. Rental charges were automatically billed to users' bank accounts. The Metronaires were barely three meters long. Their use greatly eased the problems of congestion and pollution that had afflicted cities in the late 20th century.

Billy's thoughts were far from problems of the past. He lolled against the soft seat of the tiny car while visions flitted through his mind. He saw himself driving an enormous tractor and toiling beside other sun-bronzed youths stacking bales of hay and doling out corn to fat cows. Billy had decided to look for work on a farm.

When he reached his exit point, Billy flipped a switch to release his Metronaire from the automatic guideway. He steered the little electronic car down the ramp and into a parking spot. Billy waved to his friend, Mike Hope, across the parking lot. Mike was waiting in a Dodge van. Billy looked the van over appreciatively as he climbed in beside Mike. Vehicles like this were seldom seen in Midland City. Many families used the city-owned Metronaires for commuting, shopping trips, and other short journeys. They rented sedans, station wagons, or vans for long trips and vacations.

Billy and Mike had met at basketball camp the previous summer. As Mike steered the van along a curved road, they talked of sports—basketball, hockey, and Ricco-Bound. Billy wondered whether he should bring up the subject of a job. Actually, he had no idea whether Mike's family might need a hired hand. He decided to wait.

A few kilometers from the superhighway, Mike turned the van off the blacktop road into a narrow lane. He drove directly to the base of a massive building that sprouted abruptly from a level field 100 meters from the road.

Billy looked puzzled. "Looks just like a high-rise apartment," he said.

"It is in a way," Mike answered, "but the tenants are all four-footed."

An elevator whisked the boys to the top floor. From there, they could see the entire farm—some 2,000 hectares. Thin, shiny rails cut every field into parallel strips. Mike explained that all the field work, from plowing to harvesting, was done by robot tractors that ran on rails and drew their electric power from overhead wires.

The Hope family wasted no land. The ground was cultivated almost up to the very edge of the barn. The highrise was the site for a hog-feeding enterprise that would have covered many acres on a farm of the past. Trucks constantly brought in new feeder pigs and hauled away grown hogs to slaughter. At any one time, some 20,000 hogs were in the building. All the hogs were housed on the middle floors of the building. The manure was automatically collected on each floor and channeled to huge vats on the ground floor, where it nourished protein-converting bacteria. The resulting protein was processed into feed and hoisted to the top floor, where it was stored until needed by the hogs. Antibiotics, hormones, and other additives were blended with the feed.

The entire south side of the building was a huge solar collector. Solar energy provided the heating and air conditioning needed to keep the hogs at comfortable temperatures and generated enough electricity to power the barn's elevators, pumps, mixers, and other machines. As Mike explained the farm operations, Billy became more and more discouraged. He wondered if there was a place for him amid all the scientific apparatus.

"I was sorta hoping your dad might give me a job driving a tractor or something," Billy said.

Mike grinned. "We've got a little tractor. But the only thing we use it for is to haul robot plows or other implements from one field to another. You couldn't make a career out of driving a tractor. But don't look so sad. Let's go to the house. I told Mom you'd be eating with us this evening."

As they descended past the vats of protein-producing bacteria, Billy asked, "With all this automatic equipment, what's left for you to do?"

"Machines do the muscle work, but farmers still have to do the brain work," Mike replied. "Dad and my brother have been working with a computer simulation all afternoon. They're looking for the right combination of crops. Corn brings a good price, but it's expensive to grow. That's because it takes a lot of nitrogen fertilizer to get a good yield. Alfalfa gives good yields without any added nitrogen. That's why it's become such an important crop. Dad gets all the information he can on interest rates, fertilizer prices, and other variables and feeds it into the computer. The computer will work out different alternatives and then Dad can make a decision. He spends a lot of time in the office working on problems like that."

Billy was still taking in all he had heard when his WristCom began to buzz. It was his mother. He could tell from the sound of her voice that she was worried.

Medical Technology

The tilting movement was hardly noticeable to David Niray and the 634 other passengers aboard International Aircraft's Maxiranger as it banked. The huge airliner was completing its journey from Rio to Midland City and was scheduled to arrive in 30 minutes. Passengers sat in rows of 12. Narrow aisles separated the seats into groups of four. Essentially, the plane was a lengthened version of the 747, but numerous refinements had made it more economical to operate than its predecessor.

Dave had cut short his South American holiday. He just could not shake off his feeling of exhaustion. He was beginning to think that something besides overwork might be responsible for his tiredness and frequent headaches. Dave felt very tired. His face was hot and his throat dry. He called to a passing flight attendant for a drink of water. Her startled expression was the last thing he saw before he pitched forward, unconscious.

Some two hours later, Dave's wife and son were conferring with a somber-faced surgeon at a hospital on the south side of Midland City. Ava quickly signed the papers to authorize emergency surgery, then she and Billy went to a nearby room to wait. The medical team had discovered that a tumor had been slowly strangling Dave's pancreas. This had led to his increased feeling of fatigue and headaches.

The surgery was a success, but there was the inevitable bad news as well as good news. The good news was that the tumor was benign. The doctors did not think there was a chance of cancer. The bad news was that they had to remove Dave's pancreas. The pancreas produces insulin, which is essential to digestion. Without insulin to utilize carbohydrates, an organism will starve. In the distant past, diabetics, those who lost the ability to produce insulin, faced sure death. In more recent times, their lives could be maintained by daily injections of insulin. By the early 21st century a new lifesaving technique was available.

Shortly after the operation to remove the tumor, Dave underwent surgery a second time. The surgeons implanted an artificial pancreas. The new pancreas was a small soft-plastic container moored inside Dave's abdomen on the right side just below the rib cage. Within the tank dwelled a colony of Insul-Orgs, descendents of a strain of bacteria produced some 30 years before by scientists using recombinant DNA. By manipulating the genetic material, the scientists created a new kind of bacteria that could synthesize insulin. The little bugs inside Dave's abdomen now performed the task for him.

A small pump injected insulin into David's blood in response to measured biologic needs. By sensing chemical changes in the peritoneum, the machine detected the level of nutrients in the body and the need for an anabolic hormone such as insulin. David checked the function of the device with a magnet and felt the palpable buzz which indicated adequate function. . . .

He glanced at the calendar, which was open to Dec. 28, 2001. He was pleased that he would get to spend New Year's Day at home with his family. He looked to the future with confidence.

Glossary

Account One's version of an incident; often an excuse or justification of inappropriate behavior.

Achieved status A person's position or ranking achieved at least partly through personal efforts (such as becoming a college student) or failings (such as becoming a skid row alcoholic).

Alienation The sense that one's world is meaningless, that one is isolated, estranged, and has no control over the social world.

Anomie Normlessness; conflict between norms, weakened respect for norms, or absence of norms.

Anticipatory socialization Learning the perspectives of a role before entering it. See *Role* and *Socialization*.

Ascribed status A person's position or ranking assigned on the basis of arbitrary standards over which the individual has no control, such as age, race, or sex.

Authority Power that is regarded as legitimate or proper by those over whom it is exercised.

Background expectancies The taken-for-granted assumptions people have about the way the world is. See *Social construction of reality*.

Belief An idea about some part of the natural or social world; a view of reality.

Body language Giving and receiving messages through the movement and positioning of the body.

Bureaucracy An organization with a hierarchy of offices dividing function and authority and operating under explicit rules and procedures.

Case study An in-depth investigation of a single event, experience, organization, or situation in order to better understand or to abstract principles of human behavior.

Charisma Being assumed to possess extraordinary personal qualities, on the basis of which the individual sometimes exercises leadership or authority; varies from simply a "magnetic" personality to qualities so extraordinary they are assumed to be supernatural.

Charismatic authority Leadership exercised on the basis of charisma. See *Charisma*.

Class *See Social class.*

Class conflict The struggle between social classes; generally thought of as the struggle between the rich and powerful and the poor and powerless, or those who own the means of economic production and those who do not.

Collective behavior Relatively spontaneous, unstructured, and transitory ways of thinking, feeling, and acting that develop among a large number of people.

Community Its primary meaning is that of people inhabiting the same geographical area who share common interests and feel a sense of "belonging." From this sense comes a derived meaning of people who share common interests and have a sense of "belonging" but who do not inhabit the same geographical area, such as in the phrase "a community of scholars."

Conformity Following social norms or expectations.

Control group The subjects in an experiment who are exposed to the independent variable, as opposed to the experimental group who are not subjected to this variable. See *Experiment*.

Covert participant observation See *Participant observation*.

Crime An act prohibited by law.

Cultural diffusion The process by which the characteristics of one culture are adopted by members of another culture.

Cultural relativity The view that one cannot judge the characteristics of any culture to be morally superior to those of another. See its opposite, *Ethnocentrism*.

Culture A way of life, or shared ways of doing things; includes nonmaterial culture (such as norms, beliefs, values, and language) and material culture (such as art, tools, weapons, and buildings).

Culture lag (Cultural lag) A term developed by William F. Ogburn to refer to a dislocation or imbalance due to the material culture's changing more rapidly than the nonmaterial culture. Thought by some to be a primary factor in a social change.

Culture of poverty The distinctive culture said to exist among the poor of industrialized societies, some of whose central features are defeatism, dependence, and a present time orientation.

Culture shock   The disorienting effect that immersion in a strange culture has on the unprepared visitor as he or she encounters markedly different norms, values, beliefs, practices, and other basic expectations of social life.

Data   The information scientists gain in their studies.

Definition of reality   A view of what the world or some part of the world is like. See *Social construction of reality.*

Demography   The study of the size, distribution, composition, and change in human populations.

Dependent variable   That which is being explained as the result of other factors; a variable or social phenomenon thought to be changed or influenced by another variable. See *Independent variable.*

Deviance   Violation of social norms or expectations.

Deviant   One who violates social norms or expectations. As used by sociologists, a neutrally descriptive rather than a negative term.

Deviant career   The main course of events during one's involvement in deviance; generally refers to those who are habitually, or at least for a period of time heavily, involved in some deviant activity.

Differential association   If a person associates with one group of people he or she will learn one set of attitudes, ideas, and norms, while associating with a different group teaches a different approach to life; thus such differential association is highly significant in influencing people either to conform to or violate the law.

Disclaimer   An excuse or justification for inappropriate behavior that is *about* to take place. Examples are: "Now don't get me wrong, but. . . ;" and "Let me play the role of the devil's advocate for a minute."

Discrimination   The denial of rights, privileges, or opportunities to others on the basis of their group membership.

Division of labor   A concept developed by the French sociologist Emile Durkheim to refer to the work specializations in a society (the various ways in which work is divided, with some people specializing in production, others in advertising and distribution, and so on).

Double standard   More stringent expectations being applied to one group than another. *The* double standard refers to attitudes and ideas more favorable to males than to females—often to more lax standards of sexuality being allowed males.

Downward social mobility   Movement from a higher to a lower social position.

Dramaturgical analysis   Developed by Erving Goffman, this term refers to viewing human interaction as theatrical performances. People are seen as actors, their clothing as costumes, what they do as parts they play, what they say as delivery of lines, where they interact as a stage, and so on.

Dramaturgy   Refers to theatrical performances. See *Dramaturgical analysis.*

Ecology   The study of reciprocal relationships between organisms and their environment.

Education   Systematically teaching values, skills, and knowledge.

Ego   Commonly used as a term to refer to the self; technically, Freud's term for the conscious, rational part of an individual.

Endogamy   A cultural pattern of marrying within one's own social group.

Ethnic group   A group of people with a sense of common ancestry, generally sharing similar cultural traits and regarding themselves as distinct from others.

Ethnic stratification   Hierarchical arrangements based on ethnic group membership. See *Social stratification*.

Ethnocentrism   Using the standards of one's own culture or subculture to evaluate the characteristics of other cultures or subcultures, generally from the point of view that one's own are superior.

Ethnography   A report or study that details the major characteristics of the way of life of a social group; can be of an entire preliterate tribe or a smaller group within a large society, such as a study of urban cabdrivers.

Ethnomethodology   Developed by Harold Garfinkel, the term refers to the study of the worlds of reality that people construct, their taken-for-granted background expectancies, and the ways by which different people make sense out of their experiences.

Exogamy   A cultural pattern of marrying outside one's social group.

Experiment   A study in which the researcher manipulates one or more variables (independent variables) in order to measure the results on other variables (dependent variables). See *Variable*.

Experimental group   The subjects in an experiment who are exposed to the independent variable, as opposed to the control group who are not subjected to this variable. See *Experiment*.

Extended family   A family consisting of two or more generations (extended beyond the nuclear family), usually living together. See *Nuclear family*.

False consciousness   A person's understanding of his or her social class membership that does not square with objective facts; often used to refer to people identifying with social classes higher than the one to which they belong.

Family   People related by ancestry, marriage, or adoption who generally live together and form an economic unit, and whose adult members assume responsibility for the young. The form of the family varies remarkably from one culture to another.

Family of orientation   The family into which one is born. See *Family of procreation*.

Family of procreation   The family created by marriage. See *Family of orientation*.

Folk society A term developed by Robert Redfield to refer to small, traditional societies in which there is little social change.

Folkways Developed by William G. Sumner, this term refers to norms people are expected or encouraged to follow, but whose violation is not considered immoral; the ordinary rules, usages, conventions, and expectations of everyday life, such as, in American society, the use of deodorant. See *Mores*.

Formal organization A social group brought into existence to reach specific goals that utilizes a bureaucratic mode of operation to achieve those objectives. See *Bureaucracy*.

Formal sanction A social reward or punishment that is formally applied, often a part of ritual recognition for achievement or failure (such as receiving a passing or failing grade in school or being promoted or dismissed at work).

Future shock Developed by Alvin Toffler to refer to the dizzying disorientation brought on by the rapid arrival of the future.

Generalized other An internalized idea of the expectations of a major reference group or of society in general.

Genocide Killing an entire population.

Gestures Symbols under the purposeful control of the actor that involve the movement and positioning of the body. See *Body language*.

Heterosexuality Sexual acts or feelings toward members of the opposite sex.

Holocaust The Nazi destruction, in death camps and by means of death squads, of Jews, gypsies, Slavs, homosexuals, the mentally retarded, and others considered threats to the purity of the so-called Aryan race.

Homosexuality Sexual acts or feelings toward members of the same sex.

Horizontal mobility Movement from one social position to another that is approximately equivalent.

Human ecology Study of the reciprocal relationships between people and their environment.

Hypothesis A prediction about the relation between variables.

Ideal culture The way of life represented in people's values and norms, rather than by their actual practices. See *Real culture*.

Ideal type Developed by Max Weber, this term refers to a model or description of something that is derived from examining a number of real cases and abstracting what appears to be the essential characteristics of those cases.

Ideology Statements or beliefs (especially of reasons and purposes) that justify a group's actions or interests; they buttress, uphold, or legitimate the existing social order.

Incest Socially forbidden sexual intercourse with specific categories of kinfolk.

Incest taboo The social prohibition against sexual intercourse with specific categories of kinfolk.

Independent variable That which is thought to affect or to cause change in some other factor; the variable thought to influence another variable. See *Dependent variable.*

Informal sanction A social reward or punishment informally applied, often being a spontaneous gesture of approval or disapproval. (Examples include staring or smiling.)

Ingroup The group to which an individual belongs, identifies, and feels loyalty. See *Outgroup.*

Institution See *Social institution.*

Institutional(ized) racism The use of social institutions to discriminate, exploit, or oppress a racial (or ethnic) group. See *Racism.*

Institutional(ized) sexism The use of social institutions to discriminate, exploit, or oppress either males or females as a group. See Sexism.

Interaction See *Social interaction.*

Internalization Experiences becoming part of one's "internal" consciousness.

Interview A face-to-face meeting for the purpose of formal conferences on some point; a technique used by sociologists to gain data.

Involuntary association Groups to which people belong, but about which they have little or no choice. Examples include grade school for youngsters and military service during periods of conscription.

Kin People who are related by birth, adoption, or marriage.

Kinfolk See *Kin.*

Kinship The network of people who are related to one another by birth, adoption, or marriage.

Labeling theory or perspective The sociological perspective that holds that acts are not inherently deviant or criminal but are such only because those acts are so labeled (or defined). Deviants are those on whom the label of deviant has been successfully applied.

Life chances The likelihood that an individual or group will benefit from their society's opportunities, goods and services, and other satisfactions in life.

Life cycle The biological and social sequencing through which individuals pass; these cluster around birth, childhood, maturity, old age, and death.

Life expectancy The average number of years a person can expect to live.

Looking-glass self Charles Horton Cooley's term for the process by which people see themselves through the eyes of others. As people act, others react. In those reactions people see themselves reflected. Perceiving this, they interpret its meaning, which yields a particular self-image.

Life-style   The general patterns that characterize an individual or group, including their clothing, manners, recreation, mating, and childraising practices.

Mass media   Forms of communication that reach a large audience, with no personal contact between the senders and receivers of the message. Examples are movies, radio, television, newspaper, magazines, plays, and books.

Material culture   See *Culture.*

Methodology   The procedures scientists use to conduct their studies.

Military-industrial complex   The relationships between top leaders of the Pentagon and American corporations by which they reciprocally support one another and thereby influence American politics on their behalf.

Minority group   A group of people who are treated unequally because of their physical or cultural characteristics.

Mores   (Pronounced more-rays) Developed by William G. Sumner, this term refers to norms whose violation is considered a moral transgression. Examples are the norms against murder and theft. See *Folkways.*

Negative sanction   Punishment for disapproved behavior.

Neutralization   Deflecting social norms, allowing one to continue activities for which there is social condemnation; the means of doing this are called *Techniques of Neutralization.* An example is saying, "The circumstances required it" or, "I didn't know what I was doing."

Nonmaterial culture   See *Culture.*

Nonverbal communication   Communication by the use of symbols other than language. Examples are *Body language* and traffic lights.

Norms   Rules concerning appropriate and inappropriate behavior by which people are judged and sanctions applied. See *Sanctions.*

Nuclear family   A family consisting of a husband, wife, and their children.

Organization   A social unit established for the purpose of attaining some agreed-upon goals.

Outgroup   A group to which an individual does not belong and with which he or she does not identify.

Overt participant observation   See *Participant observation.*

Participant observation   A method of studying social groups in which the researcher participates in the group being studied. If the people being studied know a researcher is in their midst, this method is called *overt participant observation;* if they do not know they are being studied, it is called *covert participant observation.*

Particular other   An internalized idea of the expectations of specific individuals.

Peer group   Associates of similar social status who are usually close in age. Examples are one's playmates as a child and workmates as an adult.

Personality   An individual's tendency over time to act (and think and feel) in ways similar to those he or she did in the past; the stable behavior patterns we come to expect of people.

Positive sanction   A reward for approved behavior.

Power   The ability to control others, even over their objections.

Power elite   C. Wright Mills's term to refer to a small group of people with interlocking interests who appear to make the most important political decisions.

Prestige   Favorable evaluation, respect, or social recognition.

Prejudice   Negative attitudes, ideas, and feelings, usually about people one does not know.

Primary group   People whose relationship is intimate, face-to-face, expressive, and extended over time. Examples are one's family and close friends.

Prostitution   The relatively indiscriminate exchange of sexual favors for economic gain.

Questionnaire   An interview taking a written form.

Race   A large number of people who share visible physical characteristics on the basis of which they regard themselves as a biological unit and are similarly regarded by others.

Racism   One racial or ethnic group dominating or exploiting another, generally based on seeing those they exploit as inferior.

Real culture   A people's actual way of life, rather than the way of life expressed by their ideals. See *Ideal culture*.

Reference group   The groups to which people refer when they evaluate themselves, their behavior, or actions they are considering.

Relative deprivation   Feeling deprived relative to what others have; based on comparison with others, the sense that the gap between the resources or rewards one actually has and what others have is unjust.

Resocialization   Learning norms, values, and behaviors that contrast with one's previous experiences.

Respondent   A person who has been interviewed or who has filled out a questionnaire. (He or she has *responded* to the request for data.)

Rising expectations   A situation in which people who have accepted existing conditions in the past now feel they have a right to better conditions.

Rites of passage   Formal, customary rituals marking one's transition from one social status to another. Examples include bar mitzvahs, confirmations, first communions, weddings, graduation ceremonies, and funerals.

Role The part a person occupying a particular status plays.

Role conflict If a person playing two or more roles find himself or herself torn between their conflicting demands, that person is said to be experiencing role conflict. Examples include a student wanting to date on the same night he or she is supposed to study for a final examination.

Role taking Putting ourselves in the shoes of someone else and seeing how things look from that perspective.

Sanction A social reward for approved behavior, or punishment for disapproved behavior.

Secondary group The more formal, impersonal, and transitory groups to which people belong, such as a college class in introductory sociology.

Self The sense individuals have of themselves as a distinct, personal identity; this sense, idea, or conception is acquired through social interaction.

Self-fulfilling prophecy A false definition of a situation ("The bank is in trouble.") that causes people to change their behavior ("People rush to the bank to withdraw their savings.") and makes the originally false statement come true ("The bank is now in trouble as it does not have enough cash on hand to meet the unexpected demand for immediate withdrawals.").

Sexism Males or females dominating or exploiting the other, with the exploitation generally based on seeing the other as inferior; usually used to refer to males dominating females.

Sex role The behaviors and characteristics a male or female is expected to demonstrate, based on stereotypical cultural concepts of masculinity or femininity, assigned on the basis of one's sex organs.

Social change Alteration in the patterns of social structure, in social institutions (or some small part of them), and in people's behavior.

Social class A number of people having about the same amount of social power; based on different characteristics in different societies. In ours some sociologists see the primary bases as the amount of one's income and education and the prestige of one's occupation.

Social construction of reality The process by which definitions of reality (views of what some part of the world is like) are socially created, objectified, internalized, and then taken for granted.

Social control The techniques used to keep people in line or, if they step out, to bring them back into line. Examples include persuasion, coercion, and education.

Social group Any human group.

Social inequality Refers to *Social stratification*.

Social institution Standardized practices (clustered around a set of norms, values, beliefs, statuses, and roles) that develop around a basic need of society. Examples include government and politics (for social order), education (for training in conformity and the transmission of skills and knowledge), and the military (for protection from external enemies and the implementation of foreign policy).

Social interaction People acting in anticipation of the reactions of others; people influencing each other's feelings, attitudes, and actions.

Socialization Refers to learning; the process of social interaction by which people learn the way of life of their society; centers on learning to play roles.

Social mobility Movement from one social position to another. See *Downward, Horizontal,* and *Upward social mobility.*

Social stratification Large groups of people ranked in a hierarchy that yields different access to the rewards their society has to offer.

Social structure The ways in which the basic components of a group or society are related to one another.

Society A group of interacting individuals who share the same territory and participate in a common culture.

Sociobiology The study of the biological basis of social behavior.

Sociology The scientific study of human society and social behavior.

Status One's position in a group or society, such as woman, mother, and plumber.

Stereotype A generalization about other people or groups; a rigid mental image that summarizes what is believed to be typical of some people or group.

Stigma A mark of social disgrace.

Stratification See *Social stratification.*

Subculture A group that shares in the overall culture of a society but also has its own distinctive values, norms, beliefs, and life-style. Examples include cabdrivers, singles, prostitutes, muggers, and physicians.

Subjective interpretation See *Verstehen.*

Symbol Any act, object, or event that represents something, such as a traffic light, a gesture, or this definition. See *Symbolic interactionism.*

Symbolic interaction People's interaction based on symbols. See *Symbolic interactionism.*

Symbolic interactionism Developed by Herbert Blumer, this term refers to the school of thought (or theoretical perspective) that focuses on symbols as the basis of human behavior—the signs, gestures, and language by which people communicate with one another and change or refine their courses of action in anticipation of what others might do.

Techniques of neutralization See *Neutralization.*

Theory A statement that organizes a set of concepts in a meaningful way by explaining the relationship between them.

Total institution Erving Goffman's term to refer to a place whose inhabitants are confined, are cut off from the rest of society, and come under the almost absolute control of the administrative authorities. Examples include prisions, the military, and convents.

Traditional authority Authority that is legitimated by custom and practice. The justification (or explanation) for something is, "We have always done it that way."

Trust The willingness to accept the definition someone offers of oneself and to play a corresponding role based on that definition.

Upward social mobility Movement from a lower to a higher social position.

Values An idea about what is worthwhile.

Value conflict Basic disagreement over goals, ideals, policies, or other expressions of values.

Value judgment A personal, subjective opinion based on one's own set of values.

Variable Any condition or characteristic that varies from one situation or person or group to another. Examples include age, occupation, beliefs, and attitudes. See *Dependent variable* and *Independent variable*.

Verstehen A term used by the German sociologist Max Weber to refer to subjective interpretation of human behavior; that is, because one is a member of a group or culture, one gains insight and understanding into what others are experiencing, allowing one to interpret those experiences.

Vertical social mobility Movement to a higher or a lower social position.

Voluntary associations Groups that people join voluntarily, often because they wish to promote some goal or be with like-minded people. Examples include a church, a college class, and a bowling league.

White collar crime Crimes committed by "respectable" persons of high status, frequently during the course of their occupation.

Appendix:
Correlation Chart

TWENTY-SIX BASIC SOCIOLOGY TEXTS are listed alphabetically across the top of the correlation chart. The chapters of these texts are the basic reference point for the chart. They are located in the column to the left of the boxes. The numbers within the boxes refer to the articles in *Down to Earth Sociology*.

I have tried to make the correlation chart for the 4th edition more helpful. When the primary emphasis of an article matches a chapter, the article number is listed without qualifiers. If a major emphasis of the article matches the chapter, the article number is italicized or slanted. If only secondary emphases of an article match a chapter, the article number is placed within parentheses.

Because the selections in *Down to Earth Sociology* have various emphases, it is possible to correlate them with the basic texts in a number of ways. Depending upon your particular approach to teaching the course and the sociological principles that you want to abstract from the articles, you may wish to rearrange the ordering suggested in this correlation chart.

The numbers within the boxes refer to selection numbers in **Down to Earth Sociology**.

The numbers directly below refer to chapters in the various basic texts:	Hobbs & Blank 3rd Edition 1982	Hess, Markson, & Stein 1st Edition 1982	Hagedorn 1st Edition 1983	Goodman & Marx 4th Edition 1982	Federico & Schwartz 3rd Edition 1983	Eshleman & Cashion 1st Edition 1983	Eitzen 2nd Edition 1982	Denisoff & Wahrman 3rd Edition 1983	Coser, Rhea, Steffan, & Nock 1st Edition 1983	Conklin 1st Edition 1984	Champion, Kurth, Hastings, & Harris 1st Edition 1984	Broom, Selznick, & Broom 3rd Edition 1984	Babbie 3rd Edition 1983
1	1, 2, 3	1, 2, 3	1, 2, 3	1, 2, 3	1, 2, 3	1, 2, 3	1, 2, 3	1, 2, 3	1, 2, 3	1, 2, 3	1, 2, 3	1, 2, 3	1, 2, 3
2	8, 9, 10, 11, (17), (18), (24), 28, 34	2	2	2	2		10, 13, 15, 16, 24, 32		2	2	4, 5, 6, 7, 13	2	
3	4, 5, 6, 7, 13	4, 5, 6, 7, 13	4, 5, 6, 7, 13		4, 5, 6, 7, 13, 21, 35	2		2	4, 5, 6, 7, 13	4, 5, 6, 7, 13	12, 13, 14, 15, 16, 17, 36	4, 5, 6, 7, 13	2
4	18, 19, 20, 21, 22, 23, 24, 36	10, 13, 15, 16, 17, 24, 32, 35, 36	8, 9, 10, 11, (17), (18), (24), 28, 34	10, 13, 15, 16, 24, 32	8, 9, 10, (17), (18), (24), 34	4, 5, 6, 7, 13	38, 39, 40, 41	16, 17, 32, (33), 35, 36	12, 13, 14, 15, 16, 17, 36	8, 9, 10, 11, (17), (18), (24), 28, 34	8, 9, 10, 11, (17), (18), (24), 28, 34	8, 9, 10, 11, (17), (18), (24), 28, 34	4, 5, 6, 7, 13
5	16, 17, 32, (33), 35, 36	8, 9, (10), 11, (17), (18), (24), 28, 34	18, 19, 20, 21, 22, 23, 24, 36	4, 5, 6, 7, 13	11, 28	8, 9, 10, 11, (17), (18), (24), 28, 34	4, 5, 6, 7, 13	4, 5, 6, 7, 13	8, 9, 10, 11, (17), (18), (24), 28, 34	18, 19, 20, 21, 22, 23, 24, 36	18, 19, 20, 21, 22, 23, 24, 36	6, 7, 10, 11, 12, 13, 14, 34	8, 9, 10, 11, (17), (18), (24), 28, 34
6	13, 15, 16, 25, 26, 27, 29, 32, 39	18, 19, 20, 21, 22, 23, 24, 36	8, 9, 10, 11, 28	8, 9, 10, 11, (17), (18), (24), 28, 34	16, 17, 23	6, 7, 10, 11, 12, 13, 14, 34	(17), (18), (24), 34	8, 9, 10, 11, (17), (18), (24), 28, 34	16, 17, 32, (33), 35, 36	6, 7, 10, 11, 12, 13, 14, 34	13, 15, 16, 25, 26, 27, 29, 32, 39	16, 17, 32, (33), 35, 36	12, 13, 14, 15, 16, 17, 36
7	8, 9, 10, 11, 28, 29, 30	25, 26, 32		18, 19, 20, 21, 22, 23, 24, 36	18, 19, 20, 21, 22, 23, 24, 36	18, 19, 20, 21, 22, 23, 24, 36	8, 9, 10, 11, 28	8, (9), (27), 31, (39), 40	13, 15, 16, 25, 26, 27, 29, 32, 39	13, 15, 16, 17, 32, (33), 35, 36	29, 30	8, 9, 10, 11, 28	16, 17, 32, 35, 36
8	31, 32, 33, 34, 35, 36, 37, 40	13, 15, 16, 19, 27, 29, 39	29, 30	12, 13, 14, 15, 16, 17, 36	13, 15, 16, 25, 26, 27, 29, 32, 39	13, 15, 16, 25, 26, 27, 29, 32, 39	24, 36	33	18, 19, 20, 21, 22, 23, 24, 36	13, 15, 16, 25, 26, 27, 32, 39	8, 9, 10, 11, 28	29, 30	13, 15, 16, 25, 26, 27, 29, 32, 39
9	12, 14, 17, 28, 29, (33), 36	8, 9, 10, 11, 28	13, 15, 16, 25, 26, 27, 29, 32, 39	16, 17, 32, (33), 35, 36	29, 30	29, 30	18, 19, 20, 21, 22, 23	25, 37	29, 30	29, 30		13, 15, 16, 25, 26, 27, 29, 32, 39	29, 30
10	38, 39, 40, 41	29, 30	8, (9), (27), 31, (39), 40	13, 15, 16, 25, 26, 29, 32, 39	31	8, 9, 10, 11, 28	13, 15, 16, 19, 25, 26, 27, 32, 39		8, 9, 10, 11, 28	8, 9, 10, 11, 28	16, 17, 32, (33), 35, 36		8, 9, 10, 11, 28

426

	C1	C2	C3	C4	C5	C6	C7	C8	C9	C10	C11
11	18, 19, 20, 21, 22, 23, 24, 36	12, 14, 17, 28, 36, 37, 38, 41	8, (9), (27), 31, (39), 40	8, (9), (27), 31, (39), 40	25, 26	26, 29	16, 17, 32, (33), 35, 36	16, 17, 32, (33), 35, 36	27, 32	33	8, (9), (27), 31, (39), 40
12	25, 29, 37	8, (9), (27), 31, (39), 40	(10), (27), 32, 39	25, 29, 37	13, 15, 16, 27, 28, 29, 32, 39	29, 30	8, (9), (27), 31, (39), 40	(12), 15, (23), 41	29, 30	25, 37	25, 29, 37
13	(10), (27), 32, 39	(10), (27), 32, 39	33	(10), (27), 32, 39	29, 30	8, 9, 10, 11, 28	33	8, (9), (27), 31, (39), 40	8, 9, 10, 11, 28	(10), (27), 32, 39	25, 37
14	33	33	25, 37	(5), 14, 21, 28, 35	18, 19, 20, 21, 22, 23, 24, 36	8, (9), (27), 31, (39), 40	(10), (27), 32, 39	33	8, (9), (27), 31, (39), 40	34	(10), (27), 32, 39
15	8, (9), (27), 31, (39), 40	25, 37	24, 36	33		33	25, 37	(10), (27), 32, 39	(10), (27), 32, 39	12, 14, 17, 28, 29, (33), 36	33
16	(12), 15, (23), 41		25, 29, 37	25, 37	25, 29, 37	25, 29, 37	25, 29, 37	25, 29, 37	33	(12), 15, (23), 41	(5), 14, 21, 28, 35
17		(12), 15, (23), 41				25, 37		25, 37	25, 37	16, 32, (33), 35, 36	18, 19, 23, 24
18	38, 41	38, 39, 40, 41	(12), 15, (23), 41	38, 39, 40, 41	38, 39, 40, 41		(5), 14, 21, 28, 35	38, 39, 40, 41	12, 14, 17, 25, 28, 29, (33), 36, 37		
19	38, 39, 40, 41		38, 39, 40, 41				(12), 15, (23), 39, 41		(12), 15, (23), 41		(12), 15, (23), 41
20						(12), 15, (23), 39, 41	38, 40, 41		38, 39, 40, 41		
21											38, 39, 40, 41
22											
23											

427

The numbers within the boxes refer to selection numbers in **Down to Earth Sociology**.

The numbers directly below refer to chapters in the various basic texts:	Horton & Hunt 6th Edition 1984	Light & Keller 3rd Edition 1982	Perry & Perry 4th Edition 1983	Persell 1st Edition 1984	Perucci & Knudsen 1st Edition 1983	Popenoe 5th Edition 1983	Ritzer, Kammeyer & Yetman 2nd Edition 1982	Schaefer 1st Edition 1983	Shepard 2nd Edition 1984	Smith & Preston 2nd Edition 1982	Stokes 1st Edition 1984	Tischler, Hunter & Whitten 1st Edition 1983	Zeitlin 2nd Edition 1984
1	1, 2, 3	1, 2, 3	1, 2, 3	1, 2, 3	1, 2, 3	1, 2, 3	1, 2, 3	1, 2, 3	1, 2, 3	1, 2, 3	1, 2, 3	1, 2, 3	1, 2, 3
2	2	2	13, 15, 16, 32	2	2	2	2	2	2	2		2	4, 5, 6, 7, 13
3	4, 5, 6, 7, 13	4, 5, 6, 7, 13	4, 5, 6, 7, 13	13, 15, 16, 24, 32	4, 5, 6, 7, 13	4, 5, 6, 7, 13	10, 12, 13, 14, 15, 16, 17, 24, 32	4, 5, 6, 7, 13	4, 5, 6, 7, 13	4, 5, 6, 7, 13	2	4, 5, 6, 7, 13	8, 9, 10, 11, (17), (18), (24), 28, 34
4	8, 9, 10, 11, (17), (18), (24), 28, 34	10, 13, 15, 16, 24, 32	8, 9, 10, 11, (17), (18), (24), 28, 34	6, 7, 10, 11, 12, 13, 14, 15, 16	16, 17, 32, (33), 35, 36	10, 13, 15, 16, 24, 32	38, 39, 40, 41	10, 13, 15, 16, 24, 32	10, 13, 15, 16, 24, 32	8, 9, 10, 11, (17), (18), (24), 28, 34	4, 5, 6, 7, 13	8, 9, 10, 11, (17), (18), (24), 28, 34	12, 13, 14, 15, 16, 17
5	7, 10, 11, 12, 13, 14, 16, 28, 31	8, 9, 10, 11, (17), (18), (24), 28, 34	18, 19, 20, 21, 22, 23, 24, 36	4, 5, 6, 7, 13	12, 13, 14, 15, 16, 17, 19, 20, 36	6, 7, 10, 11, 12, 13, 14, 16, 34	8, 9, 10, 11, (17), (18), (24), 28, 34	8, 9, 10, 11, (17), (18), (24), (28), 34	8, 9, 10, 11, (17), (18), (24), 28, 34	7, 10, 13, 15, 16, 24	8, 9, 10, 11, (17), (18), (24), 28, 34	6, 7, 10, 11, 12, 13, 15, 16, 24	16, 17, 32, 35, 36
6	8, 9, 10, 11, 28	8, 9, 10, 11, 28	13, 15, 16, 19, 25, 26, 27, 32, 39	8, 9, 10, 11, (17), (18), (24), 28, 34	8, 9, 10, 11, (17), (18), (24), 28, 34	8, 9, 10, 11, (17), (18), (24), 28, 34	8, 9, 10, 11, 28	12, 13, 14, 15, 16, 17, 32, 36	8, 9, 10, 11, (17), (18), (24), 28, 34	12, 13, 14, 15, 16, 17, 36	6, 7, 10, 11, 12, 13, 14, 34, 36	12, 13, 14, 15, 16, 17, 32, 39	13, 15, 16, 19, 27, 32, 39
7	18, 19, 20, 21, 22, 23, 24, 36	6, 7, 10, 12, 13, 14, 15, 16, 17	29, 30	12, 13, 14, 15, 16, 17, 32, 35	18, 19, 20, 21, 22, 23, 24, 36	12, 13, 14, 15, 16, 17, 19, 36	35	12, 13, 14, 15, 16, 17, 32, 36	12, 13, 14, 15, 16, 17, 32, 35, 36	16, 17, 32, (33), 35, 36	16, 17, 32, (33), 35, 36	(12), 15, (23), 41	25, 26, 37
8	16, 17, 32, (33), 35, 36	16, 17, 32, (33), 35, 36	38, 39, 40, 41	18, 19, 20, 21, 22, 23, 24, 36	13, 15, 16, 19, 25, 26, 27, 32, 39	8, 9, 10, 11, 28		13, 15, 16, 19, 25, 26, 27, 32, 39	13, 15, 16, 19, 25, 26, 27, 32, 39	13, 15, 16, 25, 26, 27, 32, 39	13, 15, 16, 25, 26, 27, 32, 39	5, 15, 17	29, 30
9	14, 28, 35, 37	18, 19, 20, 21, 22, 23, 24, 36	(12), 15, (23), 41	10, 13, 15, 16, 24, 32	16, 17, 32, (33), 35, 36		13, 15, 16, 19, 25, 26, 27, 32, 39	29, 30	25, 26, 27, 32	8, 9, 10, 11, 28	29, 30	18, 19, 20, 21, 22, 23, 24, 36	8, (9), (27), 31, (39), 40
10	8, (9), 27, 31, (39), 40	13, 15, 16, 25, 26, 27, 29, 32, 39		25, 26, 32	8, 9, 10, 11, 28	18, 19, 20, 21, 22, 23, 24, 36	(12), 15, (23), 41	8, 9, 10, 11, 28	29, 30	29, 30	8, 9, 10, 11, 28	13, 15, 16, 25, 26, 27, 32, 39	33

11	12	13	14	15	16	17	18	19	20	21	22	23
	18, 19, 20, 21, 22, 23, 24, 36	(12), 15, (23), 41	38, 39, 40, 41									
29, 30	8, 9, 10, 11, 28	8, (9), (27), 31, (39), 40	33	(10), (27), 32, 39	25, 29, 37	25, 37		(5), 14, 21, 28, 35	38, 39, 40, 41			
18, 19, 20, 21, 22, 23, 24, 36	8, (9), (27), 31, (39), 40	33	(10), (27), 32, 39	25, 29, 37	(5), 14, 21, 28, 35	(12), 15, (23), 41		38, 39, 40, 41				
8, (9), (27), 31, (39), 40	33	(10), (27), 32, 39	25, 29, 37	18, 19, 20, 21, 22, 23, 24, 36	12, 14, 17, 28, 29, 34, 36	(12), 15, (23), 41		38, 39, 40, 41				
8, 9, 10, 11, 28	8, (9), (27), 31, (39), 40	(10), (27), 32, 39	12, 14, 17, 25, 28, 29, 36, 37	33		(12), 15, (23), 41	38, 39, 40, 41					
8, (9), (27), 31, (39), 40	33	25, 37	25, 29, 37	25, 29, 37	(10), (27), 32, 39		38, 39, 40, 41					
16, 17, 32, (33), 35, 36	29, 30	8, (9), (27), 31, (39), 40	(10), (27), 32, 39	12, 14, 17, 28, 29, (33), 36	33	25, 37	34					
13, 15, 16, 19, 25, 26, 27, 32, 39	29, 30	16, 17, 32, (33), 35, 36	8, (9), (27), 31, (39), 40	(5), 14, 21, 28, 35	(10), (27), 32, 39	33	25, 29, 37					
29, 30	8, (9), (27), 31, (39), 40	25, 29, 37	33	25, 27	(10), (27), 32, 39	(12), 15, (23), 41	38, 39, 40, 41					
29, 30	8, 9, 10, 11, 28	8, (9), (27), 31, (39), 40	12, 14, 17, 25, 28, 29, 36, 37	25, 37	(10), (27), 32, 39	33	38, 41	38, 39, 40, 41	14, 21, 28, 35	(12), 15, (23), 41	20	34
33	(10), (27), 32, 38, 39, 41	25, 29, 37	13, 15, 16, 25, 26, 27, 32, 39	27	29, 30	(12), 15, (23), 41	(12), 15, (23), 41	38, 39, 40, 41	38, 39, 40, 41			

Name Index

Note: An asterisk (*) indicates that the individual is a contributing author to this anthology. Background information on the individual is given in "About the Contributors," pages xv–xx.

Subject Index